William D. Strathallan

The Genealogy of the Most Noble and Ancient House of Drummond

William D. Strathallan

The Genealogy of the Most Noble and Ancient House of Drummond

ISBN/EAN: 9783744754873

Printed in Europe, USA, Canada, Australia, Japan

Cover: Foto ©ninafisch / pixelio.de

More available books at **www.hansebooks.com**

GENEALOGY

OF THE

HOUSE OF DRUMMOND

This FAC-SIMILE REPRINT *of* Dr. DAVID LAING'S *Edition of* 1831, *which
has now become rare, is on* '*Maitland Club*' *paper, and
the impression has been limited to*
One Hundred Copies.

No. 56

Gulielmus Drummond.

THE GENEALOGY OF THE

Most Noble and Ancient House of

DRUMMOND

By The Honourable WILLIAM DRUMMOND

AFTERWARDS FIRST VISCOUNT OF STRATHALLAN

1681

GLASGOW

PRIVATELY PRINTED

MDCCCLXXXIX

Printed by T. & A. CONSTABLE, *Printers to Her Majesty, at the Edinburgh University Press.*

THE GENEALOGY

OF THE

MOST NOBLE AND ANCIENT

HOUSE OF DRUMMOND.

BY

THE HONOURABLE WILLIAM DRUMMOND,

AFTERWARDS FIRST VISCOUNT OF STRATHALLAN,

M.DC.LXXXI.

EDINBURGH : M.DCCC.XXXI.

PRINTED BY A. BALFOUR AND CO.

1164698

HE present Genealogical History, which is now printed for the first time, was compiled in the year 1681, and has always been esteemed a work of authority. The Author enjoyed the best advantages for the prosecution of his labours, not only in obtaining the use of the several accounts drawn up by previous writers, but in having free access to original papers, and to every other source of information regarding the collateral branches of a Family to which he himself was nearly related, and finally became so distinguished an ornament.

The Honourable WILLIAM DRUMMOND, youngest son of John Second LORD MADERTY, was raised to the dignity of the Peerage, on the 6th of September 1686, by the title of VISCOUNT OF STRATH-ALLAN. At the time of his decease, which happened in January 1688, he held the appointment of General of the Forces in Scotland. —He was interred at Innerpeffry on the 4th of April, when Principal

Monro of Edinburgh preached his Funeral Sermon, mentioning several curious and interesting particulars of his life, which will be found in the Appendix.

In the Appendix also, along with occasional Notes and Illustrations of the Pedigree is inserted an account of the Family written by William Drummond of Hawthornden, the celebrated poet, which was thought worthy of preservation as a literary relique, although the information it contains is completely embodied in the fuller and more detailed work of Lord Strathallan.

The impression of this volume, which is intended for private circulation, is limited to One hundred copies, and four upon large paper.

EDINBURGH,
DECEMBER M.DCCC.XXXI.

THE GENEALOGIE

OF THE

MOST NOBLE AND ANCIENT

HOUSE OF DRUMMOND.

CONTAINING

A TRUE ACCOMPT OF THE ORIGINAL EXTRACTIONE,
THE OFSPRING, AND ALLAYES OF THAT FAMILY.

DEDUCED FROM THE FIRST OF THAT NAME
ANE HUNGARIAN GENTLEMAN,

AND CONTINOWED TO THE PRESENT AGE.

BY A FREIND TO VERTUE AND THE FAMILY.

The memory of the Just is blissed : bot the name of the Wicked shall rot.   PROV. 10. 7.
Stemmata quid faciunt ? quid prodest, Pontice, longo
Sanguine censeri ——— JUVEN.
Satius est me meis rebus gestis florere, quam majorum opinione niti, et ita vivere ut sim posteris
nobilitatis et virtutis exemplum.   CICERO.

COLLECTED IN THE YEAR 1681.

Nobility is that which cannot be bought, for it consists in a high descent and undegenerat race
of Ancient Worthies, more adorned with eminent vertues than riches or outward pomp.
HATHORNDEN IN EPIST. AD COM. PERTH.

TO THE RIGHT HONOURABLE

JAMES EARLE OF PERTH,

LORD DRUMMOND AND STOBHAL, HERETABLE THANE, SENESCAL, OR STUART OF STRATHERN AND BALWHIDDER, CORONER OF THE SAME, BAYLY OF THE ABTHANY OF DULL, LORD JUSTICE GENERAL OF SCOTLAND, AND ONE OF THE LORDS OF HIS MAJESTIES MOST HONOURABLE PRIVY COUNCELL, &c.

My Lord,

Take heire a view of youre noble and renowned Anceftors, of whofe blood yow are defcended in a right and uninterrupted male lyne; as alfo of fo many of the confanguinities and ancient affinities of youre Family in the infancy thereof, as the penurie of our oldeft records and the credit of our beft traditions hes happily preferved from the grave of oblivion: bot which are in the fucceeding and modern times, with all the ftems ifhewed from that fruitfull root, more clearely and more certainely layd before yow. It hes been the regraite of many weill affected to youre Name and Family, that ane orderly collection of the pedegree of a trybe fo confiderable and of fo long ftanding fhould find no hand, in fo many ages, to fet about and accomplifh the fame; for albeit diverfe learned and judicious perfones have offered at fome parts of it, who, through defect of Authentick documents, made bot fmall progres, and wanted not theire own miftakes, yet not one hitherto hes adventured to draw the entire fcheme, and finifh the work defyred.

Sir Robert Drummond of Midhoop left fome Memorialls upon this fubject; and fo did Sir Patrick Drummond, Confervator for the

THE DEDICATION

Scots nation at Camphyre in Zeland ; Mr. Ninian Drummond, parfon at Kinnoull, a man well verfed in the antiquities of youre Houfe, gave fome informations to advance the defigne ; and the famous Mr. William Drummond of Hathornden framed a breefe relation of the pedegree of the Family, and erected a goodly tree of the ftock, branches and neareft allayes thereof. Bot Mr. John Freebairn, minifter at Maddertie, beftowed moft labour, was fuplyed with the beft helps, and came neareft to the point, if he had treated upon that head only :

Semper ego auditor tantum.

My Lord, from the well-founded relations of all thefe fyve men, bot more from the remnants of youre own authentick evidences, the particular wrytts and charters of fome Cadets of youre Houfe, with other hiftorical remarks, traditions, and manufcripts, the following narration is gleaned and fet together. In deduceing whereof, if any errors bees found, (and upon fo ancient a fubject who dare affirme pofitively upon every particular), I fhall humbly fubmit to better inquyries, and either produce authority to exoner me, or bear the blame ; neverthelefs, if any perfon will difcover the miftakes that have efcaped my informers, it fhall be very acceptable and thankfully receaved by me ; for praife I deferve none, except it be for fome finall paines in fearching of old records, and delivering the collections of fome, and traditions of others, in a worfe method and more vulgar ftyle then themfelves could have done, which me thinks merits bot very litle. The work is defigned only for youre Lordfhips fatisfaction, and fuch as yow think fit to communicat it too, bot not for publick view. And I am fo well fupported againft all criticifms in this undertakeing, by the hopes of youre acceptance, which I am accuftomed fo chearfully to meet with in every thing wherein I propofe to ferve yow, that I ftand in fear of no cenfure or detraction elfwhere.

My Lord, this Genealogie I now prefent to yow will clear the uncontroverted antiquity and excellent renowne of youre Family in the general; bot it fhal ferve that I give you heire only a couple of compendious inftances to demonftrat the fame in particular.

Firft, our Soveraigne Lord and Monarch King Charles the Second is the twentieth perfon in a right line from Walter, the Firft great Stuart of Scotland, fprung from the ancient ftock of our 108 Scots Kings; and yow are in direct order of fucceffion alfo the twentieth head of youre family, from Maurice Drummond the firft Thane of Lennox, defcended from the ancient nobility of the Kingdome of Hungary, who was contemporary with that Walter, the firft great Stuart of Scotland; and both with King Malcolm the Third, called Keandmore, in whofe time the degrees of nobility and diftinctions of fyrnames tooke begining in this land.

2. His Sacred Majefty is lineally defcended from one daughter of youre Houfe in the ninth, and from ane other daughter in the fixth degree; and I think few families in the nation can boaft of the lyke honour, faveing the famous houfes of Douglas and Lennox, who make bot up two of the fteps of thefe fex degrees, and confequently both come of youres, as will appear in the body of this collection.

The fplendor of youre Family needs no commendation more then the fune does a candle, and even a litle of the truth from me may be obnoxious to the flander of flattery or partiality, by reafon of my intereft in it; therefore I'le fay the lefs; only this is generally known for a truth, that juftice, loyaltie, and prudence, which have been bot incident vertues and qualities in others, are all three as inherent ornaments, and hereditary in youres.

For juftice, as a poor ftranger, often thruft out of doors from great houfes, where grandor and utility are commonly the idolls thats worfhipped—*quid non mortalia pectora cogis*—hes alwayes found fanctuary in youres, which hes been ever ane incouragement to the good, a terror to the bad, and free from the oppreffion of either. The unrewarded fervices done to, and the unrecompenfed fufferings fuftained for the Crowne by youre Family, are fufficient teftimonys for the loyaltie thereof; albeit no body fhould doe yow the right to mind either. Nor will I fet down the particular inftances of both, which for theire number would requyre more roome then can well be heire allowed. The fubfequent difcourfe will make it appear there was never a blot upon any of your Anceftors for difloyalty, bot that in all commotions they conftantly adhered to their duty, and ever followed the fortune of the Royal Family. But the prudence of youre Progenitors hes been admired by all who obferved it, efpecially in theire difcreet manadgement and wyfe conduct of theire own affaires; for they alwayes lived handfomly lyke themfelves, and ftill preferved or improved theire fortunes fince the firft Founder, without the emoluments of publick and profitable offices, or the advantages of court favors and preferments, which, by theire quality, theire pairts, and theire near relation in blood to the Royall Race, they might as juftly have pretended to as any elfe whatfomever. Neverthelefs, God hes hitherto richely bliffed, and I truft will ftill profper the Noble Family.

Now, My Lord, feeing yow have received from his Sacred Majeftie eminent marks of his Royall bountie, in confideration of youre fingular loyaltie and of the faithfulnes of youre Family, may yow live long to injoy his favor, and be fo happy as to perform great fervices to the Crowne in that high fphere wherein he hes placed yow, whereby yow may not only equal, bot even outfhyne the glory of youre famous Predeceffors.

    Ut fis menfura voti matribus
    Cum bene blandis precantur liberis.

And that youre Pofterity may imitate youre fingular vertues, is the heartie wifh of,
    My Lord,
   Youre moft humble fervant,
    And moft affectionat Cufine,
         W. D.

THE

RACE OF THE ROYAL FAMILY OF THE STUARTS,

FROM THE FIRST OF THAT NAME, WALTER, GREAT STUART OR SENESCALL OF SCOTLAND, THE SONE OF FLEANCHUS, SONE OF BANCHO THANE OF LOCHABER.

1. Walter, by divers authors, is ſtylled *Dapifer* or *Æconomus Regis, Seneſcallus Regni*, and *Totius Scotiae Stuartus*. From this office grew the name Stuart: for his great ſervices againſt the Rebells of Galloway he was made the firſt Seneſcall or Stuart of Scotland by King Malcolm the Third, called Keanmore, about the year 1062. He begot   1062.

2. Allan Stuart, known in old wrytts by the name of Alan Walterſone, a valiant warriour in the Holy land, with Godfrey de Bulloigne, and at the ſiege of Antioch made Duke of Lorraine in the reigne of King Edgar, anno 1099. He begot   1099.

3. Walter, called ſometimes Alanſon, *Magnus Scotiae Seneſcallus*, according to John Fordon, who ſayes, *Walterus filius Alani Dapifer Regis obiit* 1177, in the time of King William. He begot   1177.

4. Alexander, the Firſt of that name, who built the Abbay of Paſlay anno 1169, in King Williams time. He begot   1169.

5. Allan. Allan begot

6. Walter the Third, who about the year 1198 is called Allanſon, and was made firſt Lord of Dundonnald by King Alexander the Second. He dyed 1241: Fordon ſayeth, *Obiit Walterus filius Alani junioris*, 1241. He begot   1198. 1241.

7. Alexander the Second of that name, who beat Acho the Danes King at Larges 1263, in the reigne of King Alexander the Third.   1263.

His brother, Robert Stuart of Torbolton, married the heretrix of Cruxtone, of whom are come the Lords Darnly, Earles and Dukes of Lennox. This Alexander begot

8. John Stuart, who married the heretrix of Brukeland. He was called the Stuart of Buite, becaufe his father Alexander married the heretrix thereof. He was killed at Falkirk, anno 1298. He begot — 1298.

9. Walter Stuart, the Fourth of that name, who married Marjorie Bruce, daughter to King Robert Bruce, anno 1314. He begot — 1314.

10. King Robert the Second, called Blair Ey, Firft King of the Stuarts in his mothers right. He was crowned anno 1371. He begot upon Elizabeth Muire — 1371.

11. King Robert the Third, called John Fairnyear, who married Queen Annabella Drummond. They were both crowned at Scoone, anno 1390. He begot upon Queen Annabella — 1390.

12. King James the Firft, murdered at Perth by Walter Stuart, Earle of Atholl, anno 1437. He begot — 1437.

13. King James the Second, killed at the fiege of Roxburgh Caftle by the fplinter of a fprung cannon, anno 1460. He begot — 1460.

14. King James the Third, beat at the Sauchenfoord, and flaine at Bannocburn miln, anno 1489. He begot — 1489.

15. King James the Fourth, flaine at the battle of Flowden, anno 1513. He begot — 1513.

16. King James the Fifth, who dyed at Falcolland, anno 1542. He begot — 1542.

17. Queen Marie, beheaded in England, anno 1586. She bore to Henry Stuart, Lord Darnley — 1586.

18. King James the Sixth, who fucceeded to the crowne of England 1603, and dyed at Theobalds anno 1625. He begot — 1625.

19. King Charles the Firft, murdered by the Ufurper Olyver Cromwell, anno 1649. He begot — 1649.

20. King Charles the Second, crowned at Scoone, anno 1651, 1651. whom God long preferve.

The Table of the Royal Family of the Stuarts may be queftioned, becaufe fome names in the beginning are otherwife recorded by divers authors, who yet aggree not well amongft themfelves. Bot the teftimonies of the old and beft wrytters, the moft authentick records, with the trueft and moft rational chronological accompts, will conclude this to be the exacteft of any that hes yet appeared ; which might be inftructed by good arguments, if it were proper for this place.

A CATALOGUE OF THE NAMES OF
THE CHEEFE HEADS OF THE DRUMMONDS.

SINCE THEIRE FIRST COMEING TO SCOTLAND, AS THEY SUCCEEDED ONE TO ANE OTHER.

1. Maurice Drummond, the Hungarian, and firft Heretable Thane of Lennox.
2. Malcolm Drummond, his fone.
3. Maurice Drummond, his fone.
4. John Drummond, his fone.
5. Sir Malcolm Drummond, his fone.
6. Malcolm Beg Drummond, his fone.
7. Sir John Drummond, his fone.
8. Malcolm Drummond, Earl of Mar, his fone.
9. Sir John Drummond, his brother.
10. Sir Walter Drummond, his fone.

11. Sir Malcolm Drummond, his fone.
12. John, Lord Drummond, his fone.
13. William, called the Firft Mafter of Drummond, his fone.
14. Walter, the Second Mafter of Drummond, his fone.
15. David, Lord Drummond, his fone.
16. Patrick, Lord Drummond, his fone.
17. James, Earle of Perth, his fone.
18. John, Earle of Perth, his brother.
19. James, Earle of Perth, his fone.
20. James, now Earle of Perth, his fone, *quem non solum excellentia generis verum etiam mores virtutesque nobilitaverunt.*

James Lord Drummond, his fone.

THE GENEALOGIE OF THE MOST
NOBLE AND ANCIENT HOUSE OF DRUMMOND;

CONTAINEING A TRUE ACCOMPT OF THE ORIGINAL EXTRACTIONE, THE OFSPRING, AND ALLAYES OF THAT FAMILY, DEDUCED FROM THE FIRST OF THAT NAME, A NOBLE HUNGARIAN, AND CONTINOWED TO THE PRESENT AGE.

THE PREFACE.

IN the reigne of Malcolm, King of Scots, Second of that name, and about the year of Our Lord 1012, Sueno, King of Denmark, Sueden, Norway, Goths and Vandals, made invafion upon England, to revenge the maffacre committed upon the Danes there. The Englifh King Egeldred or Etheldred, of the Saxon Race, made oppofition, bot was beat and forced to fly the Kingdome ; whereupon Sueno, with common confent and univerfal applaufe, was crouned King of England at London, which fell out after the conqueft of that nation by the fraud of Hengiftus, captaine of the Saxons, about 560 yeares. 1012.

To Sueno, the firft Danifh King of England, fucceeded Harrald, his eldeft ; and then Canutus, his fecond fone, againft whom Edmond Ironfyde, the eldeft fone of Etheldred, continowed the war ; and after diverfe encounters with various fuccefs, it happened at laft that both theire armies, ftanding in array ready to joyne battle near the River of Severn and towne of Glocefter, proffer is made and accepted, that to fpare the great effufion of blood the Kingdome might be determined to whom it fhould belong by a duel to be fought betwixt the two Kings Canutus and Ironfyde, who immediatly in view of both armies entered the combat ; bot being both wounded and wearied fell a treating, and agreed in thir tearmes to divyde the Kingdome betwixt them dureing the life of Ironfyde, after whofe death Canutus was to injoy all. Not long after this agreement Edmond Ironfyde was treacheroufly murdered at Oxfoord by a fubject of his owne called Ederick; and fo the whole kingdome, with the tuo fones of Ironsyde, Edward and Edmond or Edwyn, fel into the hands of Canutus, who, to fecure himfelfe and the crowne to his pofterity, fent thofe tuo young princes for Sweden to be made away and deftroyed theire by the Governour Valgarius. Bot he, pitying the age and innocency of thefe Royal youthes, conveyed them away fecretly, and giveing out they were dead, fent them to Solomon, King of Hungary, who, obferving in them a fpirit fuitable to theire noble defcent, ufed them with much kindnefs; for he gave Agatha his daughter, or, according to fome authors, the fifter of Sophia his Queene, who was daughter of the Emperour Henry the Second, to the eldeft called Edward the Outlaw, in marriage; who begat on her Edgar Athelin, that is in theire language Prince Edgar, Margaret afterward Queen of Scots, and Chriftiana who became a Nun.

Harrold, a natural fone of Canutus, reigned after his father, and left the crowne to his brother, Hardy Canutus; in whofe time ceaffed the rule of the Danes over England.

So the Englifh being free of the Danifh yoke, called home from Normandy Edward, fyrnamed the Confeffor, a fone of Ethelreds by a Second wife, and fo halfe brother to Ironfyde; whom they made King about the year 1043.

1043.

Edward the Confeffor, now King of England, haveing no children, fent to Hungary for his nephew Edward the Outlaw, and his family, to whom he offered the croune as haveing beft right theireto, for he was the eldeft fone of Ironfyde, who was elder brother to Edward the Confeffor; bot he modeftly refufed to accept theireof dureing his Uncles life, and dyed at London anno 1057. And Edward the King,

1057

THE HOUSE OF DRUMMOND. 13

who was the laſt of the Saxon race that governed the Kingdome of
England, dyed anno 1066.   1066.

Edward the Confeſſor being dead, the right of the crowne juſtly
belonged to Edgar Athelin, ſone of Edward the Outlaw, who being
young and haveing litle power to make good his title, Harrold, the
ſone of Goodwyne, Earle of Kent, ſtept into the throne ; bot William,
Duke of Normandy, ſoone after invaded, beat and killed him in a
battle near Haſtings in Suſſex, and was upon this victory crowned at
Weſtminſter anno 1066.   1066.

Edgar Athelin, ſon to Edward the Outlaw, being now apprehen-
ſive of his danger by the juſt pretenſion he had to the crowne, whereof
tirſt he was diſappointed by the uſurpation of Harrold, and now againe
by the Norman Conqueſt, tooke ſhippeing with his mother Agatha,
and his two ſiſters Margaret and Chriſtiana, to eſcape back for
Hungary ; bot, through Divine providence, he was driven by a
violent ſtorme upon the Scots coaſt, and forced to land upon the
north ſide the Firth of Forth, in a harbour a litle be-weſt the Queens
ferry, ever ſince called St. Margurets Hoop, from the name of Edgars
ſiſter Margaret ; whom, for the rare perfectiones of her body and mind,
Malcolm, then King of Scots, and Third of that name, called Keandmore, to the great ſatiſfaction of all the Kingdome, married for his
Queen at Dumferline in the year 1066, or according to Melroſs   1066.
Chronicle anno 1067. And for the kindnes he had receaved from 1067.
Edward the Confeſſor, grand uncle to this Edgar, who had aſſiſted him
with 10000 men in armes againſt MᶜBeath the Uſurper, he not only
maintained Edgar againſt Duke William the Norman, untill a peace
was ſetled wherein Edgar was honourably included, but alſo receaved
many of his freinds with great favour, whereof ſome came with him
and others for ſafety fled after him ; upon whom King Malcolm
beſtowed lands and offices, and whoſe poſterity grew noble and potent
families in the Kingdome.

In the traine of thefe Royal perfones who arrived fafe in that haven near to King Malcolms court at Dumferline, were many brave and worthy gentlemen, both Englifh and Hungarians, who have given beginning to divers families confiderable in the nation; amongft whom was an Hungarian, eminent for his faithfull fervices, and particularly for his fkilfull conduct of Edgar his mother, and his fifters, in that dangerous fea voyage. He was highly efteemed by the Queen, and earneftly by her recommended to the King, who for his merit honoured him with lands, offices, a coat of armes fuitable to his quality, and called him DRUMMOND.

Before thefe times men were commonly diftinguifhed either by patronimicks, adding theire fathers name to theire own, or by agnames, makeing up a word taken from fome accident of theire lyfe, fomething remarkable in the body, or fome fingular quality of the mind, which served only in place of a fyrname to him who got it, and did not defcend to the pofterity. Bot about this age the cuftome from neceffity was introduced, to affix a fyrname to every worthy hero, which was faftened to all his race, whereby every one of that Generation was diftinguifhed from other familys, fo that it was knowen what perfon or trybe he came of; and the reafon of the fyrnames thus impofed was often taken from fome notable action, from the birth place, the office, the lands, fome fingular marks, coulor, or quality of the body, or fome other fuch emergent; as Stuart, Douglas, Cumin, Hay, Scot, Campbell, Butler, Sterlin, Forrefter, Erfkeen, Sckrimgeor, Banerman, &c. And fo it feems this Hungarian Gentleman got his name either from the office, as being captaine director or Admiral to Prince Edgar and his company; for Dromont or Dromond in diverfe nationes was the name of a fhip of a fwift courfe, and the captane theire-of was called Dromant or Dromoner: for proveing this affertion theire are authors very famous, fuch as William of Newberrie, Minfeus in the emendations of his Guide to the languages, John Piccard channon of

St. Victor, Caffiodorus, Sigebert the hiftorian, Mathew Paris, Goldaftus, &c.

Pliny tells of a fifh fwift in fueeming called Dromon ; *et Græcis* Δρωμον *cursum denotat.* Ifiodorus [fays], *Longæ naves sunt, quas Dromones vocamus.* So were the Argonautæ named from the fhip Argos, in which they failed to Colchos. Or otherwayes, the occafion of the name was from the tempest they endured at fea ; for Drummond υδωρ mont, made up of the compound υδωρ and mont fignifying the high hills of waters ; or Drummond from *drum*, which in our ancient language is a hight, and in Latine *dorsum*, a rigging or back, and *und* or *ond* from the Latine *unda*, a wave ; and to this the barrs called *unds*, as they are blazoned in the Drummonds armes, not only agrees, but retaine ane exact refemblance ; and its a maxim in Herauldry, *A nominibus enim ad arma bonum deducitur argumentum.*

The firft lands given to this Hungarian, Drummond, by the King, did ly in Dumbartonfhyre and jurifdiction of Lennox, a country full of rivers, woods, lochs and mountains, emblematicaly expreffed in the coats of armes then given to him, wherein hunting, waters, hounds, inhabitants wild and naked, are reprefented. He had in property the lands of Rofeneth, Cardros, Achindounan, the parifh of Drummond in Lennox and Balfron ; which can be inftructed by old wrytts yet extant, as alfo how thefe lands have been alienated from the poffeffion of the pofterity of this Hungarian by his fucceffors ; for Rofeneth was given to the Monteiths for ane afythment of flaughter, Cardrofs mortifyed for ane alms to Inchmahomo, Achindounan was difponed by Malcolm Beg Drummond to Malcolm Fleeming, about the year 1290. Sir John Drummond, about the year 1440, and Sir Walter, his fone, and Sir Malcolm, his grand chyld, poffeffed the lands of Muithlaw, Kippon, Caufhlie, and Fenwick in Lennox, and Finlarick in Broadalbine. Thomas Drummond, the third fone of Malcolm Beg

1290.
1440.

1305. Drummond, in the year 1305, mortifyed the patronage and teynds of Balfron parifh to the Abbay of Inchaffray. John Lord Drummond,
1470. in the yeare 1470, excambed the lands of Caufhlie and Fenwick in Lennox for the barronie of Strageth in Strathern. And John Earle of Perth fold his lands of Drummond in Monteith to William Earle of Monteith, bot about 50 yeares agoe.

King Malcolm haveing beftowed upon this new Hungarian ftranger a competent inheritance, dignifyed him alfo with ane honourable office, and made him Thane, Senefcal, or Stuart heretable of Lennox; all which titles fignify the fame thing materially, but altered the denomination with the times; the charge whereof was to be gufticiar and guardian of that country, to lead furth the men appointed for the war according to the rolls and lifts made up for that effect, and to be Collector or accomptor to the Abthane of the Kingdome for the Kings rents within that circuit. The Abthane was the higheft Officer under the King, the cheefe Minifter of ftate, general Queftor, principal Thefaurer, and great Stuart of Scotland; and the Thanes were next in degree of honour to him, and were the firft whom King Malcolm advanced to the new titles of Earles: for M‘Duffe of Fyfe and Ferchard of Strathern he made Earles of the countrys whereof they had been Thanes; and Dumbar, Thane of Lothian, was the firft Earle of March. It was alfo the cuftome of thefe times to fubfcrive their names Earle M‘Duffe, Earle Ferchard, without addition, as may be feen in many old charters.

Buchanan, in the lyfe of Malcolm the Second, hes this defcription of Thane: *Superioribus sæculis præter Thanos, hoc est præfectos regionum, sive nomarchas, et quæstorem rerum capitalium, nullum honoris nomen equestri ordine altius fuerat.* And againe, in the lyfe of Malcolm the Third: *Rex Walterum totius Scotiae Stuartum, quasi dicas œconomum fecerit. Hic magistratus census omnes Regios colligit, jurisdictionem etiam qualem conventuum præfecti habent, et prorsus idem est*

THE HOUSE OF DRUMMOND.

cum eo quem priores Thanum appellabant atque nunc sermone Anglico patrium superante Regionum Thani, Stuarti vocantur et qui illis erat Abthanus nunc Stuartus Scotiae nuncupatur.

Finally, this Drummond had given him as a lafting badge of honor from the King, a noble coat of Arms, fitly contrived to reprefent his prefent condition and former atcheivements. Thus

[A BLANK IN THE MANUSCRIPT.]

Which is fo blazoned : *Or*, 3 barrs unds *G* ; a helmet, wreath, coronet, and manteling fuitable to his degree ; and for a creft a bloodhound of the 2d langued, armed, coloured of the 1 ; with two wyld naked men for fupporters, wreathed about the body and head with ivy, each beareing on his fhoulder a club raguled, and gaulthrops lying fcattered about theire feet ; with this motto, GANGE WARRILY.

He was now naturalized a Scot, and had all the parts of his coat armour ingenioufly devyfed and fignificantly to exprefs him, his adventures, his name, his office, and the nation; for fo the Poet defcribes them.

> Illa pharetratis et propria gloria Scotis,
> Cingere venatu faltus, fuperare natando
> Flumina, ferre famem, contemnere frigora et æftus,
> Nec foffa aut muris patriam, fed Marte tueri.

All thefe favors were conferred upon this ftranger foon after the Kings marriage, whom he thankfully ferved againft William the Conquerour, who raifed war againft King Malcolm becaufe he refufed to deliver up to him his owne brother-in-law Edgar, whom he requyred as his fugitive and competitor; bot in end, a peace was treated, wherein Edgars fafety was articled.

William the Norman being dead, his fone, William Rufus, fucceeded; who, without any provocation given, haftily invaded that part of Northumberland which then pertained to the Scots, furpryfed the Caftle of Alnwick, cut off the garrifon, and poffeft himfelfe of the place; which injurie King Malcolm hafted to repair, bot was there unfortunately killed by the fraud of that firft bold Percie, before that action, called Robert Moubray; whereat the young prince Edward, the Kings eldeft fone, was so furioufly enraged, that he run headlong with a few upon the enemy not far from the Caftle, and receaved a wound, whereof foone after he dyed; and in the fame encounter with the prince, the Hungarian Drummond, fighting valliantly, ended his dayes, which fad
1093. accident hapened anno 1093.

It is very probable this Hungarian Drummond's propper name wes Maurice, albeit fome fay John, for it is originally a Dutch name, and wrytten Mauritz, as fome of the Emperoures have been called before this time. Its alfo ordinary amongft the Hungarians, and it hes been frequently ufed amongft his fucceffors without doubt in honour of his memorie; as one wrytting of thofe times fayes, *Fuit illius seculi moribus receptum ut præstantes viri nomen suum ad posteros transmitterent, putaverunt enim grata in vulgus nomina commendationem personis adferre prosse.*

Bot the records of that, as alfo whom he married, and what children he left, are inlackeing, and thereby the names of tuo heads of the family who immediatly followed him not fo certaine as the reft of the generation, yet fo inftructed by probable prefumptiones and tradition that they can not eafily be difproved. And this is no extraordinary thing, if we confider, that even the records of the nation in generations long after him are fo defective that they doe not inform us of the particular names of all the heads of our ancienteft trybes, nor of fome of the male children of the Royal Family; fuch as the fones of David Earle of Huntingtoune, King Williams brother, from whofe daughters a fucceffor behoved to be found to King Alexander the Third; and even amongft the ofspring of thefe daughters there wants not miftakes concerning the names and primogeniture of the fifters from whom the competitors pleaded theire rights; neither does our Genealogifts agree upon all the names and order of the fucceffors of Walter the Firft of the Royal Family of the Stuarts. It may be alfo confidered, that this Hungarian, himfelfe being a stranger, leaveing his children young in a time of much trouble, occafioned both by the invafions of England, inteftine warrs betwixt the fucceeding kings, and the rebellious commotions amongft the fubjects, when either litle was committed to wryte, or if any hes been relateing to him, might, by the injurie of the times, or the following feads and quarrells which befell that family, readily have been loft; ane accident which alfo hes befaln many of the ancient trybes of this nation, whereby fome uncertaintyes or blanks may happen amongft the names of the heads of theire families, by the fame or fome fuch lyke contingents, yet nothing derogateing from the truth and fufficient knouledge of the fucceffions extraction.

A Francifcan frier, called Adam Abel, in his hiftorie of our nation, which he calls the Wheele of Time, hes thefe words: The Drummonds,

Leflies, Creichtons, Borthwicks, Giffards, Fotheringhams and Maulds, came into Scotland from Hungarie with Queen Margaret, whereof the pofterity have preferved ane uninterrupted and fixed perfuafion.

John Leflie, Bishop of Rofs, in his Chronicle, reckning the families whofe prediceffors cam hither immediatly after King Malcolm Keandmore, makes mention amongft others of Cargill, which he miftakes for Drummond; for Cargill is bot the name of one of the barronies which the Drummonds of old hes and does now poffefs, and it may be that error flowed from hence, that fome of the heads of that family have been in old wryttings fo ftyled, as Sir Walter of Cargyll, and Sir Malcolm of Cargyll, &c.

1418. About the year 1418, a young cadet of this family, who had a bold adventureing fpirit, went abroad to travell, and after variety of accidents in diverfe foreigne parts fetled himfelfe at laft under the King of Portugalls dominions, in one of his Illands about the Latitude of 32° or 33° fome 4° benorth the Canarie or Fortunat Ilands, a litle fouthward of the Straits of Gibralter, called Madera, where he lived under the name of John Efcortio; bot about the time of his death gave this accompt of himfelfe, that he was a Scots Gentleman, born of the family of Stobhal, that his name was Drummond, a fone of Sir John Drummond, the brother of Annabella Drummond, Queen to Robert Third, King of Scots, and that his eldeft brother was Sir Walter Drummond of Stobhall. This information he left to direct his children to fearch out his pedegree when they fhould find occafion, whereby they being ftrangers might make it appear that they were Gentlemen by defcent of this John Efcortio his fucceffion. Ane information from Portugal was fent to Scotland, in the minority of King James the Fifth, fignifying that the number of men, women and children, who acknowledged them felves come of him were no lefs then 200 perfones; one of the principal whereof called Manuel Alphonfo Ferriera Drummond, fent a meffage to David, then Lord

Drummond, with a gentleman, Thomas Drummond, who in his travells met with this Manuel himfelfe, his brothers, and divers others of the Drummonds at Porto Sancto. Manuel Alphonfo, by this meffenger, fent a relation of the ftorie of his prediceffor John Efcortio, according as himfelfe had revealed it at his death, and earneftly defyred ane accompt of the Family from which he was defcended, with a teftificat or borebreife of theire gentility, and the coat of arms pertaineing to the name. Whereupon David Lord Drummond, with his cheefeft freinds, made adrefs to the Councell of Scotland, who granted him his demand, and gave him a noble teftimony, under the great feal of the Kingdome, with the particular fealls appended, and fubfcriptiones added of every one of the councellors then prefent, wherein the defcent of the Drummonds from that firft Hungarian Admiral to Queen Margaret in her voyage to Scotland, is largely attefted; and it is underwrytten thus:

  James, Archbifhop of St. Andrews.
  Gavin, Bifhop of Aberdeen.
  James, Bifhop of Dumblane.
  Archibald, Earle of Angus, Lord Douglas.
  George, Earle of Huntly, Lord Gordon.
  Colin, Earle of Argyle, Lord Campbell and Lorn.
  John, Earle of Lennox, Lord Darnlie.
  Cutbert, Earle of Glencairn, Lord Kilmars.
  John, Lord Lyndfay.
  John Sterlin of Keer.
  James Toures of Innerleith.   Knights.
  John Charters of Amersfeild.
  Mr. David Kinghorn.   Alex. Scot, &c.

Upon which deed, Sir Robert Barton of Overbarton, controller and councellor, Tutor and Guardian to David Lord Drummond, then under minority, afked and took inftruments in the hands of Mr. John

THE GENEALOGIE OF

Chapman, Notarie and Clerk to the Counceell. The Lord Drummond fent this to his Cufins in Madera, with letters full of civility and kindnes; whereof the coppies are preferved amongft the wrytts of the family, and are mentioned in theire own place heireafter.

There are fome of late who, contrary to what hath been faid and already cleared, doe alledge that the firft Drummond was one Duncan Drummach, a brother to Euen Campbell, firft knight of Lochaw, the fone of Gillefpick, the fone of Gillicallom, brother to Paul O duyne, the fone of Duyne Faldarg, all knights of Loch Crochan; which Loch was firft fo called becaufe it lyes at the foot of the great hill Crochan-Ben, bot now called Loch Awah, from a daughter of Paul O duyne of that name, heretrix of the eftate, and married to Euen Campbell, the firft knight of Lochawah, her cufine; and it is from this Paul O duyne that the tribe retaines the denomination to this day of Clan O duyne: bot the ftorie of this Duncan, they have founded upon as groundlefs and conterfit traditions, as the reafons they bring to prove the original of either name or arms of Drummond are weake and infignificant. This Duncan, fay they, defcending from the Highlands to the Low countrie, parted from his friends upon a remarkable place in his way called Carndrum, upon the confines of Argyle and Perthfhyres, where there is a Carn made up with three rifeing tops; and as from Drumach or Carndrum they derive the name Drummond, fo doe they the armes from the three rifeing tops in the Carns; and to gaine credit to the fable, they pretend a record wrytten in the Saxon character, preferved in Argyle and the Ifles fince the year 1085. 1085, wherupon this fiction is grounded; and they add, that the old forbeares of both fydes haveing knouledge heireof, it produced mutual marriages and bonds of freindfhip, with a long continowed amitie betwixt the families.

Bot to confute the whole alledgeance, thefe following confiderations may ferve. And, firft, as to the name:—It is known to be a conftant practife, both with us and elfe where, that alwayes the pofterity zealoufly retaines amongſt them the names of theire famous anceftors, efpecially of thofe who have been the firft worthie authors of theire families ; whereof might be given innumerable inftances. Therefore, if any truth were in this matter, how comes it that never one of the Drummonds fhould have been named after this Duncan, theire firft devyfed parent ; nor have the names of Archbald, Ewen, Donald, Collin, Neil or Gillefpick, fo ordinary amongft the heads and other confiderable perfones of the Campbells, ever been once heard to be ufed by any perfon of quality called Drummond ; bot contrarywife, the names of Maurice, Malcolm, Walter, Gilbert, &c. much ufed amongft the firft of the Drummonds, are as unfrequently, if at all, to be found amongft the Campbells. Next, for the original reafon of the fyrname of Drummond, we have already given it a better and more rational derivation then from either Drummach or Carndrum ; and it had been a better fancy to have alledged that Drummond fhould be Trimont, and the family Trimontanti, either from the three hills upon Carndrum, or from Duncan Drumach his goeing beyond the mountaines, if Italian had been in thofe dayes the language of Argyle.

Bot let us now behold the two Coat Armoures, and we will find in herauldrie that the waves or barrs unde in the Drummonds armes, efpecially being thryfe repeated, are as unlyke to hills or carns as the gyrons and fhips in the Campbells are to waved barrs in the Drummonds ; and when we compare the whole atcheivement of the armes of the two families together, it will appear there is no part nor charge that hes any refemblance in the one lyke the other, which may ferve for a demonftration, according to the rules of herauldrie, that none of the families are lineally defcended of the other ; for in that art this is granted, that if tuo families of one fyrname bear feveral Coats of Armour, its no argument they are originally ifhewed from the fame anceſtors, becauſe unleſs there be a reſemblance betwixt the tuo coat armoures, the agreement of the ſyrnames is bot a probability, and no proofe that both are extracted from the ſame root; bot where the tuo families are diſtinct, with different ſyrnames, and beares ſeverall coats, there is left us not the leaſt appeareance of probability to ſuſpect them to have flowed from the ſame fontaine.

And where its told, that a wrytte in the Saxon character, ſo long preſerved in Argyle and the Iſles, is the ground of the tradition, and that the forbeares of both families underſtood how they were related to other, which produced marriages, mutual bonds of ffreindſhip, and long continowed love betwixt them: It is anſwered thereto, Firſt, Will any man beleive a Saxon character to have been ſo long legible theire, who knowes how that reading and wrytting of any language, ſave the Ireiſh only, and that very rare, have been bot meere ſtrangers, except of late, in theſe parts. Next, as to the marriages, bonds of freindſhip and amitie, betwixt the tuo houſes, its found mentioned amongſt the Earle of Perths wrytts that a ſiſter of Queen Annabella 1390. Drummond, about the year 1390, was married to the knight of Lochow, which made up the firſt freindſhip betwixt the Campbells and Drummonds, who were in enmitie bot a litle before upon a quarrell betwixt the Drummonds and Monteiths, with whom the Campbells ſyded; and its not improbable that King James the Firſt, Queen Annabellas ſone, upon that relation, made either that knight of Lochaw, or his ſone, the firſt Earle of Argyle; bot whether there were any children of that marriage, I know not. Again, about the 1474. year 1474, Sir John Drummond, ſtyled of Cargyll, afterwards Lord Drummond, indents with Colin Earle of Argyle, Lord Lorn, etc. to marrie his ſone and air, Malcolm Drummond to Lady Iſſobella Campbell, the Earles daughter, and to give them 30 merk land in preſent portion, lying in the Earledome of Lennox, and faylzieing of Malcolm, the next ſone ſhould be ſubſtitute; to which Indenture Andrew

Stuart, Lord Evendale, Chancellor of Scotland to King James the
Third, is a witnes, and which marriage was accordinglie folemnized
with William the fecond fone, after the death of Malcolm the eldeft.
Moreover, David Lord Drummond, grandchyld to the faid William,
Mafter of Drummond, by the Lady Iffobella Campbell, about the
year 1533, and after him Patrick Lord Drummond, his fone, great   1533.
grandchyld to William by that fame Lady Iffobella, in anno 1573   1573.
re-entred in mutual bonds of freindſhip with Collin, Earle of Argyle,
Chancellor and Juftice General of Scotland, wherein they both
acknouledge theire defcent from the Earles houfe; bot its plainly
underftood to be by the Lady Iffobella, and no otherwayes. All
thefe bonds are yet extant in the Earle of Perths cuftody.

Ane other argument may be drawen from the bloody quarrell
which happened betwixt the Drummonds and Monteiths, begun about
the year 1330, and fo folemly reconciled by the authority of King   1330.
David Bruce, and the mediation of the Earles of Strathern, Douglas
and Angus, in the year 1360, as fhal be related in its proper place. 1360.
Had it not been very unnatural in the Campbells (who not only fyded
with the Monteiths againft the Drummonds the whole time of the difference, bot alfo refufed theire affent to the conditions of agreement
when the principall parties were fatisfyed) to have ufed that of theire
own kindred and lineal defcent fo unkindly, had there then been any
fuch blood relation underftood by either.

To fumme up the matter, the forefaid Colin, Earle of Argyle, had
never fealed nor fubfcrived the teftificat from the Councell of Scotland,
given to David Lord Drummond as a bore breiff for his Cufines in Madera, declareing ane other true original to the Drummonds, if they had
been directly and lineally defcended from his own houfe. This long
digreffion is extorted to anfuere a paper framed by Mr. Alexander Colvill, Juftice deput of Scotland, (otherwife a man well verfed in the antiquities of the nation), bot who, to flatter the late Marques of Argyle,

E

his patron, was author or outgiver of the ſtorie, that the Drummonds were come of this Duncan of Lochaw, brother to the anceſtor of the Marques. What ever was Colvills miſtake upon the poynt, yet in this he hes done the Drummonds ſome right, to make theire beginning in this nation as ancient as the firſt knight of Lochaw, which wants nothing in effect of ſex hundreth yeares, and to obſerve the many tokens of freindſhip betwixt the tuo houſes long agoe ; when the truth is, the Drummonds were Thanes of Lennox as ſoone as the Campbells were Knights of Lochaw ; and the tyes of mutual freindſhip betwixt the Families entertained by theire predeceſſors, is not for any thing known as yet difcontinowed.

CONCERNING THE FIVE FIRST HEADS OR CHEEFS OF THE DRUMMONDS,
WHO SUCCEEDED TO BE THANES OR SENESCALLS OF LENNOX, EACH
AFTER OTHER.

THE FIRST PARTITION.

It being in the preface fufficiently made appear, that the Hungarian gentleman, Maurice Drummond (who came into Scotland with Queen Margaret the faint), was the firft root of that family, from whom have grown a numerous offspring; the laws of orderly method will now requyre that the particular names of the cheef heads defcended from him, following the right lyne, whom they married, what children they begot, and how they were difpofed upon, with the times wherein they flourifhed, be all rightly marfchalled; and with each cheef theire propper branches as they iffewed from him, and how they profpered, in theire due places feverally difcuffed; that fo the Genealogie of the whole generation, with theire allies, may be (fo far as we have right) prettie well underftood.

The Hungarian, Maurice Drummond, firft heretable Thane or Senefcall of Lennox, came to Scotland in anno 1066, where he lived about 27 yeares, and with his foveraigne Lord the King Malcolm Keandmore, and his fone prince Edward, dyed in the feild at Alnwick in anno 1093; as is in the preface before related. He left behind him, as fome fay, tuo young fones, the eldeft he called, after his mafter and benefactor the King, Malcolm, and the other Maurice. From this Hungarian are lineally defcended all the worthie families of the Drummonds, and by their daughters in feverall ages, not only the greateft

The First Drummond Thane of Lennox.
1066.

1093.

and moſt ancient of our Nobility, but alſo the whole Royal Family ſince King Robert the Third, beſides many Queens and Princeſſes of forraigne nations, as will appear by the enſewing relation. Many paralell paſſages might be inſtanced betwixt that famous Trojan prince, founder of the Roman nation, and this Hungarian ſtranger, father to the tribe of the Drummonds, *si parva licet componere magnis;* bot a word borrowed from Maro, ſhal only be applyed:

>Multum ille et terris jactatus et alto.

And

>Tantæ molis erat *Drummondam* condere gentem.

1093.   2. Malcolme Drummond, the eldeſt ſone of Maurice the Hungarian, ſucceeded to be the ſecond Thane or Seneſcal of Lennox. He lived in the times of Edgar and Alexander, the ſones of Malcolme Keandmore, both Kings of Scotland after other, and ſome yeares longer. He begot a ſone who ſucceeded to him, whom he named after his father Maurice. Of this Malcolms brother, ſecond ſone to Maurice the Hungarian, there is no certaine accompt to be made, through the defect of ancient wrytts.

1142.   3. Maurice Drummond, the ſone of Malcolme, was the third Thane or Seneſcall of Lennox, and contemporarie with King David, the youngeſt ſone of Malcome the Third, and alſo with King Malcolme the Fourth, called the Maiden, whoſe father was Henrie the prince, ſone to King David. We can tell no more of him, bot that he left a ſone to ſucceed him, called John Drummond.

1184.   4. John Drummond, the ſone of Maurice, was the fourth Thane or Seneſcall of Lennox. He was head and cheefe of the family of Drummond, when William, called the Lyon, brother to Malcolme the Maiden, wes King of Scots. He had a ſone who ſucceeded, called Sir Malcolme Drummond.

5. Sir Malcolm Drummond, the fone of John, was the fyfth Thane 1228. or Senefcall of Lennox, and lived in the time of King Alexander the Second. He had two fones, Malcolme who fucceeded, called Malcolme Beg, and Gilbert Drummond. We have nothing material recorded of this Sir Malcolm the father; bot of his fecond fone Gilbert it feems one Bryce Drummond was defcended, whome the Monteiths bafely killed about the year 1330, when the quarrell begune betwixt them and the Drummonds; as fhall be declared in the third partitione following.

Albeit there be no wreat extant to give us a precife accompt of all the fones and daughters of thefe foregoeing heads of the family of Drummond, nor whom they married; yet there is fufficient ground to beleive that they matched both themfelves and theire children with none of the fmall or inconfiderable trybes of the nation. For makeing this appear, there is found amongft the Earle of Perths old evidents (whereof many are loft) one wonderfully preferved, which is a large fkin of parchment, writen in very ornat Latine, containeing ane Indenture of aggreement betwixt the Drummonds and Menteiths before the judges delegat be King David Bruce for compofeing theire bloody difference, (as fhal be more particularly mentioned in its proper place), wherein the Nobles who interpofed, and did ftipulat as furcties that both fydes fhould fland to the arbitrators determination, are faid to be in the fame degree of kindred to both the differing parties; and thofe noble mediators who ratifyed the treatie were Robert Stuart, the Kings nephew, then Earle of Strathern, afterward King Robert the Second, William the firft Earle of Douglas, and Thomas Stuart Earle of Angus, three of the prime perfones of the kingdome. Robert is mentioned in this maner, *Insuper Robertus Dominus Senescallus Scotiæ Comes de Strathern, tanquam principalis parentelæ utriusque partis, &c.:* fo that from hence it appeares, that the Drummonds have been long before that time nearly related not only to the ancient houſes of Douglas and Angus, bot even then alſo to the Royal Family of the Stuarts; albeit the records be wanting which ſhould inſtruct the particulars: Only this much is clear, without controverſie, that Ada, wife to Malcolme Beg Drummond, was neece to John, Stuart of Scotland, killed at Falkirk, and ſo cuſin german to Walter Stuart who married Marjorie Bruce, daughter to King Robert the Firſt, and mother to King David the Second, &c. And where it is made appear, and clearly informed, from what families the cheefs of the ſubſequent generations both immediatly following and conſtantly thereafter did make choiſe of theire wives, it cannot be denyed bot that they were alwayes allyed amongſt the cheife nobility of the nation, as will be by the enſueing Narration better underſtood.

Concerning Malcolm Beg Drummond, and the Branches descended from him.

PARTITION THE SECOND.

MALCOLM Drummond, the ſone of Sir Malcolm, ſucceeded to his father, and was the ſext Thane or Seneſcal of Lennox. He was a man of a low ſtature, and therefore was nick named or ag-named Beg, that is, in the ancient language of the nation, litle Malcolme; yet he had a ſpirit as great as any of his equals in quality whatſomever. He married Ada or Adama, only daughter of Malduine or Maldonich, Earle of Lennox, and ſiſter to Malcolm, his only ſone, who was Earle after him. Malcolm Beg Drummond begat with Ada four ſones, John, Maurice, Thomas and Walter Drummonds. Before we proceed any further, it will not be amiſs, for the better underſtanding the Genealogic of this Ada, and what this Maldwine, Earle of Lennox, her father, was, to deduce his pedegree from his anceftors as far upward as either our hiftories or old manufcripts can guid us.

In the lyfe of King Malcolm the Second, and at the battle fought by him befyd Murthlake in Marr againft the Danes, under the conduct of Olaus and Enechus, generals for King Sueno, about the year 1013, we read, that Kenneth of the Ifles, Grimus of Strathern, and Dumbar of Lothiane, three valiant Thanes of theire own countries, were all flain in the begining of the fight, to the great terror and difcouradgment of the Scots; which accident had weel near endangered a great victorie obtained by the Kings good conduct and valour at that time. This King Malcolm had with great contention confirmed the new law made by King Kenneth the Third, ordaineing, that the children of the defunct King fhould immediatly injoy the kingdome in theire order, and in caice of pupillaritie be governed by a Tutor until the 14th year of theire age; and fo abrogated the old law made in King Feritharis reigne, whereby in the caice of minority of the Kings children the next of the blood Royal, and fitteft to govern, was to rule for his lyftime, and the former Kings children to reigne thereafter; which was the practife of the Nation for 1025 yeares.

For all this care King Malcolme had no male children, only tuo daughters, Beatrix and Doaca; the eldeft, Beatrix, he beftowed upon Albanach Crinen, Thane of the Ifles, Abthane of Dull or Dow, and Stuart of Scotland (for all thefe are identick tearmes, and fynonimoufly fignify the fame thing), the fone of Kenneth who was killed as is before mentioned, and who begat King Donald the father of King Malcolm Keandmore; and the youngeft, Doaca, he gave to Sinel, Thane of Angus or Glames, the father of McBeth.

It was Albanach Crinen, whofe valor gained that victory at Achnavaid in Glenquaich, where King Malcolm overcame and killed King Grimus the ufurper; for reward of which fervice he got Beatrix, the

Kings daughter, in marriage. Now he being to propagate the Royal line, provyded his brother Grimus to be heritable Thane of Strathern, and to manage the Abthanes charge, for which he had the title of Baylie of the Abthanie of Dull, but was killed as is related. After, when King Malcolme Keandmore came to the Crown, he conferred the Abthanes office upon Walter, the fone of Fleanchus, grandchyld of Bancho, Thane of Lochaber, who was firſt called *Dapifer* or *Seneſcallus Regis*, and afterwards *Seneſcallus Scotiæ*, or great Stuart of Scotland, whoſe office became his firname, and in fome old wryts is defigned only Walter Seneſcal. Upon this preferment, Ferchad, then a young man, grandchild of Grimus, Thane of Strathern, became very difcontented with the King for beſtowing that office upon Walter Stuart, (which he judged, becaufe of his near relation to Crinen, due to himſelfe), and plotted treafonable defignes for furpryfing the King at Bertha, a place near to his government; bot King Malcolm diſcovering the confpiracy, ufed great magnanimity and clemencie in rebukeing and pardoning Ferchad; for he not only forgave him upon his confeſſion, bot alfo, in recompenfe of his Abthanes office, which he pretended too, erected the Thanerie of Strathern in a Countie Palatine, and made him Earle thereof; continowing alfo to him and his poſterity the Bayliſhip of the Abthanie of Dull; which office of the Bailliſhip, after a long feries of fucceſſions, at laſt fell to be and now is one of the antiquated titles of the Earles of Perth, who, becaufe the profits belonging thereto are fallen from it, have fuffered both title and benefit thereof in a maner to prefcrieve.

<small>Vide Freebairn upon the Abthanie of Dull & Apindow.</small>

Ferchard Earle of Strathern, we find, had tuo fones and tuo daughters, Gilbert and Malice, Arabella and Chriſtiana. The youngeſt, Chriſtiana, married Walter Olyffard, who got with her the parroch of Strageth, called now Blackfoord, which Walter his fone reſtored or excambed with her brother Gilbert, the fecond Earle of Strathern, and he mortifyed the patronage thereof to the Abbacie of Inchaffray, about

THE HOUSE OF DRUMMOND.

the year 1200. Ferchad, with his eldeſt daughter Arabella, gave in portion the barronie of Nethergaſk to Sir Robert Quincie, the father of Sir Seier or Saer, and grandfather of Sir Roger Quincie, Earle of Wincheſter, who had to wife Helen, the eldeſt of three daughters, coheireſſes of Allan, Lord of Galloway, Conſtable of Scotland; in whoſe right he ſucceeded to the Conſtables office after the death of Allan. Of this marriage many of our hiſtorie wrytters ſeem to be ignorant, when they relate the paſſages of the competitions for the crown after the death of King Alexander the Third. This Sir Roger Quincie, Earle of Wincheſter and Conſtable of Scotland, gave the name of Quincies burgh to the village in Kirkliſtoun pariſh, a part of his inheritance. He had no ſones, and Alexander Cumin, Earle of Buchan, married his daughter Elizabeth Quincie, with whom he got the barronie of Nethergaſk; which went with a daughter of John Red Cumin, Alexanders grandchild, to Maurice Murray, Lord of Bothwel; and he left it to Sir Malcolm Murray, his ſecond ſone, the father of Sir William Murray, the firſt laird of Tullibardine.

Earle Ferchads eldeſt ſone was Gilbert, who, in his charters of donations to the Church to ſhew his magnificence, wreats himſelfe, *Dei indulgentia Comes de Strathern.* He married Mathildis or Maud, daughter to William of Aubignie, Earle of Arundel, of whom are deſcended in order three Earles of Strathern, to wit, Robert and two Maliſſes; the laſt whereof was forfaulted be King Robert Bruce for adhereing to the Cumins.

Earle Ferchads youngeſt ſone was Maliſe, whom he made Seneſcall of Strathern and Baylie of the Abthanie of Dull. He conſtitute under him three Thanes of Aughterarder, Strowan and Dinning, in imitation of the Kingly government. This Malice married Ada, the youngeſt daughter of David Earle of Huntingtown, and widdow of Henrie Lord Haſtings, one of the ten poſtulators of the Croun, when the deciſion of theire pretentions was unhappily ſubmitted to Edward the

34 THE GENEALOGIE OF

Firſt of England. David Earle of Huntingtoun beſtowed upon this Malice, his ſone in law, the Earledome of Lennox ; which was the firſt title of Nobility he had from King William his brother, as appeares by his charter dated about 1184. Malice got from his father, Earle Ferchad, a great pairt of Muthil pariſh, the patronage whereof he mortified to the Abbay of Lundores, founded by David, father to his lady Ada.

Malice, Earle of Lennox, begot with Ada tuo ſones, viz. Malice and Gillineff. Malice was Earle of Lennox after his father, and begot Maldwine. Maldwine ſucceeded to be Earle, and married a daughter of Alexander Stewart, Great Stuart of Scotland, ſecond of that name, and ſone of Walter Lord Dundonald. He begot Malcolm, who was Earle of Lennox after his father, and a daughter Ada, the wife of Malcolm Beg Drummond.

Malcolm, the ſone of Maldwine, was the laſt Earle of Lennox of that name. He married a daughter of Sir John Menteiths, Captaine of Dumbarton Caſtle, bot had no ſones. It was he who did ſo great and faithfull ſervices to King Robert Bruce dureing the time of his troubles, and the teſtimonies of kindnes and loyalty which he ſhew to the King in his lyftime he confirmed by a reſignation of his fortune to him at his death ; which the King beſtowed not upon Sir John Menteith (as himſelfe expected), bot upon Robert Stuart of Tarbolton, Earle Malcolms uncle, and ſecond ſone of Walter Lord Dundonald ; with whoſe poſterity it continowed under the titles of Lords of Darnly, Earles and Dukes of Lennox, untill oure time. For this aſſertion I lean to the authoritie of Mr. John Freebairn, who poſitively avers that there was no Earle of Lennox of that name.

Gillineff, the ſone of Malice, and uncle of Maldwine Earle of Lennox, ſucceeded to be Seneſcal of Strathern. He againe begot Malice, who married Muriel, the daughter of Congal ſone to Duncan Earle of

Mar, the widdow of Fergus the fon of Gilbert Earle of Strathern; and he got with her the lands of Tullibardine. She bore to Malice a fone, Henrie, and a daughter, Ada. The daughter married Sir William Murray, the fone of Sir Malcolm Murray. He got the lands of Tullibardine in portion confirmed to him, with confent of Henrie her brother, by Malice the firft of that name Earle of Strathern, in a court holden at Dunfay upon the laft of October 1284.

Henrie fucceeded to be Senefcal of Strathern after his father Malice, and had only a daughter, who married Sir Maurice Drummond, the fecond fone of Malcolm Beg Drummond. He got with her both the office and lands which pertained to her father Henrie. This was the firft Drummond who was Senefcal or Stuart of Strathern, and the firft of the Knights of Croncraige. To inftruct upon what grounds the cheife preceeding affertions are founded, we will heire infert the coppies of fome old charters, whereby it will appear that what is alledged is not *gratis dictum*. 1164698

1. "WILLIAM, by the grace of God King of Scotland, to all Bifhops, Abbots, Counts, Barrons, Jufticiars, Vifcounts, Provofts, Minifters, and to all good Subjects of my realm, Clerks and Laicks, Greeting,— Be it known to all who are prefent or to come me to have given and granted, and by this my charter confirmed to David, my brother, the Earledome of Levenox, with all the pertinents thereof, Lundores, Dundee, Forgend, Petmothel, Newtyle, Fintrich, Rothlod, Inneraw, Monkegin, Boverd, Dornoch, Uven ad Uven, Garrioch, and Myrtoune which is in Lothian befyde the Maiden Caftle. I will, therefore, and command that the forefaid David, my brother, and his aires, fhal hold of me and my heires, in few and heritage, all the faid lands, &c. pay- and to me and my aires the fervice of ten fouldiers: Witneffes, Hugo Bifhop of St. Andrews, Jocelin Bifhop of Glafgow, Mathew Bifhop of Aberdeen, Simon Bifhop of Murray, Adam Bifhop of Caitnes, Earle Duncan, Earle Gilbert, Earle Walden, Malcolm Earle of Athol,

Gilchrift Earle of Angus, Earle Colvan, Richard Morvil our Conftable, Robert Quincie, Walter Olyphard, Alan McWalter Senefcal, William Hay, Rodrick Vere, Richard Montficket, William Lyndfay, Malcolm the fone of Earle Duncan, Patrick fone to Earle Walden, William fone to Richard Morvill, David de Souls: Apud Perth." Confider the witneffes, and albeit the charter wants date, it will be found to be about the year 1184.

2. "To all the faithful children of the Kirk, prefent or to come, who fhal fee thir letters, Ada, daughter to David Earle of Huntington, and fpoufe to Malice the fone of Ferchad Earle of Strathern, Be it known me to have granted, and by this my charter confirmed to the Kirk of St. Marie and St. Andrew of Lundores, and the monks ferving thereat, in a free and perpetual alms, ane plough gang of land, together with my corps, lying in the village of Bellimach, with the common pafturage of the fame, free and abfolved from all fecular burden, before thir witneffes : Henrie and Peter my chaplains, Malcolm Bartholfone, William Vafceline, Henry Malerbie, Angus his brother, Ralfe Gilkirk Vinemer, Juan Reynold, and many more." This feems to have been after the year 1228.

3. "To all and fundrie the children of the Holy Kirk, prefent or to come, who fhall fee thir letters, Maldwine, Earle of Lennox, Greeting, Be it known to yow me to have given, granted and confirmed to God and the Kirk of St. Marie at Kelfo, and the Monks ferving God thereat, the Kirk of Campfay, with all the pertinents and liberties thereof, in a free alms as freely and quietly as any Laick patron in the Kingdome of Scotland hes given any Kirk in alms to any religious men, even as it is contained in a charter of Earle David, and confirmation of William his brother, and Jocelin fometimes Bifhop of Glafgow; and for fecurity thereof, I have appended my feal to this prefent wreat befor thir witneffes : Walter, Senefcal to the King, Malcolm Beg my Senefcal, Gilbert my Judge, and Duffen my Cham-

THE HOUSE OF DRUMMOND.

berlane, and divers others." This was near about the year 1299, and Walter, Senefcal, was he that married Marjorie Bruce.

Haveing thus traced the defcent of Maldwine, Earle of Lennox, back through divers generationes, for the better knouing of Ada his daughter (whom Malcolm Beg Drummond took to wife); and alfo the pretenfions her children had to the Earledome of Lennox, after the death of Earle Malcolm, her only brother, who dyed without iffhew: We now return where we left, to Malcolm Beg Drummond his fones; bot thal begin with the youngeft, and proceed to the eldeft, who fucceeded to his Father, and fhal be treated of in the partition following. He lived to be a man of great age, and no lefs efteem: he dyed when he was above 90 yeires, and much about the fame time with King Robert Bruce.

Vide Mr. Freebairn upon Lennox. B. B.

[A BLANK IN THE MANUSCRIPT.]

Malice Earle off Strathern's Charter, to be remembred heire.

Walter Drummond, his youngeft fone, was Clerk Regifter or Secretarie to the King, whom Stow mentions in this maner in his Annalls. In the year 1323 there was a dyet appointed betwixt King Robert Bruce and King Edward of England, for eftablifhing a peace, or rather ceffation of armes, who met by theire Commiffioners at the Neucaftel upon Tyne the 30th of May: for the King of England, Aimer de Valence Earle of Pembroke, Hugh Spenfer the younger, Robert Baldoch Archdean of Midlefex, Sir William Herle knight, William de Aizewine channon of York, and Galfrid de Scroop; for the King of Scots, William Bifhop of St. Andrews, Thomas Randal Earle of Murray, John Monteith and Robert Lauder the father, knights, together with Walter Drummond Clerk to the King of Scots.

Thomas Drummond, third fone to Malcolm Beg, got from his father for patrimonie the lands of Balfrone, and mortifyed the patronage and tythes thereof to the Abbay of Inchaffray; whom Pope Clement the 5th, in his Bul and confirmation of the charter thereupon, in anno 1305, which was a year before King Roberts Coronation, calls Thomas Drummond *Hominem nobilem.*

I have feen a charter granted be Murdoch Earle of Menteith, the fone of Alexander, fometime Earle of Menetheth, to Walter Meneth, the fon of Sir John Meneth, of the lands called Thom in the countrie of Meneth, exactly marched and meithed, wherein there is no date ; only the witneffes makes us know it was about the year 1296, who ftands thus : *Testibus dominis Johanne de Meneth, Malisio de Strathern, Willelmo de Montefixo, Militibus, Alexandro de Meneth, Gilberto de Drummond et Malcolmo de Drummond.* From the time, we conclud that this Gilbert was brother to Malcolm Beg, uncle of Thomas and Walter before fpecifyed ; bot we have nothing bot conjecture for it, nor any further accompt of them, except in ane extract from the Records in the Tower of London, be Mr. John Prine, the lawyer; where, amongft many fheets full of names fubfcriveing fidelity to King Edward the Firft of England, this Gilbert Drummond is infert, called of the countie of Dumbreton, in the year 1296 ; and apparently one Malcolm was his fone and one Bryce his grandchild.

Sir Maurice Drummond, fecond fone to Malcolm Beg, was the firft Stuart or Senefcal of Strathern of that name ftyled Knight of Concraig, whofe Ofspring we will reckon in theire due order, and the families that are come of him : and then return to the principal Houfe, whereof Sir John Drummond, the eldeft fone of Malcolm Beg Drummond, and elder brother of this Sir Maurice Drummond, was head, and the feventh Thane of Lennox.

THE HOUSE OF DRUMMOND.

THE OFSPRING OF SIR MAURICE DRUMMOND OF CONCRAIG, SECOND SONE TO MALCOLM BEG DRUMMOND, THANE OF LENNOX. — Drummonds of Concraig.

Sir Maurice Drummond married the only child and airefs of Hen- — The First Steuart of Strathern, Laird of Concraig. rie, heritable Senefcal or Stewart of Strathern. Of the defcent of this Henrie we have already faid fufficiently. By this match, and the deceafs of his father in law, Maurice came to ane honourable office and a plentifull fortune; for albeit his pretenfions, by the right of his wife, were non of the ftrongeft, yet, by the favor of King David Bruce and the kindnes of Robert Stuart, the Kings nephew, Senefcal of Scotland and Earle of Strathern, there was made up to him a folid right; for befydes the charter and confirmation he got of the office and of the lands belonging to Henrie, Robert the Earle granted him a new gift of Forreftrie to reach over all the forrefts in the country, makeing him Heritable keeper. This was the firft Knight of Concraig, and the firft Senefcal or Stuart of Strathern of that name.

Sir Maurice Drummond had three fones, Maurice the eldeft who fucceeded, Malcolm the fecond who was the original ftock of the houfe of Culqualzie, and a third called Walter Drummond of Dalcheefick. Of Malcolm and the family of Culqualzie, becaufe it is the — Culqualzie firft branch from Concraig, we fhall make mention in due order.

2. This Sir Maurice Drummond was a brave gentleman, and lived in good credit; and both he and his lady were honourably burried in the queere of the church of Muthil. Sir Maurice Drummond, fone to the former Sir Maurice, was the fecond of the houfe of Concraig, and Senefchal of Strathern. He married Marrion Erfkin, daughter to Sir Robert Erfkine of Balhagartie in Mar, chamberlane of Scotland, and had with her tuo fones; John who fucceeded and Malcolm

Pitzallonie. Drummond, the author of the houfe of Pitzallonie, and the fecond branch from the family of Concraig.

I find a charter granted to this Maurice of Concraig, by Robert Stuart Earle of Strathern, of fome lands in Strachmafin called Dalkelrach and Sherymare, with the Coronerfhip of the whole countie and the keeping of the north Catkend of Ouchtermuthel, with efcheats and other priviledges thereto belonging; wherein he calls Maurice our beloved Cufine, and the witneffes are, John, Senefcal, our brother, Robert of Erfkine, Hugh of Eglingtoun, and Thomas of Fauffyde, knights, &c. This was given and fealed at the Caftle of Methven about the year 1362.

This Maurice Drummond had made a purchafs of the lands of Cairnbadie, in the barronie of Melginfh and fherifdome of Perth, from Sir Thomas Biffet, barron of Glafcun, who grants a Charter thereupon to Maurice Drummond and Marion Erfkin, his fpoufe, with warrandice of 40 merk land in the barronie of Glafdun or Lethindies at theire option. The witneffes are, William Bifhop of St. Andrews, Patrick Bifhop of Aberdeen, Chancellor of Scotland, Robert, Senefcal of Scotland, Earle of Strathern. Sir Robert Erfkine, chamberlane of Scotland. (vide Cartam, &c.) This Charter is firft confirmed be King David Bruce, next by Thomas Earle of Mar, laft Earle of Mar of that name, fuperior of the lands; dated and fealed at Amon the 1st of June 1372.

Maurice had alfo fome intereft in the fuperiority of the lands of Inneramfay, Pethie, and Newlands, in the fhyre of Mar; which was a good time after, by one of his fucceffors, Maurice of Concraig, his great grandchild, difponed to a cufine of the family, John Drummond of Inneramfay and Culqualzie, to whom the propertie belonged; which he is faid to have gotten for a reward of his fervice at the batle of Harelaw.

3. Sir John Drummond of Concraig, the fone of the laft Maurice,

was the third Senefcal or Stuart of Strathern. Hathornden calls him Malcolm, bot both Hector Boethius and Bifhop John Leflie more rightly John: he married firft the laird Craigies daughter, a barron of a confiderable and old family near Perth, fyrnamed Ros. After her death, he married a fecond wife, Maud or Matildis de Græme, daughter to Patrick Lord Grahame; and fifter to Patrick Græme, who fome yeares after became Earle of Strathern by marrying the heretrix thereof, Eufame Stuart, the only chyld of David Stewart, firft ftiled Lord of Brechin, and then made Earle of Strathern, the eldeft fone of King Robert the Second by Eufame Ros, the daughter of Hugh Earle of Rofs.

Sir John Drummond produced his Fathers charter from Robert Earle of Strathern, to be tranfumed by Nicolaus de Mair Normannus, notar publick, as appeares by ane Inftrument dated at Perth, June 7th 1399. He had fones by the laird of Craigies daughter, Malcolm, who fucceeded; John, nicknamed Gyloch, i. e. crooked; he was the firft of Mewie, next called Lenoch, now Meginfh; Maurice called Gorum, i. e. bleuifh; and Walter Drummond the youngeft. 1399

Sir John himfelfe was a gentleman of a noble fpirit, bot very unhappy by a fad accident which fel in his hand; and becaufe it is remembred by fo many of our Hiftorians, we can not pafs it over in filence: bot for the better underftanding the matter, we fhal begin at the fource from whence the mifcheife flowed.

About the year 1391, Sir Alexander Murray of Ogilvy, who was either fone or grand child to Sir Maurice Murray of Drumfhyrgart, brother to Andrew Murray the governour, defcended from the Murrayes of the family of Bothuell in Clidfdale, who had married a daughter of Hugh Earle of Rofs, fifter to the Queen, and by fome fatal misfortune had killed a gentleman named William Spalden; for which he was fummoned to a certaine day for appeareing before Sir John Drummond of Concraig, Jufticiar Coroner and Stuart of

Strathern, in a Juftice court, to be halden at Fowls. Bot Sir Alexander, either out of fear or through pryde and difdaine, made fhifts; yet at the laft found it convenient to prefent himfelfe, and by a formal inftrument, declined the Court by ane Appeal to the law of Clan M'Duffe, one of the three old priviledges granted be King Malcolm Keandmore to M'Duffe, the firft Earle of Fyfe; whereby it was provyded that if any perfon within the ninth degree of kindred to him or his aires, Earles of Fyfe, fhould commit unpremeditat flaughter, and perform fome ceremonies at the Crofs M'Duffe which ftands betwixt Fyfe and Strathern, near the Neubrugh, in that cafe he fhould be only judged by the Earle; or, as Buchannan wryts, pay 24 merks for the flaughter of a gentleman and 12 for a common man, and fo be free of the blood. The practife of this, he alledges, continowed even to the dayes of his forbeers, to wit, fo long as any of that Earles pedegree remained. The Judges tooke a time to advyfe the declinature, bot not being fatisfyed therewith ifhewed forth new fummonds, chargeing Sir Alexander again, which he obeyed, bot gave in the Appeal and Proteftation following, viz.

"In the year of God 1391, upon the 7th day of December, in prefence of ane Notar publick, and the witneffes underwrytten, perfonally conftitute a noble and potent man Sir Alexander Murray knight, with his prolocutors Sir Bernard Hadden knight, and John Logie, being called and fummoned be the Rolls of indytement concerning the killing of William Spaldin, compeared before the juftices, Sir John Drummond knight, Malcolm Drummond and John M'William, in judgement fitting at Fowlls in a Juftice court; and did proteft, that fince he was once before indyted for the killing of the faid William Spaldin, and called in judgement before them, and was repledged to the law of Clan M'Duffe by Robert Earle of Fyfe, he was not nor could be halden to anfuere before any other Judge for the forefaid flaughter, fo long as the faid law of Clan

M‘Duffe did ufe its priviledge concerning him and was in vigour; and therefore he did Appeal to the faid law, protefting with all that he fhould not be any more vexed by them or theire indytements."

The Judges takeing this to confideration, promifed they fhould decern nothing prefently againft the faid Sir Alexander, bot with efpecial regaird to him and his defyre; bot that they would continow the matter until the Lord Brechen, General Jufticiar, fhould give his deliverance upon the petition and proteftation as he and his counfel fhould think fit. Upon the which Proteftation and Anfuere of the Judges, the faid Sir Alexander took Inftruments in the hands of John Simon notar publick, before thir witneffes prefent and requyred, Maurice Archdean of Dumblane, William de Graham and Unfra Cuningham knights, Maurice of Drummond and Walter of Murray efquyres.

The Juftice general being acquainted with the matter, gave fentence; bot the reafon is not expreffed that the law [of] Clan M‘Duffe fhould not liberat Sir Alexander Murray from his ordinary Judge, bot that he fhould return and make his defences before the fame Court which he had declyned. This he was neceffitat to doe with fome difadvantage as he thought, and yet it feems not with fuch feverities and rigour of law as might have been fhewn: however, this bred fuch difcontent and animofitie betwixt the two names that Sir Alexander and his freinds, for fome ages after, ufed all means how to be freed from theire fubjection to that jurifdiction, or to procure the power thereof in theire own hands, which the other fyd as vigoroufly oppofed; untill upon a new occafion in the reigne of King James the Third, a liberation was granted to fome of the Murrayes and fecured to theire pofterity.

In the mean time, the heats and animofities from fo fmal a begining grew to a great hight; and Patrick Graeme fome yeires after this haveing married the heretrix of Strathern, and thereby become Earle

thereof, Sir Alexander Murray of Ogilvie and his freinds tooke occafion to importune him to thruft Sir John Drummond out of the office of Stuartfhip, and prefer another thereto of his own election. The Earle being thus perfwaded, endeavored by all means to prevail with Sir John Drummond to refigne the office in his hands as fuperior thereof; bot he obftinatly refufed, prefumeing that himfelfe and his predicefsors had ane unqueftionable title thereto long before the Earle had any to the Earledome. Thus the Earle, and his brother in law Sir John, were once fet at variance; bot to prevent any further breach, fome freinds did mediat betwixt them, and as John Fordon wreats, brought them in teftimonie of reconciliation to communicat together at the Holy Sacrament. Notwithftanding whereof, foone after Sir Alexander Murray, takeing advantage of the Earles good nature, and plying the intereft he had by his lady with the countefs heretrix, who was her fifters grandchild, extorted one day a promife from the Earle that he fhould either have power to difpofe of the Stuarts office or not be Earle of Strathern. Thus they incenfed him of new againft his brother in law to that degree, that in
1413. perfuance of his rafh promife upon ane ordinary Court day, 1413, he mounts his horfe in a paffion at Meffen, the place of his refidence, and with his followers refolves to diffipat Sir Johns court then fitting at the Skeat of Creiffe; bot Sir John, getting intelligence of the defigne, advanced with the freinds he had prefent with him to meet the Earle, whom at the firft encounter he killed without any more bloodfhed, for non of the Earles company offered to revenge the flaughter, bot fuffered the actors to efcape.

Sir John and his company fled immediatly firft to Ireland, and from thence intending for England were forced be ftorms upon the Scots fhoare, apprehended and brought to publick execution, as Bifhop Leflie and Adam Abel both of them, in theire hiftories of Scotland, reports; bot John Fordon fayeth, that non fuffered by the hand of publick juſtice fave William and Walter Olyphards, and that the unfortunat Knight himfelfe dyed of a dyffenterie in Ireland long after.

Hathornden gives ane other reafon of the quarrel betwixt the Earle and Sir John; alledgeing the Earle to have boafted that he had a better title to the crown then King James the Firſt, as being by his lady preferable to the race defcended of Elifabeth Muire, for which Sir John killed him: bot the true ſtorie is otherwife related, and appeares fo as Biſhop Leſlie tells, for Sir John was forfaulted for the crime in the time of the government of Robert, Duke of Albany, Earle of Fyfe.

4. Malcolm Drummond, the eldeſt fone of Sir John, was the fourth laird of Concraig and Stuart of Strathern. There is ane inſtrument of fafine given to this Malcolm of the Stuartrie lands and pertinents upon his Fathers refignation, under the figne of Robert Waddal nottar publick, in anno 1408; whereby it feems Sir John his father being long in mifunderſtanding with the Murrayes upon the occafion before mentioned, and fearcing that theire power with Patrick Earle of Strathern ſhould withdraw or alienat his affection from him, apprehended fome danger, and therefore tooke this politick courſe before hand to fecure his fone, being very young, if the worſt ſhould happen. 1408.

In the year 1416, this Malcolm, fone and air to Sir John Drummond of Concraige, prefents a precept of faifine to Walter Earle of Athol, tutor to Malice Grahame, the fone of Patrick Earle Palatine of Strathern, at the Caftle of Methven, to be infeft in the Senefcalſhip of Strathern, and the priviledges thereto belonging; which wes granted be the Earle, and inſtruments taken thereon. 1416.

Malcolm Drummond of Concraige married   Monteith, daughter to the laird of Carſe, and begot with her Maurice, who fucceeded, and James Drummond, the firſt of the houfe of Balloch; of whom is defcended the families of Milnab and Broich, whofe generations ſhal be fet doun in theire own places. Balloch, Milnab and Broich.

I have feen ane Indenture, dated anno 1441, betwixt Sir David 1441.

Murray of Tyllebardine and this Malcolm Drummond of Concraig, of mutual freindſhip, wherein the conditions are, That Malcolms eldeſt ſone Maurice Drummond ſhould marrie Iſabella Murray, daughter to Sir David, with a portion of 10 lib. worth of land; and that the office of Stuartrie, with the profits thereof, pertaineing heritablie to Malcolm, ſhould be divyded betwixt Sir David and him dureing their lives, with a penaltie of 200 merks in caice of failzie. This match we find did not hold, for Malcolm diſpoſed otherwiſe upon his ſone Maurice ; bot Sir Davids contryvance was heireby to wind himſelfe once in poſſeſſion of the Steuartrie, to which both he, upon this ground, and after him his ſone Sir William Murray kept up a pretention, untill that office fell in the hands of John Drummond of Cargill, afterwards Lord Drummond ; in whoſe time I find a diſcharge or diſhonoration of the Seneſcalſhip of Strathern brought by his brother Andrew from King James the Third to Sir William
1474. Murray of Tullibardine, dated 1474. And it was at this time when both the lairds of Tullibardine and Ogilvye found theire advantage to purchaſe from the King a liberation of theire lands from the Juriſdiction of the Stuartrie of Strathern in all time comeing; a thing they had long endeavored to compaſs.

5. Maurice Drummond, the ſone of Malcolm, wes the next laird of Concraig and Stuart of Strathern. He was ordinarly called Old Maurice, becauſe both his ſone and grandchild were called Maurice. He married firſt a gentlewoman of good qualitie called Marrion Douglas, cuſine to the Earle of Angus : after her death he married Margaret Mercer, daughter to the laird of Innerpeffrie. His children were Maurice Keer Drummond and a daughter Iſobella Drummond. In his time the eſtate became very low ; for ever ſince the killing of the Earle of Strathern, the family had no ſetled peace, bot were forced to keep houſe to ſo many freinds and ſervants for theire ſecuritie that it brought a conſumption upon the fortune, ingadged it

THE HOUSE OF DRUMMOND.

in burdens, and made him pairt with many of his lands to releive his
debts. In the year 1447 he fold to John Drummond of Innerramfay, 1447.
fecond laird of Culqualzie, his Cufin, the fuperiority of Innerramfay,
Pethie and Newlands, and made refignation thereof in the hands of
Sir Robert Erfkine (called in the wryte) Lord of that ilk, barron of
Balhagartie, fuperior thereof: Witneffes, Marrion Douglas his wife,
and others. He difponed alfo the lands of Dulchonie and Garrioch-
throw to John Drummond Gilooch, the firft of Lennoch, called then
of Mewie, the fone of Sir John Drummond of Concraig, his uncle
who was, as appeares by the inftrument of refignation in the hands of
King James the Second, under the figne of Thomas Tewquythill,
dated the 10th of December 1452.   1452.

There is alfo ane other inftrument of refignation about the fame
time made be Maurice, of the lands of Drummond, two merk land
of Cultiwhaldich, 3 quarters of Mewie, Donira, Straitht, Blairedarg,
Dalwhilra and Sherrimare; referving his own lyfrent and a reafonable terce to his wife Margaret Merfer, if fhe furvives him; under
the fame notars figne.

There is a charter granted to this John Drummond Gyloch, by King
James the Second, in the 16 year of his reigne 1453, of the lands of 1453.
Dolchony and Garrichthrow which pertained to Old Maurice Drum-
mond of Concraig, and which he refigned in the Kings hands in favors
of the faid John Drummond and his aires at the Caftle of Down in
Menteith. The charter is granted at Stirline, and the witneffes are,
William Creichton Lord Chancellor, Andrew Gray Mafter Houf-
hold, Patrick Lord Hales, Mr. John Lyndfay of Lincluden Keeper of
the Privie Seal, Alexander Nairn of Sandiefoord Comptroller, and
Mr. George of Shorefwood, Chancellor of Dunkeld, Clerk, &c.

6. Maurice Keer Drummond, the fone of Maurice, fucceeded to
be the Sext laird of Concraige and Stuart of Strathern. He married
a daughter of Sir Andrew Murray of Ogilvie and Abercairny, and

48   THE GENEALOGIE OF

got a portion with her of ane hundreth merks in pennie and pennie-
1460. worth, as the difcharge beares, dated anno 1460. With her he
begot a fone, Maurice Drummond, who fucceeded.

Sir Andrew Murray, confidering this Maurice Keers eftate to be burdened and his family decreffed far from the condition it had been in, drew on this match with a defygne upon the Stewarts office; bot the other, perceiveing the project, and being alfo ftraitned, refolved in makeing a bargaine to preferr his Cheife thereto, John Drummond of Cargill, afterward Lord Drummond, and to him difponed moft of his lands, with his office, in the 13th year of the reigne of King James the Third, and in the 14th year of the faid Kings reigne,
1474. being the year of God 1474. Winfridus de Murray of Abercairnie, Andrew Murray of Ogilvies fone, Sheriffe deput, upon a precept direct to him by deliverance of a whyte rod, gave feafine to John Drummond of Cargill, of the offices of the Senefcalfhip, Coronerfhip, and of the keeping of the north Cathekend of Ouchtermuthill, forrestries of Strathern, efcheats, forfaultries, and fees, &c. all furrendred and refigned in the Kings hands at Edinburgh, by Maurice Keer Drummond in favors of John Drummond of Cargill, the yeare before.

7. Maurice Drummond, the fone of Maurice Keer Drummond of Concraig, fucceeded to his Father, whofe fortune was now contracted within a fmal circle. He had nothing left him of the old
Borland. and faire eftate of Concraig, fave the Barronie of Boorland, and from thence tooke his ftyle accordingly. He married a daughter of the laird of Fordons, and begot a fone John.

8. John Drummond, the fone of the laft Maurice, wes the fecond Barron of Boorland. He married a daughter of Malcolm Drummond, commonly called McKie of Kilbryd; and begot tuo fones, Malcolm and Mr. Mungo Drummonds. I have feen a tack fet to this John Drummond of Boreland, of halfe the fex lib. land of Culqualzie, by Duncan
1534. McCarter of Thorrowrige, dated at Muthul the 4th of May 1534.

THE HOUSE OF DRUMMOND.

9. Malcolm Drummond of Boorland was air to John. About the year 1559 he married a daughter of Sir John Drummond of Innerpeffrie, and had by her tuo daughters, and fones, Mr. John Drummond who fucceeded, Mr. Maurice, Abraham, Malcolm, Isaac, and Mr. David Drummonds. Mr. Maurice fell to be tutor of Boorland to his brother's fone, Sir John Drummond, in his minoritie, and wes married to Agnes Drummond, daughter to George Drummond of Balloch; with whom he had a daughter, Anna Drummond, fpoufe to Walter Cheefholme, Baylie of Dumblane, the father of Alexander Cheefholm, now Baylie there. Maurice had also a daughter, called Jean, married to William Pitcairn, laird of Pitlour, of whom that family is come; and Anabella, married to Struan Murray.

1559.

Abraham was called Drumduy, and was father of James of Drumduy.

Malcolm, called French Malcolm, had a daughter married to Andrew Garrie, at Perth, her name was Jean.

Mr. David Drummond, Malcolms youngeſt fone, married Helen Menteith, daughter to Alexander Menteith of Maner, fone to the laird of Carfe, and begot with her four daughters only; Agnes, Margaret, Marrion, and Elifabeth Drummonds. Agnes, the eldeſt, married James Menteith of Alcathie, befyde Linlithgow, and had children, James, Hellen, Margaret, and Jean Menteiths. James Menteith the fone of James, now of Alcathie, married Chriſtian Mill, fiſter to Alexander Miln, prefent provoſt of Lithgow, and hes with her James, Alexander, Margaret, and Jean Menteiths. Helen Menteith, James eldeſt daughter, married George Bel, fone to George Bel, provoſt of Lithgow, and had George and Jannet Bells. Margaret Menteith, James' 2d daughter, married Henrie Graham, fone to Gartur. Jean Menteith, James' third daughter, married Robert Graham, brother to Gartur.

Margaret Drummond, fecond daughter to Mr. David, married

H

Captain David Muire, now liveing in Kyntyre, whofe children are Mr. David, Patrick, Robert, Jean, and Urfula. Marrion Drummond, Mr. David's third daughter, married William Stuart, and had no children. Elifabeth Drummond, youngeft daughter to Mr. David Drummond, married William Wallace, fone to Collonel James Wallace, fometimes of Achens; theire children are James and John, Hellen and Anna Wallaces. This Mr. David was acquainted with Theodore de Beza, at Geneva, who, in his epiftle prefixed to a book of Mr. Robert Rollos, wreats of Mr. David, that he was *homo doctus et pius*,—Mr. David lived to be near ane hundred yeares of age.

10. Mr. John Drummond, the fone of Malcolm, was Barron after his father; he married a daughter of Sir James Cuningham, laird of Glencarnock, with whom he had fones, Sir John who fucceeded, and Malcolm.

11. Sir John Drummond, the fone of Sir John, married Marjorie Hamilton, daughter to the laird of Blair Hamilton. He was the laft Barron of Boorland; for he fold the Barronie to John Earle of Perth, and with the money paft to Ireland, where he made a purchafe of land, called Kefh Caftle, in the county of Tyrone; and dyed chyldlefs about the year 1630.

12. Malcolm Drummond, his brother, wes his air, called Litle Malcolm; he married Marjorie Drummond, daughter to James Drummond of Pitzallonie, and had with her fones, William, John, and Mungo Drummonds.

13. William Drummond, the fone of Malcolm, had no vifible eftate left to him. He married Anna Hamilton, daughter of William Hamilton, laird of Baderfton; theire children are William, Robert, Thomas, and Jean Drummonds.

THE HOUSE OF DRUMMOND.

THE FAMILIE OF CULQUALZIE, THE FIRST BRANCH FROM THE HOUSE OF CONCRAIG. Drummonds of Culqualzie.

Malcolm Drummond, the fecond fone of Sir Maurice Drummond, the firft Stuart of Strathern, and knight of Concraig, purchafed the halfe lands of Culqualzie, and had his title from it; the other halfe his fucceffors conquefed. He married   Barclay, daughter to the laird of Colernie, in Fyfe, and begot John, who fucceeded. Malcolm was a man of great action and courage; he and his brother Maurice of Concraig did fingular good fervice under the command of Alexander Stuart, Earle of Mar, the fone of Alexander, Earle of Buchan, who was the youngeft of the fones of King Robert with Elizabeth Muire, at the battle of Harlaw, in Garrioch, againft Donald of the Ifles, who, pretending right to the Earldom of Rofs, pofeft himfelfe thereof by force, and wafted all the country as far fouthward as Aberdeen. The battle was fought with great obftinacie on both fydes, and much bloodfhed, and the victorie uncertaine; Alexander Earle of Mar, and many brave gentlemen, were killed. After the fight Robert Duke of Albany, then governour, rewarded Malcolm and his brother Maurice with the lands of Innerramfay, Pethie, and Newlands, in Mar; Maurice with the fuperioritie, and Malcolm with the proppertie. Malcolm's burial place is in the church of Muthul, where his father lyes with this infcription—*Malcolmus de Drummond dominus de Innerramsay.*

2. John Drummond, the fone of Malcolm, was the fecond laird of Culqualzie. He married   Campbell, daughter to a brother of the Earle of Argyle, and had by her Maurice, Walter, William, and Andrew Drummonds, and a daughter married to a rich merchant in Sterline, called Bet. He difponed to a natural fone, Thomas, and

his aires, which faylzieing, to Walter Drummond, his fone and aires, the lands of Duchlas, Petchur, and a third pairt of the lands of Meggor: the witneffes are Andrew Drummond rector of Kirkconnel his fone, and Robert Merfer of Innerpeffrie ; the difpofition is dated
1461. anno 1461, and confirmed by Marie, Queen Regent, mother to King James the Third, that fame year.

3. Maurice Drummond fuccceded to be laird of Culqualzie after his father John Drummond, about the year 1466. He married   Cuninghame, daughter to the laird of Glengarnock, with whom he had only one daughter, called Margaret Drummond, who was heretrix, and fucceeded to the eftate.

4. Margaret Drummond, heretrix of Culqualzie, the daughter of John, married John Inglis, a gentleman in Lothian, and domeftick fervant to King James the Fourth. He begot with her three fones, John, William, and Alexander, who all died without children, and two daughters, Marrion and Margaret; the eldeft married Patrick
1516. Murray, fone to the laird of Tullibardin, in the year 1516. She difpones to Malcolm Drummond of Kilbryd, with confent of Patrick Murray, her hufband, the lands of Meggor and Duchlas. Margaret Inglis, the youngeft daughter, got the lands of Culqualzie for her portion, and married David Drummond, the third fone of Thomas Drummond of Drumon Irenoch, who, by her right, was next laird of Culqualzie.

5. David Drummond of Culqualzie, third fone to Thomas, firft laird of Drummonerinoch, begat, upon his wife, Margaret Ingles, a fone, John Drummond, who was his air, and a daughter, Elfpet Drummond, married to John Drummond, laird of Pitzallonie.

6. John Drummond, the fone of David, fucceeded. He married   Cambel, daughter to   Cambel, Abbot of Coupar, who was brother to the laird of Arkindlas ; he got with his wife the lands of Blacklaw, in Angus, which continows with the family. John

begot with the Abbot's daughter, three fones and five daughters; the firſt, Sybillia Drummond, married William Riddoch of Aberlednock, and after his death ſhe married the laird of Lochinzel Cambel; the fecond, Iſſobella, married Mr. Alexander Ingles of Byres; the third, was married to Duncan Tofcheoch of Pitenzie; the fourth, to John Mufchet, brother-german to the laird of Mufchet; and the fifth to Patrick Drummond of Milnab. The fones were John, who fucceeded; James dyed without children; and Thomas, who was laird of Drummawhence, he married

[A BLANK IN THE MANUSCRIPT.]

7. John Drummond of Culqualzie, eldeſt fone to the laſt John, married Jean Mauld, daughter to the laird of Melgum, in Angus. He had with her four fones and four daughters; the eldeſt daughter, Margaret, was married to James Drummond of Drumduy, bot had no children; the fecond, Iſſobel, married John Græme of Gartur, who bore to him, Walter, John, and Robert Grahams; the third, Elſpet Drummond, married James Gray of Eaſt-Hill, who had only a daughter; the fourth Catharine Drummond, wes married to Mr. Robert Laurie, a learned and eloquent preacher; he was long miniſter of Edinburgh, and afterwards Biſhop of Brechin; He had, with Catharine, his wife, only two daughters, Jean and Bathia Lauries; the firſt married Mr. Colin M'Kenzie, brother-german to the Earle of Seaforth, who hes two fones, Robert and George, and a daughter, Barbara M'Kenzie, married to the laird of Bachelton Olyphant, to whom ſhe hath children; the youngeſt, Bathia, married David Rollo, a cufin-german to my Lord Rollo, who hath children.

This John of Culqualzie his eldeſt fone, was John who fucceeded; the fecond was James, a Collonel in the Sueddiſh fervice; he married Elizabeth Clerk, daughter of Admiral Clerk, Admiral to that Croun, with whom he had a fone, John Drummond, and tuo daughters, who continow in Suedden.

The third fone was Mr. David Drummond, a worthie man, and of good pairts; he was firſt miniſter at Linlithgow, and laſt at Moneydy; he married Catharine Smyth, fiſter to Patrick Smyth of Methwen, and had with her tuo fones, Mrs. David and John Drummonds, both hopeful youthes. Harrie Drummond, the youngeſt, married Margaret Moncreef of Weſtwood; fhe bore to him Mr. John Drummond, miniſter at Fowls, David, Harie, William, and Lodovick Drummonds, and tuo daughters; Helen Drummond, married to Mr. John Blair, miniſter at Kilſpindie; and Catharine, married to Mr. Archibald Cameron, clerk to the Kirk-feſſions at Edenburgh.

8. John Drummond of Culqualzie, eldeſt fone and air to the laſt John, married Barbara Blair, daughter to the laird of Tarfappie, and fiſter to Sir William Blair of Kinfauns. He had with her three fones and three daughters: Iffobel, the firſt married John Scot; Elſpet, the fecond, married firſt Mr. George Weems, miniſter at Scoone; the fecond time fhe was married to Mr. John Weems, miniſter at Dumbarnie; and the third time to Major James Stuart of Banchrie, and hes children to all the three hufbands. The three fones were John who fucceeded, William and Harie.

9. John Drummond, now of Culqualzie, fon and air of the laſt John, married Anna Grahame, daughter to David Grahame of Gorthie, and begot with her fones, John, David, Robert and James Drummonds.

The Family of Pitzallonie, the Second Branch from the House of Concraig.

1. Malcolm Drummond, the fecond fone of Maurice Drummond of Concraige, who was the fecond Stuart of Strathern of that name, got from his father in portion the lands of Fintolich, Lintibbers, and Dalwhyne. He was the fir laird of Pitzallonie, haveing purchafed that place from Sir John Bruce of Airth for 100 lib. Scots money of dines groats, and 40 pennie groats, delivered at the high altar of Stirline, as the deed beares : whom he married I find not, bot he had tuo fones, Duncan Drummond, who fucceeded, and Andrew Drummond, who was a church man. *Drummonds, lairds of Pitzallonie.*

2. Duncan Drummond, the fone of Malcolm, was the fecond laird of Pitzallonie. He married Agnes Riddoch, daughter to the laird of Cultabregan, and had with her a fone called Maurice Drummond.

3. Maurice Drummond, the fone of Duncan, was the third. He married Janet Strageth, daughter to the laird of Strageth. She did bear to him three fones, John, who fucceeded, Andrew and Malcolm Drummonds. Andrew was a viccar I think of Strageth, Malcolm was heritor of Cardnies, and of him came James Drummond of Cardnies or Hehill, fometime fheriffe clerk of Perth, and others from him ; James' fone, was Harie, called gentle Harie for his good company. His fifter married Ingles of Byres, father to Alexander Ingles in Perth. This Maurice, I find, gives a feafine with his oun hands to Donald France of tuo tenements in Muthull, Feb. 4, 1496 ; to which William Drummond of Muthull is witnes, who it feems was a brother of John Lord Drummonds. Thomas Youngman, chapellan of Strefillan, grants this Maurice of Pitzallonie a charter to him, and Janet *1496.*

THE GENEALOGIE OF

Strageth his fpoufe, of the halfe lands of Pittennendrie, dated at
1512. Doun the 7th of May 1512.

This Maurice Drummond of Pitzallonie, and a number more of his
name, and theire dependers, were cited before a Juftice Court holden
at Edenburgh, in prefence of the Juftice General, for deftroying and
burning of above 20 perfones in Monyvard church; bot by ane affyfe
were affoilzied, as appears by ane abfolvitor to which the feal of
King James the Fourth is appended.

4. John Drummond, the fone of Maurice, was the next laird of
Pitzallonie. He married Jannet Cheefholm, daughter to Thomas,
the fone of Edmond Cheefholm, the firft laird of Cromlix, the father
of Sir James Cheefholm and of William Cheefholm Bifhop of Dumblane, begotten upon a daughter of James Drummond of Coldoch.
Jannet Cheefholm did bear to John, three fones and three daughters:
the firft daughter married to Barron Reid of Pitnacree in Athol; the
fecond to Maine of Bruntimiln in the Barronie of Stobhal; the third
to one Hallyburton befyd Couper of Angus. The eldeft [fon], John,
fucceeded to his father; the fecond, James, dyed without children;
and the third, William Drummond, called black Willie, pofeft the
lands of Fintelich. He was great grandfather to John Drummond
of Fintelich, called John the Baylie of Muthill, who was ane officer
of the Scots army in Ireland againft the rebells there, anno 1642,
and was killed at a fort called Green Caftle. He had married
Chriftian Kippon, and had with her tuo fones and tuo daughters:
the fones, John, killed in the late Scots wars againft Oliver the Ufurper; and Thomas, married at Ochterarder to Elifabeth Grahame,
daughter to Patrick Grahame, one of the family of Garvock, who hes
a fone, David Drummond. The daughters of John, were Catharine
and Anna Drummonds: the firft married James Drummond, a
merchant in Perth; and being a widdow married David Scot,
Apothecarie in Edinburgh, to whom fhe hath a fone, Hugh, and

THE HOUSE OF DRUMMOND.

tuo daughters, Anna and Magdalene; the eldeſt married to George Drummond, late town thefaurer of Edinburgh, and hes children. Anna Drummond, the youngeſt daughter of John Drummond, married Archbald Oliphant, fone to Sir Laurence Olyphant of Gaſk.

This John Drummond, the fourth laird of Pitzallonie, hes a remiſſion for afiſting and being in company with Archbald Earle of Angus, when he carried the young King James the Fyfth, with his brother the Duke of Roſs, from Sterline, where for fecurity he was placed by the advice of John Duke of Albanie, his Tutor and Governour, and of the Three Eſtates of Parliament. It is dated at Edinburgh the 16th of Apryle 1516, James Beton Archbiſhop of Glaſgow being then chancellor. 1516.

5. John Drummond, fone to the laſt John, fucceeded, and was fyfth laird of Pitzallonie. He married Elſpet Drummond, daughter to David Drummond of Culqualzie, begotten upon Margaret Ingles. John had with Elſpet three daughters, Margaret, Sybilla, and Elſpet Drummonds. Margaret was thryce married, firſt to George Grahame of Callender, and had to him a daughter married to Andrew Baine of Findal; next to Mr. Mungo Drummond, brother to the laird of Boorland, Malcolm Drummond; and laſtly, to Mr. John Davidfone, miniſter at Muthill, to whom ſhe had a daughter married to Grahame of Ochterarder. John Drummond of Pitzallonies fecond daughter, Sybilla, married John Cambel, brother to the laird of Lawers; and the youngeſt, Elſpet, married Mr. Alexander Gall, miniſter of Gaſk.

John of Pitzallonie had alfo tuo fones, John who fucceeded, and Patrick who poſſeſt the lands of Dalwhynie. There is ane Inſtrument of feafine of the lands of Pittenendrie, holden of the chappellanrie of Strafillan, fituat under the Caſtle of Down in Menteith, mentioning a precept of feafine granted to this John, and his fpoufe Elſpet Drum-

ɪ

58   THE GENEALOGIE OF

mond, by his father John Drummond of Pitzallonie, for infefting
1542. them therein, dated March the 6th 1542, John Bryfon notar.

6. John Drummond of Pitzallonie fucceeded to his father John, and was the fexth laird. He married Elfpet Comrie, daughter to the laird of Comrie of that ilk, and had by her tuo fones James and Patrick Drummonds. There is a letter of Reverfion granted by James Drummond of Kirkhill to this John Drummond of Pitzallonie, and his fpoufe Elfpet Comrie, for payment of 400 money ftamped (pennies and placklees being excepted) for redeemeing ane annuellrent of 40 merks upon the lands of Pittenmendrie and the miln of Pitzallonie, which he oblidges him and his forefaids to perform, lealy and truely by the faith and truth of their bodies, dated at Aughterardour
1587. the 23d of December 1587.

7. James Drummond, the fone of the laft John, was the feventh laird of Pitzallonie. He married Marjorie Grahame, daughter to the firft laird of Orchill, then called Sir Mungo Grahame of Raterns, fone to William Earle of Montrofe. They had tuo fones, John who fucceeded, and David Drummond, and four daughters, Marjorie, Jean, Agnes and Iffobella Drummonds. The eldeft married Malcolm Drummond of Boorland, who was called litle Malcolm; the fecond married John Bool in Cumra; the third James M'Mefker; and youngeft to one Erfkine.

8. John Drummond fucceeded to his father James Drummond of Pitzallonie. He married Jean Olyphant, fifter to Sir Laurence Olyphant of Gafk: theire daughters were Lilias and Jean Drummonds; the firft married to Mr. James Drummond of Kildees, the fecond married John Drummond of Dilpatrick. This John of Pitzallonie had alfo with Jean Olyphant four fones, John who fucceeded, James loft
1658. at fea anno 1658, Mr. George, prefent minifter at St. Madoes; he married Margaret Drummond, daughter to Mr. James Drummond of Deanfton, fometyme Minifter at Fowls: and the youngeft, William

THE HOUSE OF DRUMMOND.	59

Drummond, who went to the Mexican Iflands. John Drummond of
Pitzallonie was a captaine in Ireland againft the Rebells, and was
killed before the fort of Charlemont in the countrey of Armagh, and
burried in that Cathedral Church anno 1644. 1644.

9. John Drummond, now of Pitzallonie, the fone of the laft John,
is the ninth laird. He married firft Catharine Calwhoune, daughter
to Sir John Caluhown of Lufs. They had tuo fones and tuo
daughters, John, Laurence, Margaret and Beatrix. After Catharin
Caluhouns death, he married to his fecond wife, Mrs. Jean Rollo,
widdow and relict of   Rollo, laird of Powes, and the daughter
of Andrew, firft Lord Rollo.

[A BLANK IN THE MANUSCRIPT, IN WHICH THERE IS NO MENTION MADE OF THE
THIRD BRANCH FROM THE HOUSE OF CONCRAIG.]

THE FAMILY OF BALLOCH, the FOURTH BRANCH FROM THE HOUSE
OF CONCRAIG.

1. James Drummond, fecond fone to Malcolm Drummond of   Drummonds
Concraig, the fourth Stuart of Strathern, and the fecond brother of   of Balloch
Maurice, laird of Concraig, the fyfth Stuart thereof, was firft defigned burges of Aughterarder, and pofeft fome lands and crofts
thereof called Quarrell holls, which ftill continows in the family of
Balloch: it feems he got alfo from his father Malcolm a pairt of the
lands of Concraige, which they alfo retaine to this day. His firft

wife was a daughter of the laird of Aberdagies. She had to him one fone, Walter Drummond, who fucceeded. His fecond wife was the laird of Craigie Rofs daughter, with whom he had tuo fones, John Drummond, who was the firft of Milnab, and David Drummond, his brother, who was the fecond.

2. Walter Drummond, the eldeft fone of James, was firft defigned Walter of Broich, and afterward of Balloch, whereof he got the firft few charter for fervice done to King James the Fourth, wherein the King calls him Armiger nofter. He married   Rollo, daughter to the laird of Duncrub, and begot William Drummond, who fucceeded.

3. William Drummond, the fone of Walter, was the third laird. He married Jean Cramond, daughter to the laird of Aldbar, and begot tuo fones, George who fucceeded, and Andrew Drummond, the author of the family of Broich, called firft Andrew of Strageth; and four daughters, Gilles Lady Monzie, Jean Lady Coffans, Margaret goodwife of the Caftle of Aughterarder, and Dorothie married to John Drummond of Lennoch.

4. George Drummond, the fone of William, was the fourth laird of Balloch. He married Margaret Drummond, daughter to Harie Drummond, firft laird of Riccarton, and had with her a fone, Harrie who fucceeded, and three daughters; firft, Jean Lady Corrivachter, Agnes married to Mr. Maurice Drummond of Auchtermuthell, third, Lilias Drummond Lady Lochland.

5. Harrie Drummond, the fone of George, was the fyfth laird of Balloch. He married Beatrix Grahame, daughter to the laird of Inchbrakie, and had with her a fone, George who fucceeded, and three daughters, to wit, Margaret Drummond, married to the laird of Strowan Murray, Agnes to John Fit of Glen Sheris, and Catharine to Robert Grahame of Cairney.

6. George Drummond, the fone of Harrie, was the fexth laird of

Balloch. He married Agnes Naper, fifter to Archibald Lord Naper and Marchiftoun. He begot fones, John who fucceeded, George who was cruelly fhot to death by order of the Comittie of Eftates who ruled Scotland in the time of our late civill warrs, Harrie now of Balloch, and Robert Drummonds; and a daughter married to Grahame of Garvock. George Drummond of Balloch had alfo a fecond wife, Margaret Grahame, widdow of George Drummond of Blair, and fifter to David Graham, laird of Gorthie. She bore to him fones, David, Archbald and William Drummonds, and a daughter, Jean, married to William Stuart of Kinnard in Athol.

7. John Drummond, the fone of George, was the feventh laird. He was efteemed a valiant Gentleman, and was a cheife officer under James Marques of Montrofe in his expeditions; was killed at the feige of Dunkirk anno 165 , and left the inheritance to his brother,—

8. Harrie Drummond, now of Balloch, of whom we entertaine fome hopes that he will not extinguifh the memorie of fo honeft and ancient a family.

The Family of Broich.

Andrew Drummond, fecond fone of William Drummond, third laird of Balloch, was the firft of the houfe of Broich. He married . . . .

Drummonds of Broich.

[A BLANK IN THE MANUSCRIPT.]

THE GENEALOGIE OF

[THE FAMILY OF MILNAB.]

Drummonds of Milnab.

1521.

1. John Drummond, fecond fone to James Drummond of Aughterarder, the firft of the houfe of Balloch, was fomething lyke Mafter of work or Artillerie to King James [the] Fourth; and for his fervice done to that King and to his fone King James the Fyfth, he got a charter of the third pairt of the lands of Balnacreefe in Eaft Lothiane, near to Haddingtoune, and within the conftabularie thereof; and of the lands and miln of Milnab, with the lands of Galdermore in Strathern, wherein he is defigned *Machinarum bellicarum Ejaculator et Carpentarius nofter*, dated anno 1521.

He wrought for King James the Fyfth the fine timber work in the Caftle of Stirline; and fet the roofe upon the Caftle of Drummond anno 1493, for which he got a tack of fome lands within the barronie from John Lord Drummond. He married the laird of Logie Biffets daughter, and begat with her one only daughter. She was married to Sir Robert Logan of Reftalrig, who got with her in heritage John Drummonds pairt of Balnacreefe. He left his other lands to his brother David.

2. David Drummond of Milnab fucceeded to his brother John. He married a daughter of the laird of Balcanquil of that ilk in Fyfe, and with her begat three fones; William who fucceeded, James and Thomas Drummonds, and one daughter, Catharine, married to the barron of Fenduy in Athol. James, the fecond fone, married Maxton, daughter to the laird of Cultowhay, and by her had Mr. David Drummond fometyme minifter at Creefe, and Mr. Daniel his brother. Thomas, the youngeft, dyed abroad in the King of Denmarks fervice. David Drummond had been bred as a domeftick

in John Lord Drummonds familie, and was too-named 'Davie the doctor.' He had the ill fortune to get a pairt of that potion which killed three of the Lord Drummonds daughters at a breakfast, wherewith albeit he hardly efcaped with his life: he was all his days infirm in his eyes.

3. William Drummond of Milnab fucceeded to his father David. He married Jannet Stirline, daughter and airefs of the laird of Ballindooch, bot the laird of Keer kept the lands, and fatisfyed her with a fourne of 500 merks, which was a portion confiderable at that time. William begot, with Jannet his fpoufe, two fones; Patrick, who fucceeded, and Andrew, who married Mr. John Malloch of Cairnies fifter; with whom he had William, John, and Andrew Drummonds. William Drummond of Milnab gives feafine to Patrick Lord Drummond anno 1573.   1573.

4. Patrick Drummond of Mylnab, the fone of William, married Elfpet Drummond, daughter to John Drummond of Culqualzie, the fone of David: he had three fones, James, who fucceeded, William, and John Drummonds. William dyed abroad; John married Ben of Findalls daughter, who bore to him Mr. James Drummond, a minifter, Patrick and John, and a daughter, Anna Drummond: John and his fone Patrick were both killed at the battle of Prefton in the year 1648.   1648.

5. James Drummond of Milnab, the fone of Patrick, married Marrion Murray, the daughter of Antony Murray of Dollorie; his children were Mr. David Drummond, who fucceeded, and was long minifter of Creefe; William, George, and Robert Drummonds; with three daughters, Iffobella, Jean, and Catharine Drumnonds. William, the fecond, dyed in Pole; George plyed the merchant trade very happily abroad and at home, was divers times Baylie of Edenburgh, and purchaffed the lands of Milnab from his nephew John. Robert Drummond, the youngeft fone, married Sybilla Murray, daughter to

Murray of Lochland, and lies with her a fone, Mr. George Drummond, and a daughter, Jean.

6. Mr. David Drummond of Milnab, the fone of James, married Iſſobell Sibbald, daughter to David Sibbald, baylie of Perth. He begot with her John, who fucceeded, and Mr. David Drummond; he purchaſſed the lands of Callender, in the parroch of Creiffe. He went to Ireland, where he was a preacher at Clocher; and dyed there, moſt unfortunately, by a fudden fire.

7. John Drummond of Milnab fucceeded to Mr. David his father. He married a daughter of Andrew Miln, provoſt of Linlithgow, father of Alexander Miln, prefent provoſt there. John had no children, he difponed the lands and miln of Milnab to his uncle George Drummond, bayllie of Edenburgh, and retained only the Barronie of Callendar.

8. George Drummond, now of Milnab, fone to James, and uncle to the laſt John of Milnab, married, firſt, Elizabeth Hay, daughter to the laird of Moncktown, befyde Edenburgh, by whom he had feven fones, without intermiſſion; three whereof [are] alive, the firſt John, the fecond George, the third Francis. George Drummond of Milnab married a fecond wife, Helen Gray, daughter to Sir William Gray of Pittendrume: her brother was Maſter of Gray. She had to him a fone, Archbald, and a daughter, Lillias Drummond.

THE THIRD PARTITIONE.

Concerning Sir John Drummond the Seventh Thane, or Senescal of Lennox and his Posteritie.

7. Sir John Drummond was the feventh Thane or Senefcal of Lennox, and fone to Malcolme Beg Drummond; he had to wife Marie Montefex, or, de Monte Fixo, vulgarly called Montfichet, fhe was the eldeft daughter of three, who were aires-portioners to Sir William Montefex. Upon her Sir John Drummond begat three fones, Malcolm, John, and William Drummonds, and four daughters; the firft Annabella Drummond, who was Queen to King Robert the Third of that name; the fecond was married to Archbald Cambell, whofe fone or grandchild was knight of Lochaw; the third to Alexander M‘Donald, Lord of the Ifles, and fone to Donald Lord of the Ifles, who fought the battle of Harelaw; and the fourth to Sir   Stuart, knight of Duallie, one of the natural fones of King Robert the Second, begotten upon his concubine Marrion Cardenie.

Sir John Drummond haveing ftrong pretenfions, in right of his mother Ada, to the Earledome of Lennox, for fhe was the only daughter of Maldwine, and only fifter of Malcolm the laft Earle, who dyed without ifhew, as hes been already declared; and finding himfelfe diffapointed be Sir John Menteith, who had bewitched or befooled Earl Malcolm, his fone in law, to refigne the fee of that eftate (referving his own lyfrent) and the title freely to King Robert Bruce, with defigne to carry all for himfelfe as the pryce of Dumbartoun Caftle; Sir John Drummond afhamed to be thus abufed, full of revenge, had a long conceaved wrath and implacable hatred againft the

1330.

K

66   THE GENEALOGIE OF

Monteiths; and albeit, the feeds of that inimitie fown upon this ground were permitted to grow without mifcheife in the tyme of King Robert Bruce's lyfe, yet they produced bitter fruits imediately after his death.

Bot the King, notwithſtanding of the refignation, and the promotter thereof, found it convenient to difpofe otherwayes of that Earldome then to Sir John Menteith (whom he was in other things kind enough to) both to fhun over great offence to the Drummonds, and alfo to gratifie a freind he more regairded; fo he beftowed the fortune upon Robert Stuart of Tarboulton, the fecond fone of Walter Stuart lord of Dundonald, uncle both to Walter Stuart, who married Marjorie Bruce, the King's daughter, and to Earle Malcom himfelfe alfo; with whofe pofteritie it continowed fucceffively untill our dayes.

In the time of King David Bruce's minoritie, amongſt other difcords frequent then in the nation, the Drummonds and Monteiths waxed fo furious againſt each other, that wherever they did meet they parted not without blows. One cruel act amongſt many of the Monteiths infolencies wes, that they found themfelves at a lofs be fevere encroachments they fuffered by one Bryce Drummond, who feems to *See Prynnes historie of King John, &c. page 657.* have been Sir John's cufine by his uncle Gilbert, whofe death out of revenge they confpyred; and for that effect hounded out of theire adherents fome flight men, fuch as Gillefpick and Cruffan M'Gillifarricks, Donald M'Gilbert, Duncan Neilfon, and others, who furpryfed Bryce, and bafely murdered him. Whereupon the Drummonds, with affiftance of theire cufine Sir Walter Murray of Tyllibardine, perfued the Monteiths, and theire accomplices the Campbells and the Buchannans, whom one day they incountred on equal termes, and fought it obftinately on both fydes: bot the Monteiths and their pairtie were worfted, and many of theire men killed, and particularly three principall perfones of theire name, Walter, Malcom, and William Monteiths. This unlucky action was followed with flaughters,

robberies, and depredationes for the fpace of about 30 years ; untill
at laft the Monteiths complained to King David, fone after he returned from his captivitie ; who, confidering the ground of the difference fomewhat touched his father King Robert, was very defireous
to have the matter compofed ; and therefore gave commiffion to Sir
Robert Erfkine of Alloway, Sir Hugh Eglinton, General Jufticiars of
Scotland, to whom he joyned Sir Patrick Grahame of Kincardine, to
call the parties before them, examine the whole affaire, and if poffible
to fettle and agree them for the future. Both parties made appeareance, accompanied with theire freinds and kinfmen. There came
Robert Stuart, Earle of Strathern, the King's nephew, William Earle
of Douglas, Thomas Steuart Earle of Angus, John Monteith Lord of
Arran, &c. The meeting was held in the feilds upon the banks of
the river Forth, over againft Sterline, upon Sunday the 17 of May
1360, where a Submiffion was agreed to, and a Decreit thereupon 1360.
pronounced, whereof one double was appointed to be given to each
partie, ratified by the fealls and fubferiptions of the other, and the
nobles prefent ; containeing, that Sir John Drummond fhould for
ever give over his right, clame, and pofeffion of the lands and barronie
of Rofneff in the Lennox, with all its pertinents, in the hands of
Alexander Monteith, guardian for the Minor the fone of umquhill
Walter Monteith his ufe, as ane affythment for the flaughter of his
Father and freinds committed by the Drummonds ; the Judges and
the other nobles promifeing that the King fhould make recompence
to them ane other way. So the fentence was aggreed to by both
parties and theire freinds, only Gillespick or Donald the cheefe of the
Cambells, and his fone Coline, who was grandfather to the firft Earle
of Argyle, refufed to fubmit to the Articles ; for remedie whereof
both the Menteiths and Buchannans did firmly oblidge themfelves,
that feing the Campbells would not confent to the termes of Agreement, that if the Campbells, or any of theire kindred fhould refent or

perfew the former quarrel, then, in that cafe, they fhould joyne with the Drummonds to refift them as common enemies, otherwayes be lyable to reftore the lands given for the affythment then agreed upon.

Heire it appeares the Campbells were then enemies to the Drummonds, bot fone after this time they were reconciled, for the fame Coline Campbell's fone, knight of Lochaw, married a daughter of Sir John Drummond's; fo that, by this marriage, it feems, the Earles of Argyle may be defcended of the Drummonds, as the Drummonds by ane other of theire daughters afterwards are defcended of the Cambells.

The Drummonds authentick double of this tranfaction, and decreit fairly wrytten upon a large parchment, in ane ornat ftyle of Latin, after the form of ane Indenture, is intirely preferved. DDD.

DDD.

Thefe paffages fell happily out in a time when there was great jealoufies and heart-burnings betwixt King David and his nephew Robert, Earle of Strathern; the King being ftill full of apprehenfions that both he and the Earle of March had purpofely deferted him on that fatal battaile of Durham, anno 1348, where he was taken prifoner, and lay in Nottinghame Caftle the fpace of 12 yeares. At his return, he expreffed his refentment, by refolveing to provyde the crown, failzieing aires of his own body, to Alexander the Earle of Sutherland's fone, born of his uterin fifter, whofe mother was the Earle of Ulfter's daughter, and upon that confideration was inclinable to reconcile the differences betwixt his fubjects to unite them for ferving his ends; nor was Earle Robert, his nephew, lefs watchfull to gaine freinds to ftrengthen himfelfe, being provyded by Taylie to fucceed to the crown by King Robert Bruce, in cafe his fone King David fhould have no children of his own lawfully begotten.

1348.

After the agreement of the Drummonds and Monteiths, King David wes very favourable to Sir John Drummond, as the Arbitrators had promifed. For, in divideing the eftate left be Sir William

THE HOUSE OF DRUMMOND. 69

Montefix to his three daughters, who were the King's wards, he gave the largeft fhare, to wit, the barronies of Aughterarder, Cargill and Kincardine for his portion with the eldeft Marie, which lands remaines ftill with the family to this day. The other two fifters became difcontented with the King's divifion, and run into England to complaine ; for which they were both forfaulted, and theire inheritance difpofed upon be the King, to wit, Dornagilla Montefex her pairt, Pitfour and Drumgraine were given to Duncan Napier ; Pitcook in the fhyre of Perth, and halfe Kilmahew in Dumbartonfhire, to William Naper ; and the third fifter Margaret's pairt to Hugh Danielftoune, whofe fucceffor was lord Lyle : the Coppies of King David's gifts, taken off the publick regifters, and dated at Dumbarton anno 1366, are at prefent in the Earle of Perth's cuftody. 1366.

Now, upon the occafion of the blood that was fhed betwixt the Drummonds and the Menteiths, and the invitation Sir John Drummond had from the acceffion of lands fallen to him in Perthfhyre, by his lady Marie Montefix, he removed his feat, and qwytted the fhyre of Lennox and Dumbarton, with the Senefcalfhip thereof ; unwilling to remaine any more near that Earldome to which he had fo juft right, bot was diffappointed thereof, and fetled his refidence at Stobhal, a pairt of the old inheritance of the family in Perthfhyre, next to the barronie of Cargill ; which gave occafion that the fucceffion afterward were fometimes ftyled by Stobhall, bot moft pairt by Cargill, as is to be feen on the old charters of the houfe. Sir John Drummond dyed about the yeare 1373, when he and his prediceffors 1373. had for near 300 yeares lived in the fhyre of Dumbarton, and countie of Lennox, whereof they were alwayes heritable Thanes or Senefcalls.

We told you that Sir John Drummond had, by his lady Marie Montefix, three fones and four daughters ; the two eldeft fones were fucceffively heads of the Family, as will appeare by the following par-

70   THE GENEALOGIE OF

tition of William the youngeſt; and ſomewhat of the pedegree of Sir John's lady and his daughter's mention ſhal be now made.

THE FAMILY OF CARNOCK.

Drummonds of Carnock.

1. William Drummond, commonly called of Ernore, the youngeſt ſone of Sir John Drummond, married Eliſabeth Airth, one of the daughters and coheireſſes of Sir William Airth, laird of Airth, and Carnock, and Plaine: he got with her the lands of Carnock and Plaine, and by the death of her ſiſter, ſucceeded to the barronie of Airth, which he excambed for Bannockburn. William begot with Eliſabeth a ſone, who ſucceeded to him, called David Drummond.

2. David Drummond of Carnock, the ſone of William, wes the ſecond laird of Carnock. He married Marrion Cuninghame, daughter to the laird of Weſter Polmaiſe, and begot with her Robert Drummond, who ſucceeded.

The charter granted to William, the father of David, by King Robert, runs in thir words, "Robertus Rex &c. dilecto nostro fratri Wilhelmo de Drummond, domino de Carnock," and lykwiſe the confirmation granted by King James the firſt to him, containes theſe words, "James, by the grace of God, &c. to our welbeloved uncle, William Drummond of Carnock."

3. Robert Drummond, the ſone of David, was third laird of Carnock. He married Marrion Monteith, ſiſter to William Monteith of Weſtcarſe, and begot with her only one ſone, called Alexander Drummond.

4. Alexander Drummond, the ſone of Robert, ſucceeded. He

married Marjorie Bruce, fifter to Robert Bruce, laird of Auchinbowie, and with her he begot three fones; Sir Robert, who fucceeded, Alexander, who was the firft laird of Midhoop: and Charles Drummond of Kingffeild. He had alfo tuo daughters. Margaret Drummond, the eldeft, firft married to the laird of Arncapel in Dumbartonfhyre, built that houfe; and of her Sir Aula McAula of Arncapel, and the reft of that family are come. She married, to her fecond hufband, Balfoure, laird of McKareftowne, and built that houfe alfo; fhe bore to him Collonell Bartholomeus Balfoure, the father of Sir Philip Balfoure, both knowen for valiant men in the wars of the Netherlands.

Alexander Drummond's youngeft daughter was lady Skemore and Frofk, mother to Sir Patrick and Sir David Abercrombies well known at the Court of England. This Alexander Drummond was ane intimate freind of that Archbald Earle Douglas, who married the relict Queen of King James the Fourth, and a fufferer with him in all his troubles. In the year 1527, he was banifhed with the Earle by the parties of John duke of Albanie, the Governor, bot foon recalled by King James the Fyfth, and reftored to his libbertie and fortune. Buchan: lib. 14. "In comitijs aqua et igni interdictum fuit Comiti Angufiano, fratri et patruo, præterea Alexandro Drummanio Carnocenfi, eorum intimo amico."

1527

5. Sir Robert Drummond of Carnock, the fone of Alexander, was Mafter and furveyor of all the King's works to King James. He married firft Margaret Kircaldy, fifter to that laird of Grange, who is famous in all our hiftories for keeping the Caftle of Edenburgh. Margaret had to Sir Robert only a daughter, Margaret Drummond, married to   Erfkine of Cambufkenneth, and was mother to Annabella Erfkine, Lady Buchannan, and to   Erfkine, Lady Tyllibodie. Sir Robert Drummond, married to his fecond wife, Marjorie Elphingfton, fifter to Robert Lord Elphingftone, and neece

to Alexander Lord Elphingſtoune, ſlaine at Floodon with King James the Fourth. Marjories mother was the Lord Erſkines daughter. She bore to Sir Robert tuo ſones, Patrick Drummond who ſuccceded, and Sir John Drummond, the firſt laird of Hathornden; and tuo daughters, Margaret, Lady Sheyffield, and Jean Drummond, lady Lea . . . .

6. Patrick Drummond of Carnock, the ſone of Sir Robert, married Margaret Scot, heretrix of Monzie. She had to him three ſones and a daughter, who was Lady Kippenrofs; Sir Alexander the eldeſt ſone, who ſuccceded, Mr. James and Patrick Drummonds. Mr. James, the ſecond, married   and begot Mr. Patrick, Robin, and Jean Drummonds; Mr. Patrick, a learned ſcholar and religious gentleman, Robine his brother, a courtly youth, both dyed unmarried; Jean theire fiſter married . . . .

7. Sir Alexander Drummond of Carnock, the ſone of Patrick, was the ſeventh laird of Carnock, he married Eliſabeth Heburn, daughter to Sir Patrick Heburn of Wachton, knight, and had with her a ſone, Sir John Drummond.

8. Sir John Drummond of Carnock, the ſone of Sir Alexander, married   Rollo, eldeſt daughter of Sir Andrew Rollo of Duncrub, afterwards created Lord Rollo. She bore to him a ſone, John Drummond, a gentleman of the King's guard. This Sir John was the laſt of that family; for, in his time, the lands changed from the name of Drummond, himſelfe was ſlain in the laite civill warrs at the batle of Alfoord, under the Marques of Montroſe, in the year 1645; and his ſone John dyed anno 1680.

1645.
1680.

THE HOUSE OF DRUMMOND.

[THE FAMILY OF MIDHOOP.]

1. Alexander Drummond, the fourth laird of Carnock, his second Drummonds fone was Alexander, and the firſt laird of Midhoop. He married of Midhoop. Blanch Bruce, daughter to   She did bear to him Sir Robert Drummond, who ſucceeded; Mr. John Drummond of Woodcockdale, a gentleman of King James the Sexth his privie chamber: Major William Drummond, killed at the ſeige of Groll in Holland; and Sir Robert Drummond, the youngeſt, who came alſo to be laird of Midhoop.

2. Sir Alexander, the fone of Alexander, ſucceeded to his father; he was one of the Lords of the Colledge of Juſtice, and therefore was ſtyled Lord Midhop. He had no children bot Robert, who was ſlaine in Ireland, and the eſtate went to his brother, Sir Robert Drummond the youngeſt: He dyed anno 1619.   1619.

3. Sir Robert Drummond, the youngeſt fone of Alexander, firſt laird of Midhope, and brother to Sir Alexander, was the laſt laird thereof. He married   Hamilton, ſiſter to the laird of Binnin. She bore to him a fone, Alexander Drummond, who was a captaine in the late warrs, and unfortunately ſlain at the batle of Aldern, in the year 1645. Sir Robert Drummond had alſo with his wife tuo 1645. daughters, the firſt Lady Kincavel, mother to the Bruces of that family, whereof Mr. Robert Bruce, miniſter of Aberdowr, was the moſt famed for his ſingular piety and his travells to Paleſtina; the youngeſt was Lady Kennet, mother to Mr. Alexander Hay, and the brothers of that family.

L

74   THE GENEALOGIE OF

THE FAMILY OF HATHORNDEN.

Drummonds   1. Sir Robert Drummond, fifth laird of Carnock, had by his fecond
of Hathorn-
den.   wife Marjorie Elphingftoun, fifter to Robert Lord Elphingfton, a
fone, Sir John Drummond, who wes the firft laird of Hathornden.
He was gentleman ufher to King James the Sixth, and married
Sufanna Fouler, fifter to Sir William Fouller, fecretary to Anna,
Queen of Great Brittaine. She did bear to him one fone, Mr.
William Drummond, who fucceeded; and tuo daughters Anna and
Rebecca Drummonds. Anna married Sir John Scot of Scotftarbet;
he was one of the King's Secret Councell, and Director of the
Chancery, and a Lord of the Colledge of Juftice. She had to him a
fone, Sir James Scot, who married   Carnegie, fifter to the Earle of
Northefk, who did bear to Sir James David Scot, now of Scoftarbet;
married to   Greer, daughter to the laird of Lag, [who had one
only daughter married to the Vifcount of Stormond.] Sir John
Drummond's fecond daughter was Rebecca Drummond, married to
William Douglas, laird of Bonjedward, and had to him . . . .
 2. Mr. William Drummond of Hathornden, the fone of Sir John,
married Elifabeth Logan, daughter to the laird of Cotfeild, and
grandchyld to Sir Robert Logan of Reftalrige. He begot with
Elifabeth tuo fones, William, who fucceeded, and Robert Drum-
mond; and a daughter Eliza Drummond, married to Mr. Henrie
Henderfone, a famous doctor of phyfick in our time; by whom fhe
had only a daughter, Elifabeth Henderfone, married to Sir John
Clerk, laird of Pennicook; her children are John, Henrie, Elifabeth,
Marie and Barbara Clerks. Robert Drummond, the fecond fone of
Mr. William of Hathornden, married Anna Maxwel, fifter to the
Laird of Hills.
 Mr. William Drummond of Hathornden gave a noble prefent of

books to the librarie of Edenburgh Colledge; and dyed about the
year 1649. He was a learned gentleman, famed for his wryttings 1649.
both in profe and verfe; his hiftorie of the Fyve King James, and a
few of his poems, are only made publick; many more of his elaborat
peices are ftill lying in manufcripts. He was renowned amongft the
Poets of his time, particularly by Michel Draytone, and the Author
of the Vindication of Poefie, two famous Englifh poets. Arthurus
Johnfton gives him this epigrame—

> Quæfivit Latio Buchananus carmine laudem,
> Et patrios dura refpuit aure modos.
> Cum poffet Latiis Buchananum vincere Mufis
> Drummundus, patrio maluit ore loqui.
> Major uter? Primas huic defert Scotia, vates
> Vix inter Latios ille fecundus erit.

3. William Drummond, now of Hathornden, the fone of Mr.
William, is left the only perfon of a family to reprefent the ancient
Houfe of Carnock. He married firft Sophia Achmutie, daughter to
Sir John Achmutie, laird of Gosfoord, mafter of the robes both to
King James the Sixth and King Charles the Firft; with Sophia
Achmutie he had only a daughter, Sophia Drummond. The fecond
time he married Barbara Scot, daughter to Sir William Scot of
Clerkington, one of the Senators of the Colledge of Juftice; he
begot with Barbara tuo fones, William and Robert Drummonds,
and five daughters, Barbara, Elifabeth, Anna, Margaret, and Marie
Drummonds.

OF QUEEN ANNABELLA DRUMMOND, THE ELDEST DAUGHTER OF SIR JOHN DRUMMOND, BEGOTTEN UPON HIS LADY MARIE MONTEFIX, AND THESE COME OF HER;

Queen Annabella Drummond.

Haveing given ane accompt of the offspring of William Drummond of Eremore, first laird of Carnock, youngest sone of Sir John, seventh thane of Lennox, knight of Stobihal, and the severall branches sprung from Sir John Drummond's daughters; leaveing the accompt of the tuo eldest sones, Malcolm and John, who succeeded one another to be heads of the family to the next Partition.

Queen Annabella wes the eldest, of whom one observes well, that she wes a lady born under a most happie conjunction of starrs; for Robert, the Third of that name, King of Scots, enamoured with the perfections of her vertues and singular rare beautie, tooke her to wife when he was Earle of Carrick, Senescal of Scotland, and apparent heir of the Crown. Upon this marriage a certaine Poet wryttes—

> Ecce autem quærenda fuit, quæ ventre beato,
> Ederet hæredem sceptri; jam certa per omnes,
> Ut mos, Europæ discurrit cera potentes,
> Nuncia famosi vultus, tabulæque loquaces
> Nativum exhibuere decus; sed principis ardor,
> Non ultra Oceani fines, sua regna, vagatur.
> . Digna Annabella thoris legitur regalibus una,
> Olim Fergusio magnos paritura nepotes.

1390. King Robert, and his Queen Annabella Drummond, were both crowned at Scoone in one day, in the moneth of September 1390. She is recknd amongst the best of our Queens; and her death, 1401. about the year 1401, wes considered as a common loss to the Nation

THE HOUSE OF DRUMMOND.

It hapned fo that Archbald Earle of Douglas, called Auſtere, and Walter Trayle, Biſhop of St. Andrews, both dyed about the ſame time with the Queen; the removal of which three did prognoſticat a ſad revolution in the ſtate; and in that common calamitie, the queſtion being moved, which of the three were moſt uſeful to the kingdome? it was reſolved, That as the Douglas had mantained the glorie of the War, and Traile the authority, ſplendor, and diſcipline of the Church, ſo had Queen Annabella the dignity and reputation of the Court, which was well underſtood after her death by what followed. Solomon's commendation of a good wife, Proverbs xxi. might have been pertinentlie applyed to her, Many daughters have done vertuouſly, but thou excelleſt them all. She did bear to King Robert tuo ſones and tuo daughters; the eldeſt ſone was David the Prince and Duke of Rothſay: He married Marie or Marjorie Douglas daughter to Archbald the Grim, third Earle of Douglas, four yeares before his cruel Uncle ſtarved him in the Caſtle of Falcoland, about the twenty-third or twenty-fourth year of his age. He was the firſt that ever was inſtalled to be a Duke in this nation, for he was made Duke of Rothſay or Roſa, and with him Robert Earle of Fife and Monteith, his uncle, was made Duke of Albany in the year 1396. 1396.

Queen Annabella's ſecond ſone was James, who ſucceeded to be the firſt King of Scots of that name. She had alſo to King Robert tuo daughters, Margaret and Marie Stuarts. Margaret was married to Archbald the fourth Earle of Douglas, Lord Bothwel, Galloway, and Annandale, the firſt Duke of Turaine, the ſone of Archbald the Grim. He was called Archbald Tynman, for the loſs of the batles of Hamildon in Northumberland, and Vernoil in France; yet he gained great renown at the batle of Shreuſberrie upon the Earle of Northumberlands ſyde againſt King Henry the Fourth of England. He begot with Margaret Stuart tuo ſones Archbald and James

Douglaffes. Archbald was the fyfth Earle of Douglas, and the firft called Earle of Wigton, &c., for it was to him that Thomas Fleeming Earle of Wigton fold that Earledome. He married David Earle of Craufurd's daughter, who bore to him William Earle of Douglas. James the fecond fone of Archbald Tyneman was called Grofs James Earle of Abercorn, and fucceeded to the Earledome of Douglas, when his nephew Earle William, the fone of Archbald, was killed in the Caftle of Edinburgh; and married the daughter of Henrie Sinclar Earle of Orknay, her name was Beatrix.

Archbald Tyneman had alfo by Margaret Stuart tuo daughters; Margaret Douglas married to William Sinclar Earle of Orknay, the fyfth in line from the Earle of St. Clarences' brother, the firft Sinclar that came to Scotland; and Elifabeth Douglas married to John Stuart Earle of Buchan, and Conftable of France, fone to Duke Robert the Governour, and killed with Archbald Tyneman at the batle of Vernoil in France, anno 1423.

1423

Margaret Stuart, the eldeft daughter and wife to Archbald Tyneman, lyes burried in the church of Lincluden with this infcription on her tomb:—

HIC JACET MARGARITA SCOTIE REGIS FILIA, COMITISSA DE DOUGLAS, VALLIS
ANNANDIE ET GALLOVIDIE DOMINA.

King Robert's fecond daughter with Queen Annabella wes Marie Stuart; fhe was firft married to Sir Gilbert Kennedy of Dunure, and did bear to him, John firft Lord Kennedy; James Kennedy, Bifhop of Dunkeld, thereafter Bifhop of St. Andrews; and Sir Alexander Kennedie, beheaded.

1398. Marie Stuart was the fecond time married, about the year 1398, to George Douglas, fecond Earle of Angus of that name, fone to William firft Earle of Douglas, whom he begat upon Margaret

THE HOUSE OF DRUMMOND.

Stuart, Comtess heretrix of Marr and Angus; and had to him two fones William and George Douglaffes, both Earles of Angus after other. Marie Stuart was the third time married to Lord John Grahame of Dundaffmure, and did bear to him, Patrick Grahame, firft Archbifhop of St. Andrews, and James Grahame firft laird of Fintrie. It's faid, fhe was yet a fourth time married to the Laird of Ednim, and bore to him the firft Laird of Duntreath Edmonfton, and built that houfe.

King James, the Firft of that name, the fone of King Robert the Third, begotten with Queen Annabella Drummond, married Jean Seymour, daughter to John Beaufort Earle of Somerfet, coufine to Henrie the Sexth King of England, and begot James the Second King of that name, and fex daughters. The eldeft, Margaret, married to Lues the Daulphine after King of France, called Lues the Eleventh, fone to Charles the Seventh of France; the fecond, Elifabeth or Hellen, Dutchefs of Brittanie; the third, Eleonora, married to Sigifmund Duke of Auftria; the fourth, Marie firft Comtefs of Camphyre, then married to James Douglas the firft Earle of Morton, created be King James the Second; the fifth, Jean, firft Comtefs of Angus then of Huntly; the fixth, Annabella, dyed unmarried. [King James the First.]

King James the Second took to wife Marie of Edgmond, daughter to Arnold Duke of Gueldria, fifter daughter to Charles Audæum laft Duke of Burgundy. He begot King James the Third, Alexander, John, Marie or Margaret, and Cicile. [King James the Second.]

Alexander was Duke of Albanie, and married, firft, the daughter of   Earle of Orknay. With her he had a fone, Alexander alfo Duke of Albanie, who married Margaret Stuart the Lord Gordon's widow, whom King James the Fourth begot, under promife of marriage, upon Margaret Drummond, daughter to John Lord Drummond; Alexander begot with Margaret Stuart Lady Gordon a daughter, Margaret, married to David Lord Drummond.

THE GENEALOGIE OF

Alexander the King's fone Duke of Albanie, married to his fecond wife the Duke of Bulloign's daughter in France, and begot with her John alfo Duke of Albany, governour in the minoritie of King James the Fyft.

John the King's youngeft fone was Earle of Mar, alledged to be
1479. guiltie of defigning the King's death, was bled to death, 1479.

Marie or Margaret the eldeft daughter was firft married to Thomas Boyd, Earle of Arran; bot divorced from him and married to James Hamilton of Cadzow knight. They had James Earle of Arran, and Margaret or Marie Hamilton. James Earle of Arran married the fifter of Alexander Earle of Hume, and begat James Duke of Caftelherauld, Regent of Scotland in the minoritie of James the Sixth. Margaret or Marie Hamilton, fifter to James Earle of Arran, married Mathew or John Stuart Earle of Lennox: this Mathew or John Earle of Lennox, had tuo daughters one married to the Earle of Athol, the other to the laird of Tullibardine, and tuo fones, Mathew Earle of Lennox, and John Duke of Aubignie. Mathew Earle of Lennox married Lady Margaret Douglas, begoten by Archbald Earle of Angus on King James the Fourth's widow: Mathew had with Lady Margaret, Henrie Lord Darnlie, who married Queen Marrie; and Lord Charles his brother, father to the Lady Arabella Stuart, begotten upon Elifabeth Cavendifh, daughter to Sir William Cavendifh. Lady Arabella married to the Earle of Hartford, dyed childlefs, whereby the Earledome of Lennox fell in to the houfe of Aubignie.

Cicil, the youngeft daughter of King James the Second, married William Lord Creichton the fone of Chancellor Creichton. William begot a daughter with her called Margaret Creichtone; married to the Earle of Rothes, who had to him a fone the firft laird of Findreffie; bot the Earle found a way to divorce Margaret Creichton and difherit her fone.

THE HOUSE OF DRUMMOND.

King James the Third of that name, married Margaret daughter to Chriſtianus the Firſt, ſyrnamed Dives, King of Denmark; and begot with her King James the Fourth, Alexander Archbiſhop of St. Andrews, and John Earle of Marr. *King James the Third.*

King James the Fourth married Margaret Teudors, daughter of Henrie the Seventh King of England and Eliſabeth daughter to Edward the Fourth. She did bear to him King James the Fyfth. *King James the Fourth.*

King James the Fyfth married firſt Magdalen of Vallois, daughter to Francis the Firſt, King of France. After her death he married Marie of Lorraine, ſiſter to Francis, and daughter to René or Claud, Dukes of Guiſe, widdow of the Duke of Longueville. Marrie of Lorraine did bear to the King only one daughter, Marie Queen of Scots, mother to King James the Sixth. *King James the Fyfth.*

Marie Stuart Queen of Scots, the only chyld of King James the Fyfth, married to her firſt huſband Francis, the Second of that name, King of France: He lived not long. Then ſhe married Henrie Stuart, Duke of Albanie and Lord Darnlie, eldeſt ſone to Mathew Steuart, Earle of Lennox, begotten upon Margaret Douglas, the daughter of Archbald Earle of Angus, and Margaret Teudors, the widdow Queen of King James the Fourth; ſo that Queen Marie and her Huſband were couſines, and both great grandchildren to King Henrie the Seventh of England. Queen Marie had only a ſone to her huſband Henrie, King James the Sext. *Queen Marie.*

King James the Sext married Anna, daughter of Frederick the Second, King of Denmark, whoſe mother was Sophia Ulricus, Duke of Meckelburgh's daughter. Queen Anna's children to King James were Henrie the Prince of Wales, who dyed about the age of 18; Charles the Firſt, King of Great Brittaine; and one daughter, the Lady Eliſabeth, who married Fredericus, the Fifth of that name, Prince Elector Palatine of the Ryhne, after unfortunat King of Bohemia. Eliſabeth Queen of Bohemia did bear to Frederick many *King James the Sexth.*

M

fones and daughters: the fones were Charles Lodovick Henrie, who fucceeded to be Prince Elector Palatine, Prince Philip, Prince Rupert, Prince Maurice and Prince Edward; the daughters, Princefs Elifabeth ane Abbefs in Germanie, Princefs Loues ane Abbefs in France, Princefs Sophia, married to Erneft Auguftus Duke of Brunfwick Lunneburgh and Bifhop of Ofnabrugge, who hes many children.

The Princes Philip, Rupert, and Maurice all dyed without fucceffion. Prince Edward married the Duke of Niverfe' daughter, had by her only daughters; one married to the Duke d'Anguien, aire to the Prince of Condé, ane other married to John Frederick Duke of Brunfwick Lunneburgh and Hannover; bothe thefe daughters have children.

Charles Lodovick Henrie, Prince Elector Palatine, married a daughter of the Landgrave of Heffe, and begot a fone, Charles, now Prince Elector Palatine; married to the King of Denmark's daughter; and a daughter married to the Duke of Orleans, brother to Louis the Fourteenth, King of France, who was formerly married to Princefs Henrietta, youngeft daughter to King Charles the Firft of Great Brittaine, and who did bear to him two daughters, the eldeft now Queen of Spaine, and the fecond a young lady called Madamoifele de Vallois.

King Charles the Firft. King Charles the Firft married Marie of Burbon, daughter to King Henrie the Fourth of France; fhe had to him King Charles the Second, James Duke of York, Henrie Duke of Glocefter, Marie Princefs of Orange, the Princefs Elifabeth who dyed young, and the Princefs Henrietta. James Duke of York married firft Lady Anna Hyde, daughter to Edward Earle of Clarendon, Lord High Chancellor of England, by whom he had only tuo daughters, the lady Marie, now Princefs of Orange, and the Lady Anna. He married the fecond time to Marie d'Eftée daughter to the Duke of Modena, who hes born to him only the Lady Iffobella, dead. Henrie Duke

of Glocefter dyed unmarried. Marie, Princefs to William Prince of
Orange, had to him a fone, William now Prince of Orange, married
to the Lady Marie daughter to his Royal Highnes James Duke of
York. Princefs Henrietta had two daughters to the Duke of Orleans,
the eldeft prefent Queen of Spaine, the other Madamoifelle de Vallois.

Charles the Second, King of Great Brittaine, married Catharine, daughter to   King of Portugal.

<small>King Charles the Second.</small>

All thefe and many more are lineallie come of that renowned
Queen Annabella Drummond, of whofe fifters are alfo defcended
very confiderable perfons; as of the fecond, who married the laird
of Lochaw, the family of Argyle; of the third, the race of the
M'Donalds of the ancient houfe of the Lords of the Ifles; and of the
fourth, many knights and gentlemen of the name of Stuart, who
pofeffed old eftates in the Stormonth, come from the houfe of Duallie
and Arntullie; the firft whereof was a natural fone to King Robert
the Second, whofe care to provyde for his natural fones may appear
by the Charter following, which was granted about eight yeares
before his death, anno 1382.

<small>1382.</small>

"John, eldeft fone to the moft illuftrious King of Scotland, Earle of
Carrict and Stuart of Scotland, Robert Earle of Fyfe and Menteith,
Alexander Lord Badenoch, fones alfo to the forenamed King, Greeting: forfuameikle as oure lord and progenitor, King of Scotland
forefaid, hes given feverall lands, to wit, the lands of Rait, Kinfawns,
Kinclevin, Clackmannan, Lounnan and Forteviot, and 10 lib. land
within the fheriffdome of Aberdeen, to his natural fones begotten on
Marrion Cardeny, under certaine conditions and forms, as is contained in his Charter made to his faid fones more fullie beares:—" Be
it known to all that we have faithfullie promifed by the tenor of thir
prefent letters, that as we may, and ought in juftice, we fhall main-
taine and defend them, that they nor none of them fhal fuftaine any
injurie in the poffeffion of the faids lands, or violence wherethrough

they may be hindered to freely ufe and enjoy the famen notwithftanding of any eftate we may poffibly come to, in witnefs whereof we have appended our feals to thir prefents to remaine with them for their fecuritye. Given at Edinburgh, the 21 of June, 1382. *Ita est per me dominum Adam Turbull Cappellanum et notarium publicum.*"

There is a burial place, amongft the undefaced monuments within the wall of the church of Dunkeld, where it's written : "This is a place ordered for the burrieing of the Stuarts of Arntullie, defcended lineallie from King Robert, the firft of the Stuarts."

The Extraction of Lady Marie Montefex, the Wife of Sir John Drummond and Mother to Queen Annabella.

<small>Lady Marie Montifex.</small>

Sir Harie Montefix, originallie of a French family according to the Roll of Batle Abbay, whofe predeceffor came into England with the Conquerour, and became Lord of Stanfted in the countie of Effex, of which generation fpeaking, Cambden calles them *summæ nobilitatis viros*. This Sir Henrie accompanyed King William returning from his captivitie, when he had been prifoner with King Henrie the Second of England, about the year 1179. In recompence of his kindnes the King beftowed upon him feverall barronies in the fhyres of Perth and Dumbarton, which his pofteritie pofeffed for many years; untill at laft thefe lands became the portions of Sir William Montefixes daughters, the eldeft whereof, Mary, wes this fpoufe to Sir John Drummond, as is mentioned already.

<small>1179</small>

Sir Richard Montefix was fone to Sir Harie; I find him a witnes in a charter granted be King William, to his brother David of the Earledome of Lennox, about the year 1186. 1186.

Sir William Montefix was fone to this Sir Richard; and I find him a witnes in a charter granted be King Alexander the Second, to the convent of Inchaffray of the teynds of the King's revenue of the lands of Auchterarder, and he is there written Willielmus de Montfichet. This charter is dated at Clunie the 13th of Auguſt and eleventh year of the King's reigne, which falls to be the year of God 1227. 1227.

Sir William Montefex was fone to the laſt Sir William, and father to Sir William, whoſe daughter was this Lady Marie Montefix. King Robert Bruce grants a charter to this laſt Sir William of the lands of Aughterarder, paying to the King the foume pertaineing to the fervice of halfe a knight, and referving the liberties of the brugh and burgeſſes as they had them in the time of King Alexander the Third; the date of this charter is in the year 1328. 1328.

The Mufchets in Monteith doe alleadge theire name to be corrupted from Montefichet to Mufchet, as if one of their prediceſſors had married one of the three daughters of Sir William Montefix: bot the true original of the name of the Mufchetts, which came hither from England, thus, Robert Earle of Strathern, fone of Earle Gilbert, married a daughter of Sir Robert Mufchamp, barron Willover in the countie of Northumberland, and a cuſine of his called Mufchapp married ane heretrix in Menteith, of whom are the Mufchetts, fo called for Mufchamps, or de Mufco campo. And Cambden, in his herauldrie, makes it clear by the difference of the tuo coat armors; for the Montfichets, fayes he, beares Gules, three cheverons, Or, and the Mufchamps, Azure, three butterflyes, Argent; which flyes are the Mufchets' arms to this day, and very propper to the name according to its derivation.

CONCERNING MALCOLM DRUMMOND AND JOHN HIS BROTHER, THE EIGHTH AND NINTH CHEEFE HEADS OF THE FAMILY, SONES OF SIR JOHN DRUMMOND, BEGOTTEN ON THE LADY MARIE MONTEFIX.

THE FOURTH PARTITION.

<small>Malcolm Earle of Marr, the Eighth cheef of the Drummonds.</small> Malcolm Drummond, the eldeſt ſone of Sir John Drummond, begotten upon the Lady Marie Montefix, the Eighth cheefe head of the family : He married Lady Iſſobella Douglas, heritable Comteſs of Marr and Garrioch, and by her right was heritable Earle of Marr all the dayes of his lyfetime. William the firſt Earle of Douglas was the father of this Lady Iſſobella; for he married Margaret Mar, daughter to Donald or Duncan Earle of Mar, who through defect of males became heretrix of that earledome: on her he begot the Lady Iſſobella Douglas.

Duncan or Donald Earle of Marr was governour of Scotland benorth Forth in the abſence of King David Bruce, and killed in his tent at the unhappie ſurpryze of his army beſyde Dupline by Edward Balliol. He left bot one ſone Thomas and one daughter Margaret Mar. Thomas his ſone, Earle of Mar, married Margaret Stuart, heretrix of Angus, bot dyed without iſhew; ſo theire was none remaineing of Earle Duncan's race ſave this Margaret Mar, only ſiſter of Thomas, who married William Earle of Douglas, and was mother to the Lady Iſſobella, who was alſo heretrix thereof.

Malcolm Drummond Earle of Mar dyed without children, left his lady a widdow, and his own propper inheritance to his brother Sir John Drummond.

THE HOUSE OF DRUMMOND.

The Lady Iſſobella, after the death of her huſband Earle Malcolm, married Alexander Stuart, the ſone of Alexander Earle of Buchan, the youngeſt brother of King Robert the Third, whereby he became next Earle of Marr.

William Earle of Douglas, after the death of his Lady Margaret Mar, married Lady Stuart, Comteſs-Dowager of Mar and heretrix of Angus, widdow of Thomas laſt Earle of Mar, in the year 1381 : he begot with her George Douglas, ſecond Earle of Angus of that name. She was the daughter of Thomas Stuart, the laſt Earle of Angus of the Stuarts, lineallie come of John Stuart, great Stuart of Scotland, killed at the batle of Falkirk in the year 1299. Of George Douglas Earle of Angus, the ſone of William Earle of Douglas, we have made mention that he married Marie Stuart, the daughter of King Robert the Third, begotten upon Queen Annabella Drummond.

1381

I underſtand, there was a charter granted be Robert Stuart Earle of Strathern, who was afterwards King Robert the Second, and confirmed by King David Bruce to Malcolm Drummond Earle of Mar, of divers lands within the Earledome of Strathern, to wit, Tullieravan, Drum of Concraig, &c.; which lands are ſtill poſeſt be the Earle of Perth to this day. Ane other charter there is paſt by King David Bruce in favors of this ſame Malcolm Earle of Mar, conſtituteing him Heritable Corroner of the ſhyre of Perth, which was compted a very honourable office in thoſe dayes. I find John, fifth Lord Glames, got the office of Corronrie of the ſhyres of Forfar and Kincardine—Lyke to that office of Corronerſhip of the countie of Strathern, belongeing to the knights of Concraig, who were alſo Stuarts or Seneſcalls thereof, both which offices are long agoe antiquated and become obſolete.

88   THE GENEALOGIE OF

This Malcolm Earle of Mar, as he was a man noble and generous, allyed with the cheife nobles of the nation, in great efteem with the Kings David Bruce, Robert the Second and Third, fo was he no lefs honoured for his valor and gallantrie. He accompanyed his brother-in-law, that valiant warriour James the fecond Earle of Douglas, fone to William the firft Earle thereof, at the famous and bloody batle of Otterburn in the year 1388, where his courage eminently appeared; for he was one of them who tooke prifoner Sir Randolphe or Sir Ralph Percie, the brother of Henrie Percie, called Hotfpurs, Earle of Northumberland; for which fervice† he got a gift of penfion of 40 lib. Sterline yearly, payable during his life, out of the cuftomes of Invernefs, from King Robert the Third, in the firft year of his reigne 1393 : the tenor whereof begins, " Robert, by the grace of God, King of Scots, to our welbeloved brother Malcolm Drummond Earle of Mar, &c." It feems Mr. George Buchannan and others of our wrytters have been ignorant of this in the relations of the particulars of that battle.

OF SIR JOHN DRUMMOND, THE NINTH CHEEFE OF THE NAME,
BROTHER TO MALCOLM DRUMMOND EARLE OF MAR.

Sir John Drummond, brother to Malcolm Drummond Earle of Mar, fucceeded to be the Ninth cheife head of the family. He is fometimes ftyled Sir John of Stobhal, as his father was, after he diferted

Sir John Drummond, the Ninth cheife head of the family.

† There is a Charter in the Chartulary of Aberdeen, wherein King Robert Third, anno 1394, gives him seven hundred merks out of Strathbogy for the same cause.— *Vide Annot. on Friebairn's Buchannan, fol.* 434.

THE HOUSE OF DRUMMOND.

the Lennox, bot more frequently Sir John Drummond of Cargill, as wes alfo his fone and grandchild. There is one authentick inftrument of feafine carries it thus:—" In the year of Chrift 1407, Sir John Drummond Lord of Cargill gave feafine with his own hands of the lands of Ochtertyre, within the barronie of Kincardine and fhyre of Perth (which lands belonged to my Lord Henrie Sinclar Earle of Orknay) to a potent man Sir John Forrefter Lord of Corftorphin, and Margaret his fpoufe, &c."

I find Sir John Drummond got from the King a particular gift of the Ballyrie of the Abthanie of Dull, which feems to have been with the confent of his Coufine the Laird of Coneraig, who was Stuart of Strathern. This office of Baylerie hes been a dignitie of great honour, and wanted not its profit: whoever enjoyes the benefit, the right and title contained in the gift belongeth as juftly and heritablie to the Earles of Perth as any thing elfe they injoy.

Sir John married Elifabeth Sinclar, daughter to Henrie Lord Sinclar, Earle of Orknay, Barron of Roflin, Pentland, &c. He got with his lady from the Earle the lands of Murthlach, in the fhyre of Bamfe, by the refignation of his father-in-law, and confirmed by a charter granted be Robert the Third King of Scotland, in thir tearmes: "To our welbeloved brother Sir John Drummond of Stobhal, and Elifabeth Sinclar, daughter to the Earle of Orknay, his fpoufe." It wes from this Earle Henrie and his daughter that a foreft, ever fince, and now pofeft by the familie, had the name of Glenorknay, which lyes not above five milles from the caftle of Drummond.

Henrie Sinclar, Earle of Orknay, was the third Earle of that name, and the next perfon in a lineal defcent from William Sinclar, the Earle of St. Clarence's fecond fone, who was the firft of that name that came from France to this nation. Henrie maried Egidia or Giles Douglas, daughter to William Lord of Niddefdaile, called the black Douglas, a gallant perfon, and highly commended by all our wrytters: this William Lord of Niddefdaile married the fair Egidia Stuart, the wonder for beautie of her time, daughter to King Robert the Second and Elifabet Muire. Hector Boethius wrytts that Charles the Sixth of France, heareing the fame of her beautie, fent a painter to Scotland privately, who haveing drawn her picture exactly to the lyfe, prefented it to the King, who was fo enamoured therewith, that incontinent he difpatched ambaffadors to defire her in marriage, bot they came too late.

William Lord of Niddifdale begot with her only this daughter Egidia Douglas, who married Henrie Earle of Orknay, and did bear to him a fone William, who ucceeded, and a daughter Elifabeth Sinclar, married to this Sir John Drummond; fo that King Robert the Third was brother-in-law to Sir John, and great uncle to his lady. Henrie Earle of Orknay's father was William, and his mother Florentina, daughter to the King of Denmark. Amongft other lofty titles given to Henrie, he is called Knight of the Garter and Prince of Orknay, as appeares by a wreat extant of the defcent of the Sinclars. Henries fone, William Sinclar Earle of Orknay, married Elifabeth Douglas, daughter to Archbald fourth Earle of Douglas, begotten upon Margaret Stuart, daughter to King Robert the Third and Queen Annabella Drummond. Earle William Sinclar was Chancellour of
1453. Scotland to King James the Second, anno 1453; from whom he got the earledome of Caithnes in compenfation of his claim to the lordfhip of Niddifdale, offices, and penfions, contracted by King Robert the Second to William the Black Douglas Lord of Niddifdale, with his daughter the fair Egidia.

By this deduction it appeares, that as Sir John Drummond was brother-in-law to Earle William himfelfe, fo was he great uncle to his lady Elifabeth Douglas, who was grandchild to King Robert the Second and his Queen Annabella.

I had given me, from a very worthie friend S. J. C., the double of a Difclamation given by Sir John Drummond and his lady Elifabeth Sinclar, wreatten in very good Latine, wherein they both oblidge themfelves to a noble and potent Lord Henrie Earle of Orknay, Lord Roflin, &c., theire father, that they nor theire aires fhall never claime any intereft or right of propertie to any lands or pofeffions belonging to the faid Earle or his aires, lying within the kingdome of Norroway, fo long as he or any air-male of his fhall be on lyfe to inherit the fame; bot if it happen (which God forbid) the faid Earle to die without any air-male to fucceed to him, that then it fhall be lauful for them to claime fuch a portion of the forefaids lands as is knowen by the Norvegian laws to appertaine to a fifter of the family. Sealled at Rofline the 13th of May 1396. By this it feems that 1396. Earle Henrie hes pofeft lands in Norroway by right of his mother Florentina, the King of Norroways daughter, and that the law of that kingdome allowes inheritances to be divyded amongft the children upon the fathers death, unlefs it be otherwayes provyded by a deed, which may feclude the granters.

I find ane inftrument taken by Sir John Drummond in the year 1410, in prefence of Robert Duke of Albanie, fitting in councell with 1410. Walter Earle of Atholl, Archbald Earle of Douglas, George Earle of March, Alexander Earle of Mar, Patrick Earle of Strathern, William Lord Grahame, and John Senefcall of Innermay, concerning his lands of Ledcreiffe, Arguthie, and Smithifton, in the barronie of   .

Sir John Drummond begot upon Elifabeth Sinclar a daughter, called after the mother Elifabeth Drummond, and divers fones. The eldeft was Walter, who fucceeded; Robert was fecond; and the youngeft John, afterwards called John Efcortio: If there were any other, we find nothing but only theire names, and therefore paffes by them. Elifabeth Drummond was married to Thomas Kinnaird, the fone of Allan Kinnaird of that ilk, who was laird of   . I have feen the difcharge of her portion, wherein Thomas Kinnaird is witnes,

92   THE GENEALOGIE OF

and his fathers feal appended in wax, quarterly quartered; the 1st a faltier betwixt four crefcents, the 2d three mullets or ftarrs, the 3d as the firft, and the 4th as the 2d. They got the ftarrs in theire coat quartered with theire awn armes by a marriage with the Murrays.

Innes.

Robert Drummond, the fecond fone of Sir John Drummond, went out of the countrey, and became a notable fea captaine, and in the time of the war did great prejudice to the Englifh fhips: he was well knowen abroad in France, Flanders, Holland, &c. by the name of Robin of Bartane, in the place of Robin of Brittaine: by this trade he became rich, returned home, was made Controller to King James the Firft, and married the heretrix of Barnbougal, called Moubray, and fo betooke himfelfe to the name and armes of the Moubrayes. Of him all that were of that family are defcended; bot of late it's extinct.

CONCERNING JOHN ESCORTIO DRUMMOND AND HIS PROGENIE IN THE ISLAND OF MADERA.

Drummonds of Madera.

John Drummond, the youngeft fone of Sir John Drummond, 1419, travelled abroad, and was for a long time thereafter judged to have been dead; becaufe his friends never heard of him. untill it was accidentally, in the year 1519, that one Thomas Drummond, a cadet of the family, going on a fea voyage to the fouthward, was put in upon the Ifle of Madera, where he encountred with many fyne gentlemen of his own name; bot efpeciallie converfed with one call Mannuel Alphonfo Ferreira Drummond and his brothers, who related to him the whole ftorie of the lyfe of this John Drummond their prediceffor, how he fetled himfelfe in that ifland, and paft under the name of John Efcortio untill the time of his death, and then difcovered himfelfe, his nation, and kindred. After long conference, they ingadged Thomas Drummond to bring them from Scotland a perfect accompt of their pedegree, with the armes belongeing to the houſe they were come of; which Thomas performed accordingly, carrieing letters from them for that effect to David Lord Drummond, the cheefe of the family, then a yowng man, who, with the aſiſtance of his cuſins Archbald Earle of Angus, George Earle of Huntly, and others his neareſt relations, addreſſed himſelfe to the Councell of Scotland, and haveing inſtructed by many faire evidences the original extraction of the name in general, and the particular defcent of this John Efcortio, he obtained a large and noble Atteſtation upon the whole matter; wherewith the forefaid Thomas Drummond returned to his Cuſins at Madera, as hes been already mentioned in the Preface to this Collection. He had alfo letters with him from David Lord Drummond to Manuel Alphonfo Feriera Drummond, and his brothers, a coppie whereof, for further illuſtration of the point, as it is preſerved amongſt the Earle of Perth's wreats, I judged proper to infert in this place.

DAVID LORD DRUMMOND'S LETTER TO HIS CUSINES MANUEL ALPHONSO FERIERA DRUMMOND, AND HIS BRETHEREN IN THE ISLAND OF MADERA.

"Dear and welbeloved Cuſines, I have receaved, and underſtood much to my comfort, and with a very good will, your letter from the Ile Madera, of the 2d of July, in the year of our Redemption 1519, brought to Scotland by Thomas Drummond, our kinſman; and according to youre plenarie and full information, I find that a certaine gentleman, John Drummond, about 100 years agoe, departed from Scotland, and ſetled himſelfe in the Ile of Madera, where his generation happily increaſſed to the number of 200 men, women, and

1519.

children, and grand-children, defcended of him; and that the faid John Drummond, youre prediceffor, concealed to his latter time from them of the Ifland, and thofe he converfed with, his name, blood, and generation, whereby the original of his extraction, and what belonged to his pofterity therein, remained till then covered; fave that about his end, he difclofed to his ghoftly father in confeffion, and others called for witneffes, that he, accommodating himfelfe to the Portugal tongue, went by the name of John Efcortio, whereas his own proper name was John Drummond.

"For giveing you a full and fufficient certaintie of the nativitie and extraction of youre progenitor and his forbeers, you fhall receave the following relation. A noble Lord, John Drummond of Stobhal, our great-grandfather's great-grandfather, was brother to the illuftrious Lady Annabella Drummond, Queen of Scotland, from whom lineallie are defcended Five moft excellent kings of Scotland, whereof the Fifth at this time moft glorioufly reigneth. This John was alfo brother to Malcolm, Earle of Mar, who dyed without children; and to whom John his brother fucceeded, who married Elifabeth, daughter to the right noble My Lord Henrie Sinclar, Earle of Orkney, by whom he had diverfe children; the firft Walter Drummond, lord of Stobhal, our great-grandfather's grandfather, and the youngeft John youre anceftor; who, being a gallant and heigh fpirited gentleman, according to the true information of the ancienteft of our trybe, about 100 yeares agoe, went to France to feek honor and reputation; of whom we never heard any tydings before youre letter, the contents whereof we have with the oldeft men of our kindred, particularly examined, and after much fearch, it's found that he only about that tyme, and of that name, went from Scotland; fo that we are affuredly perfuaded, and, with the reft of our freinds, affirm, that the forefaid John Efcortio, youre grandfather's grandfather was fone to the faid John Drummond, lord of Stobhall, and brother to Walter Drummond, and that he defcended from our ancient Houfe and predeceffors; as lykewife have done the cheafe dukes, earles, and barrons of this Kingdome, and even the Royall race of our Kings alfo.

"Furthermore, to the end, that the maine ground and foundatione of our gentilitie in the kingdom of Scotland, may more cleerely be known unto youre Worthines, underftand that near 500 yeares agoe, a King of England, righteous aire to the crown, albeit he never injoyed it, called Edward the Outlaw, fone to Edmond Ironfyde, being an exile in Hungarie, married Agatha, fifter to Queen Sophia, wife to Solomon king of Hungarie, and daughter to the Emperour Henrie the fecond, and begot a fone, Edgare Atheling, and tuo daughters, Margaret and Chriftian. Edward the Outlaw came from Hungarie with his children to England, where he dyed; his fone Edgar Atheling and his fifters flying from William Duke of Normandie, then conquerour of England, back to Hungarie for fafety for fear of danger, becaufe of theire title to the crown, tooke the fea under the conduct of ane Hungarian gentleman, their Cufine and Councellor, bot by the violence of a ftorme, were driven upon the Scotifh fhore, and landed at a place, called to this day, Queen Margaret or St. Margaret's Hoop.

"Malcolm Keandmore, then King of Scots, haveing his court near the place, went himfelfe, as fome fay, or, as others, fent ane honourable meffage to invite them to his court, where they were royally entertained, and the King being taken with the beautie and deportment of Edgar's fifter Margaret, married her for his Queen, to the great contentment of all his fubjects.

"And to the end the root and original of our Pofteritie and kindred through lapfe of time fhould not decay, the forefaid King and Queen gave unto our Hungarian forefather, a Lordfhip and name of Gentrie, to wit, Drummond, and to him and his pofteritie, a coat of armes, as a badge of honour: Sea waves of red collour in a golden fhield, fupported by tuo favage or wyld men; all which you may read, attefted

under the great feal of Scotland, with the feals and fubfcriptions of
every member of the Councell then prefent, fent to you heirewith;
which armes, as we bear them oure felves, fo we fend them to yow for
youre ufe by the bearer heireof, to whom you fhall be pleafed to give
credit. Bot if you would be pleafed to fend us one of youres, who can
fpeake the Latine tongue, becaufe the Portugal language is altogether
unknowen to us, we fhould ufe and treat him as our own fone.

"In the mean time thanking you heireby, and accepting youre
letters more gratefullie out of the hands of the faid Thomas Drummond, then if he had brought us ten thoufand crowns, for none can
doe us a more acceptable kindnes then to bring us certaine tydings
of the welbeing and increafs of oure generation and kindred amongft
ftrangers, as we underftand by youre letters, which we pray God to
blefs with the increafe of all pofteritie and happines.

DAVID LORD DRUMMOND.

"At Oure Caftle of Drummond,
"the 1 of Decemb. 1519.

> "For our dear and welbeloved Cufines Manuel Alphonfo
> Feriera Drummond, and his bretheren, Gentlemen in the
> Ile of Madera."

Thomas Drummond, with this letter, and the fealled atteftation,
arrived at Porto Sancto in Madera, which he delivered to his Cufins;
whereof they were not a litle rejoiced, and refolved, with all convenient
fpeed, to difpatch one of theire principal freinds therewith to Portugal
for makeing addrefs to the King, that feeing they could inftruct the
gentilitie of theire lineage by theire defcent in fo noble a maner, they
might alfo have the priviledges belongeing to fuch granted to them in
the ufual forms; and accordingly fent Diego Perez Drummond for
Portugal for that purpofe. The King gracioufly commanded that

the matter fhould be furthwith put to tryall, that upon report of fuch as were deputed for that end, he might declare his Royall will; which at laft was publifhed in the form following, tranfcribed word by word out of the original.

"Don John, by the grace of God, King of Portugal and of the Algarbes on this fyde, and on the other fyde of the fea, in Africa, Lord of Guinee and of the conquered navigation and trafick of Ethiopia, Perfia, Arabia, Indies, &c. To whomfoever the fight of thefe my prefent Letters fhal come, I make known that Diego Perez Drummond, refidenter in my Ifle of Madera, hes by his Petition fhewed unto me that he is defcended by direct line, without baftardie, from the ftock of the Drummonds in Scotland, who are gentlemen that beares a coat of armes, and a family in that kingdome, known for fuch, and accompted amongft the beft and ancienteft houfes of the faid Kingdome; intreateing for the favor and grace for the continouation of the memorie of his prediceffors, who, through their good defervings, and noble fervices in former ages, were known to be gentlemen, and had all the badges thereof, that he might enjoy theire armes, with fuch other priviledges, honors, and immunities, as the laws of nobilitie does allow for continouance of the honor and reputation of Gentrie, to him and his; and, moreover, that I would be pleafed to command my Letters to be given him of his coat of armes, regiftrat in the records of my King at armes, amongft the reft of the noblemen and gentlemen of my Kingdome of Portugal, to remaine in the hands and cuftodie of my cheife herauld at armes: Of the which Petition I takeing notice, did caufe inquirie to be made by fuch officers and minifters of my Court whom it did concern, who found that the faid Petitioner proveth himfelfe to be come of the houfe and pedegree of the Drummonds in Scotland, being lawfull and legittimat great grandchild to Andreffa Gonfales Drummond, daughter to John Efcortio Drummond, great grandfather's father to this Petitioner, and

fone to Don John Drummond, lord of Stobhal, in Scotland, brother
to Annabella Drummond, Queen of Scotland, defcended with the
principal nobles of Scotland, of the illuftrious houfe of Drummonds,
according to the evident proofes thereof, by publick and authentick
wryttings and inftruments under the great feal of the kingdome of
Scotland, and other nobles his councellors of that kingdome: All
which premiffes were allowed and approven by my forefaid officers
and controllers of my Court in lyke cafes, fo that, according to juftice,
the faid armes doe belong to this Petitioner; which, by thefe my
Letters, I command to be delivered to him accordingly, with the
blazon of his helmet, creft, fheild, and difference to be regiftrat in the
records and book of Portugal, my king at armes, in maner and forme
following: Upon a golden feild, three red waved panes, or ftreames,
and, for a diftinction, a green Briza, with a diadem of gold, and a red
garland, or corronet, betwixt helmet and creft, with a hound, haveing
a golden coller above all for a creft; which fheild armes and infeigne,
the faid Diego Perez Drummond fhal, and may wear, in forme and
maner as his prediceffors have done, and all noble and gentle men
ufed to doe in all places and affemblies of honor in the dayes of the
moft high and excellent Kings, my prediceffors; and that it fhal be
lawfull for him, with the faid armes, to enter in feilds, batles, combats,
challenges, fkirmifhes, defyances, practifeing therewith all lawful acts
whatfomever, in time of peace or war, ufeing them in theire fubfcriptions, fealls, fignets, houfes, edifices, and buildings, caufeing them be
put or graven upon theire tombs and monuments; finally, to make
ufe of them in all places of honor, and enjoy them at theire pleafure,
freely, and wherever occafion fhal requyre, and to nobilitie may appertaine: Therefore I will and command, all governors, majors, fheriffs,
juftices, judges, and other officers, efpecially my King at armes, to
whofe fight thefe my Letters fhal come, to give way, obferve and
accomplifh, to doe all points of the premiffes according to the tenor

thereof, without any difficultie, hinderance, or difturbance to be made, done, or offered in the performance thereof, for fuch is my will and pleafure. Given in my royall and ever loyal citie of Lifbon the 19th of March.

THE KING.

And by his command the Bachelour ANTONIO ROIZ, his Majeflies cheife Herauld at armes. ANTONIO DELANEO Peco Duca, Notarie for the Nobility. In the year of our Saviour Jefus Chrift, 1538.

PORTUGAL King at Armes.

And was payed for the fees of the Office of Herauldrie, the 28 of the fame moneth fourtie Reys.   1538.

PEDRO GOMEZ.   PEDRO ALUREZ.

Regiftrat and Ingroffed in the Chancerie, and a coppie taken out of the Original, which remaineth in the cuftody of Gonfalo Alwes Feriera."

This warrant and provifo of the King's, with all its formalitie, publifhed and recorded, feems not to have been made more ufe of at that time, by reafons of the warrs and confufions which happened then betwixt Spaine and Portugal; which alfo interrupted the correfpondence from the Drummonds in the Portugal dominions to theire freinds in Scotland, untill the year 1604, when Martine Mendez de Vafconfelles Drummond, of the town of Porto Sancto in Madera, indeavoured to recover ane Extract of the former papers : and for that end did fupplicat the Office to which the power thereof belonged, declareing how he had occafion to make ufe of a certaine letter fent from Scotland by the Lord Drummond to Manuel Alphonfo Ferriera Drummond, great grandfather to the Petitioner, as alfo ane Extract of the fentence of the auditor of the town of

Funichall, and the provifo from the King our foveraigne, conform to the faid letter; which wryttings are under record in the cuftodie of Henrico Coelo, notarie publick; the Petitioner's purpofe being to annex the fame unto ane authentick teftimonie and inftrument of his blood and gentrie, for better proofe thereof, according to equitie and juftice.

THE PROVISO.

"Whereas the above mentioned wrytting are recorded and in the hands of Henrico Coelo, notarie, it is ordered that he deliver unto the forefaid Petitioner, ane extract thereof, in due and competent forme, to the end they may ferve him as a laufull and competent proofe and teftimoniall upon any occafion that may offer. Given the 15th of November 1604.

ANT.º BAPTISTA DE SPINOLA.

On the 15th of November 1604, in the town of S.ᵗ Cruz, was prefented unto me, publick notarie, the above mentioned Petition and provifo of Antonio Baptifta de Spinola, on the behalfe of Martine Mendez de Vafconfelles Drummond, who demandeth a coppie of the forenamed letters, and fentence, for prefervation of his nobilitie, which tuo acts are in my cuftodie; the coppie whereof, *de verbo ad verbum*, are in form and maner delivered to him, and wreatten out by me

HENRICO COELO, Notarie."

This Martine Mendez whom we have mentioned, liveing in the Ile of Madera, had got notice from the Court of Spaine, that the right noble James, Earle of Perth, his cheife, had been at Madrid with Lord Charles Howard, Earle of Nottinghame, Ambaffadour from England for confirmeing the peace treated betwixt the tuo kingdomes; and that the Earle of Perth, and his fifter, Lady Jean Drummond, Comtefs of Roxburgh, were both in great favor with

the King of Brittaine ; he fent unto them, intreating that by theire
favor and moyen, he might have theire King's letters of recommendation, and the Spanifh Ambaffadoures refideing at the Court of
England, to his mafter the King of Spaine ; which the Earle procured and fent to Madera, with one William Craufurd, a gentleman
who performed the meffage, and from Madera returned the Earle this
accompt of his negotiation.

"MY NOBLE LORD,
After I came out of England, bound for this place, I was robbed
by pirrats, and forced to goe to Barbarie, which hes been a great
prejudice to youre Honors kinfman Martine Mendez de Vafconfelles
Drummond, in regard the letters I carried to him were of ane old
date. I arrived heire upon the 10th of Aprylle 1614, where many
Gentlemen of the Drummonds did exceedingly rejoice. I delivered
the Kings letter and youre Lordfhip's to the faid Martine, who is
now gone to the Court of Spaine, not doubting of good fuccefs with
his Majeftie there by youre Honors means ; for we have heard
already that the King of Spaine hes conferred upon him the honor
of being one of the Knights of St. James. Neverthelefs it was his
defyre youre Honor fhould recommend him to the Englifh ambaffador at Madrid ; and if it were poffible to purchafs a new letter from
youre King to his Majeftie of Spaine, and alfo others from the
Spanifh ambaffador to fome of the nobles at Madrid ; for he doubts
nothing of youre Lordfhips care of what concerns him. The original
certificat, teftifying his defcent and his friends from youre Honors
houfe, and the accompt of the begining of youre family, I have feen,
with many fealls affixed thereto ; whereof he and his freinds make fo
great accompt, that they preferve it as the rareft jeuel in the world,
whereof youre Lordfhip fhal receave with his own letter ane exact
tranfumpt, with all that followed thereon.

1614.

In the fhip with thir papers goes foure chefts of excellent fweet-meats, directed to the right noble Lady Jean Drummond, Comtefs of Roxburgh, whereof tuo for herfelfe, and tuo for youre honor, one with dry succads, and the other with wett: upon your tuo chefts there is wrytten "For the Ry^t Honourable the Earle of Perth," which is fufficient to know them by. He fent to Barbarie for a fine horfe to youre honor againft next fpring. Moreover, if youre honor will permit me to bring one of his little fones to be a page to yow, I fhall doe it, for he is very willing to fend him. So, expecting youre Honors anfuere, I commit yow to the protection of the Almightie.
Youre Honors humble fervant till death.
W. CRAUFURD.
From the Ifland of
1614. Madera, July 3d, 1614."

Here I thought fit to infert a juft coppie of Martines own letter, in the language he fent it.

"ILLUSTRISSIME DOMINE COMES AMPLISSIME,
Dominationis veftrae praeclariffimae fuaviffimas literas, feftivo applaufu et tota pectoris alacritate, a me acceptas, meoque (ut par erat) capiti impofitas, fumma animi veneratione et reverentia femel legi, et faepius, alacrique tripudio, noftris oftentavi Dromondaeis, quas omnes hilari vultu et laeto accepere finu; immortali immortales perfolventes Chrifto grates, qui tam fingularem fibi patronum, fautorem et fuae noftraeque Drumondeae familiae elargitus fit firmiffimam columnam: Ii omnes quotquot funt, veftrae illuftriffimae Dominationi fe fubjectos, ne dicam fervos, profitentur, quae ut indies accrefcat, feliciterque procedat, rogant fuperos.
In veftro fafciculo literarum venerat Regia epiftola in mei com

mendationem, quam ego, utpote tanti principis et regis invictiffimi, a veftra Dominatione diligentiffime folicitatam, habitamque, atque meis negotiis tam neceffariam, maximi duco ; et cum veftra Dominatio tantam mihi ingerat fiduciam, velocefque mihi imponat audaciae alas, ut ad altiora volitare poffim, refque arduas atque difficiles aggrediar, iis, veftrae benevolentiae, nec non ampliffimis acceptis beneficiis innixis, recentiora, fed maxime mihi neceffaria, funt expetenda beneficia.

Cum ampli fit temporis tranfactum fpatium, tredecem fcilicet menfium, ex quo veftrae Dominationis, veftrique regis et legati confcriptae funt literae (moram trahente tabellario, quippe a Mauris capto, fpoliato et in Africam ducto, et ad hanc Infulam nuper pervento), cum item in procinctu, jamjam in aulam profecturus regiam, ad meorum expeditionem negotiorum, atque hae literae fint aliquantulum antiquatae, fintque tam utiles quam neceffariae aliae recentiores, veftram Dominationem fubmiffe rogo, aliam curet a rege veftro ad Regem Hifpaniarum, in mei favorem, in qua fignificet, me ex Drummondea effe familia : quod fi id haud quaquam fieri poffit, faltem unam procuret, ab eodem Rege, ad fuum in Hifpania legatum, in qua oftendat fuam erga me benevolentiam, eique jubeat, ut mearum rerum et negotiorum gerat adminiftrationem, mihi auxilietur, et prefens, me prefentem exhibeat, offerat et praefentet meo Regi : abfque hac enim ad Legatum litera, non eft cur ad aulam Regiam proficifcar.

Ad eundem legatum a veftra Dominatione unam, et ab illuftriffima domina Johanna Drummond alteram, in quaram unaquaque exprimatur et apperte declaretur vefter in noftros Drummondeos favor, amor et benevolentia, nobis quippe tam fanguine conjunctos.

A legato item Hifpaniarum in veftra Curia commorantem aliam defidero, de eadem re, ad regem fuum et noftrum, in qua manefefte affirmet veftro regi facturum gratiffimum, fi meis rebus bene confulat.

meis negotiis faveat, meque foveat benigne; aliam etiam ab eodem legato ad Lufitaniae proregem; quia jam eft vita functus, cui altera venerat; et, fi aliis magnatibus fibique familiaribus dynaftis plures velit fcribere, in mei commendationem, mihi faciet gratiffimum.

Super omnia autem exopto veftrae Dominationis literas, quae me de valetudine, ftatu, rebufque veftris, deque noftris Drummondeis faciant certiorem, quorum ego profapia et fanguine glorior et exulto, ut clariffime videri poterit, in hac fcriptione, five, ut aiunt publico inftrumento, quod meo proavo Jacobo Perez Drummond miferunt ex Scotia viri praeclariffimi, ibidem nominati et fubfcripti; ejus prototypon, five examplar eft penes me, quod ad aulam regiam cum aliis litteris et fcriptionibus mecum oportet deferre, in quo funt figilla multa pendentia, Drummondeorum arma gentilitia, et aliorum illuftriorum dominorum ftemmata; ad cujus fimilitudinem effecta eft, diligentiffime et fideliter, hujufmodi inclufa confcriptio.

Pro fingulari veftrae Dominationis in me benevolentia, collatifque non vulgaribus beneficiis, me in veftram fervitutem in perpetuum offero, nec non mei amoris fignificationem in ifto munufculo (noftrae Infulae et regionis funt fructus minutiffimi, non vero lautiffima bellaria) ut veftris fecundis menfis admifceatur: quod fi irritamentum videatur gulae, veftroque fuave palato, pace habita, cum facultate, mittam quam plurima; Magni etiam ducerem, fi ire una poffit nobilis et generofus equus, quem fumma anxietate et folicitudine ex Africa expecto, qui, ubi primum pervenerit, quam citiffime mittetur.

Si veftrae Dominationi fuerit gratum, mittam et ex liberis meis multis unum puellum, ut fit mei amoris et fervitutis pignus certiffimum: fi placuerit et velit veftra Dominatio, ibit, idque mihi apperte fcribat; fin minus non mittam: et quando ipfe a Curia revertar, alium etiam puerum ex Drummondea familia in mei folatium et honorem a veftra petam Dominatione, cui noftra Infula et idioma minime difplicebit.

Prolixae epiftolae jam imponenda eſt coronis, quare, cum ſim in procinctu ad curiam, nullaſque traham moras, niſi dum Olyſippone dictas expecto litteras, precipue vero ad veſtrum legatum, expeditionem et brevitatem obnixe rogo ut omnes mihi mittantur. Deum optimum maximum peto, ut felicem veſtrae Dominationis ſtatum, ad feliciorem, ne dicam feliciſſimam perducat finem, quod omnes Drummondeae profapiae efflagitamus alumni. Datum Funchali in Infula Maderia, ultimo Junij anno 1614.   1614.

Fui oblitus petere a veſtra Dominatione aliam epiſtolam ad dominum Alonſum de Valefco, qui fuit noſter legatus in Anglia et modo reſidet in curia, mihique mirandum in modum favebit, propter veſtrum Dominationem; qui, cum abſens erat, et tum in Anglia, in mei commendationem ſcripſit luculentiſſime.

MARTINE MENDEZ VASCONSELLES DRUMMOND.

Illuſtriſſimo Domino de Drummond
   Comiti de Perth in Scotia.

In the year 1623, John, Earle of Perth, receaved a letter wrytten in the Portoguefe language, and ſigned by three brothers, from the Citie of Liſbon, the 12th of May, thus tranſlated by S. J. W.

ILLUSTRIOUS LORD,

The ſplendid Family of Drummond, whereof youre Lordſhip is the cheife and principal head, is fo illuſtrious in the world that, lyke ane other fone, it doth communicat its light to the utmoſt places of the earth. We three brothers who wrytte this letter to youre Lordſhip are natives of the Iſle of Madera, and, although bot ſlender branches in refpect of fuch a ſtock, we doe proceed in a right and legittimat line alfe well on the father's as on the mother's fyde from the Lord John Drummond, who heiretofore came from the Kingdome of Scotland to affiſt Don Ferdinando and Donna Iſſobella, theire Catholick

Majefties of Arragon and Caftile, againft the Moores for recovery and conqueft of Granada, and from thence went to the Ifland of Madera, where he married a noble Portuguefe, who bore to him thefe children, from whom we and many others our relations liveing in the faid Ifland and in Brazile, doe defcend. The faid Lord John Drummond, our progenitor, was fone to the Lord John de Drummond of Stobhal, brother to the Lady Annabella, Queen of Scotland, as is already certifyed to youre Lordfhip by Martine Mendez Vafconfelles Drummond, our kinfman, at prefent governor of the Ifland Porto Sancto; and albeit the length of time, the difference betwixt kingdomes, and diftance of places, hath hitherto hindered a deu correfpondence and communication between us, now, fince our Lord God is pleafed to open a way by the above-named Martine Mendez &c. for our correfpondence, and alfo a better occafion for it by the good fuccefs of that happie marriage (which we hope for) between the moft ferene Prince of England and the Infanta Maria, it will not be reafonable that we fhould defift, from this time forward, to offer and to fhelter ourfelves under the fhade of fuch great trees as are youre Lordfhip and the reft of thefe noble perfones in thefe kingdomes of youre illuftrious family ; who, being fo eminent and generous perfones, will not deny theire protection and favour, it being the duty of princes to aid thefe who requeft it of them, and to confer favors on thofe who afk them of them ; principallie, fince, in thir parts where we live, we doe not degenerat from our anceftors, bot indeavours in all things we doe to preferve that nobility and honor which we inherit from them whom the former Kings of Scotland (at the inftance of youre Lordfhip's anceftors) have tenderly recommended as theire relationes, to the ancient Kings of Portugal; and fo lykwife hath done, at the requeft of youre Lordfhip's felfe, the moft ferene King James, who now reignes in England, by his letters, dated the 12th of Auguft

1613. 1613, wreatten to the late King Phillip, who is now in glorie ; for which we ought to efteeme the fyrname of Drummond, as moft illuftrious above all others in the kingdome, albeit there are many moft noble and moft worthie therein. Ane other principall favor which we yet defyre of youre Lordfhip, is, that yow will pleafe to honor us as youre relationes, and command us as youre fervants; and, in the fecond place, that youre Lordfhip will pleafe to procure from the moft ferene King of England his letters to his Highnes the moft ferene Prince of Wales, his fone, (who is at prefent in Madrid) wherein he may recommend to him the trybe of the Drummonds, who live in the Kingdomes and Segneories of Portugal, and particularly us youre fervants who wreats this letter; and that youre Lordfhip would alfo, at the fame time, fend youre recommendation to fignifie to his Majeftie, our King Philip, that we are defcended from youre illuftrious familie, and to defire him that he will honor us, and doe us the favor to make ufe of us in his fervice and employments. And that youre Lordfhip may fullie underftand that the perfons yow fhall pleafe to beftow thefe favors upon are not incapable of them, we fhall heire fet down the name, condition, and office of each of us three brothers who fend this prefent letter: The eldeft of us is called Antonio de Freitafcorrea and Drummond, Clerk and Cannon in the Church of Funchale; the fecond brother is called Remigio de Affumpfatione and Drummond, Monk of the Ciftertian Order, Doctor and Mafter in Theology, who hes been heretofore Abbot, General, and Reformer of the faid Order in the Kingdome of Portugal, and at prefent is deputed in the holy office of the Inquifition; the third brother is called Simon de Freittafcorrea and Drummond, a laick man and a Captaine of Foot in the Ifland of Madera. When yow fhall pleafe to doe us thefe favors yow may fend youre letters by the way that this comes, that fo it may arrive fafely to our hands, and thereafter one of us fhal goe to the court at Madrid to kifs the hands, in name of us all three brothers, of the moft ferene Prince of England, and to fhew to his Heighnefs the blazon

108   THE GENEALOGIE OF

that we have of the armes of the family of Drummond, given to us by the kings of that kingdom, they being well fatiffyed that they belong to us both by the father's and the mother's fyde, as is above-mentioned; the which armes we doe not fend heirewith to youre Lordſhip for its confirmation, and the authentick tranſlation of the whole matter, and that certificat of our defcent, (which anciently came from Scotland to our anceftors by order from thefe of youre Lordſhip) by reafon of the danger and uncertainty of thir prefent letters comeing fafe to youre Lordſhips hand, bot with youre Lordſhips anfuere we fhal doe it. God keep your Lordſhips moft illuftrious perfon long to live, and all thofe noble worthies of the illuftrious family of Drummond with 1623. increfs of eftate, etc. Wrytten from Lifbon the 12 of May 1623.

| Od^{res} Frat. Remigio Dasumpsa^t & Drummond. | Antonio de Freitas Correa & Drummond. | Simeon de Freitas Correa & Drummond. |

For the illuftrious Lord
John, Earle of Perth in Scotland.

1634.   Againe, in the yeare 1634, John Earle of Perth receaved ane other letter in Latine; the coppie whereof follows,

ILLUSTRISSIME DOMINE COMES AMPLISSIME.

Accepta beneficia gratiis perfolvantur neceffe eft, neque feram beneficii recordationem, dumunodo oblivio non intercedat, culpandam judico. Tua in me maxima merita, excell: Comes, mihi adeo ante oculos obverfantur, ut fi bellorum eventus mutuae familiaritatis commercio non obftarent tuam in me benevolentiam fcripta teftarentur; tuo enim prefidio fultus (fereniffimo Angliae Rege favente) in Equitum D. Jacobi ordinem adfcriptus fum, ut ex Regia Hifpaniae Curia certiorem te feci, et dominam meam Comitiffam Johannam Drummond, quam, accepti muneris parentem maximam fuiffe fcio, ut etiam praefecturae Infulae Sancti Portus, elapfis jam annis 14, a Catholica Regis majeftate mihi conceffae, etiamfi infula divitiis nequaquam afflueret, ob illatum detrimentum a Turcis Argelencibus: femiobrutam clade ego erexi, et in priftinam reftitui dignitatem. Nunc ardenter exopto, ut regis majeftas in altiore me tranfferat dignitatem. Jam, ut in ramos vegetantis humoris affluentia, ab arboribus, ubi nafcuntur, derivatur, ita profecto tuam in me redundare benevolentiam et dominae Johannae Drummond, cui nunc fcribo, contendo; itaque a tua excellentia obfecro, ut ei notum facias, munera a me petita, ab abnepote D. D. Johannis exorari, ut tibi fatis conftat: et te fummis rogo precibus, ut gentilitiam generis cartam, quam in ftemmate quinque filii fequaces infignem habeat concedas, uno certe fiquidem negotio impedior, immortales tuae excellentiae grates jufte perfolvere, ob fingularem in hanc domum noftram beneficentiam. Felices dignitatis tuae et rerum fecundos eventus coelum fuppeditet. Regiae tuae Arboris palmes et cliens amantiffimus.

     MARTINE MENDEZ DE VASCONSELLES DRUMMOND.
Infula Portus Sancti, 16 Maij A. D. 1634.   1634.

  Illuftriffimo Domino Johanni de Drummond,
    Comiti de Perth in Scotia.

To this letter John Earle of Perth returned anfuere in thefe words:

  COGNATE MI DILECTISSIME,

Quanta folent laetitia, ex naufragio emerfi, et gravi periculo reduces (quos conftans jam olim fama in demortuorum gregem annumerabat) amicos et propinquos fuos domi afficere, tanta equidem, et majore, infperatae illae tuae, jucundiffimae tamen, literae, Cognate dulciffime, me affecerunt. Quid enim mihi incogitanti poterit accedere optatius, quam poft tantam annorum feriem, antiquam noftram familiam, non priftinis, majorum in patria continente, finibus contentam, oceanum tranfmififfe et ultra Herculis columnas pofuiffe fedem. Itaque lubens facio, ut veterem Cognatum meum (quem celeberrima duarum gentium monumenta literis eundem effe comprobant) poftliminio gratulabundus agnofcam. Quod quidem, non folum omnia humanitatis et verae amicitiae jura, verum ipfius etiam naturae, quae fpeciei fuae quam diutiffime confervationem amat, poftulant fieri. Quare de cetero, pro mea fumma erga te benevolentia, omnem in te, ut quam ampliffima fis dignitate, ornando, curam adhibebo, daboque operam, ut quem propria, in externo folo, virtus, apud exteros (frendente invidia, et fortuna obluctante) magnis honoribus auxit, aliquis etiam cumulus, mea commendatione, eidem accedat: Eft tamen (ignofcas velim) quod non injuria expoftulem tecum, qui Scotiam rem notiorem multo quam nos Maderam veftram habueris, nec citius ad nos fcripferis, fed nomen et memoriam tui, oblivione altiffima, tamdiu apud populares et amicos, obrueris; prefertim hac tempeftate, qua tam commoda et frequens illinc in has oras navigatio recepta eft. Igitur obnixe a te contendo, fiquidem prefentes tuae literae, tam felicem viam invenerint, ne committas poftea, ut excufatione, aut longo locorum intervallo, potius quam literarum affiduitate fcribendi officium expleas. Hoc autem tempore molefte fero, quod ab Aula et Rege tam longe diffitus fum, ne tuo plane defiderio, ut velim, fatiffaciam Magnaeque Regis Britanniae literas, quas tibi ufui fore fpero, impetrem: verum fi tibi opus effe cenfueris, dabo operam, eafdem liberales fatis, una cum magno Scotiae diplomate, cum fervo quodam ex familiaribus meis, ut locus tempusque poftulaverit, mittendas. Proximas tuas literas in Aulam Anglicanum, ubi ego conjunctiffimos habeo, qui eas ad me perferendas curabunt, dato. Haec ego Latine, quod eam linguam communiffimam, qui mihi tuas tradidit, dicebat, exaravi. Vale.

PERTHE.

Dat. Apud Arcem noftram de
Drummond, 24 Novembris anno 1634.

THE HOUSE OF DRUMMOND.

CONCERNING SIR WALTER DRUMMOND, THE TENTH CHEEFE OF THE FAMILY, AND THE BRANCHES DESCENDED FROM HIM.

THE FIFTH PARTITIONE.

Sir Walter Drummond of Cargill, in order the tenth cheefe of the name and family of Drummond, fucceeded to his father Sir John Drummond about the year 1440. He married Margaret Ruthven, a daughter of Sir Patrick Ruthven, the cheefe of that name, from whence came the Lords Ruthvens and Earles of Gowrie; and begot with her Malcolm Drummond, who fucceeded to him; John Drummond, a churchman; and Walter Drummond, ftylled of Ledcreefe, from whom are come the Lairds of the Neuton of Blair, and divers families fprung from them.

Sir Walter Drummond, the tenth Cheefe. 1440.

Off this Sir Walter there is a wrytting extant, dated the third year of the reigne of King James the Second, wherein Alexander Seaton alias Gordon, Lord Gordon, retoures himfelfe neareft and laufull air of the lands of Bad, Camfdranie and Weftwood, to the Lady Elifabet Keith, his grandmother, who laft deceaffed infeft in the faids lands, and which were then fallen in the hands of Sir Walter Drummond of Cargill, Knight, of whom they are holden ward, and at that time lying in Nonentrie, &c. The lands are a part of the Barronie of Kincardin, in Monteith, which came to the houfe of Drummond by the Lady Marie Montefix, the fuperioritie whereof did ever fince appertaine to the family, and now of late the proppertie alfo, which had been in diverfe other hands, fuch as the Earles of Huntlie, Earles of Wigtoune, &c.

John Drummond, Dean of Dumblane and Perfone of Kinnowll,

was fecond fone to Sir Walter: he feems to have been a very hardy and bold churchman, and to have thruft himfelfe in that office at his own hand; for the proverb tooke beginning from him, ufed when any thing is pofeft without warrant—Yow take it (they fay) as the Drummond tooke the order. He was one of the Popes knights, and called Sir John. He had a fone Sir William Drummond, who was Dean of Dumblane after his father, and feverall daughters, whereof one married to the Laird of Coldoch Douglas; ane other to a Laird in Lothian, called Hepburn; ane other to the Laird of Neuton; ane other to James Hay; and the laft to one called Abernethie. Sir William Drummond, fone to Sir John, and Dean alfo of Dumblane, had fones Mr. Malcolm Drummond, a notar, and David Drummond; for albeit they were ecclefiaftick perfones, and then under the vow of chaftitie by theire order, yet very few outwent them in propagation of their kindred: of thefe fones feverall fmal families about Dumblane had beginning.

Sir John, Dean of Dumblane, after the death of his brother Sir Malcolm Drummond of Cargill, fell to be tutor to his nevoy John Drummond of Cargill in his minoritie, to whofe fafine he is witnefs anno 1478. Sir William Drummond, Dean alfo of Dumblane, Sir John's fone, was perfon of Forteviot before he was Dean, as appeares by a wryte, wherein King James the Fyfth, in the third year of his reigne, with advyce of John Duke of Albany, his tutor, protector and governor of the realme, gives to Sir William Drummond, whom he tearmes our familiar Clerk, Perfon of Forteviot, a gift of the ward of William Mufchet, the fone of John Mufchet of Wefter Cambfheeny, under the privie feal.

1478.

THE HOUSE OF DRUMMOND.

THE FAMILY OF BLAIR DRUMMOND.

Walter Drummond of Ledcreefe, the youngeſt ſone of Sir Walter Drummond of Cargill, was the firſt of the Drummonds of the familie of Newton of Blair; of whom all of that houſe are deſcended in a right line. There is a charter of the lands of Ledcreefe, granted by John Lord Drummond in the year 1486 to this Walter, wherein he calls him Walter Drummond, our deareſt uncle. This Walter left tuo ſones, John, who ſucceeded, and James; of whom I find a commiſſion by Malcolm Drummond of Cargill, the ſone of Sir Walter, conſtituteing them, to wit, John of Drummond and James of Drummond, his loveing nevoys, to be his baylie deputs, dated anno 1447.

Drummonds of Blaires familie.

1486.

1447.

2. John Drummond, the ſone of Walter, ſucceeded; he was called John of Fliſkhill and Ledcreefe. I neither find, who was his mother, whom he married, nor any accompt of his brother James; only that John had a ſone, who ſucceeded to him, called George Drummond.

3. George Drummond, the ſone of John, ſucceeded, who appearantly purchaſed the lands of Newton of Blair, for he is the firſt whom we underſtand to have been ſtyled George Drummond of Blair. He married Jannet Halyburton of Buttergaſk; ſhe had to him tuo ſones, George, who ſucceeded, and William Drummonds. George Drummond the father, and William his youngeſt ſone, were both treacherouſly killed together at an unhappy rencounter by the
                    upon the 3d of June 1554; bot moſt of them that were preſent or guilty of the ſlaughter were either brought to publick execution, or by theire ſubmiſſions and ſatiſfactions made theire peace with the parties wronged, as appeares by theire applicationes extant.

1554

4. George Drummond, the eldeſt ſone of the laſt George, commonly

diftinguifhed by the name of 'Old George Drummond of Blair,' married Katharine Hay, Lady Ballunie, daughter to Hay of Meggins. He had by her five fones, George, who fucceeded, John, Harie, Andrew, James, and four daughters, Sibylla, Elifabeth, Catharina, and Jannet.

George was infeft in the lands of Ledcreefe by a charter granted
1554. from David Lord Drummond, dated in November 1554. He did good fervice to Queen Marie in the time of her troubles againft the Englifh; and in revenge of his fathers flaughter, did a handfome exploit at Dumferline, which is reported thus:—

[A BLANK IN THE MANUSCRIPT.]

John Drummond, the fecond fone of Old George Drummond of Blair, dyed young. Harie Drummond, the third fone, was a valiant man: of him Bifhop John Leflie, in his Cronicle of Scotland, gives a notable accompt, when he relates the ftorie how Queen Marie for hir
1559. fafety betooke herfelfe to Leith, in anno 1559, and ftrengthned it with a garrifon of Scots and French forces; His words are, *Regina Leithum ipsa ingreditur; ac tandem magnas Gallorum et Scotorum copias militum, ducibus Kennedio et Drummondo, eo traducit;* and againe, telling of the fayllies made out of Leith againft the Englifh, *Galli vero creberrimis eruptionibus factis, praelia levia, sed non sine sanguine committebant quibus in praeter alios, occubuerunt Kennedius Scotorum peditum, et Henricus Drummondus equitum duces strenuissimi.*

Mr. Andrew Drummond, the fourth fone of old George, was minifter of Parbyrde in Angus. He had four fones, Mr. Henrie, Sir Patrick, Mr. James, and Archbald Drummonds. The eldeft, Mr. Henrie Drummond, married his cufine Jean Drummond, daughter to John

Drummond of Blair, his uncles fone; he purchafed the lands of
Gardrum, four miles from Perth, and left it to his fone James Drum- Drummonds
mond, now of Gardrum. of Gardrum.

Sir Patrick Drummond, fecond fone to Mr. Andrew, went to France
very young, where he ferved the Duke of Bowillion; who, being well
fatiffied with his learning and difcretion, very foone made him governor to his children. He continowed in the Dukes fervice, at the
court of France, untill the Duke dyed; then he came to the court of
England, where, by King Charles the Firft, he was advanced to be
one of his gentlemen ufhers; then preferred to be Confervator for the
Scots at the ftaple of Camphere, in the Low Countries, where he lived
to a great age, in much credit and honour. He married Dame Margaret Porterfield, daughter to the Laird of Comiftown, in Lothian,
bot had no children with her. Mr. James Drummond, third fone to
Mr. Andrew, was a minifter in the diocefs of Durham, in England;
where his pofteritie continows to this day. Archibald, the youngeft
fone of Mr. Andrew, married in Angus, and left a familie behind
him there.

James Drummond, the fifth and youngeft fone of Old George Drummond of Blair, had three fones and tuo daughters; to wit, Mr. James,
Robert, Daniel, Chriftian, and Sufanna Drummonds: He purchafed
the lands of Fordew, in the parifh of Clunie, and Boghal, near to
Cowper of Angus. Mr. James Drummond, his eldeft fone, was minifter at Kinloch, fucceeded to the lands of Boghal, and had children
George, and Thomas, and Jean Drummonds. Robert Drummond, the
fecond fone of James, had four fones, James, John, Gavin, and George.
James, the eldeft, had children, Robert, John, and Griffel Drummonds.
John, the fecond, a factor in Edinburgh, married
daughter of   Gavin and George are fine hopeful young
men: thefe are the fones of Robert. Daniel Drummond, the youngeft
fone of James Drummond of Boghal, was a liveteunant in the garrifon

of Hulſt, belongeing to the States-General : he married there, bot we hear not what children he left. Chriſtian, the daughter of James Drummond of Boghal, was married to Alexander Stewart of Dalguiſſe ; and her ſiſter Suſanna to   Herring of Lenings : All theſe were come of the ſones of Old George of Blair.

5. George Drummond, called George Drummond younger of Blair, the eldeſt ſone of Old George, whereby it ſeemes they lived long together, had alſo tuo ſiſters ; Sibilla, married to   Tyrie, Laird of Drumkilboe, and Jannet Drummond, to   Ratray of Craighal, in the Storemonth. George married Gilles Abercrombie, Lady Mugdrum, daughter to the Laird of Abercrombie, and had with her tuo ſones, John, who ſucceeded, and George Drummond, and a daughter, called Jean Drummond.

George Drummond, ſecond ſone to the laſt George, married Griſſel Cargill, daughter to Daniel Cargill of Haltown, and had with her ſones Daniel and Patrick Drummonds. Daniel had onlie a daughter, Marjorie Drummond, married to Thomas Whitſone, wreater in Ratray, and heritor of a pairt of the lands of Ratray. Jean Drummond, the daughter of young George, went with Lady Jean Drummond, Comteſs of Roxburgh, to the court at London, and was married to Mr. Thomas Murray, provoſt of Ayton Colledge, and governor to King Charles the Firſt when he was Prince of Wales. She did bear to Mr. Thomas, Harie, Charles, William, and Anna.

6. John Drummond ſucceeded to his father, George Drummond younger of Blair. He married Agnes Herrin, daughter to Sir David Herrin of Lethintie and Glafchuine ; theire children were George, who ſucceeded, Andrew, James, David, William, and Jean Drummonds. Andrew Drummond, the ſecond ſone, dyed in a voyage to the Eaſt Indies. David, the third, was a factor in Campheere, married to   Skeen, and had only one daughter, Margaret Drummond. James and William both dyed unmarried. Jean, the daughter of

THE HOUSE OF DRUMMOND.

John Drummond of Blair, married Mr. Harie Drummond of Gardrum, whofe children we mentioned before.

7. George Drummond of Blair fucceeded to his father John, and married Marjorie Graeme, fifter to David Graeme, Laird of Gorthie: they had children, George, who fucceeded, Margaret, and Lilias Drummonds. Margaret married Patrick Monteith of Eaglefhaw, in Orknay, to whom fhe had only three daughters, Marjorie, Margaret, and Marie Monteiths. Margaret Monteith married to Sir Douglas of Spinie. Lilias Drummond, the youngeft daughter of George Drummond of Blair, married Andrew Grant of Balhagells.

8. George Drummond, the fone of the laft George, now of Blair, married Elifabeth Ramfay, daughter to Sir Gilbert, Ramfay of Bamfc, who hes already born to him four fones, James, John, William, and Patrick Drummonds.

OF MARGARET RUTHVEN, SIR WALTER DRUMMONDS LADY, AND THE FAMILY OF SIR PATRICK RUTHVEN, HER FATHER, OF WHOM THE LORDS RUTHVEN AND EARLES OF GOWRIE ARE DESCENDED, MENTION IS MADE IN THE LIFE OF DAVID LORD DRUMMOND; WHO MARRIED ALSO OUT OF THAT FAMILIE, A DAUGHTER OF WILLIAM LORD RUTHVEN, CALLED LILIAS RUTHVEN.

118   THE GENEALOGIE OF

CONCERNING SIR MALCOLM DRUMMOND, THE ELEVENTH CHEIFE OF
THE FAMILIE, AND SUCH AS DESCENDED OF HIM.

THE SIXTH PARTITIONE.

Sir Malcolm Drummond, the eleventh Cheife.

Sir Malcolm Drummond fucceeded to his father, Sir Walter, and is moft ordinarly defigned by his title of Cargill. He married Marrion Murray, daughter to Sir David Murray, knight and laird of Tullibardine; with whom he had many fones: John, who fucceeded; Walter, who was the firft of Deanftown; James, who was the firft of Corrivauchter; Thomas, the firft of Drummonerinoch; Andrew and William Drummonds. Andrew was viccar of Strageth, William was called of Muthill.

Sir Malcolm was married anno 1445; and that fame year his mother, Margaret Ruthven, relict of Sir Walter Drummond his father, indents with her fone Malcolm, to give him her conjunct fee lands of Murthlaw, Kippon, Cathlie, Fenwyck, and Furlarge, for payment to her of a yearly annuitie.

Sir Malcolm Drummond lived in the reigne of King James the Second, and fome years with King James the Third.

Drummonds of Deanstown.

1. His fecond fone, Mr. Walter Drummond, in the year 1496, was chancellor of Dunkeld, in the time when George Brown was Bifhop; and in the year 1500, he was dean of Dumblane, perfon of Kinnowll, and Clerk both of the regifters and councell of Scotland to King James the Fourth. There is a chamber in the Caftle of Drummond, called after him, Walter's chamber, to this day. He was the firft that fewed the lands of Deanftown in Monteith; fo called after him.

becaufe he was a Dean, (for before that time Deanftown was called Sachentowne,) and the firft of the Drummonds of that familie.

[2.] He begot John Drummond, the next dean of Dumblane and perfon of Kinnowll. He folemnized the marriage of Queen Margaret with Archbald Earle of Angus, in Kinnowl. And feeing marriage, by the tyrannie of the church of Rome, was not permitted to the Clergie, this Mr. John, by particular difpenfation, was allowed to cohabit with Chriftian Scot, lawfull daughter to the laird of Balweery, in Fyfe, one of the ancienteft barons of that countrey: with whom he begot Malcolm Drummond, the third of Deanftown. Walter Drummond the father, and John his fone, were burried within the Drummonds Ifle of Dumblane church, upon the fouth wall; where all of that familie have fince been burried in the fame place, and next to that fame tomb. Thefe who have alleadged that the familie of Deanftown defcended from Walter, the fourth fone of Thomas Drummond of Drummonerinoch, or from Mr. William Drummond, dean alfo of Dumblane, bot long after this time, have been miftaken: for many evidences which I have feen teftifie the contrare.

3. Malcolm Drummond, the fone of Mr. John, fucceeded to the lands of Deanftown; his infeftment, and his mothers, Chriftian Scot, are yet extant, and his legitimation alfo under the Kings great feal. He married a daughter of   Cornwal of Bonhard, with whom he had children; John, who fucceeded, Andrew, Robert, and Thomas. Andrew was a churchman.

Robert purchaffed the lands of Gibliftown in Fyfe; of him defcended Archbald Drummond of Gibliston; and after him Alexander Drummond baylie of Cockenie; and Mr. Alexander Drummond his fone, now liveing in Edinburgh, and is chamberlane to the Earle of Winton, and wrytter to the fignet.   *Drummonds of Gibliftoun and Corfkeply.*

Thomas Drummond, the youngeft, was proprietar of Corfkeplie. His fone was Thomas, who built the houfe in Dumblane; he married

Elifabeth Stirline, daughter to William Stirlin of Ardoch; fhe had to him [a] fone John Drummond, and daughters

4. John Drummond, the fone and air of Malcolm Drummond of Deanfton, begot a fone, James, who fucceeded, on Janet Stuart, a near coufine to James, Earle of Murray, who dyed at Dunibyrfell; and daughter to John Stuart, brother fone to the Lord Ochiltrie, begotten with Agnes Grahame, neece to William Grahame, Earle of Montrofe.

5. James Drummond, who was the fifth of the houfe of Deanftown, had, with Janet Stuart, his wife, fones, Mr. James, Mr. Harie, Mr. Patrick Drummonds, &c.

6. Mr. James fucceeded to be the fixth laird of Deanftown to his father James: He was fourteen yeares minifter at Fowlls, in Strathern. He married Janet Malcolm, alias Maxwell, the daughter of a learned reverend and pious preacher Mr. John Malcolm, minifter at Perth; whofe propper fyrename was Maxwell, as may be feen by his armes engraven upon his lodgeing in Perth, and by his fathers wryts, wherein he defignes himfelfe and fubfcrives Andreas Malcolm, alias Maxwell. He had with his wife, Janet   , fones; John Drummond the eldeft, Mr. Archbald Drummond the fecond, Mr. James the third, &c. and   daughters

Mr. Archbald Drummond was minifter of Ochterarder. He married firft Sufanna Douglas, daughter to the laird of Dallenie, in Nithifdale; the fecond time to Jean Drummond, natural daughter to William Earle of Roxburgh, but had no children. He was generally beloved by all that knew him, and particularly by all in the parifh, where he ferved, fuch was his mild temper and pleafant converfe, that he oblidged every man, and never difoblidged any: he was profundly learned in maters of antiquitie, and a great mafter, not only in the original languages of the fcripture, bot alfo in all the heads of polemical and pofitive theologie, and yet had fo plaine a way of expreffing his deepeft thoughts when he fpoke to the people, that the meaneft capacities underſtood him. He dyed at Aberuthven the 22d of January 1680, and was burried in his firſt wife's grave at Innerpeffrie.

His brother, Mr. James Drummond, miniſter at Muthull, a man every way qualifyed for the miniſtrie, and ane ornament of the clergy in the country where he lived. They were tuo brothers, hardly to be paralelled either in moralls or miniſteriall gifts, theire lives being as exemplary virtous as theire doctrine was powerfull to perfuade: in a word, they were tuo excellent fones, worthy of fo good a father. Mr. James, their father, haveing betaken himfelfe whollie to the miniſteriall function, difponed the inheritance of Deanſtown to his brother, Mr. Harie Drummond, and dyed in Fowlls, November 10. 1634, where he was burried. 1634.

He had ane other brother, Mr. Patrick Drummond, who was a preacher in England, near Newcaſtle; where he dyed and left his fones, of whom we have not any accompt.

7. Mr. Harie Drummond was the feventh laird of Deanſtown; he married Helen Atchefon, daughter to the laird of Golfoord, ane ancient familie in Eaſt Lothian, and begot with her a fon, John Drummond, who fucceeded. Mr. Harie was a fharp man, and very active in the affaires of William laſt Earle of Monteith, when he was cheife miniſter of ſtate to King Charles the Firſt in Scotland.

8. John Drummond, now of Deanſton, married Elifabeth Dog, daughter to David Dog, laird of Ballengrew, ane old family in Monteith, whofe predicessors got that name for being huntfmaſter to the King. John is Stuart-deput of Monteith for the Earle of Murray, and hes only a daughter, Ifobella Drummond.

R

THE GENEALOGIE OF

THE ORIGINAL OF THE DRUMMONDS OF CREEFE, AFTER COMMONLY
CALLED CORRIVAUCHTER.

Drummonds of Corrivauchter.

1. James Drummond, third fone to Sir Malcolm Drummond of Cargill, was ftyled laird of Coldoch and Ballochard. I doe not find whom he married; bot his fone was Malcolm Drummond, called Mackie of Kilbryd, and his daughters, the firft   Drummond, married to John Bane Drummond of Innerpeffrie, of whom mention fhall be made in his own place. The fecond daughter was Janet Drummond, married to Edmund Chifolme, the firft of the houfe of Cromlix; whofe offspring, being fo oft to be fpoken of becaufe of the frequent matches betwixt the Drummonds and Cheefolms, fhal have a paragraph apart in the tenth partition. The third daughter of James Drummond married   Sinclair of Galdermore, forbear to Edward, William, and Henrie Sinclairs of Galdwalmore and Glaffingall-beg.

2. Malcolm Drummond, the fone of James, called Mackie of Kilbryde, married a gentlewoman called Grahame; begot James Drummond and Gavine Drummond of Kildees.

3. James Drummond, the fone of Mackie of Kilbryd, begot Alexander Drummond upon Elifabeth Cheefolm, daughter to Bifhop William Cheefolm.

4. Alexander Drummond, the fone of James, begot a fone William Drummond of Corrivauchter: I find Alexander Drummond, in anno 1577, and William, his fone, in anno 1588, both ftyled of Megore.

5. William Drummond of Corrivauchter, the fone of Alexander, married a daughter of George Drummond of Balloch, and begot Patrick Drummond. He fold the lands of Port and Yle to Patrick Lord Drummond.

6. Patrick Drummond of Corrivauchter, the fone of William, married Dorothea Stewart, daughter to John Stewart of Fofs in Athol, and begot William Drummond. He was ane ill manager of the fortune left him by his forbeares, for he debauched and fpent all.

7. William Drummond, the fone of Patrick, was a foldier in all the late wars in Ireland and Scotland. He attained to the degree of a ferjeant-major to a regiment under command of General Thomas Dalyell. He married Elfpet Lidderdale, daughter to the laird of Ile at Kirkcubright, and begot a fone John Drummond.

Drummonds of Kildees.

1. Gavine Drummond, the fecond fone of Mackie Drummond of Kilbryd, was the firft of the houfe of Kildees. He married Jean Strageth, daughter to the laird of Strageth, and had a fone called George Drummond.

2. George Drummond married Margaret Thomfon, relict of Drummond of Boreland his father. Gavin was killed at the feild of Pinky, 1547, in defence of David Lord Drummond, his cheife, who narrowlie efcaped. George, alias Gavine, had many fones; the eldeft Gavine who fucceeded; George who lived and dyed at Drummond of the Lennox; John at Queenfbrug in Spruce; David, called 'Glauren Davie,' gentleman penfioner to King James the Sixth; whofe fone John was a Rutemafter under Major-General Hurrie, when his army was beat by the Marquis of Montrofe at the fight of Oldearn; after which defeat, Hurry, to palliat his bad conduct, accufed the Rutemafter as if he had kept correfpondence with the enimie, and fo occafioned the lofs of the battle, for which he made a facrifice of him, and caufed fhoot him to cloak his own fault.

1547.

1645.

124   THE GENEALOGIE OF

Drummonds in Cuilt.   James Drummond, the youngeſt ſone of George Gavine, was the firſt of the Drummonds in Cuilt. His ſones were James, who lived there after him, and Andrew in Strageth. James had ſones, Mr. John Drummond, miniſter at Monzie, and George Drummond. Andrew, James' brother, had ſones, James and George Drummonds.

3. Gavin Drummond, eldeſt ſone of George Gavine, married Elſpet Murray, only daughter of Andrew Murray of the Kildees. He had many ſones; John, who ſucceeded, James, William, and Gavin Drummonds, who all dyed without any ſucceſſion. David Drummond, the youngeſt, was a Livetennant-Collonel in the ſervice of the great Zaar of Muſcow; and left there a ſone Jacob Drummond, a collonell of horſe, and two daughters.

4. John Drummond of Kildees married Elſpet Bane, daughter to Andrew Bayne of Findal, and had three ſones, Mr. James Drummond, who ſucceeded, Gavine, and Mr. John Drummond, who dyed a preacher in England. Gavine, the ſecond ſone, married Jean Oliphant, ſiſter to Sir Laurence Olyphant of Gaſk, relict of John Drummond of Pitzallonie; and begot a ſone Gavine Drummond, laird of Belliclon. He married Eliſabeth Oliphant, daughter to Sir Laurence Oliphant of Gaſk, and begot Gavin and Lilias Drummond.

5. Mr. James Drummond, the ſone of John of Kildees, married Lillias Drummond, daughter to John Drummond of Pitzallonie, and had four ſones; John, now of Kildees, James, George, and Laurence Drummonds.

THE FAMILY OF DRUMMONERINOCH.

Drummonds of Drummonerinoch.   1. Thomas Drummond, the fourth ſone of Malcolm Drummond of Cargill, was the firſt laird of Drummon-Irenoch. In his time that

THE HOUSE OF DRUMMOND.

unluckie action of burning the kirk of Monyvaird fell out; after which he being in the Caftle of Drummond in company with his nephew David Drummond, fecond fone to John Lord Drummond, and brother to Malcolm, then mafter of Drummond, the hous was rendered to King James the Fourth; bot this Thomas Drummond, refufeing to give himfelfe up with the reft upon fuch unfecure tearmes, (feareing what happened foone after,) leaped over the caftle wall, and fo efcaped into the wood clofs befyde the hous, and was for that and fome other bold pranks called 'Tom unfained.' He fled firft to Ireland, thereafter to London, where he procured favor from King Henrie the Seventh of England; by whofe mediation and interceffion he got a pardon from King James the Fourth. After that he returned to Scotland, and ftayed at Kincardine with his neece Annabella Drummond, daughter to John Lord Drummond, and lady to William, then Lord Grahame, who gave to this Thomas Drummond the lands of Drummondirenoch, (which fignifies the Irifh Drummonds lands,) formerly called Waigtowne. He married   Scot, daughter to the laird of Monzie, who had to him many fones; firft, Thomas, who fucceeded; Mr. James Drummond, called James of Ward; third, David Drummond, who married the heretrix of Culqualzie, Margaret Inglis, of whom mention is made before; fourth, Walter Drummond alias Freer Drummond; fifth, Gavine Drummond; and the fixth, Gilbert Drummond. I find this Gilbert was a natural fone of Thomas Drummond's, and the firft of thefe Drummonds called of Achlaick.

2. Thomas Drummond of Drummonerinoch, the fone of 'Tom unfained,' wes the fecond laird. He maried Duncan M'Kingie's daughter; he had bot one fone, called John Drummond, who fucceeded to him, and divers daughters. I find this Thomas upon an aflife at a court holden anno 1532.   1532.

3. John Drummond, the fone of Thomas Drummond of Drum-

monderinoch fucceeded. He married James M'Gruder's daughter, and had three fones; firft, John, who fucceeded to his father; the fecond, David Drummond, who for his quantity was called 'Mikel Davie;' he was author of the family of Innermay; the third, and youngeft fone was Thomas Drummond of Pitcairnes; and a daughter, married to James Stuart of Ardvorlich's father.

4. John Drummond of Drummond Irenoch, fone to the former John, was the fourth laird; he married   Livingfton, daughter to the laird of Glentirran, and had fones and daughters. His eldeft fone was alfo John, who fucceeded; Thomas and Oliver dyed young without children; David, the youngeft fone of John, was called 'Davie of the vault,' and was the firft of the Houfe of Comrie. John Drummond, the father of thefe children, was killed by the Clangreigors, anno 1589.

1589.

5. John Drummond of Drummond Irenoch, the fone and air of John, killed by the M'Greigors, married Iffobel Pitcairnes, ane gentlewoman near Abernethie, and had fones and daughters; the eldeft fone, David Drummond, fucceeded; the reft dyed without lawfull children. John married to his fecond wife,   Ibret, widdow of the lard of Cultobregane, and begot Robert Drummond, and daughters.

6. David Drummond of Drummond Irenoch, fucceeded to the former John, and was the fext laird. He married Margaret Drummond, daughter to Patrick Drummond of Maler, who was motherbairns with David Drummond of Innermay. This David had three fones; the firft David dyed young, the next, James, who fucceeded to David, and Patrick Drummond, the youngeft, now liveing at Dalchonie.

For this accompt of the original of this familie, I have seen authors; I had it also from themselves, albeit some others there are who relate it far otherwayes. *Sit fides penes legentem.*

7. James Drummond of Drummonderinoch, the fone of David the feventh laird, married Margaret Smyth, fifter to Patrick Smyth, laird of Methven, and les with her tuo fones, James and David Drummonds, and a daughter, Catherine.

The Familie of Innermay.

1. David Drummond, fecond fone to John Drummond, the third Drummonds laird of Drummond Irenoch, was the firft of Innermay. He married of Innermay. Elifabeth Abercrombie, daughter to the laird of Caffie and Frofk, whofe brother was Sir Patrick Abercrombie, famous at the court of England for extraordinary danceing. David Drummond had with the faid Elizabeth, tuo fones, David, who fucceeded, and Mr. James of Cultmalundie, and three daughters; the firft, Iffobel Drummond, married Mr. James Grahame of Monzie, the fone of Patrick Grahame of Inchbrakie, by a fecond wife. Mr. James had with Iffobella a fone, George Grahame, called of Pitcairnes, who married Rollo, daughter to Sir John Rollo of Bannockburn, and had children. Jean Drummond, the fecond daughter to David Drummond of Innermay, married Mr. James Pearfon, laird of Kippenrofs, and dean of Dumblane; fhe had to him tuo fones and a daughter: James, the eldeft fone, now of Kippenrofs, married Rollo, daughter to Sir John Rollo of Bannockburn, and hes tuo fones and three daughters. Alexander Perfon, the lady Kippenrofs' other fone followed the wars, and is now ane officer in the Earle of Dumbartons regiment in Tangeires. Jean Perfon, the ladyes daughter, married a gentleman of the houfe of Tofts, in the Mers, called James Belfhes.

Margaret Drummond, third daughter to David Drummond of Innermay, married Sir George Mufchet of Burnbank, laird of that ilk; and had with her James Mufchet, who dyed.

2. David Drummond of Innermay, the fone and air of David, the firft laird, wes the fecond laird of Innermay. He married Helen Cheefolm, daughter to the laft Sir James Cheefolm, laird of Cromlix;

with her he had tuo fones; David, who fucceeded, and James, *qui difficulter frugi faciet*, and three daughters. The firft, Jean Drummond, married Mr. William Oliphant of Coltewcher, and had children, David, Ifobella, Margaret, and Catherina Oliphants; Jean Drummond, lady Coltewcher, married a fecond hufband, Thomas Stuart of Ladywell, and hes to him a daughter, Amelie Stuart.

David Drummond's fecond daughter, Elfpet Drummond, married David Drummond of Comrie, and hes to him children, James, David, and Thomas Drummonds. His third daughter, Margaret Drummond, married Paul Dog of Ballengrew, ane old family in Monteith, and hes children.

David Drummond of Innermay, fiar fone to the former David, married Annabella Rollo, daughter to Sir John Rollo of Bannockburn, and hes with her a fone, David.

The Family of Cultmalundie.

Drummonds of Cultmalundie.

1. Mr. James Drummond, fecond fone to David Drummond, firft laird of Innermay, was the firft of Cultmalundie. He married Elifabeth Stuart, daughter to Mr. Harie Stuart, brother to Sir Thomas Stuart of Garntullie; fhe had to him tuo fones, David, who fucceeded, and John Drummonds; and three daughters, Jean, Anna, and Helen Drummonds.

2. David Drummond, now of Cultmalundie, the fone of Mr. James, yet a minor, but very hopeful.

THE HOUSE OF DRUMMOND.

THE FAMILIE OF PITCAIRNES.

1. Thomas Drummond, third fone to John Drummond, third laird of Drummond Irenoch, married   heretrix of Pitcairnes, and hes with her only tuo daughters; the firſt Margaret Drummond, who was nexte heretrix, and married William Drummond, fecond fone to Harrie Drummond, the firſt laird of Riccarton; the other, Lilias Drummond, married to Patrick Drummond, a fone of Patrick Drummond, laird of Carnock, who, for his great bulk, was commonly called Meikel Patrick; he had fones,   and a daughter, Jean Drummond, married to Andrew Naper at Burnbank.

_{Drummonds of Pitcairnes.}

William Drummond of Pitcairnes, the fecond fone of Harie Drummond, firſt laird of Riccartowne, in right of his wife Margaret Drummond, was the fecond of the Drummonds of Pitcairnes. He begot with her

---

THE FAMILIE OF COMRIE.

1. David Drummond, the youngeſt fone of John Drummond, the fourth laird of Drummonerinoch, was the firſt laird of Comrie. He married Margaret Hay, daughter to George Hay of Pitfowre, and had with her a fone, David, who fucceeded, and tuo daughters; Jean Drummond, married to Robert Stuart of Ardvorlich, who had to him tuo fones and tuo daughters; and Anna Drummond, married to James Stuart in Balwhidder, who hes children.

_{Drummonds of Comrie.}

2. David Drummond of Comrie, fone and air to the firſt David, married Elſpet Drummond, daughter to David Drummond of Inner-

s

130   THE GENEALOGIE OF

may, and fecond laird thereof: he dyed young, and left children David, James, and Thomas Drummonds.

3. David Drummond, now of Comrie, the fone of the former David, fucceeded to a good father, and is yet to give teftimonie, if alfo to his vertues.

ACHLAICK DRUMMONDS.

Drummonds of Achlaick.

Gilbert Drummond, a natural fone of the firft Thomas Drummond of Drummond Irenoch, begot a fone John Drummond. John Drummond, the fone of Gilbert, had four fones; the eldeft Walter Drummond; the fecond George Drummond, dyed without ifhew; the third Patrick Drummond, killed by the laird of Lenie; the fourth James Drummond, killed at Prefton bridge, in England, under the Duke of Hamilton's armie, in anno 1648.

1648.

Walter Drummond, the eldeft fone of John Drummond, had fones John Buy Drummond, and Patrick Drummond in Brackly. John Buy had no children; bot Patrick had a fone Walter Drummond, now in Brackly.

It may be faid of thir Drummonds of Achlaick, that as they are baftards in nature, they are no lefs in vertue.

THE DRUMMONDS OF SMITHIESTOWNE.

Drummonds of Smithieftowne.

Andrew Drummond, fifth fone to Sir Malcolm Drummond of Cargill, and brother to John Lord Drummond, got for patrimonie from his father the lands of Smithieftown, in the barronie of Cargill. He begat a fone William, who had a wadfet upon Cargil, and thereupon was called William Drummond of Smithieftown and Cargill. This William Drummond had tuo fones, Patrick and George Drummonds; to Patrick he gave Smithieftown, and to George the wadfet of Cargil, who was otherwayes defigned of Halholl. William Drummond of Smithieftown had the manadgement of the lands of Stobhal and Cargil, in the minoritie of David Lord Drummond, from Sir Robert Barton, donator to the waird, from the year 1519 to the time of David Lord Drummond's age of majoritie.

Patrick Drummond of Smithieftown, the fone and air of William, had a fone called John Drummond; and John had a fone called Robert Drummond of Smithieftown; which Robert difponed the inheritance to John Earle of Perth; fo that he left his fone William Drummond in a mean condition.

George Drummond, the fecond fone of William Drummond of Smithieftowne, had a fone defigned Laurence Drummond of Bruntihill, whom I find mentioned in feveral papers. Laurence had a fone William Drummond of Bruntihill; he fold the poffeffion alfo to John Earle of Perth about the year 1635.   1635.

William Drummond had a fone called David Drummond, now of Halholl.

OF MARION MURRAY, SIR MALCOLM DRUMMOND'S LADY.

[A BLANK IN THE MANUSCRIPT.]

THE GENEALOGIE OF

CONCERNING JOHN, THE SONE OF SIR MALCOLM DRUMMOND, THE FIRST LORD DRUMMOND.

THE SEVENTH PARTITION.

John Lord Drummond, the twelfth cheefe.

John Drummond, the eldeſt ſone of Sir Malcolm, ſucceeded to his father, and wes in order the twelfth cheefe of the familie. He was ſtylled John Drummond of Cargill, untill King James the Third, anno 1487, created him a Lord of Parliament; about which time the Hume, Olyphant, Creichton of Sanquair, Hay of Yeſter, and Ruthven of that ilk, were alſo made lords. He married Lady Eliſabeth Lindſay, daughter to David Lindſay, Earle of Craufurd, who was weell known by the deſignation of 'Earle Beardie, or beard the beſt of them;' he begot with her three ſones, Malcolm, who dyed young; William Drummond, the ſecond, called the Maſter of Drummond; and the third John Bane Drummond; and five daughters, the firſt Margaret, the ſecond Eliſabeth, the third Eupheme, the fourth Annabella, and the fyfth Sybilla Drummonds; ſhe died a maid. Of his younger ſones and daughters and theire offſpring mention ſhal be made in this Partitione. We told yow in the Second Partition how Maurice Keer Drummond, the laſt of the barrons ſtylled of Concraig, diſponed moſt part of his lands, with his offices of Stuart of Strathern, &c. Coroner Keeper of the Northkathkend of Ochtermuthull, forreſtries of Strathern, eſcheats, forfaultures, and fees thereto belongeing, to John Drummond of Cargill, all refigned and furrendred in the hands of King James the Third, his ſuperior, in the 13th year of his reigne, for a new infeftment to be granted in favors of this John Drummond of Cargill, his cheefe: this reſignation was made at Edinburgh, in the 1473; and in the following year Winfridus de Moravia, of Abercarny, ſheriffe-deput,

1487.

1473.

upon a precept directed to him from the Chancery, gave feafine of the forenamed offices, &c. to the faid John, be deliverance of a whyte rod. The charter granted be King James the Third, anno 1473, is confirmed be King James the Fourth 1488; whereupon he altered his old refi- 1488. dence from Stobhal to Strathern, and there, in the year 1491, by a 1491. fpecial licence from King James the Fourth, under his own hand and feal, built the ftrong caftle of Drummond; to which, in the year 1508, 1508. being the 20th of King James the Fourth, he mortifyed the Collegiat Kirk of Innerpeffrie, with ane aliment to the Provoft thereof, and eftablifhed it as a burial place for the familie in all time comeing; nominateing Walter Drummond Provoft, and ordaineing Walter Drummond of Broich, John Drummond, Maurice Drummond of Pitzallonie, with divers others, to give him inftitution and poffeffion. The witneffes to the inftrument are John Drummond, the Lord's fone; Walter Drummond of Ledcreefe, his uncle; and John Drummond of Pitzallonie younger.

In the year 1484, John Lord Drummond, was imployed by King 1484. James the Third, as one of his commiffioners, in company with Colin Earle of Argyle (Lord Campbel) Chancellor of Scotland, William Elphingfton Bifhop of Aberdeen, Robert Lord Lyle, Laurence Lord Olyphant, Archbald Quytelaw Archdeacon of Lothiane Secretary to the King, and the Lyon King at Armes Duncan Dundas, all of his Majeftie's privy councell, to meet at Nottinghame with John Bifhop of Lincoln Lord Chancellor of England, Richard Bifhop of St. Afaph, John Duke of Norfolk, Henrie Earle of Northumberland, Thomas Lord Stanley, George Lord Strange, John Gray Lord Powes, Richard Lord Fitfhugh, John Gunthorp Keeper of the King's Privie Seal, Thomas Barrow Mafter of the Rolls, Sir Thomas Bryan Lord Cheife Juftice of the Common Pleas, Sir Richard Ratcliffe, William Catfby and Richard Salkeld, efquyers, all deputed by King Richard the Third of England, to treat upon a ceffation of armes a perfect amitie and inviolable peace ; which they concluded, to ſtand betwixt the two realmes for the ſpace of three yeares, to begin September 9th 1484 and continow to September 1487.

I find, in the year 1474, before John was made Lord, ane indenter betwixt him and Coline Earle of Argyle, wherein John oblidges himſelfe, that his eldeſt ſone Malcolm, Maſter of Drummond, ſhall marry Lady Iſſobella Campbel, the Earles daughter, both then under age ; and in caſe of failzie, by death or other chance, the next ſone and next daughter to be ſubſtitute for makeing up the marriage, for which end John provydes for maintinance to his ſone, the ten merk lands of Fenwick, twenty merk lands of Caſhlie with the miln, lyand in the earledome of Lennox and ſhire of Sterlyne : Witneſſes, Andrew Stuart Lord Evendale Chancellor of Scotland, William of Drummond, Robert of Drummond, &c. This Malcolm, Maſter of Drummond, dyed before the fulfilling of this contract, and his brother William came in his
1474. place, for the contract is dated 1474 ; and in a charter granted by John Lord Drummond, a year before he was made Lord, 1486, to Walter Drummond of Ledcreefe, his uncle, one of the witneſſes, ſtands thus : *testibus Willielmo Drummond, filio meo et haerede apparente.*

John Lord Drummond, was made Juſtice General of Scotland, but ſo deeply ingadged in friendſhip with the familie of Douglas, with whom he joyned on a ſtrict allyance, by giveing one of his daughters in marriage to George Douglas, ſone and air to Archbald Earle of Angus, ſyrnamed, 'Bel the Cat ; ' that he run many hazards upon
1482. theire accompt ; for in the year 1482 he aſſiſted them to purge the court at Lauder of ſome unworthie obſcure plebeian perſones, who had abuſed and miſgoverned King James the Third ; whereof Robert Cochran, from being a maſon and ſurveyor of the King's buildings, wes made Earle of Mar, William Rogers of a muſician, made a knight,
1488. and James Homyl were principal ; and, again, in the year 1488 he was, by the Earle of Angus, ingadged, amongſt the confederat lords,

with the Sone againſt the Father at the Sauchenfoord befyde Sterline; bot foone after he gave fingular evidences of his loyaltie and fidelitie to King James the Fourth, while he was bot about fixteen years of age, when the Earle of Lennox, Lord Lyle, and a great power of theire faction, drew together in a hoſtile maner againſt the King, upon pretext that he had unlawfullie taken armes againſt his Father; bot in effect rageing with malice that others were admitted to his intimat favor, and they neglected, for which they defigned to put him from the crown; and to that purpofe had marched with a confiderable force from the weſt towards the river Forth, for joyning theire confederats, the Earle Marifchal, the Lord Gordon, and Alexander, Lord Forbes, who, upon the point of a lance, difplayed the ſhirt of the ſlaughtered King purpled with his own blood, inviteing the countrey as by ane herauld to revenge the murther, all advanceing from the north. The Lord Drummond, with his own freinds, domeſticks, and a few volunteeres, valiantly affaulted the Earle of Lennox camp lying at Tillimofs, befyde Touch, upon the river; and haveing good knowledge of the foord to which his own lands adjoines, he gave them fuch a defeat, that theire party never more appeared in that quarrel; for which fervice the King not only treated him with great kindnes and familiaritie, bot alfo rewarded him with the barronie of Drummond in the countie of Monteith.

John Lord Drummond, was a great promoter of the match betwixt his own grandchild, Archbald Earle of Angus, and the widdow queen of King James the Fourth, Margaret Teudores, for he caufed his own brother, Mafter Walter Drummond's fone, Mr. John Drummond, dean of Dumblane, and perfon of Kinnowl, folemnize the matrimonial bond in the kirk of Kinnowl in the year 1514. Bot this marriage begot fuch jealoufie in the rulers of the ſtate, that the Earle of Angus was cited to appear before the Councel, and Sir William Cummin of Inneralochy, knight, Lyon King at Armes, appointed to deliver the

1514.

charge; in doeing whereof, he feemed to the Lord Drummond to have approached the Earle with more boldnes then difcretion, for which he gave the Lyon a box on the ear; whereof he complained to John, Duke of Albany, then newly made governor to King James the Fifth, and the governor to give ane example of his juftice at his firft entry to his new office, caufed imprifon the Lord Drummonds perfon in the Caftle of Blackuefs, and forfault his eftate to the crown for his rafhnefs. Bot the Duke confidering, after information, what a fyne man the Lord was, and how ftrongly allyed with moft of the great families in the nation, wes well pleafed that the Queen-mother, and Three Eftates of Parliament, fhould interceed for him; fo he was foone reftored to his libbertie and fortune.

John Lord Drummond was a wife, active and valiant nobleman, famous in all our hiftories wrytten be Hector Boetius, Edward Hal, George Buchannan, Raphael Holinfhed, Bifhop John Leflie, Sir Thomas More Lord Chancellor of England, &c. He lived with the Kings James the Third and James the Fourth, did fee the third generation come of himfelfe, and haveing paft the age of eighty, dyed in his own caftle of Drummond, and was honourablie interred in his own burial place at the collegiat kirk of Innerpeffrie in the year 1519. He left behind him his Advyce to his pofterity, worthie to be recorded; and it is heire fet down coppied verbatim from his own original.

"JOHN LORD DRUMMOND'S COUNSEL AND ADVYCE TO HIS SUC-
CESSORS, WHO, BY GODS PROVIDENCE, ARE TO INHERIT HIS
LANDS AND ESTATE.

"Imprimis, he wills them ftudy to ken themfelves, the countrey they live in, and the laws thereof, whom they ought to obey, and to perform the fame truely and honeftly as it becometh men of worth; alwayes craveing Gods afiftance to direct them aright, that they wrong neither themfelves, theire fucceffors, nor theire forbeers verteus, bot rather by theire own deeds to illuftrat the fame; efchewing all intemperance or fleuth which may difcredit them. It being more commendable by honeft means to better our fortune left unto us by inheritance, then to diffipate the famine unworthily under falfe and unneceffary pretexts of liberalitie and fuch lyke. Bot if, by civil diforders or incident calamities, we be made unable to improve the fame, yet let us doe the lyklieft, ftriveing alwayes to preferve the ftock from all ingadgements, that juftly it be not alledged, we are degenerated from our forbeeres vertues.

"Its eafie and facile to fpend, confume, and put away our patrimonie, bot to mantaine a good name, and live honourably as it becometh noblemen, is a more difficile tafk; *expetendae sunt opes ut dignis largiamur*, fayes the ancient. In all our doeings, diferetion is to be obferved, otherwayes nothing can be done aright. We fee the fouldier undergoes many hazards to provyde for himfelfe and his pofteritie; the advocat, the phyfician, the theologue, does the like, ever affecting preheminence, with means and riches to intertaine the fame; fhould we not then at leaft be alfe careful as they are, to mantaine our eftate and condition, fo eafily befallen to us by fucceffion, as not to fuffer it, through fupine negligence, untimely fpending, drunkenefs, companionrie, or debaucherie whatfomever, to be dilapidat or bafely put away; rather let us live honeftly and foberly within our felves, as becomes good Chriftians, then to caft away that we never wan.

. "Let our fpending be conform to our yearly rent, without diminution of the ftock or ground right, elfe we fhal incur the blame of debaucherie, and fuftaine great reproach, with difreputation and lofs of thefe means which we never acquyred.

"Let us looke and confider our charter kift, how many forts of evidents are there, what confultations with lawyers, how many contracts and obligationes of diverfe natures, with other fecurities, al tending to fecure us, then we will find that fuch records and monuments hes not been put there without great paines, laboures, and expenffes; wherefore to dilapidate fuch wreats, mifchantly, upon feclefs and frivolous occafions, can no way be commended. Moreover, he by whofe mifgovernment thir miferies falls out, to the diftruction of his familie, fhal be mifpryfet of al men as unworthie of fuch parentage, or any true freindfchap; bot be the contraire conferving his eftate, he will be honoured and refpected as becomes his quality and condition. Thir, and fuch lyk reafones, fhould make us carefull to behave ourfelves aright, and to take diligent tent to our affaires, that they be no wayes mifguided till our fhame and fkaith; bot albeit no remonftrance be fufficient to correct or amend a depraved nature, yet fhould we not leave off to admonifh our fucceffors of theire duty.

>Nemo adeo ferus eft, qui non mitefcere poffit,
>Si modo culturae patientem accommodet aurem.

Perchance good may follow, and God will affift honeft intentions with theire endeavoures, which is the earneft prayer of him who does alwayes affect the well being and ftanding of his Houfe in the right and lineal defcent thereof. FAIREWEELL."

OF JOHN LORD DRUMMOND'S DAUGHTERS.

John Lord Drummond, his eldest daughter.

Margaret Drummond, his eldeft daughter, was a lady of rare perfections and fingular beautie. With her, the young King James the Fourth was [fo] deeply inamoured, that without acquainteing his nobles or councell he was affianced to her, in order to have made her his Queen; but fo foon as his intention was difcovered, all poffible obftructions were made both by the nobilitie, who defigned ane alliance with a daughter of England, as a mean to procure peace betwixt the nations, and by the clergie, who declared againft the lawfulnes of the marriage, becaufe they were within the degrees of confanguinitie forbidden by the cannon law: neverthelefs, the King, under promife, got her with child, which proved a daughter, and was called Lady Margaret Stuart. But he was fo much touched in confcience for the ingadgement he had made to the young lady, that notwithftanding the weaknefs of the royal familie, he rejected all propofitiones of marriage fo long as fhe lived: for he was crowned in the year 1488 at the age of fexteen, and did not marrie untill the year 1502, when he was near thirty, and about a year after her death, which was effected not without fufpicion of poyfon; for the common tradition goes, that a potion wes provyded in a breakfaft to difpatch her for liberateing the King from his promife, that he might match with England: bot fo it happened, that fhe called tuo of her fifters, then with her in Drummond, to accompany her that morning, to wit, Lilias Lady Fleming, and a younger, Sybilla, a maid, whereby it fell out all the three were deftroyed with the force of the poyfon. They ly burried in a curious vault, covered with three faire blew marble ftones joyned clofs together, about the middle of the queer of the cathedral church of Dumblane; for about this time the burial place for the familie of Drummond at Innerpeffrie was not yet built. The monument which containes the afhes of thefe three ladyes, ftands intire to this day, and confirmes the credit of this fad ftorie.

1488.
1502.

The King greeved for the death of his miftres, takes care for the daughter, lady Margaret Stuart, which Mrs. Margaret Drummond did bear him in the year 1497, and difpofes of her in marriage to John Lord Gordon, eldeft fone to the Earle of Huntly, a gallant hanfome

1497.

youth new come from his travells and breeding abroad. John begat
with Lady Margaret Stuart, Lord George Gordon, Earle of Huntly,
and tuo daughters, the Comtefs of Sutherland, and the Comtefs of
Athol, who was mother to the Lady Lovet and the Lady Saltoun;
fo that from Lady Margaret, fpoufe to John Lord Gordon, all thefe
four families are clearly defcended. George Earle of Huntly, the
fone of John, was killed at the batle of Corrichie, about the year
1562. 1562. He left a fone called alfo George, who was Earle of Huntly,
1567. and Chancellor of Scotland about the year 1567.

Lady Margaret Stuart, the King's daughter, after the death of her
firft hufband, was married the fecond time to Alexander Duke of
Albany, elder brother to John Duke of Albanie, regent and governour to King James the Fifth, and had to him a daughter of her own
name, married to David Lord Drummond; and after that, the King's
daughter was married a third time, to her cufine, Sir John Drummond of Innerpeffrie: the children begotten of both thefe matches,
we fhal have occaffion to mention hereafter.

John Lord Drummond's second daughter. Elifabeth Drummond, fecond daughter to John Lord Drummond,
married George Douglas, mafter of Angus, (which was the title in
thofe dayes beftowed upon the Earles eldeft fones); George was fone to
Archbald, 'Bel the Cat,' and had with her three fones, Archbald, who
fucceeded; Sir George of Pittendreich; and a third, who was a churchman, William, prior of Coldinghame; and five daughters, the firft was
Lady Yefter, the fecond, Lady Bafs, the third, Lady Drumlanrick,
the fourth, Lady Blacater, then Lady Wedderburn, the fifth, Lady
Glaimes.

Sir George Douglas of Pittendrich, was father to William [James]
1581. Earle of Morton, beheaded, anno 1581.

George, Mafter of Angus, and his brother, Sir William Douglas of
Glenbervie, were both killed at the battle of Flowdon with King
1513. James the Fourth, 1513; where Archbald 'Bel the Cat,' theire father,

THE HOUSE OF DRUMMOND.

after good counfel given to the King, and being very aged, tooke leave, bot left thefe tuo fones as the fureft pledges of his affection to his king and countrie, and proved a prophet in foretelling the event of that unhappie defeat.

Elifabeth Drummonds eldeft fone, with George Douglas, Mafter of Angus, was Archbald the next Earle of Angus. He married firft Margaret Hepburn, daughter to Patrick Lord Bothwell, bot fhe dyed of a child within the firft year, his fecond wife was Queen Margaret Teudors, relict of King James the Fourth, the eldeft daughter of King Henrie the Seventh of England, married, anno 1514. The Queen did bear to Earle Archbald, a daughter, Lady Margaret Douglas; who married Mathew Stewart Earle of Lennox, and had to him Henrie Lord Darnly, his eldeft fone, married to Marie Queen of Scots, mother to King James the Sixth; and Lord Charles Stuart, the youngeft fone, married to Elifabeth Cavendifh, daughter to Sir William Cavendifh, who did bear to Lord Charles the Lady Arabella Stuart, married to the Earle of Hartford. Archbald Earle of Angus married a third time, (being divorced from the Queen,) to Margaret daughter to the Lord Maxwell, bot had no liveing children by her. He had alfo a natural daughter, Jean Douglas, married to Patrick Lord Ruthven, whom he begat with a daughter of the Laird of Traquaire: and fhe had to Patrick Lord Ruthven, William, the firft Earle of Gowrie, created by King James the Sixth, in a parliament holden at Perth, October 24, 1581, and made Thefaurer of Scotland, bot at laft execute for treafon at Sterlin, May the 4th 1584. His lady was Dorothy Stuart, daughter to the Lord Meffen, begotten on Queen Margaret, who was divorced from Archbald Earle of Angus.

In the year 1515, John Duke of Albany wes chofen governour to the young King James the Fifth, bot becaufe Archbald Earle of Angus did not favor the election, the Governour, full of fufpicion, carried him no good will; upon this accompt Gavine Douglas, bifhop

1514.

1581.
1584.

1515.

of Dunkeld, the Earles uncle, John Lord Drummond, his grandfather, and David Panitier, fecretary to King James the Fourth, were all committed to prifon.

1528. Again in the year 1528, King James the Fifth, haveing freed himfelfe from the tutorie of Archbald Earle of Angus, at a parliament in Edinburgh, cited, condemned, and forfaulted the Earle; Sir George his brother, Archbald Douglas of Kilfpindie, his uncle, and Alexander Drummond of Carnock, his intimat freind; whereupon they fled to England, the Earle and his brother remained fifteen yeares in exile,

1543. and returned not untill the year 1543, a year after the Kings death, and then was James Hamilton Earle of Arran, Regent; he againe committed Archbald Earle of Angus prifoner, who was not relieved untill King Henrie of England fent a fleet under the Earle of Hartfoord, who landed at Leith very unlooked for by the Governour, and then he fet him at libertie. Archbald, the Earle, was a brave man, he behaved himfelf valiantly at Coldingham, where he faved the reputation of the Scots army in bringeing of the cannon; and at Melrofs, where Sir Ralph Ivers and Sir Brian Laton were defeat and flaine, and many Englifhes killed and taken prifoners; and, laftly, at Pinkie, where he and his vantguard behaved gallantly with the lofs of many freinds, where Hamilton the Governour, with the mid-batle, and Huntlie with the rear, both deferted the feild before they came to

1556. ftrocks. He dyed at Tantallon in the year 1556; he was honoured by Henrie the Second of France, with the order of knighthood, called the order of the Cockell, or of St. Michael, fent to him by a commif-
1545. fion, with Monfieur de L'Orge, in the year 1545; and dyed, &c.

Sir George Douglas, Earle Archbalds brother, fecond fone to George mafter of Angus, with Elifabeth Drummond, married the heretrix of Pittendrich in the north, called alfo Douglas; and had with her tuo fones, David and James Douglaffes. David fucceeded to his uncle Earle Archbald, who dyed without aires male, he was

THE HOUSE OF DRUMMOND.

Earle of Angus not above a year. David married Elifabeth Hamilton, daughter to John Hamilton, called John of Cliddefdale, brother-german to James Duke of Chaftelheraut, Governour; fhe had to him a fone Archbald, who alfo was Earle of Angus after his father, and tuo daughters, Margaret Douglas, firft lady Balcleuch, then Comtefs of Bothwell. Margaret had to her firft hufband, called Sir Walter Scot of Balcleuch, a fone Walter Scot, married to a daughter of Ker of Seffoord; Walter was a Collonell in Holland, and created a Lord of Parliament by King James the Sixth, upon the 17th of May 1606. He was father to Walter firft Earle of Balcleuch, married to   Hay, daughter to Francis Earle of Errol, who did bear to him Francis, laft Earle of Bucleuch, father to the prefent Duches of Balcleuch. Sir George Douglas of Pittendrich his fecond fone, James Douglas, married the Earle of Morton's third daughter, who was alfo Douglas, and in her right was made Earle of Morton by provifion; her elder fifters being married before, one of them to Duke Hamilton the Governor, and the other to the Lord Maxwell.

James Douglas Earle of Morton was Chancellor of Scotland, and a zealous promotter of the Reformation. He did enter in great frindfhip, and run all hazard with James Earle of Murray, and after the Regency of Murray, Lennox, and Marre, Morton was chofen Regent to the young King in the year 1572; which office he demitted again in the year 1577, that the King might take the goverment in his own hands; bot in the year 1580 he was accufed by Captaine James Stuart, fone to the Lord Ochiltree, for being airt and pairt of the murther of the late King Henrie. James Stuart the accufer was foone after preferred to be a privie councellor, Barron of Bothwellhaugh, Lord Hamilton, Earle of Arran, and Captaine of the Kings Guard; and Morton by ane affyfe found guiltie, condemned and execut, haveing his head cut of by the axe of the Maiden, which he himfelfe had caufed make after the pattern which he had feen at

1606.

1572.
1577.
1580.

Halyfax in England: thus ended that great man on the 2d of June
1581. 1581.

William Douglas, prior of Coldingham, the youngeſt ſone of
George Maſter of Angus, and Elifabeth Drummond, was made
1528. Abbot of Holyroodhouſe; where he dyed in the year 1528.

George, Maſter of Angus, had many daughters born him by his
Lady Elifabeth Drummond; one of them was Lady Yeſter: Of her
that familie, now Earles of Tueddale, are defcended.

Another daughter was called Alifon Douglas, firſt married to the
Laird of Blacater, of that ilk; and then, after his death, to Sir
George Hume of Wedderburn.

Another daughter was Lady Baſs; ſhe did bear to her huſband a
daughter, who was Lady Whittingham.

Another daughter was married to James Lord Hamilton, Earle of
Arran; ſhe had to him only a daughter, married to Andrew Stuart,
the Lord Ochiltree, who was father to Andrew, the next lord, and to
Captaine James Stuart, Earle of Arran. The Lord Hamilton purchafed a divorce from his lady, upon confideration of confanguinitie
within the degrees forbidden by cannon law; bot the trew reafon
was, becauſe ſhe had only a daughter and no ſones to him. This deed
was refented and repayed by a neece of the mother Elifabeth Drummond, Lady Hamilton, who was daughter natural to King James
Fourth, and married to the Earle of Huntlie, as will be obferved
afterward in the fame Partition; for the truth of this, albeit it feemes
not to be believed, I have divers grounds to convince me of it.

Another daughter of George, Maſter of Angus, with Lady Elifabeth
Drummond, was Jean Douglas, Lady Glames; married to John Lord
1537. Glames, called to a by name, 'Cleanfe the Cauſay.' In the year 1537
ſhe was accufed, by fufpected witneſſes, (if not falfe,) that ſhe and her
ſone and ſome others had gone about to take away King James the
Fifth his lyfe by witchcraft; whereupon ſhe was brunt upon the

Caftle Hill of Edinburgh, with great commiferation of the people, in regaird of her noble blood and fingular beautie, fhe being in the prime of her age, and fuffering with a mafculine courage, al men conceavcing that the King's hatred to her brothers had brought her to that end. Her fone John, who was next lord, was alfo condemned and forfaulted; yet, becaufe he was a minor, referved in prifon untill he fhould be of age to have his fentence put in execution. Bot after the King's death, in anno 1542, he was againe reftored to his lyfe, eftate, and honor, and was father to John Lyon, Lord Glames, Chancellor of Scotland; whofe fone was Patrick the firft Earle of Kinghorn, and married to Anna Murray, daughter to John, then Laird of Tullibardine, begot upon Catharine Drummond, daughter to David Lord Drummond; this Patrick, the firft Earle, was grandfather to Patrick, now Earle of Strathmore and Kinghorn. The families lineally defcended of this Lady Glames, befydes Strathmore, are Duke Hamilton, Earle of Caffils, Earle of Morton, and Lord Spynie.

1542.

Its alfo faid, that there was yet ane other daughter of that marriage, betwixt George Mafter of Angus and Elifabeth Drummond, and that fhe was either Lady Drumlanrig or Lady Cleefh Colvill.

John Lord Drummond's third daughter, was Eufame Drummond. She married John Lord Fleeming, fone to Robert Lord Fleeming, and had to him John Lord Fleeming, and five daughters. John Lord Fleeming, fone to John Lord Fleeming, by Eufame Drummond, married   and had to him a fone called Malcolm, the next lord, and a daughter, called Fair Margaret Fleeming. She was firft married to the Lord Erfkine, bot had no children; the fecond time fhe married William Earle of Montrofe, and had to him John Earle of Montrofe, firft chancellor then viceroy of Scotland; and the third time married to John Earle of Athol, the father of Jock Earle of Athol, whofe only daughter, Dorothea Stuart, married William Earle

John Lord Drummond's third daughter.

of Tullibardine, in whofe right he became Earle of Athol. Jock Earle of Athol had alfo a fifter, married   Campbel of Glenurchie.

John Lord Drummond, a year before he was made Lord, got a gift of the waird and marriage of David Fleming, fone of Robert Lord Fleeming, from King James the Third in anno 1483.

1483.

Eupheme Drummond had daughters to the Lord Fleeming; the firft was married to William Lord Livingfton, the father of Alexander Livingfton, created Earle of Linlithgow by King James the Sixth, upon the 28th of November 1600. He was father to Alexander Earle of Linlithgow, and James Earle of Callendar. Alexander was father to George, now third Earle of Linlithgow, collonel to the King's foot regiment of guards.

1600.

Eupheme Drummond, Lady Fleeming, her fecond daughter, was Lady Jean Fleeming, married to Secretarie Sir John Maitland. John, the fifth Earle of Caffills, married Lady Jean, a widdow, (vide Maitland): And one of Livingtons daughters married Robert Earle of Roxburgh; fhe bare to him Lady Jean Ker, Comtefs of Perth, grandmother to James now Earle of Perth. Of the Lady Fleemings daughters are defcended the houfe of Laderdale: John Earle of Lauderdale had with Lady Jean Fleeming, John, fecond Earle of Lauderdale.

Eupheme Drummond had to the Lord Fleeming ane other daughter, married to the Lord Sanquair, after Vifcount of Air; of whom is [defcended] the [family of] Creichtoun Earle of Dumfreis.

She had a fourth daughter, was Lady Calder, and mother to Sir James Sandilands, of whom is the Lord Torphichen. After fhe was a widdow, fhe married a fecond time to   Craufurd laird of Carfe; and of her all that familie who are of good accompt in Carrick are lineallie defcended.

She had a fifth daughter, [married] to Cuninghame laird of Glengarnock, of whom many families of that name came.

THE HOUSE OF DRUMMOND.

John Lord Drummonds fourth daughter, Annabella Drummond, married to William Lord Grahame in the year 1479, as appeares by an inftrument; where Sir William Hirdman, who joyned them in matrimonie, requyred the faid William Lord Grahame and Annabella Drummond to declare, if they had any impediment to hinder theire marriage; under the figne of James Durrow, notar publick, of the forefaid date. There is a difcharge granted by Thomas Lord Erfkine, and James Shaw of Sauchie, to John Drummond of Cargill, fome yeares before he was Lord Drummond, for the foume of 750 merks, payed to each of them for redeemeing theire gift of the waird and marriage of William Lord Grahame, married to Annabella Drummond, daited 1480.

John Lord Drummond's fourth daughter. 1479.

1480.

There is alfo a charter granted to William Lord Grahame, and to Annabella Drummond his fpoufe, of the lands of Coull and Coulfhill, of the date 1487, and ane inftrument of feafine.

John Lord Drummond's youngeft daughter, was called Sibilla Drummond: fhe dyed a maid by getting a pairt of that breakfaft which difpatched tuo of her elder fifters, as is before related.

[DRUMMOND OF INNERPEFFRIE.]

John Lord Drummond's youngeft fone was John Drummond. called to a by name John Bane, that is whyte or faire John. He was provyded to the baronie of Innerpeffrie and others, and married ——— Drummond, daughter to his uncle James Drummond of Coldoch, and begot with her a fone, Sir John Drummond of Innerpeffrie, who fucceeded, and tuo daughters. The eldeft, Sybylla Drummond, a beautiful young woman, was miftres to King James the Fifth, who beftowed on her a title of honour, makeing her Lady Kinclevin; fhe was afterwards married to Sir James Herrine of Weftergormoch, bot had never any children, that we hear. It may be, that it was upon this accompt that Cambden, in his Brittannia, giveth this commendation to the ladys of the familie of Drummond, that for theire unparalelled perfections and beautie, the Kings of Scotland made choife of them for theire paramoures.

John Bane Drummond's youngeft daughter, Iffobella Drummond, went north with her cufine Margaret, Lady Gordone: where fhe was married to   Gordon of Buckie, who begot with her tuo fones and a daughter, married to   Gordon of Cairnbarrow, called Beffie Gordon: of her are [defcended] diverfe families of that name, which were called Drummond Gordons.

John Bane Drummond's firft fone was Sir John Drummond of Innerpeffrie. He married his cufine, Lady Margaret Stuart, King James [the] fourths daughter, after fhe had been firft married to the Lord Gordon, and the fecond time to Alexander Duke of Albanie; and begot with her four daughters, Agnes, Margaret, Jean, and Elifabeth Drummonds. Agnes, the eldeft, was firft married to Sir Hugh Campbel of Loudun, fheriffe of Aire, and had to him a fone who fucceeded, and five daughters; the eldeft, Margaret, was firft married to Thomas Lord Boyd, of whom the now Earle of Kilmarnock is defcended: the fecond was married to   Cunninghame, laird of Capringtoun, which was a confiderable familie in the fhyre of Air, bot now is extinct; the third was married to the laird of Craigie-Wallace: the fourth to the laird of Lochnorris; and the youngeft to   Ker, laird of Kerfland in Cunninghame.

After the death of Sir Hugh Campbell, Agnes Drummond, his lady, being a handfome young widdow, was paffionatly beloved by Hugh third Earle of Eglington, Lord Montgomerie, bot the difficultie was he could not marrie her, for he had a lady, Jean Hamilton, daughter to James Duke of Chaftelherauld: he communicats his inclinationes to Lady Margaret Stuart, the widdow's mother, who contrives a divorce to be purchafed betwixt the Earle of Eglingtone and his lady, Jean Hamilton, purpofely to be avenged upon the Duke of Chaftelherauld, becaufe he had married to his firft wife a daughter of George Mafter of Angus, begotten upon Elifabeth Drummond, Lady Margarets motherfifter, and had got a feparation from her by a bill of divorce upon pretence of confanguinity within the degrees forbidden by the cannon law; bot in effect, either becaufe fhe had to him only a daughter and no fone, or out of love to Lady Margaret Douglas, daughter to James Earle of Morton, his fecond wife, mother to Lady Jean Hamilton, Comtefs of Eglingtoune. Lady Margaret Stuart was active in carrieing on the defigne, fent away privately to Rome, where a commiffion is obtained from Pope Pius V., and directed to John Hamilton, Archbifhop and primate of Scotland, Legat a Latere of the Appoftolick fea, for trying the truth of Hugh Earle of Eglingtons perfute of a divorce from his putative lady, Jean Hamilton, becaufe they were contingent in the fourth degree of confanguinitie againft the cannons of the church, and had proceeded to marrie without the Popes difpenfation. Many courts were holden upon the tryal, bot in end, the matter was inftructed and proven by fuorn witneffes, and fentence pronounced by Mr. John Houfton, canon of the metropolitan church of Glafgow, and commiffarie there. The whole authentick procefs of this divorce betwixt Hugh Earle of Eglington, and Lady Jean Hamilton his fuppofed fpoufe, with a difpenfation for the Earle to marrie Agnes Drummond, widdow of Sir Hugh Campbel of Lowdone, granted after the divorce, is yet to be feen intire, wrytten in a faire hand in Latine, upon a book of fyne parchment, with all the particulars of the proceedings, as it wes carried on in the year 1562. 1562.

Upon this divorce the Earle married Agnes Drummond, and begot with her Hugh, who fucceeded, and was killed by the Cunninghames;

150   THE GENEALOGIE OF

Lady Margaret Montgomerie, who married Robert Seaton, firft Earle of Winton; and   Montgomerie, Lady Semple. Robert Earle of Winton was created Earle by King James the Sixth, at Holyroodhoufe, anno 1600, on the 14th of September; he had by Lady Margaret Montgomerie, George, the fecond Earle of Winton. He had alfo Sir Alexander Seaton, who, by taylzie or adoption, fucceeded to the Earledome of Eglintowne, and tooke the name and armes of Montgomerie, becaufe of the defect of aires male in the fone of Hugh, the Earle who preceeded him. Alexander wes commonly called old Grayfteell; he married Lady Anna Livington, daughter to Alexander firft Earle of Linlithgow; with whom he begot Hugh, the next Earle, father to Alexander, who is now Earle of Eglington.

Agnefs Drummond Comtefs of Eglinton, after the deceafs of her fecond hufband, Hugh Earle of Eglington, married a third time to her own cufine, Patrick Lord Drummond, when they were both well advanced in age. About the year 1588 he difponed her conjunct fie lands to Hugh Earle of Eglington her fone, for a certaine foume of money of yearly annuity, by a mutual obligation; to which the witneffes are John Drummond of Pitzallonie, Thomas Drummond of Corfkeplie, and William Drummond viccar of Strageth.

1588.

Sir John of Innerpeffrie, his second daughter.

Sir John Drummond of Innerpeffrie his fecond daughter, Margaret, married Sir Mathew Cambel of Lowdon, the fone and air of Sir Hugh Campbel by his firft wife; fo the father and fone married tuo fifters, twins. Of this Sir Mathew and his Lady Margaret Drummond are lineally defcended the family of the Earles of Loudon.

Sir John of Innerpeffrie, his third daughter.

Sir John Drummond of Innerpeffrie his third daughter, was Elifabeth Drummond, and married to Robert third Lord Elphingfton; whofe grandfather Alexander was created firft Lord Elphingfton by King James the fourth, in the year 1510, and killed at Flowdon batle in the King's habit 1513. Robert Lord Elphingfton begot with his Lady, Elifabeth Drummond, three fones and four daughters: the

THE HOUSE OF DRUMMOND.

eldeſt ſone, Alexander, ſucceeded and married a daughter of the Lord Livingſton's, with whom he had Alexander the next Lord, and five daughters; Anna the Comteſs of Sutherland, the Lady Forbeſs, the Lady Langtowne Cockburn, the Lady Airth Bruce, and the Lady Crommartie Urchart.

Robert Lord Elphingſton had a ſecond ſone, by Margaret Drummond, called Mr. George Elphingſton, Rector of the Scots Colledge at Rome. His third ſone was Sir James Elphingſton of Barntowne, Secretarie of State, and Preſident of the Colledge of Juſtice; he was created a Lord of Parliament, and called Lord Balmerinoch by King James the Sixth, upon the 20th of February 1603; he married, firſt, Sara Monteith, daughter to Sir John Monteith of Carſe, and begot with her John Elphingſton, who was Lord Balmerinoch after his father; and, by a ſecond marriage, James Elphingſton, Lord Cowper. Robert Lord Elphingſton had alſo by his Lady, Eliſabeth Drummond, four daughters; the Lady Towie Barclay, the Lady Findlator, the Lady Innes, and the Lady Drumwhaſel.

Sir John Drummond of Innerpeffrie his fourth daughter, with Lady Margaret Stuart, was Jean Drummond. She was married to Sir James Cheeſholm of Cromlix, and had to him Sir James, who ſucceeded; William Biſhop of Vaſon in France, and Sir John Cheeſholm, and Thomas Cheeſholm portioner of Buttergaſk; her daughters were, Helen Cheeſholm Lady Kinfauns, mother to Lodovick Lyndſay, Earle of Craufurd, Jean Cheeſholm Lady Maddertie, Agnes Cheeſholm Lady Marcheſton, and Margaret Cheeſholm Lady Muſchet. Of the family of Cromlix we ſhal make mention heireafter. *Sir John of Innerpeffrie, his fourth daughter.*

Sir John Drummond of Innerpeffrie his youngeſt daughter was Eliſabeth Drummond, married to Malcolm Drummond, the third baron of Boreland; of theire children mention hath been made in the Second Partitione, where the pedegree of the family of Concraige and Boreland are ſet downe at length. *His youngeſt daughter.*

THE GENEALOGIE OF

[DRUMMOND OF RICCARTON.]

Drummond of Riccartone.

John Bane Drummond of Innerpeffrie had a fecond fone, Harie Drummond, whofe mother was Elifabeth Douglas, a neare cufine to the houfe of Lochlevin. Harie was a valiant gentleman, and of good breeding, he ferved the French King Henrie the Second, as Captaine of his Archer-Gard; after he came home, he was in good efteeme at the Scots court, under the Regencie of King James [the] fifth his relict, Queen Marie of Lorraine, and with Marie, Queen of Scots, her daughter; bot he was fecretly a great favorer of John Knox, and the Reformation; for I find it recorded, that, in the year 1555, the Earle of Glencairn allured the Earle Marifchal, who with Harie Drummond, his councellor for the time, heard ane exortation, bot it was in the night, in the Bifhop of Dunkeld's great lodgeing, from John Knox: wherewith they were all weell contented, and willed John to wryte fomething to the Queen Regent that might move her to hear the Word of God, which he did, and fent the letter to her by the hand of Alexander Earle of Glencairn.

1555.

Harie Drummond married Jannet Creichton, heretrix of Riccartowne, the daughter of Harie Creichton, laird of Riccarton, begotten by him upon his Lady   Livingftone, daughter to Alexander Lord Livingfton, who went to France with Queen Marie. Harie Creichton of Riccarton had a brother, Robert, who was Bifhop of Dunkeld; who fucceeded in that Sea to his uncle George Creichton, Bifhop of Dunkeld, of whom its wrytten, by Archbifhop Spotfwood, that in contraverfies of religion, which were much agitat in his time, he loved calmnefs and moderation, "For, faid he, I neither know the

THE HOUSE OF DRUMMOND. 153

Old nor New Teſtament, and yet I thank God I have proſpered well enough al my dayes."

The Creichtons of Riccarton feeme to be cadetts of my Lord Sanquair's family; for by Riccarton's charters, it appeares that Alexander Creichton, who wes laird of Riccarton, before Harie Creichton in the year 1506, purchaffed the lands of Pardivine, which are ſtill Riccartones; and that a little after, the Lord Sanquaire difponed to him the lands of Riccartone. Jannet Creichton, the heretrix, had a fifter married to the laird of Lochnorris, Craufurd, whofe lands foone after came alfo in to the family of Sanquaire, and now are pofeſt by the Earle of Drumfriefs. 1506.

Harie Drummond had with Jannet Creichtone five fones and five daughters. The eldeft fone, Harie Drummond, fucceeded to be laird of Riccartone after his father; the fecond, William Drummond, in the year 1580, married Margaret Drummond, heretrix of Pitcairnes, who was the only daughter of Thomas Drummond of Pitcairnes, the third fone of John Drummond the third laird of Drummond Irenoch, as is marked in the families of Drummond Irenoch and Pitcairnes.

Harie Drummond of Riccartone's third fone was Sir David Drummond, Supreame Judge of the Biſhop's Court of Vafon in France, belongeing to the Apoftolick Sea; he was Knighted by Pope Clement the Eighth, about the year 1598, and came to Scotland, anno 1600, for great matters, to King James Sixth, concerning his Succeffion to the Crown of England, and for procureing a recommendation from the King to the Pope, to get William Cheefholm, Bifhop of Vafon, a Cardinal's cape; he alfo carried back the letter to the Pope, for which Prefident Elphingfton was ftaged. 1598. 1600.

Harie Drummond of Riccarton his fourth fone, Thomas Drummond, went to France, where he dyed unmarried.

His youngeft fone, Mr. Ninian Drummond, was minifter and parfon of Kinnoull; he married Margaret Creichtone, daughter to

x

THE GENEALOGIE OF

Creichton of Lugtowne, and had with her tuo fones, Mr. James and Mr. Edward Drummonds, and a daughter, Jean Drummond.

Mr. James, the eldeſt, married Agnes Graham, daughter to Robert Grahame of Cairnie, had bot one fone, Mr. Ninian Drummond of Gaffingall Weſter, married to Helen Drummond, daughter to Duncan Drummond of Balhadie, and five daughters; the firſt, Anna Drummond, married to Thomas Grahame, brother to John Grahame of Boultone; the fecond, Helen Drummond, married to Mr. James Balfoure in Erroll, and had only a daughter, Agnes Balfoure; the third, Annabella Drummond, married to Mr. David Young, miniſter at Lethendie, in the dioceſs of Dunkeld, and hes many children; the fourth, Jean Drummond, married to Mr. Thomas Chriſtie, miniſter at Wigtowne in Galloway, and hes children; and the youngeſt, Griffel Drummond.

Mr. Edward Drummond, youngeſt fone to Mr. Ninian Drummond, married Helen Moriſon, a widdow, relict of Mr. William Foggo, miniſter at Callendar; had a fone, Harie Drummond.

Jean Drummond, only daughter to Mr. Ninian Drummond, perſon of Kinoull, married firſt, William Moncreiffe, brother to the laird of Moncreiffe, *sed propter impotentiam viri separati*. She married thereafter Mr. John Freebairn, miniſter of Madertie, and had to him a daughter, Margaret Freebairn, married to Mr. John Murray, a miniſter in England, who hes diverſe children.

Harie Drummond of Riccarton's daughters were firſt, Margaret Drummond, married to George Drummond, fourth laird of Balloch; the fecond was married to the Laird of Cowſtowne, Polwart; the third to the Laird of Logie, who did bear to him that famouſs gentleman, beheaded in Holland; the fourth married to the laird of Bearlaw, Houſtone; and the fifth to the laird of Badrige, Bruce.

2. Harie Drummond, the fecond laird of Riccarton, fone to Harie the

THE HOUSE OF DRUMMOND.

firſt laird, married Margaret Sandilands, fifter to Sir James Sandilands of Slamanno Muire, gentleman of the King's privie chamber, prediceſſor to the Lord Torphichen; and begot tuo fones, Sir William and Thomas Drummonds, and tuo daughters, Jean and Margaret Drummonds. Sir William fucceeded; Thomas dyed without iſhew. Jean Drummond, the eldeſt daughter, married Coline Campbell of Aberuchell, fecond fone to Sir John Campbell, laird of Lawers, and had to him tuo fones and two daughters. The eldeſt fone was James Campbell, next of Aberuchell; he married Hepburn, daughter to Patrick Hepburn in Edenburgh, and had with her Sir Coline Campbel, now of Aberuchell.

Sir William Drummond, the third laird of Riccarton, eldeſt fone 3. to the laſt Harie, married Jean Sterline, daughter to Sir Archibald Sterline of Keer, and begot with her a fone, William Drummond, who fucceeded, and tuo daughters; Jean Drummond, married to John Buchannan of Shirrahall, bot had no iſhew, and Anna Drummond, married to Mr. Robert Naper of Kilcreuch.

William Drummond, fourth laird of Riccartone, fone to Sir William, 4. married Magdalen Dalzell, daughter of Thomas Dalzel of Binns, cufine to the Earle of Carnwath. Her mother was Magdalen Bruce, daughter to the Lord Bruce, grandfather to the Earle of Elgin in Scotland, now Earle of Ailfberrie, in England, and a peer of the kingdom. William Drummond of Riccarton, begot with Magdalen Dalzel, three fones, Thomas, who fucceeded, Alexander and John Drummonds, who both dyed young unmarried, and four daughters, Anna and Margaret dyed maids, Catharine and Jean. Catharine Drummond was married to her cufine-german, Thomas Dalzel, fone to General Thomas Dalzel of Binns, well knowen for his loyaltie to the crowne, and his great fervices and fufferings for King Charles the Firſt and Second, at home, and his famous actiones in the wars abroad. Thomas, the fone of General Thomas, begot with Catharine

Drummond, tuo fones, Thomas and William Dalzells, and tuo daughters, Magdalen and Jannet Dalzells.

The youngeft daughter of William Drummond, fourth laird of Riccarton, was Jean Drummond.

5. Thomas Drummond of Riccartone, the fone of William, fucceeded to be the fifth laird ; he married Elifabeth Nicolfon, daughter to Sir Thomas Nicolfon of Carnock, a famoufs lawyer and advocat to the King. Thomas Drummond, begat with Elifabeth, his lady, tuo fones, Thomas Drummond, the eldeft, who fucceeded, and George, his brother, and three daughters, Iffobella, Magdalen, and Elifabeth Drummonds ; all hopefull young gentlemen and gentlewomen.

6. Thomas Drummond, now of Riccarton, is the fixth laird.

Off Lady Elifabeth Lindfay, John Lord Drummonds wife, of whom are come al the generations above mentioned, and of the familie of the Earles of Craufurd, her father, mention fhal be made when we come to Patrick Lord Drummond, who married alfo out of the fame familie in the 11th Partitione.

CONCERNING WILLIAM, MASTER OF DRUMMOND, SONE TO JOHN
LORD DRUMMOND.

PARTITION THE EIGHTH.

William Drummond, after the death of his elder brother, Malcolm, wes the eldeft fone of John Lord Drummond, and called all his lifetime Mafter of Drummond, becaufe he dyed before his father, and fo came never to be lord; yet is he reckned the thirteenth head of the family, as being the thirteenth perfon in order of generation, from the firft of the name. He married Lady Iffobella Campbel, daughter to Coline Earle of Argyle, according to the paction of agreement betwixt theire tuo fathers, in the year 1474, when Malcolm, his eldeft brother, and the Lady Iffobella, were both under age, as is fignifyed in the foregoeing Partition.

William Mafter of Drummond, thirteenth head of the family.

1474.

William begat with the Lady Iffobella tuo fones; the eldeft, Walter, called the fecond Mafter of Drummond, becaufe he alfo dyed before John Lord Drummond his grandfather; and the youngeft, Andrew Drummond, who was the firft of the houfe of Belliclon.

William, Mafter of Drummond, was a gallant youth, bot very unfortunatly concerned in a fad and cruel action which proved fatal to himfelfe, and matter of fadnes and trouble to his freinds, the ftorie whereof were fitter to be burried in eternall oblivion then curioufly to be inquyred after by the pofterity; bot in refpect the reports thereof are various, whereby wrong may be done by the liveing to the memorie of the dead, *et quanquam animus meminisse horret*, yet I judge it not amifs breefly to relate the truth of the thing as it is collected and delivered by ane impartial hand, from old manufcripts happily preferved and faln upon, and it is thus:—

THE GENEALOGIE OF

1490. There was, about the year 1490, a complaint exhibited to William Shevez, Archbifhop of St. Andrews, by George Murray, then Abbot of Inchaffray, fignifyeing that, how fome of the Drummonds (whom he calls Satan's foldiers and rotten members) had moft barbaroufly killed and burned, in the kirk of Monyvaird, a number of his kinfmen, friends, and followers, without regaird to God or the place to which they had betaken themfelves as to a fanctuary and fafe houfe of refuge, and fupplicateing for juftice and fevere proceedings againft fuch outrages, &c. The names of the dead are fet down in the paper, which I think not neceffarie for this place.

The Archbifhop, with a large aggravation of the cruelty of the fact, recommends the anathematizeing of thefe offenders to John Hepburn, Bifhop of Dumblane, within whofe diocefe the cryme was committed, to be performed with all the folemnities requyred in the Rubrick of the great Excommunication, fuch as Bell, Book, and Candell, &c.; and further, ordaines the Bifhop to intimate folemly the fame Excommunication to all the congregationes of the countrey; bot it feemes, by the reft of the ftorie, the Bifhop was not haftie in the buffines. This (fayes my author) I have feen in wryte, and the tradition of all parties intereffed confirmes, that John Lord Drummond himfelfe was abfent at the time, and knew nothing of the matter, bot that only his eldeft fone William and Thomas Drummonds, afterwards called Drummond Irenoch, his uncle, with fome other freinds and dependents were provocked by threatning words to goe to Monyvaird, where fome of the name of Murray were faid to keep a meeting in defpite of them and theire partie. The caufe of that meeting wes the rydeing of the teynds (as they called it) of the Drummonds lands in the parifh of Monyvaird, belongeing to the Abbot of Inchaffray, called George Murray; this rydeing of teynds is a kind of fevere way to confider and eftimate the value of the tenth fheaffe of all cornes in the time of harveft ftanding on the ground, and from thence to eftablifh the number of rentalled teynd bolls accordingly to be payed by the heritor to the titular yearly ; which rigour the Drummonds did not well lyke, efpecially to be done in a boafting maner, and this was the occafion of all the mifcheife. Bot it happened, unluckily, that in the fpring feafon of the fame year, one Alexander Murray, a natural fone to the Laird of Tullibardine, had killed Walter Drummond, barron of Mewie, and his tuo fones ; whereof the news comeing to Duncan Campbell, captaine of Dunftaffnage in Argyle, (he being in Ireland at the time,) who had married Iffobella Drummond, daughter to this Walter Drummond of Mewie: It fell out, I fay, in the harveft time that this Captaine of Dunftaffnage came to Lenoch, attended with a company of Hylanders, according to their maner, to try how the murther of his father-in-law might be revenged and to take care for the young child his wife's brother, al which is related in the petition, he layes hold upon this opportunity to goe in company with the Mafter of Drummond, and his followers, to hinder the rydeing of theire teynds. The Murrayes, furpryfed with theire approach, betakes themfelves to the kirk as the secureft place from al danger. The Mafter of Drummond, fatyffyed that he had put them from the feild, and from theire defigne wes returneing home, and marched by the kirk, fome unhappy perfone within made a fhot, and therewith wounded or killed one of Campbell of Dunftaffnage his men, whereat the reft of the Highlanders being fo inraged, could not be reftrained from fyreing the church, covered only with heather, and fo burned al within it. This inhumane barbaritie being reprefented to King James the Fourth, then at Sterline, he was exceedinglie offended, and goes in perfon to Drummond Caftle, whither the Mafter of Drummond and his company had retired. The Caftle was furrendred, the Mafter carried to Sterline, and there publickly execute, notwithftanding his fifter Margaret, the King's miftres, and the Lady Drummond her mother, had upon theire knees begged his lyfe from the King ; which would have been certainely granted, if the Mother, a bold, proud, and undavyfed woman, had not in her paffion uttered fome bitter and unfeafonable words, wherewith the King was fo irritated, that he commanded juftice furthwith to be done upon the Mafter of Drummond, and many others of his freinds who were his accompliffes in that ill turn, and appointed alfo an affythment to be given to the wives and children of fuch as dyed at Monyvaird. This unchriftian action, with what had paffed before, tended much to the wydening of the breach betwixt the tuo families of the Drummonds and the Murrayes, albeit they were nearely allyed together, for John Lord Drummond's mother was a daughter of the Laird of Tyllibardine's, cheefe of the Murrayes; untill it pleafed God to reconcile and cement theire hearts againe by new and ftrong bonds of mutual allyances one with ane other, fo that now they have long lived as freindly and kindly united as any other trybes of the nation.

OFF THE LADY ISSOBELLA CAMPBEL, MARRIED TO WILLIAM MASTER OF DRUMMOND, AND OF THE FAMILY OF THE EARLE OF ARGYLE, HER FATHER.

The Campbells were firft knights of Loch Crochan: the third knight called Duyne Faldarge, had tuo fones, Paul and Gillicallum. It was from this Duyne firft that the whole trybe are called Clan O'Duyne to this day. Paul, the fourth knight, had only a daughter, called Awah; from her being heretrix, came the denomination Lochawah, which in former time was called Loch Crochan, becaufe it lyes at the root of the high montane called to this day Crochan Ben.

Gillicallom or Malcolm, brother to Paul, went to France, where he married the daughter of Monſieur Beauchamps, heretrix and halfe fiſter to William the Conquerour. Malcolm begot with her tuo ſones, Archbald and Dennys, called in the Scots tongue Gilleſpick and Duncan.

Gilleſpick, the eldeſt, came to England with King William the Conquerour, anno 1066; and from thence to Argyle, where he married the only daughter of his uncle Paul, Awah, the heretrix: his name was de Beauchamp, in Latine de Campo Bello, from whence grew the name Campbell. His brother Duncan or Dennis poſeſt the eſtate of Beauchamp in France.

1066.

Gilleſpick Campbell begot upon Awah, Euen; of whom are deſcended all the knights of Lochawah, in theire order.

One of that line was Archbald Campbell, who married the heretrix of Lorne; his ſone Coline was the firſt Earle of Argyle created by King James the Firſt. Both the father Archbald and the ſone Colline partied the Monteiths againſt the Drummonds in the time of theire quarrell before related; bot either Gilleſpick, or rather his ſone Collin, married a ſiſter of Queen Annabella Drummonds, whereby the firſt freindſhip was made up betwixt the Campbells and the Drummonds.

The ſecond Earle [of Argyle] was Archbald. The third was Collin, called Collin Roy; he married a daughter of Alexander Earle of Huntly, and begot Archbald the fourth Earle of Argyle, and the Lady Iſſobella Campbell, married to William Maſter of Drummond. Archbald, called Gilleſpick Dow, his ſone, was the fifth Earle; Collin, called Buy, his brother, was the ſixth: Archbald, called Gruamach, his ſone, the ſeventh.

Archbald, the eighth Earle [of Argyle], was created Marquis by King Charles the Firſt, at the parliament in Edinburgh 1641; and forfaulted by King Charles the Second in his firſt parliament, 1660.

1641.
1660.

Archbald his fone, was reftored to be the ninth Earle, bot in the year
1681. 1681 wes againe forfaulted.

The Drummonds of Belliclon.

Belliclon. 1. Andrew Drummond, fecond fone to William Mafter of Drummond, begotten with Lady Iffobella Campbell, was the firft of the houfs of Belliclon. He married Jannet Campbel, daughter to the laird of Glenurchy, and begot with her a fone, who fucceeded, called alfo Andrew.

2. Andrew Drummond, the fecond of Belliclon, married Janet Dickfon, the daughter of John Dickfon Laird of Ballachafter, about
1550. the year 1550. He begot tuo fones, William who fucceeded, and David his brother, and a daughter, Margaret Drummond, married to the Laird of Buwhain Leflie, in the fhyre of Aberdeen. David the fecond fone, married Margaret Grahame, daughter to Edward Grahame of Arbenie, with whom he had tuo fones, Sir David and Sir Maurice Drummonds, and one daughter, Anna Drummond. Sir David was a gentleman of great honor in the warrs of Germanie; he was preferred to be Major-General by the great Guftavus Adolphus King of Sueden, and Governour of the ftrong town of Stettine in Pomerania: He married Cicile Spens, daughter to the Laird of Wormiftoune, bot had no chyld. Sir Maurice Drummond, his brother, was in good efteeme at the court of England, in the time of King Charles the Firft; he married Dorothea Lowr, a near cufine to Algernon Earle of Northumberland, and begot only four daughters, firft, Henrietta Maria Drummond; the fecond, Margaret Drummond; the third, Penelope Drummond; the fourth,

The eldeſt married, firſt   , and then Maſter Ropper; the ſecond married Mr. Carryll; the third Mr. Ployden; and the youngeſt Mr. Travanie. All of them had children of good accompt in theire own countrey.

Anna Drummond, the daughter of Andrew of Belliclon, went over to her brother, Sir David, the Major-General, to Stettine; and was married to William Monnipennie, a captaine in the war under King Guſtavus his army.

3. William Drummond, the eldeſt ſone of Andrew, was the third of that family. He married Margaret Rollo, daughter to Sir Andrew Rollo of Duncrub, and begot Andrew Drummond, who ſucceeded.

4. Andrew, the ſone of William, ſucceeded to be the fourth of that houſe. He married Margaret Campbell, daughter to the Laird of Kethick in Angus, and begot a ſone, John Drummond.

5. John Drummond, the ſone of Andrew, ſucceeded to be the fifth laird of Belliclon; he married &c., and begot only a ſone John Drummond.

6. John Drummond ſucceeded to his father John, and was the ſixth of that houſs. He married Anna Cheeſholm, daughter to Sir James Cheeſholm of Cromlix, and had with her only a daughter, married in Sterline. He unworthiely ſold the land, and ſo extinguiſhed ane honeſt old family, whereof himſelfe was the laſt of that race.

CONCERNING WALTER DRUMMOND, SONE TO WILLIAM, MASTER OF
DRUMMOND, AND GRANDCHILD TO JOHN, LORD DRUMMOND.

PARTITIONE NINTH.

Walter, Master of Drummond, fourteenth cheefe of the family.

Walter Drummond, the eldeſt ſone of William Maſter of Drummond, begotten with Lady Iſſobella Campbell, was called the ſecond Maſter, in regaird he came never to be Lord, for his grandfather John outlived both this Walter and his father William; yet is he accompted the fourteenth head in direct line of the family from the firſt.

Walter Drummond, the ſecond Maſter of Drummond, married his near cuſine Lady Eliſabeth Grahame, daughter to William Earle of
1513. Montroſe, about the year 1513: he begot with Lady Eliſabeth only one ſone David, who ſucceeded to be Lord Drummond. Walter
1519. dyed very young, and was burried at Innerpeffrie anno 1519.

OFF THE LADY ELISABETH GRAHAME, MARRIED TO WALTER SECOND
MASTER OF DRUMMOND, AND OF THE FAMILIE OF THE EARLE OF
MONTROSE, HER FATHER.

Leſlie, Grammus. Buchan. Graemus.

The original of the name of Grahame, or as ſome wryte it, Graeme or Greem, is ſaid to be ſprung from that famous Graemus who came to Scotland from Denmark with, and was father-in-law to King Fergus [the] Second. He was alſo governour dureing the minoritie of that King's ſone, his own grandchild, King Eugenius the Second. Theſe of Graemus ſucceſſors in the time of King Malcolm the Third,

THE HOUSE OF DRUMMOND.

when firnames tooke beginning for diftinction of families, made choife of the name of theire firft prediceffor Graeme or Greem for their firname. This Graemus is the firft of the name we read of, who, it feems, was general commander to King Fergus army when he fought at Carron water againft the Romans and Brittaines, commanded by Victorius the Roman Legat. He it was that broke down the old trench called Severus Wall, built from Abercorn to Kilpatrick, at the mouth of Clyde, about thirty miles in length, and beat the Roman garrifones from thence, for which notable action it got the name of Graemfdyke, which it retaines to this day; this was foone after the 400 year of Chrift. The next eminent perfon of that name was Grahame, who, with Dumbar Earle of March, refcued this Kingdome from falling in the hands of the Danes, who had conquered England, and attempted to doe the lyke with Scotland, bot without the like fuccefs. The Graemes came firft to Strathern by the marriage of Sir John Graham of Dundaffe Muire to a daughter of Malife, fourth Earle of Strathern, and firft of that name; with whom Sir John got the lands of Aberuthven, about the year 1242.

In the year 1257, and eighth of Alexander the Third, in a charter of Malife Earle of Strathern, the fifth Earle and fecond of that name, mortificing a donation to the monafterie of Inchaffray, the witneffes ftand thus: Robert Bifhop of Dumblane, Sir Patrick de Grahame, Sir John de Stryvyllin, Sir William de Moravia, the fone of Sir Malcolm de Moravia, &c.

In ane other charter which begins, *Malisius filius Gilberti quondam Comitis de Stratheren Miles*, the witneffes is dominus Patricius de Grahme, which may be the fame Sir Patrick above mentioned. In ane other of William, the fone of Malife, fealled with the common feal of the burgh of Auchterarder, the witneffes are Sir David de Grahme, Sir Thomas de Fauffyde, Walter de Moravia laird of Tyllibardine.

400.

1242.
1257.

THE GENEALOGIE OF

1292. In the year 1292, David de Grahme, Patrick de Grahme, and Nicoll de Grahme, are called amongſt thefe who were appointed by King Edward the Firſt of England to hear the claimes of the Bruce and Ballioll at Berwick.

Not long after this, that valiant champion Sir John the Grahame, companion to the renowned Wallace, of whom Buchannan gives this character, *Secundum ipsum Vallam, Scotorum longe fortissimus habitus*, wes unfortunatly killed at the batle of Falkirk; where his tomb is to be feen to this day, and the place hes its name from Graemfdyke, *Fanum Vallium*, that is, the chappel on the wall, a more propper fignification then Buchannan's *Varium Sacellum*.

1320. In the letter directed to Pope John the 22d, from the communitie of Scotland, in the year 1320, and 14th of the reigne of King Robert the Firſt, amongſt the fubfcrivers are David de Grahme, immediately following after the nobilitie, John de Grahame and Patrick de Grahme.

In the minoritie of King David Bruce there is mention of one Sir John Graham, lord of Abercorn, who had a daughter Margaret Grahame married to William Douglas, lord of Liddifdale, called the floure of chivallrie, with whom he got thefe lands of Liddifdale. There is ane other, Patrick Grahme, provocked to a duell by ane Englifh man, to whom he faid, " Pray yow dyne well, for I fhall fend yow to fup in paradyfe."

1400. About the year 1400, John Grahame, defygned of Dundaffe, married Marie Stuart, daughter to King Robert the Third, begotten on Queen Annabella Drummond. There is ane Indenture of the date 1399, in the reigne of King Robert the Third, betwixt Sir Patrick Graham of Kincardine, and Sir John Olyphant of Aberdagie, that Robin de Graham, fone of the faid Sir Patrick the Graham, fhal wed to wyffe, God willand, Marrion Olyphant, daughter of the faid Sir John, with many remarkable and fingular conditions very well worthie of the obferving.

THE HOUSE OF DRUMMOND.

In anno 1410, after the death of King Robert the Third, Sir John 1410.
Drummond of Stobhal, brother to Malcolm Drummond Earle of
Marr, takes ane inftrument, in prefence of Robert Earle of Fyfe, duke
of Albanie, and the Councell fitting, concerning fome of his lands in
the parifh of Cargyll; being then prefent, Walter Earle of Athol,
Archbald Earle of Douglas, George Earle of March, Alexander Earle
of Marr, Patrick Grahame Earle of Strathern, William Lord Grahame,
and John, Senefcall of Innermay, &c. This William Lord Grahame
feems to be the firft that was created lord, and it hes been by King
Robert the Third. In a charter by King James the Second, 1446, 1446.
createing James Lord Hamilton lord of parliament, Patrick Lord
Graham is witnefs. (Vid. Hamilton's Papers.) About 1460,
William Lord Graham was chofen by King James [the] Second his
Queen widdow, to be one of the four Governours to King James the
Third.

His grandchyld, William Lord Graham, in anno 1479, married 1479.
Annabella Drummond, daughter to John Lord Drummond; and in
the year 1504, and 16th of King James the Fourth, he was created 1504.
Earle of Montrofe, and his lands erected in an Earledom.

His fone was alfo William the fecond Earle of Montrofe; whofe
daughter, Elifabeth Grahame, was married to Walter fecond Mafter
of Drummond, the father of David Lord Drummond, anno 1513. In 1513.
the year 1542, this William Earle of Montrofe, enters in a bond of 1542.
freindfhip and manrent with David Lord Drummond, to which the
witneffes are Robert Mafter of Montrofe, and Alexander his brother;
bot it feems William [Robert] dyed young and William fucceeded.

William the fone of William, was third Earle of Montrofe, (William
Mafter of Grahame married Jannet Keith, daughter to the Earle
Marifchall killed at Pinkie), and grandfather to John the fourth Earle
of Montrofe, who was chancellor of Scotland when King James came
to the crown of England. He married Jean Drummond, and was

THE GENEALOGIE OF

created Vice Roy of Scotland, and injoyed that higheſt honour which any ſubject of the nation is capable of all his lyfetime. Sir William Graeme of Braco was his ſone. William Earle of Montroſe, this John's grandfather had alſo other children, Alexander of Cambuſ-kennet, William of Killeren, and Mungo Graeme of Roterns. John the fifth Earle, the ſone of John the Vice Roy, married Margaret Ruthven, daughter to William Earle of Gowrie; he performed honourable embaſſies for King James the Sixth, and was by King Charles the Firſt made Lord Preſident of the Seſſion, but dyed young.

James the ſixth Earle of Montroſe, John's ſone, married Magdalen Carnegie, daughter to the Earle of Southeſk, and was by King Charles
1644. the Firſt created Marques in the year 1644; then was High Com-miſſioner and the Kings Livetenant-General over all Scotland, where, with a ſmall flying army, he did faicts beyond beleife againſt the Covenanters forces, which he ſex times in one year beat and ſcattered;
1650. bot was, in the year 1650, unhappily taken and diſgracefully putt to death. Bot King Charles the Second, after his happy Reſtauration,
1660. in the year 1660, cauſed raiſe his bones and gather his diſperſed members, and bury them with pompe and great ſtate, in St. Gylles church, at Edinburgh. James his ſone was ſecond Marqueſs, and married Lady Iſſobella Douglas, daughter to William Earle of Morton, and relict of Robert Earle of Roxburgh. James his ſone, now the third Marques, married Lady Chriſtian Leſſlie, daughter to John Duke of Rothes, Lord High Chancellor of Scotland.

THE HOUSE OF DRUMMOND.

CONCERNING DAVID LORD DRUMMOND, THE SONE OF WALTER
CALLED THE SECOND MASTER OF DRUMMOND.

[PARTITION TENTH.]

David Lord Drummond, the fone of Walter called the fecond Mafter of Drummond, was borne before the death of his great-grand-father, John Lord Drummond. He was very young when he came to be Lord, and fo fell to be the King's ward; the gift whereof King James the Fifth beftowed upon Sir Robert Barton, Controller, who, as a worthy guardian, performed his office with great care and kindnefs, for he caufed educat the minor as was fit for his qualitie; and when he came to yeares of difcretion he bred him at the court, where the King did take much notice of him; for in the year 1525, John Duke of Albany, governor, in the King's name, enters in ane obligation with his tutor Sir Robert Barton, upon the Lord Drummond's behalfe, wherein he promifes to reftore him entirely, and put him in full poffeffion of all the lands which belonged to John Lord Drummond, before his forefaulture, (which [it] feems hes not been fullie done at the firft,) with fome refervationes and provifions; and, particularly, it was conditioned that David Lord Drummond fhould, when he came to maturitie of yeares, marrie Lady Margaret Stuart, the daughter of Alexander Duke of Albany, begotten with the Lady Gordon, after fhe was firft a widdow.

This Lady Gordon was the King's fifter, as he calls her in that wrytte the daughter of King James the Fourth, by Margaret Drummond, John Lord Drummond his daughter; firft married to the Lord Gordon, and thereafter to this Alexandar Stuart Duke of Albanie, and laft of all to Sir John Drummond of Innerpeffrie, of

David Lord Drummond, the fifteenth cheefe of the familie.

1520.

1525.

z

whom we have already made mention. Alexander Stuart, Duke of
Albany his father, was alfo Alexander Stuart and Duke, fone to
King James [the] Second. He was twife married, firft to
St. Clare Earle of Orkneyes daughter, who was mother to this Duke
Alexander; next to the Duke of Bulloignes daughter, the mother of
John Duke of Albany, the Governour. I find, at the Parliament
where John was elected Governor to the young King, Alexander his
elder brother protefted that the promotion of his younger brother
John to that office fhould not prejudge his right to the Crown in cafe
of the young King's death, in refpect he was the eldeft fone to theire
father, Alexander Duke of Albanie, the brother of King James the
Third, lawfullie begotten upon a daughter of the Earle of Orknayes;
and that John his brother was a younger fone begotten upon their
fathers fecond wife, a daughter to the Duke of Bulloigne in France.
Bot this proteftation fo difpleafed the Governour, that he refted not
untill he had fecured himfelfe from the danger of it by cutting off all
further hope of fucceffion from the perfon of Alexander his brother,
for he made him a church man; and the more to ingadge him thereto,
beftowed tuo confiderable benefices on him, to wit, the Bifhoprick of
Murray and Abbacie of Scoone; and yet further to content him,
oblidged David Lord Drummond to marrie his daughter, the Lady
Margaret; whereupon in a maner he gelded his brother, and divorced
him from his lady.

Some have miftaken the mother of this lady, Margaret Stuart, whom
David Lord Drummond married, and conceives fhe was daughter to
Cecillia Creichton, firft Countefs of Rothefs, againft whom the Earle
her hufband, upon fome difcontent, fued for a declarator upon the
nullitie of the marriage, becaufe of theire too near affinity, as being
attingent in the third degree; whereupon they were divorced, and
Robert Leflie, the Ladyes only fone with the Earle, difinherited, and
made laird of Findreffie, in place of fucceeding to the Earldome,

THE HOUSE OF DRUMMOND. 171

which barronie of Findreffie continows with his pofterity to this day; and that this Countefs of Rothes was, after divorce, married to Alexander Stuart, Duke of Albanie, to whom fhe hade the Lady Margaret Stuart, Lady Drummond; bot by the wreat of the date 1525, before expreffed, this alledgeance is fufficiently refuted, where David Lord Drummond's Lady is called King James the Fifth his neece.   1525.

Befydes, in the year 1538, I find a charter of the King's, granted by John Duke of Albanie's meanes, to David Lord Drummond who had married his neece, as a confirmation of the eftate (forfaulted from John Lord Drummond, and not before this *Novo damus* well fecured); whereby it appeares, that the mutual ingadgements made by John Duke of Albany for the King, and Sir Robert Barton for the young Lord Drummond, were punctuallie obferved, and that it was Lady Margaret Stuart, fifter to King James the Fifth, and widdow of the Lord Gordon, who, by a fecond marriage to Alexander Duke of Albany, was mother to David Lord Drummond's lady; who married about the year 1535.   1538.   1535.

David Lord Drummond begot with his lady Margaret Stuart only one daughter, Sybilla Drummond. She was married to Gilbert Ogilvie of Purie Ogilvy, 1556. Gilbert begot with Sybilla Drummond a fone, Thomas, who fucceeded, and a daughter, Sibilla Ogilvie, who was married to   1556.

David Lord Drummond, about the year 1559, after the death of his firft lady, Margaret Stuart, married a fecond time to dame Lilias Ruthven, daughter to William, third Lord Ruthven, whom he begat upon Jean Halyburton, one of [the] co-heires of the familie of Dirleton. This Lady Drummond was a beautifull perfon, of excellent pairts, and good breeding: fhe had to her Lord tuo fones, Patrick who fucceeded, and James, the firft Lord Maddertie; with five daughters, to witt, Jean, Anna, Lillias, Catharine and Margaret Drummonds.   1559.

Jean Drummond, the eldeft daughter of David Lord Drummond,

THE GENEALOGIE OF

David Lord Drummond's eldeſt daughter.

1562.

1563.

was married to John, Maſter of Grahame, about the year 1562. He was afterward Earle of Montroſe, Chancellor and Vice Roy of Scotland. It ſeems this John Maſter of Grahames father dyed young, and before his ſones marriage; for there is a precept granted to William Earle of Montroſe, grandfather to John Maſter of Grahame, of the foume of ſex thouſand merks from David Lord Drummond, for the tocher of Jean Drummond, his daughter, ſpouſe to the ſaid John Maſter of Grahame, his oe; before witneſſes, William Murray of Tyllibardine, Alexander, William, and Mungo Grahames, his ſones, of Cambuſkennet, Killeren and Raterens, George Grahame of Inchbrakie, Malcolme Drummond of Boreland, and John Drummond of Pitzallonie, dated in the year 1563.

John, who was Maſter of Grahame and Earle of Montroſe, begot with his Lady Jean Drummond, Comteſs of Montroſe, three ſones. John, the eldeſt, who ſucceeded: he married Margaret Ruthven, ſiſter to William, [third] Earle of Gowrie, and had with her James, the firſt Marquis of Montroſe, and his ſiſters Lady Lillias, Lady Margaret, Lady Dorothea, Lady Beatrix.

Sir William Grahame of Braco was ſecond ſone to John the Vice Roy with his Lady Jean Drummond: he married firſt the relict widdow of the Laird of Luthwharne, who was ſiſter to William Earle Mariſchall, bot had no children. The ſecond time he married Marie Edmonſton, widdow of the Laird of Cuninghamhead, and daughter to Edmonſton laird of Dunbreath; with her Sir William begot Sir John Grahame of Braco. He married Margaret Campbell, daughter to Campbell laird of Auchinbreck; ſhe had to Sir John, ſones, Sir William, who ſucceeded, James, John, Robert, and a daughter Griſſel Grahame, married to Sir James Keith of   . Sir William, the third Laird of Braco, married Marie Cowan, daughter to Mr. John Cowan provoſt of Stirline; and hes to him tuo ſones, Sir James, the fourth Laird of Braco, and John Grahame, his brother.

THE HOUSE OF DRUMMOND.

John Earle of Montrofe had a third fone with his Lady Jean Drummond, called Sir Robert Grahame of Innermeath, who died without ifhew. He had alfo a daughter Lady Lillias Grahame, married to John firft Earle of Wigton. She had to him, John, who fucceeded to be fecond Earle of Wigtoun, James laird of Boghal in Renfrew, and Malcolm Fleeming, who married Helen Bruce, the widdow of Sir Robert Murray of Abercarny. He begat fones, John, who was ane officer in all the Kings warrs, Alexander and William, who dyed both unmarried, and three daughters, Jean Fleeming, married to Adam Murray of Cardon, a fone of the Laird of Stanhope; Helen, who did not marrie; and the youngeft, Marie Fleeming, who was married to John Grahame, commiffar clerk of Dumblane, and hes a fone John Grahame, and three daughters.

Anna Drummond, fecond daughter to David Lord Drummond, was married to John, fecond Earle of Marr, Lord High Thefaurer of Scotland; fhe had to him John, the third Earle of Mar. He married Lady Jean Hay, daughter to Frances Earle of Erroll, and begat with her John, the fourth Earle of Mar, and tuo daughters, Lady Elifabeth Erfkine, and Lady Marrie Erfkine. Lady Marrie never married. Lady Elifabeth married Archbald Lord Napper: fhe had to him tuo fones, Archbald, now Lord Nappier, and John Napier, and three daughters, Mrs. Jean, Margaret, and Marie. John Napier was a hopefull youth, firft page to King Charles the Second, then cornet to his guard of horfe. He went, upon point of gallantrie, to ferve in the Englifh fleet againft the Hollanders, in anno   , where he was unhappily killed by a cannon fhot, to the great regraite of all who knew him. Mrs. Jean married Nicolfon of Carnock, [and] had a fone. Mrs. Margaret married Mr. Brifbane, and hes children. Mrs. Marie died a maid.

John, the fourth Earle of Mar, married Lady Jean Mackenzie, daughter to George Earle of Seaforth, and begot John, the fifth

David Lord Drummond's fecond daughter.

Earle, and three daughters. The firft, Lady Barbara Erſkine, married   Marques of Douglas, and hes to him a fone Archbald Earle of Angus; the fecond, Lady Marie, married   Earle of Glencairn, and hes a fone; the third, Lady Sophia, married Lord Pitfligo, and hes children. John, the fifth Earle of Mar, married Ladie Marrie Mauld, daughter to the Earle of Panmure, and hes children.

David Lord Drummond's third daughter.   David Lord Drummond's third daughter Lillias Drummond, wes married to David, thirteenth Earle of Craufurd : this was confidered fo noble a match, that there was a tocher given with her far beyond what was cuftomarie in thefe times, to wit, ten thoufand merks, and yet ſhe had no children. David had been married before to Jean Ker, daughter of the Lord Newbottle, bot was divorced from her : he was a fpender of the fortune, and a ryotous liver ; and left, by Jean Ker, a daughter, Lady Jean Lindfay.

David Lord Drummond's fourth daughter.   Catharine Drummond, the fourth daughter of David Lord Drummond, wes married to Sir John Murray of Tyllibardine, and had to him three fones, William, Patrick, and Mungo Murrayes, and five daughters, Anna, Jean, Lillias who married the Laird of Grant, Catharina, and Margaret. Anna Murray was married to Patrick, eleventh Lord of Glames; and was created Earle of Kinghorn by

1606.   King James the Sixth, in anno 1606. He dyed at Edinburgh in the
1615.   year 1615, and lyes burried at Glames. Patrick Earle of Kinghorn had a daughter, Anna Lyon, married to the Earle of Erroll ; and had to him Gilbert Earle of Erroll, and Margaret Lady Ker, after Lady Caffills. His fone John Lyon, begotten with his Lady Anna Murray, wes fecond Earle of Kinghorn. He married firſt Lady Margaret Erſkine, daughter to John Earle of Marr, bot had no children that came to age. His fecond wife was Lady Elifabeth Mauld, daughter

1647.   to Patrick firſt Earle of Panmure. He dyed at Huntly 1647, and lyes at Glames. His daughter, Elifabeth Lyon, was married to

Charles Gordone Earle of Aboyne, brother to Lues Marques of Huntly, who did bear to him children.

His Lady Elifabeth Mauld being a widdow, was married a fecond time to George Earle of Linlithgow, and had to him tuo fones and a daughter. John, fecond Earle of Kinghorne, had by his Lady Elifabeth Mauld, Patrick, the third Earle of Kinghorn. He changed his title from Kinghorn, to be now called Earle of Strathmore: he married Lady Helen Midleton, daughter to John firft Earle of Midleton, and begot children.

Margaret Murray, youngeft daughter to John Laird of Tullibardine by his Lady Catharina Drummond, was married to Sir James Hadden of Glenegles, the twelfth laird of that family: he begot Sir John, who fucceeded, and dyed anno 1624. Sir John Hadden was the thirteenth laird: he married Catharina Weems, daughter to the Laird of Weems, who after was made Earle. Sir John Hadden had with his lady, Catharina Weems, a fone, Johne, who dyed in the King of Suedens fervice in Pol, and three daughters; firft, Jean, married to Collonel Hacket, and hes a fone and a daughter; the fecond, Marie, married to David Brodie of Pitgeveny, brother to the Laird of Lethem; [and] Iffobella Hadden, married firft to Sir Harie Stirline of Ardoch, to whom fhe had one fone, Sir William Stirline, now of Ardoch: fhe married again to Collin Mackenzie, brother to the Earle of Seaforth.

1624.

Sir John Hadden of Glenegafke married a fecond time Margaret Frafer, daughter to the Lord Lovet, and widdow of Sir Robert Arburthnet. His fone Robert was made Vifcount of Arburthnet. Margaret did bear to Sir John, Mungo and Patrick Haddens. Mungo fucceeded to be the fourteenth Laird of Glenegafk: and married Anna Grant, brother-daughter of the Laird of Grant's, with whom he had tuo fones, John and David, and a daughter Margaret. Mungo married a fecond time Margaret Gray, daughter to James

176   THE GENEALOGIE OF

Gray of Ballegarney, relict of James Grahame of Monorgan; fhe had one daughter Jannet Hadden.

1606. Sir John Murray of Tyllibardine was firft created Lord of Parliament by King James the Sixth; and foone after, to wit, in anno 1606 upon the 18th of July, he was made Earle of Tullibardine. His eldeft fone William Murray, Mafter of Tullibardine, begotten upon Catharina Drummond, daughter to David Lord Drummond, married Lady Dorothea Stuart, daughter to John Earle of Atholl, begotten upon his Lady Jean Ruthven, daughter to William Earle of Gowrie, and by her right fucceeded to the Earledome of Athol. William Murray Earle of Atholl begat with Lady Dorothea Stuart a fone, John, next Earle. He married   Campbell, daughter to Sir Duncan Campbell of Glenurchie, and begat John who fucceeded, and Mungo who died unmarried. John, now Earle of Athol, was by King Charles the Second made Marques, anno 167 . He married Lady Emilia Stanely, daughter to   Earle of Derby, in England; and fell in, by the death of his Cufine, James Earle of Tyllibardine, without ifhew, to that eftate. John had with Lady Emilia Stanely, feven fones and three daughters, John Lord Murray, Lord Charles, Lord James, Lord Edward, Lord Mungo, Lord William, and Lord George; Lady Charlotte, Lady Emilia, and Lady Catharina Murrays.

Patrick Murray, the fecond fone of John Earle of Tullibardine, purchafed the eftate of Tullibarden from his elder brother William Murray Earle of Atholl, and had the title of Earle of Tullibardine, refigned by his brother in his favors, and confirmed by the King. He married   and begot James Earle of Tullibardin; who married Lady Lillias Drummond, daughter to John Earle of Perth; bot theire children dyed before they came to be married; fo the eftate went to the Earle of Atholl, afterwards made Marques of Atholl.

Sir Mungo Murray, the youngeft fone of John Earle of Tullibardine, by his lady Catharina Drummond, married a brother daughter

THE HOUSE OF DRUMMOND. 177

of David Murray of Balvaird, the firſt Lord Scoone and Viſcount of Stormonth, who dyed without iſhew; and ſo Sir Mungo Murray ſucceeded by vertew of a tailzie to be Lord Scoone and Viſcomte of Stormont, bot left no children, whereby the eſtate and honor againe returned to the family of Balvaird in Fyfe, who now are poſeſſors thereof.

Margaret Drummond, David Lord Drummond's youngeſt daughter, was married to Sir Archbald Sterline of Keer: ſhe had a ſone James, and Jean Sterlines. Jean married Sir William Drummond of Riccarton: vide Riccarton [page 155]. Sir James married Hume, daughter to the laird of Wadderburn, and begot Sir George, and tuo daughters: Marie Sterline, married to   Stewart of Blackhal, and had tuo ſones; one who ſucceeded, and ane other, Stuart, married to   Mitchell, heretrix of Kincarrochie. David Lord Drummond's youngeſt daughter.

CONCERNING JAMES DRUMMOND, SECOND SONE OF DAVID LORD DRUMMOND, FIRST LORD MADERTIE.

James Drummond, the youngeſt ſone of David Lord Drummond, was firſt called Lord Inchchaffray, becauſe of a *Commendam* he had of that Abbacy; purchaſſed from Alexander Gordon, abbot thereof, by David Lord Drummond, for a conſiderable ſoume of money, about the year 1560 or 61, in the beginning of the Reformation; and by King James the Sixth confirmed to his ſone James the Commendator, who afterward was created Lord Madertie by King James the Sixth, anno 1607. He married Jean Cheeſholm, daughter to Sir James Cheeſholm of Cromlix, third laird thereof. James Lord Madertie got James, firſt Lord Madertie.
1607.

2 A

178   THE GENEALOGIE OF

with his lady, Jean Cheefholm, the Barronie of Innerpeffrie; which barronie Jean Cheefholms father, Sir James, had with his lady Jean Drummond, daughter of Sir John Drummond of Innerpeffrie, which Sir John had no fones. James Lord Maddertie begot upon his lady Jean Cheefholm tuo fones, John Drummond, who fucceeded, and Sir James Drummond, the firft Knight of Machany, and four daughters, Lilias, Jean, Margaret, and Catharine.

OFF JEAN CHEESHOLME, LADY MADDERTIE, DAUGHTER TO SIR JAMES CHEESHOLME, SECOND OF THAT NAME, AND THIRD LAIRD OF CROMLIX, AND THE PEDIGREE OF HER FATHERS HOUSE.

The firft Laird of Cromlix.

Edmond Cheefholme, a fone of the Laird of Cheefholmes houfe in Teviotdaile, defcended from the Cheefholmes of Tindaile in England, married firft Margaret Sinclare, a widdow, and daughter of the houfe of Dryden: he begot with her James and Thomas Cheefholmes. James was a learned and wife man, firft preferred to be chapelaine to King James [the] Third; then he was fent to Rome, to Pope Innocent

1486. the Eighth, in the year 1486; who provyded him to the bifhoprick of
1533. Dumblane, where he dyed, and wes buried anno 1533. He had a halfe brother by his mother, called Sir John Ramfay of Balmane, page to King James [the] Third, much beloved by his mafter, whom the King preferred at the Road of Lauder 1482, when Cocheran, Rogers, and Homyll were hanged over the bridge.

Bifhop James had tuo natural fones, Mr. Malcolm and John Cheefholms. Mr. Malcolm begot Mathew; and his natural fone was Sir
1542. John Cheefholme, Archdeacon of Dumblane, 1542.

Thomas Cheefholme, brother to Bifhop James, and fecond fone to Edmond, had daughters Annas Cheefholme, Lady Newton and Ochtertyre ; and Janet Cheefholme, married to John Drummond of Pitzallonie, the fourth laird thereof, who had divers children with her, mentioned in the accompt of the houfe of Pitzallony.

Edmond Cheefholme, after the death of his firft wife, married Janet Drummond, daughter to James Drummond of Coldoch, brother to John Lord Drummond, and begot with her tuo fones, Sir James, who fucceeded, and William, and three daughters, Jannet, Beatrix, and Hellen Cheefholms.

William Cheefholm, the youngeft fone, was made Bifhop of Dumblane by a refignation of his uncle James, Bifhop of that fame bifhoprick, in the hands of Pope Clement the Seventh, in favors of William, who was confecrat before Bifhop James his deceafs, at Sterline, upon the 14th of Apryle 1527, by Gavine Dumbar, Archbifhop of Glafgow and Chancellor of Scotland, George Creichton Bifhop of Dunkeld, and Bifhop James Cheefholme affifting at the ceremonie. William Bifhop of Dumblaine had diverfe natural children, according to the cuftome of the clergie in thofe dayes. Jean Cheefholm, his daughter, begotten upon Lady Jean Grahame, daughter to William Earle of Montrofe, was married to Sir James Sterline of Keer, and had to him Sir Archbald Sterline of Keer, and James Sterline, his brother, killed in Dumblane by George Sinclair ; and alfo daughters, to wit, Elfpet Sterline Lady Marchifton, Helen Sterline Lady Duntreath, Barbara Sterline Lady Pohnaife, Margaret Sterline Lady Houftoune. Bifhop William wafted and put away the bifhops patrimonie, and reduced it to a mean benefice. He dyed, and was laid in the Cathedral of Dumblane, in the year 1564.

1527.

1564.

Jannet Cheefholme, the daughter of Edmond Cheefholme, begotten with his lady Jannet Drummond, was firft married to John Napier of Marchiftoune, who begot with her Archbald laird of Marchiftowne, and Jannet Napier Lady Powfowlls. Jannet Cheefholme, after the death of her firft hufband John Napier of Marchiftowne, was married a fecond time to Sir Alexander Seytoune of Touch and Tyllibodie, and did bear to him Walter Seytoune, who fucceeded, Alexander and James Seytons, with feveral daughters.

Beatrix Cheefholme, fecond daughter to Edmond Cheefholme, was firft married upon John Murray laird of Strowan, and buire to him Alexander Murray of Strowan. Alexander of Strowan married Margaret Redheuch, daughter to the laird of Cultebrogan. She bore to him John Murray of Strowan, and William his brother, and a daughter, Sybilla Murray, who was married upon David Murray of Lochland.

After the death of John Murray of Strowan, Beatrix Cheefholm his wife, married Henrie Sinclaire; fhe obtained from Bifhop William of Dumblane and chapter thereof, a few charter of the five merk land of Nether Ardoch and Drumlaw; and had to Henrie only a daughter, Marion Sinclare, who was heretrix of Ardoch. She was married upon William Sterline, brother german to Sir James Sterline of Keer, the father or grandfather of Sir Archbald Sterline of Keer. William Sterline begot with Marion Sinclar, Hendrie Sterline of Ardoch, and other fones; alfo he had   daughters, to witt, Jean Sterline Lady Kippenrofs, Elizabeth Sterline, married to Thomas Drummond of Wefter Corfkepplie, and Beatrix Sterline, married to William Sinclar of Galdwalmore, the father of old Hendry Sinclar.

Helen Cheefholm, the youngeft daughter of Edmund Cheefholm, begotten with Jannet Drummond was Lady Newton, and Dalgetie: her hufband, was called James Olyphant of Newton, and had with Helen Checfholm, Margaret, Chriftian, and Catharina Olyphants.

2. Sir James Cheefholm of Cromlix, eldeft fone to Edmund Cheefholm, with his lady Jannet Drummond, was the fecond laird of that family. He married Lady Catharine Grahame, fifter to William,

third Earle of Montrofe, and begot with her Sir James Cheefholm, who fucceeded, Mr. William and Mr. Alexander Cheefholms; and daughters, Barbara, Jannet Lady Kinfauns, Helen, and Beatrix Cheefholms. Mr. William Cheefholm, the fecond fone, was firft bifhop of Dumblane, for he fucceeded to his uncle, Bifhop William; bot that being in the time of the Reformation, his abode was fhort with that bifhoprick; then he went to France, and was made Bifhop of Vafon; which bifhoprick, after fome years, he demitted in favors of his nevoy, called alfo William Cheefholme, retered himfelfe from the world, turned Carthufian freer at Grenoble, and dyed at Rome.

Mr. Alexander Cheefholm, the youngeft fon of Sir James, begotten upon Lady Catharine Grahame, was parfon of Comrie. He married Jannet Buchannan, daughter to Walter Buchannan, natural fone to the laird of Lenie, and begot tuo fones, Walter and Alexander Cheefholmes, and daughters, Jean, Hellen, and Iffobell Cheefholmes.

Walter Cheefholme, the eldeft fone of Mr. Alexander, married Anna Drummond, daughter to Mr. Morife Drummond, the fecond fone of Malcolm Drummond of Boorland, whom he begot upon Agnes Drummond, his wife, daughter to George Drummond of Balloch. Walter Cheefholme was baylie of Dumblane: he begot with Anna Drummond many fones and daughters. The eldeft fone, James Cheefholme, dyed young; the fecond, Alexander Cheefholme, married Sara Bramftone, the widow of   , and daughter to Francis Bramftone, foveraigne of Belfaft, a town in the north of Ireland, near Carrick Fergus. She had to Alexander tuo daughters, Helen and Elifabeth Cheefholmes. Alexander himfelf hes long been Bayly of Dumblane. Walter the third fone, and Hendrie Cheefholme, the fourth fone, were both killed in the King's fervice, in our late unhappie warr. Alexander, the fifth and youngeft fone, was firft minifter at Newbottle, and thereafter at Corftorphin; he married

Margaret Coult, daughter to Mr. Oliver Coult, miniſter at Innereſk, and begot James and Jeane Cheeſholms.

Jeane Cheeſholm, the eldeſt daughter of Mr. Alexander Cheeſholm, perſon of Comrie, was married to Mr. John Sinclar, laird of Ulbſter in Catnes, a near kinſman to the Earle of Cathnes. She did bear to him Patrick Sinclar, who ſucceeded, and Henrietta Sinclar, married to Mr. William Abernethie, miniſter at   . Helen Cheeſholm, ſecond daughter to Mr. Alexander Cheeſholme, parſon of Comrie, married Hendrie Sinclar of Glaſſingall and Drumdowlls, but had no ſucceſſion. Hendrie Sinclar left his fortune to his nephew, James Sinclar. Iſſobella Cheeſholme, third daughter to Mr. Alexander Cheeſholm, parſon of Comrie, married firſt, Mr. Alexander Craig, laird of Roſecraig in the ſhyre of Bamffe, and had children to him. After the death of Mr. Alexander Craig, ſhe married Mr. Alexander Douglas, provoſt of Bamffe, and ſheriffe of that ſhyre. She did bear to him Iſſobella and Chriſtian Douglas. Iſſobella, the eldeſt, married   Cant, ſone to Mr. Andrew Cant, miniſter at Aberdeen, and hes a ſone called young Mr. Andrew Cant, now miniſter at the Colledge Kirk of Edinburgh. Chriſtian Douglas, the ſecond daughter, married

Jean Cheeſholme, the eldeſt daughter of Walter Cheeſholme, Bayly of Dumblane, was married upon James Sinclar, nephew to Hendrie Sinclar of Glaſſingall; ſhe had to him Mr. John, and Jean Sinclares. Eliſabeth Cheeſholme, the other daughter of Walter Cheeſholme, was married to Mr. James Scrimgeour, miniſter at Currie in Lothian, a kinſman to the Earle of Dundee, and hath children.

3. Sir James Cheeſholme, the eldeſt ſone of the former Sir James, begotten with Lady Catharine Grahame, was third laird of Cromlix. He married Jean Drummond, daughter to Sir John Drummond of Innerpeffrie, begotten upon Lady Margaret Stuart, widdow of the Lord Gordon, the daughter of King James the Fourth. Jean did

bear to Sir James four fones, Sir James who fucceeded, Mr. William, Sir John, and Thomas Cheefholmes; and four daughters, to wit, Jean Cheefholm Lady Maddertie, Helen Cheefholm Lady Kinfawns, Margaret Lady Mufchet, and Agnes Cheefholm Lady Marchifton.

Mr. William Cheefholme, the fecond fone, was born in Innerpeffrie, March 11th 1551, and bred up in France, and by the demiffion of William Bifhop of Vafon, his uncle, of that bifhoprick, in his favors, he was made Bifhop of Vafon, which he enjoyed all his lifetime. Sir John Cheefholm, the third fone, born in Dumblane, Auguft 1557, lived in France, married ane heretrix there, and had children, whereof we have no accompt. Thomas Cheefholme, the fourth and youngeft fone of this Sir James, begotten upon Jean Drummond, was born in Aguft 1559, he was portioner of Buttergafk, and dyed without heires. 1551. 1557. 1559.

Jean Cheefholm, the eldeft daughter of this Sir James, was born in Dumblane, upon the 13th of Jully 1555. She was married to James Lord Maddertie, and of theire fucceffion, it will fall to be fpoken in the pedigree of the family of Maddertie. Helen Cheefholm, fecond daughter, was born in Dumblane in Apryle 1562. She was married to _____ Charterefs laird of Kinfauns. Margaret Cheefholm, the third daughter, was born in Apryle 1567. She was married to Mufchet of that ilk, and had to him fones. Agnes Cheefholm, the fourth and youngeft daughter, was born in Dumblane the 4th of May 1568. She was married to John Napper laird of Marcheftowne, a fecond wife. She had fones, John Napier, Mr. Robert Napier of Kilcreuch, William and Alexander Napiers. 1562. 1567.

4. Sir James Cheefholme of Cromlix, eldeft fone to the laft Sir James, begotten with his lady Jean Drummond, was born at Muthill, upon the 10th of September 1550. He was the fourth laird of Cromlix, and married Dame Anna Beatton, daughter to Bettone laird of Creech: he begat with her Sir James Cheefholme, his eldeft fone, who fucceeded, and divers other fones and daughters. 1550.

5. Sir James Cheefholme of Cromlix, fone of the former Sir James, begotten upon dame Anna Bettone, was the fifth laird of Cromlix. He married dame Helen Sterline, daughter to William Sterline, brother to Ardoch, and begot with her tuo fones, James and John Cheefholmes, who both fucceeded to be lairds; and daughters, Helen Cheefholm, the eldeft, married to David Drummond, fecond laird of Innermay, of whofe fucceffion mention is made in the family of Innermay. Jean Cheefholm, the fecond, was married to John Grahame of Orchill, and had to him James, who fucceeded, and Mungo and William Grahames. James Grahame of Orchill married Lilias Olyphant, daughter to Sir Laurence Olyphant of Gafk, and had with her children.

Lilias Drummond, eldeft daughter to James, firft Lord Maddertie, was married to Laurence Lord Olyphant, a man of a vaft eftate, if he had underftood to manadge it. It was judged fo great a match, that James Lord Maddertie did give of tocher with her a greater foume, viz. 40000 merks, then almoft had been heard of in thofe dayes: fhe did bear to the Lord Olyphant only one daughter, Mrs. Anna Olyphant. She married Sir James Douglas, brother-german to William Marques of Douglas; he was created Lord Mordington by King Charles the Firft. The Lord Mordingtowne begot with Anna Olyphant a fone, William Douglas, and a daughter,   Douglas, married to Semple, Lord Semple.

Jean Drummond, fecond daughter to James Lord Maddertie, was married to Andrew Wood, laird of Largo, bot had no children. Margaret Drummond, third daughter to James Lord Maddertie, was married to James Muirehead, laird of Breadifholme: fhe had to him fones, James Muirehead who fucceeded, John Muirehead, and tuo daughters; the firft Lillias, married firft to Sir Walter Stuart of Minto, and afterward to Sir James Drummond of Machany, bot had no children; the youngeft, Margaret Muirehead, married to

Cleeland, laird of that ilk, who hes a fone,   Cleeland, and a
daughter, Margaret Cleeland, married firſt

Catharine Drummond the youngeſt daughter of James Lord Maddertie, wes married to Sir Andrew Rollo of Duncrub, created Lord
Rollo by King Charles the Second, 1650; he begat with her, daugh-   1650.
ters, Margaret, Jean, Anna, and Iſſobella Rolloes, and fones, James,
who fucceeded, Sir John Rollo of Bannockburn, Mr. Laurence Rollo,
Mr. Andrew, George, and Mr. William Rollo.

Margaret married Sir John Drummond of Carnock, of whom is that
family defcended. Jean married firſt, Robert Rollo of Powes, and had
to him a fone who fucceeded;   Rollo, who married Jean Murray,
daughter to the laird of Polmaife: Jean married a fecond huſband,
John Drummond of Pitzallonie. Anna Rollo was married to William
Mercer, laird of Clevadge; ſhe had to him a fone, James, who fucceeded, and married his uncle William Mercer's daughter, and begot
       Mercer, now of Clevadge; he married Jean Maxwell, daughter to Sir Patrick Maxwell of Newwark. Iſſobella Rollo was married
to   Haliday, laird of Tyllyboole, who had to him   Haliday,
now of Tylliboole, and three daughters.

Sir Andrew Rollo Lord Duncrub's eldeſt fone, was James fecond
Lord Rollo. He married firſt, Lady Dorothea Grahame, fiſter to
James firſt Marques of Montrofe, who dyed and left no children; to
his fecond wife, he married Lady Mary Campbell, fiſter to Archbald Marques of Argyle, who had to him tuo fones, Andrew who
fucceeded, and Archbald Rollo, and tuo daughters, Margaret, and
Marie Rollos. Andrew third Lord Rollo married Margaret Balfowre,
daughter to   Balfowre Lord Burghleigh, and hes children.

Sir John Rollo, fecond fone to Andrew firſt Lord Rollo, married
firſt, Iſſobella Cockburn, daughter to   Cockburn of Langton; ſhe
had three daughters, Iſſobella, Lady Kippenrofs, Anna Rollo married
to George Grahame of Pitcairnes, and Marion Rollo married to

Young, miniſter of Abbotſhal. Sir John's ſecond wife was Buchannan, daughter to the laird of Buchannan; he had by her Annabella Rollo, married to David Drummond of Innermay, younger. Sir John's third wife, Helen Sinclar, daughter to Sinclar of Roſline, had tuo daughters, Jean Lady Coxton, and Iſſobell.

Machanie.

1. Sir James Drummond of Machanie, Knight, youngeſt ſone of James Lord Madertie, married Catharina Hamilton ſiſter to John Lord Bargenie; he had with her ſones, Sir James who ſucceeded; ſecond, John a captain killed at the ſtorming of Newcaſtle, anno 1641; the third, Andrew Drummond a livetennant-collonel in oure late warrs, he dyed unmarried; fourth, Patrick; fifth, George; ſixth, David; ſeventh, William; eighth, Thomas: all dyed young in the warrs, ſome at home, ſome in France.

1641.

2. Sir James Drummond of Machanie, ſone to Sir James, was the ſecond of that family. He married firſt, Marion Halyburton, daughter to the laird of Pitcurr, bot had no children with her. He married for his ſecond, Lady Agnes Hay, daughter to Sir George Hay of Keillor, the brother of Francis Earle of Erroll, and widdow of Sir William Murray of Abercairney. Agnes Hay did bear to Sir James tuo daughters and tuo ſones, Lilias and Anna Drummonds, Sir John, who ſucceeded, and David Drummonds. Lilias wes firſt married to James Earle of Tullybardine, bot had no children to him; ſhe married a ſecond time to James now Earle of Perth, and hes born to him tuo ſones, John and Charles Drummonds. Anna Drummond youngeſt daughter to Sir James Drummond, was married to Thomas Grahame of Balgowan, and hes born to him children.

3. Sir John Drummond of Machany, ſone of the laſt Sir James, is the third laird of Machany. He married Margaret Stuart, daughter to Sir William Stuart of Innernytie, brother to Sir Thomas Stuart of

Garntyllie, and hes by her fones, James, John, and David, and tuo daughters, Anna, and Lilias Drummonds.

John, fecond Lord Maddertie, the fone of James, married Margaret Lefly daughter to Patrick, firft Lord Lundores, who was eldeft fone to Andrew Earle of Rothes by his fecond Lady, and was created Lord by King James the Sixth, 1600. Margaret Lefly Lady Maddertie her mother was Lady Jean Stuart, daughter to Robert Earle of Orknay, the fone of King James the Fifth, begotten upon Euphame Elphingftone, daughter to   Lord Elphingftone: Robert Earle of Orknay married Jean Kennedie, daughter to Gilbert Earle of Caffills, with whom he had Patrick fecond Earle of Orknay, beheaded, and Lady Jean Stuart, firft Lady Lundores, mother to Margaret Lady Madertie. Margaret Lefly Lady Maddertie had to John Lord Maddertie five fones, David who fucceeded; James and John, both captaines, dyed abroad in Germany; Lodovick a collonell in the fervice of King Charles the Second, fore wounded at Worcefter with King Charles the Second, anno 1651; after that he went and ferved Carolus Guftavus, King of Sueden, and was killed upon the wall at the ftorme of Coppenhagen, and honourably laid in the church of Elfeneour, anno 16 .

William Drummond the youngeft fone of John Lord Madertie except Lodovick, ferved long in the warrs at home and abroad; he paffed through all the degrees of military preferments, from a captaine untill he attained the honour to be a Generall-livetennant, in which ftatione he long ferved the great Zaar of Mofcovia, by whom he was noblie entertained and honourably difmiffed at the defire of King Charles the Second. After his return to Scotland he married Elifabeth Johnfton, daughter to Sir Archbald Johnfton of Warriftone, one of the Lords of the Colledge of Juftice, and widdow of Thomas Hepburn, laird of Humbie. Elifabeth Johnfton did bear to him a fone, William, and a

188   THE GENEALOGIE OF

daughter, Margaret Drummond. Elifabeth Johnfton dyed in England, and was burried in St. George his church, in Southwark, over againft London, anno 1679.

1679.   John Lord Madertie had alfo with his lady three daughters, Anna, Jean, and Margaret Drummonds. The eldeft, Anna Drummond, was married to Patrick Rattray, laird of Craighall in the Stormont, a very ancient family of above four hundred yeares ftanding. She had to him one fone, James Rattray, who fucceeded, and one daughter, Anna Rattray, who was married to John Ogilvie, laird of Balfoure in Angus, whofe children are

Jean Drummond, fecond daughter to John Lord Maddertie, was married to Patrick Grahame, laird of Inchbrakie, a family defcended of a brother of the houfe of Montrofe. She had to him tuo daughters, Anna and Margaret Grahames; the eldeft, Anna, was firft married to Patrick Smyth, laird of Rapnes in Orkney, to whom fhe had tuo daughters, Jean and Rebecka Smythes. Jean married Sir William Keith of Ludwhairn, defcended of the Earle of Marifchalls houfe, and hes to him children. Anna Grahame being a widdow, married Sir Robert Murray of Abercairney, ane old familie come from Sir Morife Murray, ftyled of Drumfhergort, of the houfe of Bothwell, and brother to Andrew Murray, the Governour of Scotland in the time of King David Bruces impriffonment in England, about the year 14 . Anna Grahame, Lady Abercairney, had to Sir Robert, her fecond hufband, tuo daughters, Anna and Emilia Murrayes, and four fones, William, Robert, John, and Maurice Murrayes.

Margaret Grahame, the youngeft daughter of Patrick Graham of Inchbrakie, was married to Sir Robert Nairne of Strathurd, one of the Lords of the Colledge of Juftice; who was created a Lord of Parlia-
1681.   ment by King Charles the Second, anno 1681, and ftylled Lord Nairne. He had only one daughter with his lady, called Margaret Nairne, heritrix of his whole eftate.

THE HOUSE OF DRUMMOND.

Jean Drummond had alfo five fones to her hufband, Patrick Grahame; George who fucceeded, Patrick, John, David, and James Grahames. George Grahame, laird of Inchbrakie, married Margaret Nicol, daughter to Patrick Nicol, a rich merchant in Edinburgh, and begot with her tuo fones, Patrick and George Grahames, and daughters. Patrick Grahame, the fecond fone of Patrick laird of Inchbrakie, married Anna Smyth, fifter to Patrick Smyth laird of Methven, who did bear to him children. John Grahame, the third fone of Patrick Grahame of Inchbrakie, now Poftmafter General of Scotland, married Margaret Drummond, eldeft daughter to David, third Lord Madertie, and had with her a fone, David, and a daughter, Emilia Grahames. David Grahame, the fourth fone, dyed in the fervice of the Eftates of Holland; and James Grahame the youngeft, is now ane Advocat at Edinburgh.

Margaret Drummond, youngeft daughter to John Lord Maddertie, was married to Sir Robert Creichton, a brother fone to William Earle of Drumfrees. She had to Sir Robert only tuo daughters, Jean and Anna; Jean was married to George Sterline, laird of Harbertihyre, and hes born to him children, William Sterline [and] Margaret Sterline.

David, third Lord Maddertie, the fone of John Lord Maddertie, married firft Alyfone Creichton, the eldeft of tuo daughters, heireffes portioners to theire father John Creichton, laird of Airelywight. She lived bot a few yeares, and left only a daughter, who dyed a chyld. David Lord Madertie, married the fecond time to Lady Beatrix Grahame, fifter to James, firft Marques of Montrofe; fhe did bear to him tuo fones, James and William, who both dyed young, and three daughters, Mrs. Margaret, Mrs. Beatrix, and Mrs. Marie Drummonds.

Third Lord Maddertie.

Mrs. Margaret was married to John Grahame, her cufine-german,

Poftmafter-General, fone to Patrick Grahame of Inchbrakie, and had to him a fone, David, and a daughter Emilia Grahames, mentioned before. Mrs. Beatrix Drummond, the fecond daughter, was married to John Lord Carmichael, and had to him, fones, James, William, Daniel, John, and David Carmichaels, and alfo daughters. Mrs. Marie Drummond, the youngeft daughter of David, Lord Madertie, wes married to John Hadden, younger of Glenegafk, the fone of Mungo Hadden of Glenegafk, reckoned amongft one of the ancienteft families in the fhyre of Perth ; his original was from Hadden of that ilk, in the fhyre of Roxburgh, who married the heretrix of Glenegafk, called Fauffyd. Mungo, now laird, is reckoned the fourteenth, from the firft that married the heretrix, diverfe yeares before King Robert the Firft, in a lineall race. Mrs. Marie hath born to her hufband tuo fones.

THE FAMILY OF LESLIE

[BLANK IN THE MANUSCRIPT.]

THE HOUSE OF DRUMMOND.

CONCERNING PATRICK LORD DRUMMOND, THE SONE OF DAVID, LORD DRUMMOND, AND THE FAMILIES DESCENDED FROM HIM.

[PARTITION ELEVENTH.]

Patrick, Lord Drummond, fucceeded to David, his father, and is reckoned the fifth Lord Drummond in order, albeit fome of his prediceffors were only Mafters, becaufe they dyed before their fathers, and fo came not to be Lords. He married Lady Margaret Lyndfay, daughter to David, laird of Edzell; who was made Earle of Craufurd by difpofition, and begot this Lady Margaret Lindfay, Lady Drummond, upon Jean Gray, daughter to the Lord Gray. Patrick Lord Drummond, had by this lady, Margaret Lindfay, tuo fones, James and John, who fucceeded one ane other to be Earles of Perth, [and] five daughters, Mrs. Catharina, Mrs. Lilias, Mrs. Jean, Mrs. Anna, and Mrs. Elifabeth Drummonds. *[Patrick Lord Drummond, the Sixteenth Cheefe of the name, 1571.]*

Mrs. Catharine Drummond, the eldeft, was married to James, Mafter of Rothes, fone and aire of Andrew, fifth Earle of Rothes, begotten upon Iffobella Hamiltone, daughter to Andrew Lord Evendale. James Mafter of Rothes begot with this lady, Catharina Drummond, tuo daughters, Lady Jean Lefly, and Lady Griffel; and a fone, John, who fucceeded to be Earle of Rothes. Lady Jean was married to Menzies of Weem: Lady Griffel Leflie was married to Alexander Earle of Dumfermline, and was his fecond wife. *[Catharina Patrick Lord Drummond's eldeft daughter.]*

John Earle of Rothes, the fone of James, the Mafter who dyed before Earle Andrew, his father, married Lady Anna Erfkine, daughter to John Earle of Marr, Thefaurer of Scotland. This Earle of Rothes was chofen Commiffioner for Scotland to treat with King Charles the Firft, concerning the differences then in debate, in the

THE GENEALOGIE OF

1641. year 1641. He begot with Lady Anna Erfkine a fone, John, who fucceeded, and tuo daughters. Lady   Leflie, the eldeft, was married to Hugh Earle of Eglingtone, who begot tuo fones, Alexander, now Earle of Eglingtone, and Mr. Frances Montgomerie, and four daughters. Mr. Frances wes firft married to Lady   Leflie, Countefs heretrix of Leven, who dyed without children; he married againe to

Alexander, now Earle of Eglingtone, the fone of Hugh, married   Creichton, daughter to William Earle of Dumfrees, and had by her daughters, and tuo fones; Alexander, now Lord Montgomerie, married to Lady Margaret Cocheran, daughter to William Lord Cochran, the fone of William, Earle of Dundonnald, and hes children. Hugh Earle of Eglingtone's four daughters were married as followes:—Lady Mary Montgomerie, the eldeft, was married to George, now Earle of Wintone, fhe dyed and left no liveing children; the fecond, Lady Chriftian Montgomerie, was married to John Elphingftone, Mafter of Balmerinoch, and hes children; Lady Anna Montgomerie, the third, was married to Sir Andrew Ramfay, laird of Wachtone, and hes children; Lady Elifabeth Montgomerie, the youngeft daughter, was married to   Dumbar of Balduine, and hes children.

Alexander Earle of Eglington's fecond fone   Montgomerie, and his daughters are

Lady   Leflie youngeft daughter to John Earle of Rothes, was firft married to Alexander Leflie Lord Balgonie, fone to Alexander Earle of Leven, and had to him a fone. Lady   Leflie, after the death of her firft hufband Alexander Lord Balgonie, fhe married the fecond time to Frances Earle of Bucleugh, to whom fhe had tuo daughters. Lady   Scot, the eldeft, was married to Walter Scot now Earle of Tarras, bot fhe dyed without children; Lady   Scot, the youngeft heretrix, was married to James

Duke of Montmouth and Bucleugh, natural fone to King Charles the Second, and hes to him children. Lady   Leflie was the third time married to David Earle of Weems, and had to him a fone and a daughter; the fone dyed young, whereby the daughter became heretrix of Weems : fhe was married to James Weems Lord Bruntifland, and hes to him children.

John Earle of Rothes, only fone to the laft John, was firft Thefaurer, then Lord High Chancellor of Scotland, General of all the Forces, Lord High Commiffioner, and at laft created Duke of Rothes. He married Lady   Lindfay, daughter to John Earle of Craufurd and Lyndfay : fhe had to him a fone who dyed young, and two daughters, Lady Margaret Leflie, and Lady Chriftiana Leflie. The eldeft was married to   Earle of Haddingtowne, in favors of whofe children of that marriage, the eftate and honour of the Earle of Rothes wes refigned : the Earle of Haddingtone hes children. Lady Chriftiana Leflie the youngeft daughter, was married to James third Marques of Montrofe, and hes to him James Lord Grahame.

Mrs. Lilias Drummond, fecond daughter to Patrick Lord Drummond, wes married to Alexander Seattone, one of the younger fones of George Lord Seatton, begotten upon Iffobella Hamiltone his wife. Alexander was firft Prefident of the Colledge of Juftice, then made a Lord of Parliament by King James the Sixth, and called Lord Fyvie; after that, he was created Earle of Dumferline, upon the 4th of March 1605; when he had been fome yeares Lord High Chancellor of Scotland. Alexander Earle of Dumferline begot with his lady, Lilias Drummond, only four daughters, to wit, Lady Anna, Lady Sophia, Lady Iffobella, and Lady Margaret Seattons. Lady Anna Seattone the eldeft daughter of Alexander Earle of Dumferline, was married to Thomas Erfkine Lord Fenton, afterward Earle of Kellie; fhe had to him three fones. The firft,   Erfkine dyed unmarried ; the fecond,   Erfkine fecond Earle of Kellie, he

margin: Lady Lilias, Patrick Lord Drummond's fecond daughter.

margin: 1605.

married   Dalyell daughter to Sir Robert Dalyell, who hes to him a fone; and the third fone Sir Charles Erſkine, Lyon King at Arms. Lady Sophia Seaton, fecond daughter to Alexander Earle of Dumferline, begotten with his lady, Lilias Drummond, was married to   Lindfay Lord Balcarras; who was a fecond fone of David laird of Edzell and Earle of Craufurd, and fo brother-in-law to Patrick Lord Drummond. This Lord Balcarras had with his lady, Sophia Seaton.

Lady Iſſobella Seaton, third daughter to Alexander Earle of Dumferline, begotten with his lady, Lilias Drummond, was married to John fecond Earle of Lauderdale; he was fone to Sir John Maitland of Thirleſtane, Chancellor of Scotland, made a Lord of Parliament
1590. by King James the Sixth, upon the 17th of May 1590, and called
1606. Lord Thirleſtane; afterward created Vifcount of Lauder, upon the
1623. 30th of Apryle 1606, and again in anno 1623 Earle of Lauderdale. Lady Iſſobella Seatone had to her hufband John Earle of Lauderdale one daughter, Lady Griſſel Maitland, who dyed a maid, and three fones; John who fucceeded, Robert, and Charles Maitlands.

Robert the fecond, married   Lundin, heretrix thereof; he had with her a fone who dyed unmarried, and two daughters, Sophia Lundin the next heretrix, and   Lundin her fifter. The eldeſt, Sophia, married John Drummond, fecond fone to James third Earle of Perth, who by her right is Laird of Lundin; he hes with her three fones and three daughters.   Lundin fifter [of] Sophia the heretrix, was married to James Carnegie of Phinheaven, fecond fone to   Earle of Northeſk, and hes to him children. Charles Maitland, the youngeſt fone of John Earle of Lauderdale, is a Lord of the Colledge of Juſtice, General of the Mint, and Thefaurer-deput: he married   Lauder, heretrix of Hattone, and is called Lord Hattone. His children are   Maitland, Lord Juſtice Clerk, married to Lady Anna Campbel, daughter to Archbald Earle of Argyle; his fecond fone, Sir John Maitland, ane advocate, married

THE HOUSE OF DRUMMOND. 195

to Lady Margaret Cuninghame, daughter to Cuninghame Earle of Glencairn.

John Earle of Lauderdale, the fone of John the fecond Earle by his lady, Iffobella Seatone, wes one of the Commiffioners of Scotland to the Parliament of England in the beginning of our late civill warrs; bot in the year 1648 he became of the Kings fyde, and in the year 1651 wes taken prifoner at Worcefter fight, and keept fo until King Charles the Second was happily reftored in the year 1660; then he was made fole Secretary of State of Scotland, and one of his Majefties Privy Councel of both Kingdomes: afterward he was honoured to be his Majefties High Commiffioner for Scotland to three or four feveral Seffions of Parliament; made Knight of the moft noble Order of the Garter, and at laft created Duke of Lauderdale. He married to his firft wife Lady   Hume, daughter to Alexander Earle of Hume, by whom he had one only daughter, Lady Marie Maitland, married upon John Hay Lord Yefter, eldeft fone and appeareand aire to John Earle of Tueddale, who hes children, fones,

John Duke of Lauderdale, after the death of his lady, married to his fecond wife Lady Elifabeth Murray, Comtefs of Dyfert, eldeft daughter and heirefs of William Murray Earle of Dyfert, and relict widdow of Sir Lionel Talmafh, ane Englifh knight; bot hes no children.

Lady Margaret Seatone, youngeft daughter to Alexander Earle of Dumferline, wes married to Colin M'Kenzie Earle of Seaforth; fhe had to him only tuo daughters: Firft, Lady   M'Kenzie, married to   Sinclar Lord Berrendaile; fhe had to him George Sinclar Earle of Caitnefs, who married Lady   Campbell, daughter to Archbald, late Marques of Argyle. The fecond was Lady Anna M'Kenzie, firft married to   Lord Belcarras.

Mrs. Jean Drummond, third daughter to Patrick Lord Drummond, wes married to Robert firft Earle of Roxburgh, and had to him one daughter Lady Sophia Ker, who dyed unmarried, and one fone, called Henrie Frederick Lord Ker. Robert Earle of Roxburgh was Lord

1648.

Jean, third daughter to Patrick Lord Drummond.

Privy Seal. After his Lady's death he married Lady Iffobella Douglas, youngeft daughter of William Earle of Morton, bot left him chyldlefs, and his eftate to his fones eldeft daughter; with this provifion, that fhe marrie Sir William Drummond, his grandchyld, youngeft fone to John Earle of Perth, which was accordingly performed.

Jean Drummond Lady Roxburgh wes a lady of excellent parts, for which fhe was preferred before all the ladyes of both kingdomes to be governefs to the young children of King Charles the Firft; which fhe performed with great applaufe and fatiffaction of both King and Queen.

Henry Lord Ker, the only fone of Earle Robert, married Lady Margaret Hay, daughter to William Earle of Errol, and had with her only four daughters, Lady Jean, Lady Anna, Lady Margaret, and Lady Sophia. Lady Jean, the eldeft, by her grandfathers appointment, was married to Sir William Drummond, youngeft fone to John Earle of Perth; who, by his Lady's right, was fecond Earle of Roxburgh, and begot with Lady Jean Ker four fones, Robert, who fucceeded, Harie, William, and John, and a daughter, Lady Jean Ker. Harie, the fecond, dyed unmarried; William, the fecond [third], is a hopefull youth; John, the youngeft, was chofen by William Lord Ballendine for his aire, and is now called John Ballendine, fecond Lord Ballendine. Lady Jean is yet a proper young maid. Robert third Earle of Roxburgh, fone to William the fecond Earle, married Lady Margaret Hay, daughter to John Earle of Tweddale, and hes with her   Lord Ker. Lady Anna Ker, fecond daughter to Henrie Lord Ker, wes married to John Earle of Wigtowne; and did bear to him only a daughter, Lady Jean Fleeming, married to Mauld, third Earle of Panmure, and hes children. Lady Margaret Ker, third daughter to Henrie Lord Ker, was married to the youngeft Laird of Innes, and hes   . Lady Sophia Ker, the youngeft of the four fifters, lives a maid, and is refolved to dy fo

THE HOUSE OF DRUMMOND.

Mrs. Anna Drummond, fourth daughter to Patrick Lord Drummond, was married firft to   Barclay, laird of Towie, and had to him a fone, Patrick Barclay, who fucceeded; and tuo daughters, Anna and Violett Barclayes. Anna Drummond, Lady Towie, was married a fecond time to   Frazer, Lord Muthell.

Mrs. Elifabeth Drummond, the fifth and youngeft daughter of Patrick Lord Drummond, was married to Alexander Elphingftone, the fourth Lord thereof; who had with her only one daughter, Mrs. Lilias Elphingftone, heretrix thereof. She was married to Alexander Elphingftone, her own cufine-germane, laird of Barnes, who, by her right was fifth Lord Elphingftone. He begot tuo fones, Alexander, who fucceeded to be fixth Lord; he married   Burnet, daughter to   Burnet, Archbifhop firft of Glafgow, then of St. Andrews, bot dyed without ifhew; and John, his brother, now feventh Lord Elphingftone, fucceeded. He married   Maitland Lauder, I know not which, eldeft daughter to Charles Maitland of Hattone, brother to John Duke of Lauderdale, and hes to him children, to wit,

Anna, fourth daughter to Patrick Lord Drummond.

Elifabeth, youngeft daughter to Patrick Lord Drummond.

Patrick Lord Drummond, after his Lady's death, married Agnes Drummond, daughter to Sir John Drummond of Innerpeffrie, after fhe had been firft wife to Hughe Campbell of Lowdone, next to Hugh Earle of Eglingtone, as hes been obferved, Partition Seventh.

OFF LADY MARGARET LINDSAY, DAUGHTER TO DAVID LYNDSAY, LAIRD OF EDZELL AND EARLE OF CRAUFURD, AND THE PEDEGREE OF THAT FAMILY.

The Earle of Craufurd, Cheefe of the Lyndfayes, deduces their original from one called Lyndfay, who did good fervice to King

THE GENEALOGIE OF

Kenneth the Second, in his warrs againft the Picts, about the year
839. 839; bot in regard theire wanted wrytes in thofe dayes, whereby to inftruct the matter, the credit of theire beginning (as alfo of diverfe other ancient families in the kingdome) depends upon tradition. Neverthelefs, we find them often infert as witneffes, amongft the great ones of the nation, in the charters granted by King Malcolm, called the Maiden, King William, King Alexander the Second and Third; efpecially one William de Lyndfay, and one Walter de Lyndfay, and after that, William the fone of Walter de Lyndfay, and David de Lyndfay of Glenefk, who went with King Alexander the Second, in company of King Lues the Ninth, of France, to the
1239. Holy Land, in the year 1239. Another, David de Lyndfay, Cubi-
1267. cularius Regis to King Alexander the Third, 1267; he it is was with the Bruce, at the killing of John Cummine in the kirk of Drumfrees. One called Willelmus de Lyndfay, Camerarius to King Robert the
1319. Firft, about the year 1319. There is one of them called Alexander
1332. de Lyndfay, flaine at the battle of Dupline, anno 1332.

There is alfo one David de Lyndfay, flaine at the batle of Halydon-hill, and James, his fone, the favorite of King Robert the Second; this James is reckoned to be the firft Earle of Craufurd, created
1373. by King Robert the Second, anno 1373. David de Lyndfay, his fone, was the fecond Earle of Craufurd; he was famous for fighting the Lord Wells, upon the bridge of London, which he was provocked to doe before King Richard the Second, on St. George's day; and for overcoming him, was rewarded by the King with the order of Knighthood of the Garter; he married a daughter of King Robert
1420. the Second, and dyed about the year 1420. The third Earle was David; he married Helen Abernethie, one of the aireffes of Hugh Lord Abernethie, and got with her divers lands in Angus; he dyed
1425. about the year 1425. The fourth Earle was David, called Earle Beardie, he was beat at the fight of Brechin, by   Earle of

Huntley, livetenant to King James the Second, 1452; and with the 1452.
Earles of Douglas and Rofs, forfaulted for rebellion, bot by the
mediation of Huntly he was reftored; for which he yeelded him the
precedencie, the fheriffhip of Invernes, the lands of Lochaber and
Badenoch. This Earle Beardie married Marie Ogilvie, daughter to
Sir James Ogilvie of Airely, thereafter Lord Ogilvy, and begot with
her David, who fucceeded, and Lady Elifabeth Lyndfay married to
John Lord Drummond, of whom mention is made in the Seventh
Partitione. David was the fifth Earle, and by King James the
Third made Duke of Montrofe, about the year 1486; he married Eli- 1486.
fabeth Hamilton, daughter to the Lord Hamiltone, but was forfaulted
by King James the Fourth, and reftored againe to be Earle, bot not to
the title of Duke; he dyed about the year 1493. Alexander was the 1493.
fixth Earle; he married Jannet Gordon, daughter to the Earle of
Huntlie, but dyed without children. John, his brother, was the
feventh Earle; he married Jeane Hume, daughter to the Lord Hume,
and was killed at the batle of Flowdon 1513, and had no ifhew. 1513.
Alexander of Auchtermonfie, his uncle, was the eighth Earle; he
married   Dumbar, heretrix of Auchtermonfie, before he came
to be Earle of Craufurd, and dyed anno 1516. 1516.

David, his fone, was the ninth Earle; he married Marrion Hay,
daughter to William, Earle of Erroll, and begot David, the wicked
Mafter of Craufurd. He married   Sinclar, daughter to the Lord
Sinclar of Ravenfheugh, and begot David. This wicked Mafter,
amongft other cruell acts, imprifoned his father, who out of dif-
pleafure againft his fone, difherifhed him, and difponed the Earledome
to David Lyndfay, laird of Edzell, who fett him at libbertie. David,
laird of Edzell, was the tenth Earle; he married firft Jean Gray,
daughter to the Lord Gray, and fhe had children to him, Margaret
Lyndfay, Lady Drummond. He, by the threats and allurements of
Cardinal Beatone, was forced to difpone the Earledome back againe

to David, fone to the wicked Mafter; and thereafter married the fecond time to   Campbell, daughter to Campbell, laird of Caddell, and begot with her fones. David, fone to the ill Mafter, was the eleventh Earle. He married Margaret Beatone, natural daughter to the Cardinal, begotten upon Marrion Ogilvie his concubine. David, his fone, was twelfth Earle; he married Jean Stuart, daughter to John Earle of Atholl. David, his fone, was thirteenth Earle; he married Jean Ker, daughter to Mark Ker Lord Newbottle and firft Earle of Lothian, the widdow of John Lord Boyd: he was a ryotous liver; he killed Sir Walter Lindfay of Balgayes; was therefore imprifoned in the Caftle of Edinburgh, where he dyed, bot had no fones. This David, the thirteenth Earle, was divorced from his firft lady, Jean Ker, with whom he had only a daughter, Lady Jean Lyndfay; and married the fecond time to Lillias Drummond, daughter to David Lord Drummond, bot had no children with her.

Sir Harie Lyndfay of Kinfaunes, was the fourteenth Earle; he was the fone of David the eleventh Earle, by Margaret Bettone, his wife; he married Beatrix Chartowres, heretrix of Kinfaunes. George his fone was the fifteenth Earle; he married Anna Sinclar, daughter to the Earle of Caithnes; he went to Germany, and was killed in the warr, and had no children.   Lodovick, his brother of the fecond marriage, begotten upon Euphame Shaw, daughter to the laird of Sauchie, wes fixteenth Earle of Cranfurd; he married Margaret Grahame, daughter to William Earle of Monteith, and widdow of the Lord Garleis; he difponed his title to John Earle of Lyndfay of Byres in Fyfe, referving his own lifetime; whereupon, after his death, John was confirmed in Parliament to that title, and it was ratifyed to him by King Charles the Firft; and now he hes his place in Parliament, which pertained to the old Earles of Craufurd: And thus the great and old family of Craufurd had an end, whereof there is not any direct cadet remaining except the Laird of Edzell.

THE HOUSE OF DRUMMOND.

CONCERNING JAMES LORD DRUMMOND, THE FIRST EARLE OF
PERTH, AND ELDEST SONE OF PATRICK LORD DRUMMOND.

PARTITIONE THE TWELFTH.

James the Fifth Lord Drummond, the eldeſt ſone of Patrick Lord Drummond, was ſent very young to be bred up in France; he came from thence to England, about a year after King James the Sixth of Scotland had injoyed the crowne of Great Brittaine. At that court he was in ſuch eſteem that the Council there did wryte him a courteous letter, imploying him in that honourable embaſſie with Charles Earle of Nottinghame, Lord Admiral of England, to Philip the Third, King of Spaine, for takeing that King's oath of ratification upon the articles of peace concluded betwixt the tuo Crowns, and for mediateing a peace betwixt Spaine and the Low Countries, which was performed with great approbation. After that embaſſie, James Lord Drummond returned to Scotland, where he, with Alexander Lord Hume, and Alexander Lord Fyvie, were all, upon the 4th of March 1605, created Earles of Perth, Hume, and Dumferline. James Earle of Perth married Lady Iſſobella Seattone, daughter to Robert firſt Earle of Wintone, and had with her only one daughter, Lady Jean Drummond. James Earle of Perth, when he was litle above twenty yeares of age, dyed at Seatton, and was burried in the collegiat church thereof. His Lady over him erected a ſtately marble monument, with this inſcription:

James Earle of Perth, ſeventeenth cheefe of the family.

1605.

Lady Iſſobella Seatton, Comteſs of Perth, after the death of her

202 THE GENEALOGIE OF

hufband, was married to Francis Stuart Earle of Bothwell, eldeft fone to Francis the former Earle, and had to him fones.

Lady Jean Drummond, only daughter to James Earle of Perth, was married to John Earle of Sutherland, who was the fixth Earle of the race of the Gordons, as will appear by the pedegree of the houfs of Sutherland. He begot with his lady tuo fones, John who fucceeded, and Robert Gordon, and a daughter. Robert dyed unmarried. John Gordon, the feventh Earl of Sutherland of that name, married

---

OF LADY ISSOBELLA SEATTONE, COUNTESS OF PERTH, AND THE FAMILY OF THE EARLES OF WINTON, HER FATHER.

The Earle of Winton is cheife of the Seatones, and he reckones his defcent from one Dougall, who, in the reigne of King Malcolm Canemore, for his good fervice got the land of Seaton, fo called becaufe they ly near the fea, in the fhyre of Lothian. This Dougal, from thefe lands, affumed the fyrname Seatone, becaufe, about thefe dayes fyrnames grew to be in fafhion. The next we find is Philip de Seatowne, to whom King William grants a charter of the lands of Seatowne, Winton, &c. and therein its faid, *quae terrae ad predecessores ejus perprius pertinuerunt.* In a charter of confirmation by King Alexander the Second, I find thefe witneffes, William de Bofco, Chancellor; Walter the fone of Alan, Senefcal; Alexander de Seaton,
1222. &c. and this is about the year 1222 or 1223.

After this Alexander, we find Sir Chriftopher Seaton, who married Chriftian Bruce, fifter to King Robert the Firft. The race of the family, he being reckoned for the firft, follows orderly as they

THE HOUSE OF DRUMMOND.

fucceeded. The fecond was Sir Alexander Seaton, governour of Berwick-upon-Tueed. I have feen a charter of King Robert Bruce, concerning the patronage of a kirk, which concludes thus: *Testibus Bernardo Abbate de Aberbrothick Cancellario nostro, Willielmo de Lyndsay Camerario nostro, Waltero Senescallo Scotiae, Jacobo Domino de Douglas, Roberto de Keith Mareschallo nostro, et Alexandro de Seaton militibus: apud Bervicum super Tueedam*, 12 *Aprilis, anno regni nostri* 13; which falls to be the year 1318. And in the year 1333, in the minority of King David Bruce, he expreffed wonderfull fidelitie and courage in maintaineing the town of Berwick againft King Edward the Third of England, where his Lady fhew a mafculin fpirit whilles a fad tragedie was acted upon her tuo fones Thomas and Alexander. This Sir Alexander, had one other fone Alexander Seaton, who married Elifabeth Gordon, heretrix of Huntly, whofe fone Alexander Gordon, was the firft Earle of Huntly, anno 1449.

The third of the family of Winton was William; he married Jean Hallyburton, daughter to Sir Walter of Dirletoune; and was the firft Lord Seatone, created by King Robert the Second. The fecond Lord was John, the fone of William; he married Jannet Dumbar, daughter to George Earle of March; he was made *Senescallus Hospitij* to King James the Firft; he dyed anno 1445. The third Lord was George; he married Jean Stuart, daughter and airefs to John Stuart Earle of Buchan and Conftable of France. The fourth was John, Mafter of Seatton; he married Jannet Lyndfay daughter to the Lord Lyndfay of the Byres, and dyed before his father. The fifth was George, his fone; he married Margaret Campbell daughter to Collin Earle of Argyle, he dyed anno 1490; and had affumed the armes of the Earle of Buchan. The fixth Lord was George; he married Jean Hepburn, daughter to Patrick Earle of Bothwell, and was flaine at Flowdone. The feventh Lord was George; who married

1318.
1333.

1449.

1445.

1490.

THE GENEALOGIE OF

Elifabeth Hay, daughter to the Lord Yefter. The eighth Lord was George ; who married Iffobella Hamilton, daughter to Sir William of Sanquair. He was fent to France for concluding the marriage betwixt our Queen Marie and Francis Dauphine of France : (His fecond fone Alexander, was Earle of Dumfermline, and Chancellor of Scotland, married to Lilias Drummond, daughter to Patrick Lord Drummond :)
1584. He dyed 1584; he hes a fine monument in the church of Seatone.

The ninth Lord was Robert; created Earle of Wintone by King
1600. James the Sixth, upon the 14th of September 1600. He married Margaret Montgomerie, the only daughter of Hugh Earle of Eglingtone. His eldeft fone was not right; George the fecond fucceeded, and Alexander the third fone was by adoption or tailzie, made Earle of Eglingtone; this is he was called Old Grayfteel. Iffobella Seaton Comtefs of Perth was this Earle Robert's daughter. George the fecond fone of Robert, was the fecond Earle of Wintone ; he married Lady Anna Hay, daughter to Francis Earle of Errol. George his fone was the third ; he married Lady Henrietta Gordon, fecond daughter to George Marques of Huntly ; he dyed before his father. George his fone was fourth Earle of Wintone ; he married his cufine Lady Mary Montgomery, daughter to Hugh Earle of Eglington, bot hes no children.

OF THE EARLE OF SUTHERLAND HIS FAMILY WHO MARRIED LADY JEAN DRUMMOND.

The old Earles of Sutherland were Cheefes of that name, and produces now the faireft evidents for theire antiquitie as noble, of any of the nobilitie extant at this day ; for they are defcended of one Allan

THE HOUSE OF DRUMMOND.

Thane of Sutherland, whofe fone Walter tooke that fyrname for the family, and was created Earle of Sutherland by King Malcolm the Third, called Keandmore, in the year 1062; from him they reckon the progrefs of the fucceffion in this order. The firft, Earle Walter, the fone of Alane the Thane. The fecond, Earle Robert, who built the caftle of Dunrobin, fo called from his own name. Third, Hugh commonly called Frefkin. He difponed the lands of Skibo, to the Archdean of Murray, in the reigne of King William. Fourth, Earle Hugh, who was imployed by King William to apprehend Harrold Guthrie, Thane of Cathnes, for killing the bifhop of that fea. Fifth, Earle William, who overcame the Danes in a battle at the Ferrie of Wnes in Sutherland; he dyed and lyes at Dornock, anno 1248. Sixth, Earle William, who was with King Robert the Firft at Bannockburn batle; he lived to a great age, and dyed anno 1325. Seventh, Earle Kenneth; he married   Mar, daughter to Duncan Earle of Mar, governour in King David the Second his minoritie. Kenneth was flaine at the batle of Hallidone Hill, 1333. Eighth, Earle William; he married Margaret Bruce, uterin fifter to King David the Second, and dyed anno 1370. Ninth, Earle Alexander, who married Mabella, daughter to George Dumbar Earle of March. King David Bruce his uncle, defygned him once for his fucceffor to the crowne : he dyed 1389. Tenth, Earle Nicolaus; he married   M'Donald, daughter to the Lord of the Ifles, and dyed about the year 1399. Eleventh, Earle Robert; he married   Dumbar, daughter to the Earle of Murray, and dyed anno 1442. Twelfth, Earle John; he married   Baillie, daughter to the Laird of Lamingtowne, and dyed 1460. Thirteenth, Earle John; he married againe a daughter to Macdonald Lord of the Ifles, and dyed anno 1508. Fourteenth, Earle John; he never married, and dyed anno 1513. He left the earledom to his fifter Lady Elifabeth Sutherland, who was ferved heirefs to her brother at Invernefs upon the 10th of October 1514.

1062.

1248.
1325.

1333.

1389.
1399.

1460.
1508.
1513.
1514.

She married Adam Gordon Lord of Aboyne, fecond fone to George fecond Earle of Huntly, and Chancellor of Scotland, begotten upon Lady Jean Stuart, daughter to King James the Firſt. Adam retained the fyrname of Gordone, which was tranfmitted to his pofterity, and the name of Sutherland fuppreffed: He was the firſt Earle of the
1531. name of Gordone by the right of his wife, and dyed 1531. Second, Alexander Gordone, his fone, who married Lady Jean Stuart, daughter to the Earle of Atholl, and dyed before his father. Third, Earle John Gordone, fone to Alexander, who fucceeded to Adam his grandfather in the Earledome of Sutherland: he was made by Queen Marie the Regent, after the death of her hufband King James the
1547. Fifth, Livetennant benorth Spey, anno 1547. He went to France with the Queen, where, by the French King Henrie the Second, he was made a Knight of the Order of the Cockell, called the Order of St. Michaell. He married Eleonora Stuart, daughter to Mathew Earle of Lennox, and widdow of William Earle of Airroll. He was
1567. poifoned at Garvie, bot dyed at Dunrobine, 1567. Fourth, Earle Alexander, his fone; he married Jean Gordone, daughter to George Earle of Huntly, divorced from John [James] Earle of Bothwell: he
1594. dyed at Dunrobin 1594. Fifth, Earle John fucceeded to his father; he married Anna Elphingſtoune, daughter to Alexander Lord Elphingſtone, Thefaurer of Scotland. John Earle of Sutherland dyed at
1615. Dunrobin, and was interred at Dornoch 1615. Sixth, Earle John fucceeded his father; he married Lady Jean Drummond, daughter to James Earle of Perth. He caufed himfelfe be ferved heir and
1630. retowred, anno 1630, to William Sutherland, the fifth Earle of Sutherland, who lived in the reigne of King Alexander the Second and dyed anno 1248: This Earle John dyed anno 16 . Seventh, John Earle of Sutherland, his fone, married Lady   Weems, daughter to the Earle of Weems, and relict of the Earle of Angus, the Marques of Douglas eldeſt fone. He begot   Lord

Stranaver, who married Lady Cochran, daughter to the Lord Cochran.

It is remarkable that this ancient Houfe of Sutherland, by the Ladyes they have matched with, is often come of the Drummonds. Firſt, Adam Gordon Lord of Aboyne, the firſt Earle of Sutherland of the name of Gordon, by the right of the heretrix Eliſabeth Sutherland his Lady, was great-grandchyld to Queen Annabella Drummond, and fecond fone to Lady Jean Stuart Counteſs of Huntly her grandchyld, the daughter of King James the Firſt, married to George ſecond Earle of Huntly. Secondly, Alexander Gordon, the fourth Earle of Sutherland of that name, married Lady Jean Gordone, daughter to George Earle of Huntley; and this George was grandchild to Mrs. Margaret Drummond, the eldeſt daughter of John Lord Drummond by his daughter Lady Margaret Stuart, begotten by King James the Fourth. Thirdly, John Gordon, fifth Earle of Sutherland of that name, married Anna Elphingſtone, daughter to Alexander Lord Elphingſtone, which Alexander was the fone of Robert Lord Elphingſtone, begotten with Margaret Drummond, daughter to Sir John Drummond of Innerpeffrie. And laſtly, John Gordon, the ſixth Earle of Sutherland of that name, married Lady Jean Drummond, daughter to James Earle of Perth, with whom he begot John, the ſeventh Earle, now liveing.

THE GENEALOGIE OF

OFF JOHN, SECOND EARLE OF PERTH, THE SONE OF PATRICK LORD
DRUMMOND, AND BROTHER OF JAMES FIRST EARLE OF PERTH.

PARTITIONE THIRTEENTH.

John fecond Earle of Perth, eighteenth cheefe of the family.

John, fecond Earle of Perth, fucceeded to his brother James, who had no fones. He was not only a great favourer of learning and learned men, bot himfelfe was alfo very learned in all kinds fit for a nobleman. He fpent his younger yeares with great improvement in the moft famous univerfities of France, where he was when his brother 1612. Earle James dyed. He fucceeded about the year 1612, and married Lady Jean Ker, eldeft daughter to Robert Earle of Roxburgh by his firft wife   Maitland, daughter to John firft Earle of Lauderdaile. John Earle of Perth, had by his lady, four fones, James who fucceeded, Robert, John, and William Drummonds; befyde Harie, who was the eldeft, and dyed a child, and tuo daughters, Lady Jean and Lady Lillias. Lady Jean Ker, Countefs of Perth, lived in great efteem with all that knew her, and dyed much regrated about the 1622. year 1622.

John Earle of Perth, her hufband, lived after her death a widdow, the fpace of near forty yeares, he dyed about the age of eighty; they lye both interred in the Collegiat Church of Innerpeffrie. He was one of his Majefties Privy Councell, and well deferved to be fo, for he was verfed in all found and folid knowledge; witnefs his library, not for oftentation, a fault many are guilty of, bot for ufe; all the volumes of thefe many bookes being marked with his own hand, where he obferved the moft material and remarkable paffages; and thus he made a furvey of all the beft men's learning, being himfelf compleat in all vertue and fingular worth. The ancient houfe fuffered

THE HOUSE OF DRUMMOND.

no prejudice, bot on the contraire became to have acceſſions by his induſtrie and acqueaſts. His loyaltie to his prince was untainted, notwithſtanding the great difficulties both himſelfe and his ſones fell into, dureing the late civill warrs; he payed great ſoumes of money as fynes, for his ſones joining themſelves with the King's party againſt the preſent governoures of the realm; his houſe was garriſoned, and moſt of his eſtate ruined by the army of Oliver the Uſurper; in all the mutationes of the time, his conſtancy was never brangled; he was juſt to all, and charitable to every one who was a trew object of it; in a word, for his rare qualities, he deſerved to have lived up to Neſtor's yeares.

His ſecond ſone, Robert Drummond, dyed on his travells through France. His third ſone, Sir John Drummond knight, of Logialmond, married Griſſell Stuart, daughter to Sir Thomas Stuart of Garntullie, and begot with her tuo ſones; Thomas, who ſucceeded him, bot left no children, and William of Ballathy, who left tuo ſones, John and Thomas.

Sir William Drummond, the youngeſt ſone, was Collonell of a foot regiment in the ſervice of the Eſtates of Holland. He was adopted heire to his grandfather, Robert Earle of Roxburgh, and married Lady Jean Ker, the eldeſt daughter of Henrie Lord Ker, who was the only ſone of Robert Earle of Roxburgh, by whoſe right he was the ſecond Earle of Roxburgh; his children are already mentioned in the Eleventh Partition, where we ſpoke of Patrick, Lord Drummond's third daughter, Jean Drummond, Lady Roxburgh, and theſe deſcended of her.

Lady Jean Drummond, eldeſt daughter to John Earle of Perth, was bred up with her aunt, Lady Jean Drummond Counteſs of Roxburgh, at the Court of England. She was courteous, beautifull, and good, to that degree as ſhe might have well been judged compareable, if not preferable to any of the ladys in her time. She was married to

John Lord Fleeming, afterwards third Earle of Wigtone, begotten betwixt John fecond Earle, and Lady Margaret Livingftone, daughter to Alexander firft Earle of Linlithgow.

Lady Jean Drummond, Comtefs of Wigtone, did bear to her Lord, tuo daughters, Lady Margaret, and Lady Lillias Fleemings; the eldeft dyed a maid, and the other was married, bot by her own advyce only. She had alfo fix fones, John, who fucceeded; the fecond, Robert, a youth of much expectation, bot he dyed unmarried; third, James; fourth, Harie, both dyed unmarried; the fifth, William, he was aire to his brother John, by defect of fones; and the youngeft, Charles Fleeming, now a Captaine in the King's fervice.

John fourth Earle of Wigtone, eldeft fone of the laft Earle John, begotten upon Lady Jean Drummond, was married to Lady Anna Ker, fecond daughter to Henrie Lord Ker, fone to Robert Earle of Roxburgh. He had by her only one daughter, Lady Jean Fleeming. married to George Mauld, third Earle of Panmuire, who hes children.

William fifth Earle of Wigtone, the fone of Earle John, begotten with Lady Jean Drummond his Countefs, fucceeded to his elder brother, Earle John, for want of ifhew-male. He married Lady Henrietta Seatone, daughter to Charles fecond Earle of Dumferline, and hes by her tuo fones.

Off the Familie of Wigtone.

The Earles of Wigtone reckons theire original from a valiant man, one Baldwine, who came from Flanders to Scotland, about the dayes of King Alexander the Third, and was called Fleeming from his countrey, for the Frenches call the men of Flanders Flammans. The firft lands they poffeffed wes Barrochen and Foolwood, in the

THE HOUSE OF DRUMMOND. 211

thyre of Renfrew. The fucceffor of Baldwine was Malcolm Fleeming, commonly called good Sir Malcolm, bot by Buchannan and Leflie, Robert Fleeming; he very opportunely met King Robert Bruce at Lochmaben, from whence he went to Drumfreefs, and was with the King at the killing of John Cummin; for which fervice and his conftant afiftance to the King thereafter, he got Cummernauld, and the lands belonging to the Cumins in Cliddefdale, and was made Lord Fleeming. His fone Malcolm was created Earle of Wigtone by King David Bruce, in the thirteenth year of his reigne, anno 1342. There is a charter granted by this King David to this Malcolm, of fome lands in Galloway. This Earle Malcolms fecond brother, Gilbert, married one of the three coheireffes of Simon Lord Frafer, and got with her the lands of Biggar, called Boghall. The firft Earle Malcolm's fone was Patrick Fleeming, fecond Earle of Wigtone. He dyed at the batle of Hallydonhill, anno 1333; and his fone, Thomas Fleeming, third Earle of Wigton, a prodigal man, fold the Earledome of Wigton, with the title, to Archbald Earle of Douglas, called the fifth Earle, the fone of Archbald Tyneman, and the reft of the patrimonie to others: So the fucceflion failed in the perfon of Earle Thomas, and then Malcolm Lord Fleeming, the fone of Gilbert Fleeming of Bigger, grand uncle of Thomas, fell to be cheefe of the family, and was bot Lord Fleeming. He purchaffed the barronies of Lainzie and Denny; and of this Malcolm are the Lords Flemming and Earles of Wigtone defcended, whereof the prefent John is the fixth Earle. They were a fecond time made Earles, by King James the Sixth, anno 1606.

1342.

1606.

The family of Wigtone are divers times allyed with and defcended of the houfe of Drummond; firft, John Lord Fleeming, about the year 1483, married Eupheme Drummond, third daughter to John Lord Drummond; and this John's male line with her lies not fince failled, for John the firft Earle was John Lord Drummond's great

1483.

grandchild. Secondly, John firft Earle of Wigtone married Lady Lillias Grahame, daughter of John Earle of Montrofe, who was chancellor and viceroy of Scotland, whom he begot upon Jean Drummond, the eldeft daughter of David Lord Drummond; fo that John fecond Earle of Wigtone, the fone of Lady Lillias Grahame, was great grandchild to David Lord Drummond. Thirdly, John the third Earle of Wigtone, the fone of John the fecond Earle, married Lady Jean Drummond, eldeft daughter to John Earle of Perth; fo that the prefent fixth Earle of Wigtone is again great grandchild to John Earle of Perth.

Lady Lillias Drummond, fecond daughter to John Earle of Perth, with his lady, Jean Ker, Countefs of Perth, after the marriage of her fifter Lady Jean Drummond, Countefs of Wigtone, was bred at court with her aunt Lady Jean Drummond, Countefs of Roxburgh; and was married to James Earle of Tullibardine, the fone of Patrick Earle of Tullibardin, who purchafed the Earledome from his elder brother William, who by marrying the heretrix of Atholl became Earle thereof. Lady Lillias Drummond had tuo fine gentlemen to her fones.

OFF LADY JEAN KER, COUNTESS OF PERTH, DAUGHTER TO ROBERT EARLE OF ROXBURGH, AND HER FATHER'S FAMILY.

1330. The Syrename of this family is Ker or Car, and had its beginning in Scotland, 1330, in the dayes of King David Bruce; for then came to Scotland, from France, Robert and Ralphe Kers. Whether they were out of the family of Barron Ker in Normandy, or from England out of the barronie of Kershall in Lancafhyre, which hes fpread it felfe through the counties of Lincoln, Bifhoprick, and Northumber-

THE HOUSE OF DRUMMOND.

land, which laſt tuo lyes near to the border of Scotland, is uncertaine. It is queſtioned which of the tuo brothers was the elder. Robert got the lands of Aldtowneburn and the country about Beaumont; and of him is the family of Cefsfoord, now Earles of Roxburgh. Ralphe got the lands about the watter of Jedd, which he named Kerſheugh; and is the original of the family of Ferniherſt, of whom are the Earle of Lothian and Lord Jedburgh : They are all confiderable families, and conteſts which of them is the cheefe, and yet all the three will yeeld to ane other ſmal familie for antiquitie, to wit, the Kers of Kerſland, in the ſhyre of Aire and Baylyrie of Cuninghame.

Off the houſe of Ceſſoord, the firſt who was advanced to the dignitie of ane Earle was Robert, created Earle of Roxburgh by King James the Sixth, anno 16 . He married firſt Lady   Maitland, daughter to John firſt Earle of Lauderdale, and Chancellor of Scotland. Earle Robert had with her three daughters; the firſt, Lady Jean Ker, Countefs of Perth, of whofe offspring we have already treated ; the fecond, Lady Iffobell Ker, married to the Viſcount of Dudhop; ſhe had   Scrimgeour, Earle of Dundie; the third, Lady Mary Ker, Countefs of Southefk, mother to   now Earle of Southefk, and Lady Catharina Carnegie Countefs of Airoll, and Lady Jean Carnegie Vicountes of Storemont. Robert Earle of Roxburgh married a fecond time to Lady Jean Drummond, daughter to Patrick Lord Drummond ; of whom alfo we have treated fullie in the Eleventh Partition. Robert Earle of Roxburghe married a third time Lady Iffobella Douglas, daughter to William Earle of Mortone, bot had no children by her.

THE GENEALOGIE OF

OFF JAMES, THIRD EARLE OF PERTH.

PARTITION THE FOURTEENTH.

James third
Earle of Perth,
nineteenth
cheefe of the
family.
1661.

James, third Earle of Perth, fucceeded to his father, Earle John, about the year 1661. He was compofed of kindnes, conftancy, and juftice. After he had been bred a whyle in France, and at the court of England, he returned home, and married Lady Anna Gordone, eldeft daughter to George fecond Marques of Huntly, whom he begot upon Lady Anna Campbell, daughter to Archbald Earle of Argyle.

James Earle of Perth, had with his lady, tuo fones, James, who fucceeded, and John, and a daughter, Lady Anna Drummond. John Drummond, the youngeft fone, married Sophia Lundin, heretrix of Lundin. She was the eldeft daughter of Robert Maitland, fecond brother to John Duke of Lauderdale, who married her mother Londy, and fhe being alfo heretrix, he was, by her right, Laird of Lundin, with provifion, that the children fhould ftill keep the name of Lundin.

The prediceffor of this family, belonging to the Lairds of Lundy of that ilk, was Robert Londy or Lundin, a naturall fone of King William's whom he begot at London, the time of his captivity with King Henrie the fecond of England, to whom King William gave the lands of Lundy in Fyfe; fo that, whether Robert had his name Lundy from the land, or the land from him becaufe of his being born at London, is uncertaine. This Robert is frequently defigned, in King William's charters, amongft the witneffes, *Robert de London filio nostro*, and in his own wryttings he calls himfelfe *Robertus de London filius Regis Scotiae*. From this Robert, the firft of the name

in that family, to the laſt, John Lundin, who was father-in-law to
Robert Maitland, there hes been about fourteen generations ſucceed-
ing in right maſculine line, without interpoſition of ane heire female,
or the ſubſtitution of one brother to ane other.

John Drummond, now of Lundy, is Conſtable of the Caſtle of
Edinburgh, Maſter of the Ordinance, and one of his Majeſtie's moſt
honourable Privy Councell; he hes, by his firſt lady, Sophia Lundy,
three ſones.

After his Lady's death, he married   Wallace, daughter to Sir
Thomas Wallace of Craigie Wallace, one of the Senatores of the
Colledge of Juſtice, and Lord Juſtice Clerk of Scotland, by whom
he hes children.

Lady Anna Drummond, the only daughter of James the third
Earle of Perth, was married upon John, twelfth Earle of Airrol, who
was neareſt in blood to the laſt Earle Gilbert the eleventh Earle, who
dyed without ſucceſſion; for John the twelfth Earle of Airroll was
ſone to Sir Andrew Hay, the ſone of Sir George Hay of Keillor,
brother [to] Francis ninth Earle of Airoll, and Gilbert the eleventh
Earle, was the ſone of William the tenth Earle, and the grand-child
of Francis the ninth Earle; ſo that to Earle Francis, Earle Gilbert
was grand-child, and Earle John his grand-nephew; and the ſucceſſion
runs thus: John, the grand-nephew of Earle Francis, ſucceeded to
Francis his grand-child Earle Gilbert.

Lady Anna Drummond hes to her Lord, ſones.

OFF THE FAMILY OF ERROLL.

The Hayes of Erroll are reckoned amongſt the moſt ancient, and
moſt noble families in Scotland. The beginning was long before ſyre-

names (excepting patronimicks) were known or ufed in the nation; to wit, in the reigne of King Kenneth the Third, about the year 980. The firft of them was a valiant dareing countrie laboureing-man, called Hay, who being at his plowing with his tuo fones, near the field where the batle of Luncarty wes fought, not far from the toun of Bertha, now Perth, and feeing his countrymen the Scots flying from the Danes, and deferting the fight, he with his fones, haveing no other arms bot the yocks of the oxen wherewith they were plowing, for it was then *furor arma ministrat*, fet themfelves in a ftrait pafs whither the army was flying, where, with fuch courage and ftrength they made refiftance, and ftopped the forerunners, that they forced the beatten army of the Scots to turn upon the victorious Danes, and put them to flight with a total route. This great victory of the Scots over the Danes, was wholly afcribed to this Hay and his fones, whom the King honoured with the Barrony of Erroll, lying in the Carfe of Gowrie and fhyre of Perth; giving him alfo a noble and remarkable coat of armes, viz. three red fheilds, within a whyte, intimateing, that Hay and his tuo fones had proven the three fheilds of theire countrey, againft the Danes. This man's pofterity, when fyrenames came in ufe, made choife of his name Hay for the fyrename of his family; which hes continowed ever fince, in great honour, dureing the government of all our Kings in ane orderly fucceffion, for the fpace of 320 yeares. And about that time, the head of the family, called Gilbert Hay, ane conftant and faithful friend and fervant to King Robert the Firft in all his troubles, was, for his good fervice, rewarded with the heritable office of Great Conftable of Scotland, which had been poffeffed by the Cumins before this time, and which continowes with the houfe of Erroll to this day.

The fifth perfon in a lineal race from this Gilbert, firft Conftable, was Sir William Hay of Erroll. He was created firft Earle of Erroll by King James the Second, anno 1452, or 1454, and was the fifth

Conſtable of the kingdome of that name. The ſucceſſion was continowed lineally from him to that Earle John, who now liveth; and is the twelfth Earle, and ſeventeenth Conſtable, ſince theſe honoures were firſt conferred upon his forbeares.

OFF THE BEGINNING AND SUCCESSION OF THE CONSTABLES OF SCOTLAND.

Before the dayes of King Malcolm the Third, we had no higher titles of honor in this nation, then Knights, excepting only the Abthane of the kingdome and the Thanes of the ſeveral diviſions and diſtricts within the ſame; bot he, being brought up long with Edward the Confeſſor in England, whither he fled from M'Beth the Uſurper, had there learned the formes of the Engliſh offices and degrees of nobility; ſo that when he returned home, and was reſtored to the Croune, he ſet up a Steuard of the kingdome and Earles of the countries, after the manner of England, in place of the Abthane and Thanes uſed of old by his progenitors.

King William, great grandchyld to King Malcolm, haveing been alſo long in England and in France with King Henrie the Second, at his return is thought firſt to have ſett up the offices of Chancellor, Conſtable, and Mariſchall in this nation, in imitation of France and England; for the firſt Chancellor we find is about his time, and is called Alexander oure Chancellor; and the firſt Mariſchall we find recorded is Gillycallum, who rebelled againſt King William, tooke part with the Engliſhes, and delivered up the King's caſtle upon the Water of Even in theire hands, then raiſed the Gallovidians in armes, bot was defeated by Gilchriſt Earle of Angus, and forefaulted by the King.

The occaſion of the firſt Conſtable created by King William was thus:—In the reigne of King Henrie the Second of England, Thomas Becket was Archbiſhop of Canterburrie, and had many ſharp conteſts with the King concerning the priviledges of the Church, for which he was depoſed and baniſhed; bot upon follicitations from the Pope reſtored againe; yet behaved himſelfe in his charge with ſuch inſolencie, that many grievous complaints came over to the King from England, he being then in France; where, on a day at dinner, there came to him ſome news, complaints for outrages ſuffered from the Archbiſhop, whereat the King was ſo inraged, that he burſt furth with theſe words, "If I had any about me that loved me, they would find out ſome way or other to free me of this trouble, which vexes me more then the French war." Some gentlemen attending the King laid hold upon the words, and reſolved to doe the King ſervice; whereupon they haſted over to England, and killed the Archbiſhop

1171. in his own church at Canterburry, about the year 1171. The actors were Sir Reinolds Fitzurſe, Sir William Tracy, Sir Hugh Morvill, and Sir Richard Britton. Bot the deed being done, the King diſouned it; ſo the actors were baniſhed by the King, excommunicate by the church, and forced to fly for theire ſafeties. Sir Hugh Morvill came to Scotland, where he was welcomed and kindly intertained by King William, and, by all appeareance, for his good ſervice, was the firſt Conſtable of Scotland. His ſone Sir William Morvill was ſecond; 1196, Chron. Melroſs. His ſone Sir Richard Morvill ſucceeded to him, and was the third Conſtable: his name is often found in King Williams charters, as one of the witneſſes; thus, *Teſte Ricardo de Morvill Constabulario.* The fourth Conſtable was Sir William Morvill, ſone to Sir Richard Morvill: he had no ſones; his eldeſt daughter was married to Rolland Earle of Galloway, who, after the death of Sir William Morvill, his father-in-law, barganed with the King, and payed 700 merks Sterline for the office, whereof he got the heritable right to him and his aires whatſomever, and not as it had been before difponed to the Morvills and theire aires male. Allan Earle of Galloway, fone to Rolland, was the fixth Conftable of Scotland : he married Margaret, eldeft daughter to David Earle of Huntingtoune, brother to King William ; upon her he begot only three daughters, Helen, Dornagilla, and Marjorie. Oure hiftorie wrytters feeme heir to miftake, for they reckon only tuo daughters, and place Dornagilla for the eldeft. Helen, the eldeft, was married to Sir Roger Quincie, Earle of Winchefter, and had by her the third part of Earle Allans eftate, with the fpecial mannor, place, and office of Conftabulary of the Kingdome, albeit he was a ftranger, which Dornagilla, the wife of John Balliol, had beft right too, and he upon her accompt, if fhe had been eldeft. Againft this Sir Roger Quincie, duelling in Galloway, a baftard fone of Allan's, called Thomas, raifed ane infurrection of the Gallowidians, whom King Alexander the Second fuppreffed with no final danger and difficultie, in the year 1236. 1236.

Sir Roger Quincy, Earle of Winchefter, and Conftable, had only by his wife Helen three daughters ; the firft Margaret, married upon William the Lord Ferriers, eldeft fone to the Earle of Derby ; the fecond, Elifabeth, upon Alexander Cumin Earle of Buchan ; and the third, Helen, upon Allan Lord Afhby de la Zough. The Lord Ferriers, in right of his wife, was the next Conftable of Scotland, and the eighth in order, only the adminiftration thereof was committed to Alexander Earle of Buchan who married the fecond fifter, in the abfence of the Lord Ferriers ; upon whofe death, without fucceffion or forfaulture by King Henrie the Third of England, Alexander became Conftable. Alexander Earle of Buchan, who had married Elifabeth, fecond daughter of Roger Earle of Winchefter, begotten upon Helen the eldeft daughter of Allan Earle of Galloway, was the ninth Conftable of Scotland ; he begot John Cumine Earle of Buchan, and other children. John Cumin Earle of Buchan married and begot John Red Cummin ; John Cummin the father was the tenth Conſtable of Scotland. John Red Cumin, Earle of Buchan, married Sponda, daughter and heirefs of Malcolm Earle of Angus; he wes the eleventh Conſtable in order from the firſt Sir Hugh Morvill, and was killed by King Robert Bruce in the kirk of Dumfreefs, and he and all his poſterity forfaulted, and the office of Conſtabularie beſtowed upon Sir Gilbert Hay of Erroll, of whofe fucceſſion we have made mention before.

In fome old charters I have feen amongſt the witneſſes Normand Conſtable, bot cannot fay what he was.

A CHARACTER OF LADY ANNA GORDON, Spoufe to James third Earle of Perth, who dyed Lady Drummond, and of the maner of her death; wrytten by the hand of JOHN EARLE OF PERTH, her father-in-law, worthie to be recorded for the excellency of the Lady and the wreatter.

AT DRUMMOND CASTLE.

" As heroic actions have ever been held in admiration, and delivered to poſterity for advancing of vertue, fo the directions and laſt words of eminent dying perfones have upon the fame reafon been tranfmitted to the fucceeding ages, not only for eternizeing the memory of the author (if that were poſſible) and graceing of theire name, bot alfo that the poſterity might learn whom to imitate, and follow in the lyke cafe, and in all vertuous and religious behaviour; for albeit this prefent age inclyneth to vice and partiall dealeing, yet it is not fo deſtitute of difcretion and goodnes, bot that notable exemples are to be found for our inſtruction, if we could make right ufe of the fame, even flowing from fome of oure own deareſt freinds, whofe worth can never be fufficiently recorded, nor admired enough either by the beholders or by fuch as are to be acquainted with them by the report of others; and albeit learned eloquence were moſt requifit for fuch a relation, yet the fimple and naked truth needs litle ornament, from fine languadge, being fufficient to infinuat itfelfe in the hearts of upright and underftanding perfones.

"This year of our Lord 1656 begune with a total eclypfe of the moon, and upon the 16th of the firft moneth thereof happened alfo a notable darknes of the fune, betwixt which tuo it pleafed God to vifit this afflicted family by calling to himfelfe the Lady Anna Gordon Lady Drummond, eldeft laufull daughter to George late Marques of Huntly, whofe worth can never be fufficiently expreffed. She was alwayes moft religioufly difpofed, of a folid ftrong wit, difcreet to all who had the happines of her acquaintance; a lady chafte, vertoufs, forfeeing, temperat, of a moft excellent behaviour and comely carriage, without pryde or vanity; in a word, no grace nor vertue were wanteing in her whereof any true Chriftian was participant. She lived with her hufband about fixteen yeares, in all dutifull kindnefs and unity, her love to him dayly increaffing, and by her generous deportment gained more and more the refpect and commendation of all her acquaintances. She was well and nobly bred from her youth fome years with her mother Lady Anna Campbell, Marchiones of Huntly, at the court of France, where fhe was highly efteemed even by thofe who pretended greateft fharpnes in cenfureing good and ready witts. She was of a lively fpirit, and naturally difpofed for every noble exercyfe of body or mind. In England, after fhe left France, fhe was no lefs efteemed by the King, the Queen, and all the nobles, frequenting that court, where fhe was never named bot with due refpect, and free from all blameifh of light behaviour: whereunto then it was thought too many were inclyned, bot perchance undefervedly, becaufe envy alwayes accompanies the moft illuftrious perfones. She was for her blood, breeding, and parts, capable of the greateft fortune, yet was contented with that lot which God had ordained for her, far below her worth and merit; and albeit, fhe had all the induements

1656.

and perfections of nature, which might have invited her to a more publick and courtly way of liveing, yet fhe choifed rather a folitary, quyet, godly, and vertoufs manner of lyfe, efhewing all vaine, oftentive converfatione whatfomever: *optima matronae laus latuisse probae.*

1656. "Bot becaufe God thought us unworthy of fo great a bliffing, he withdrew her from us to himfelfe, upon Wedenfday the 9th of January, 1656, upon the eleventh day after fhe was brought to bed of a daughter, who was named Anna, after the mother. And when we thought her in a recovering condition, and all danger paft, it proved otherwayes decreed in heaven; for fhe found herfelfe worfe, and did take fome medicine from her phifitian, Doct. P., which profited nought; then finding her diffeafe increaffing, fhe had fome conference with her hufband apart, after which, fhe called for the whole family, early before day, and did take leave of every one of them particularly, with fuch courage and confidence, as if fhe had only been goeing a fhort journey to vifit her freinds; and fhortly to returne, fhe fpoke kindly to the fervants, and exhorted them to their duties, alfe well for theire own credit, as theire mafter's profit; fhe bid farewell to her father-in-law, and to her hufband, with wonderful kindnes, and paffionate expreffions; then calling for her children, fhe bleffed them, and recommended them to God, feeing fhe was no more to help them, telling us who were about her, that in place of one Anna, who was to leave them, fhe had left ane other young Anna in her roome; and al this fhe did, without the leaft figne of trouble or diforder which was admireable, and occafion of great greiffe to us for fo fad a lofs, if we could exprefs it.

"The Minifter, after this prayed, and then fhe herfelfe, fo pertinently, and with fuch earneft and fignificant expreffions, that no perfon could fpeake better: fhe lay a whyle very quyet; at laft yeelded up her fpirit moft devotely to our Redeemer, whom I humbly befeech, at his own appointed time, to grant us the lyke delivery, in all godly and faithful affureance of our falvation, that, as fhe is now, fo we may be bleffed for ever. Amen."

This is ane fhort abridgement upon ane excellent fubject, truely recorded by him who was prefent, and out of whofe thought nothing earthly is able to delete the lafting memory of fo lamentable a parting; more happie for her who is gone, than for thofe fhe left diftreffed behind. *Non decessit, sed praecessit, in aeternum quietura; ubi fruitur, cum dilectis in Christo, Sabbato Sabbatorum.* Her funeralls were honourably folemnized at the Chappell of Innerpeffrie, the 23d of January, 1656; many fpeciall good freinds accompanyed her corps to the grave.

1656.

What follows is by the   D. D.

"To the memory of Lady Anna Gordon, Lady Drummond, eldeft laufull Daughter to the late Marques of Huntly.

" Let the curious inquyre upon this noble Lady's behavior or conditions, and they fhall find no vertue deficient in her whereof humane nature wes capable. She proved neceffary for the good of the family and education of her children : this made her health and welifare ever wifhed and prayed for. Her death was regrated by all who had the honour of her acquaintance, which will make her memory to laft fo long as true worth fhall be had in efteeme. The gifts of the fpirit cannot be meafured, as our fhort and narrow graves, wherein our bodys doe reft; therefore let us only contemplat that immortall excellency which this peece of earth could not containe, and which is now placed with the bliffed angells on high, where no corruption afchends; and with us no oblivion can delete the true efteem of fo rare induements, which once this noble body pofeffed, fet furth for ane example and true pattern for imitation to all that honoures vertue. She departed this lyfe on Wedenfday the 9th of January 1656."

OFF LADY ANNA GORDON, SPOUSE TO JAMES THIRD EARLE OF
PERTH, DAUGHTER TO GEORGE MARQUES OF HUNTLY, AND OF
HER FATHERS FAMILY.

The Marques of Huntly is the cheefe of the Gordons; his family
is thought to have had its beginning out of France from one Duke
800. de Gordon, Conftable to Charlemaine about the year 800; whofe
fucceffors ftill pofeffes the caftle of Gordon in France, under the title
1199. of Viconts thereof. There wes one, about the year 1199, Bertrand
de Gordon, a Gafcogne, that killed King Richard the Firft of England
at the feige of Cadialliar in Limofin, of the fame family. It feems
fome of thefe Gordons have come alfo to England, for about the year
1265. 1265 there was one Adam Gordon governour of the caftle of Mun-
chered, in England, who defeated the Welfhmen in Somerfetfhyre
when King Henrie the Third reigned. He alfo fought a combat,
hand to hand, with Edward Prince of Wales, upon the head of the
1267. tuo armies, in the year 1267. The Marques of Huntly reckons his
prediceffor to have come to Scotland in the time of King Malcolm
the Third, and to have gotten from that King the lands of Huntly;
and that one of the fucceffors married the heretrix of Straboggy, and
that both thefe lands continowed with the pofterity in a lineal defcent
1370. of heires male untill the year 1370; about which time Sir John
Gordon of Huntly and Straboggie dyed without aires male, leaving
his eftate to Elifabeth Gordon, his only daughter, who wes married
to Sir Alexander Seatone, a younger fone to Sir Alexander Seatone,
that renowned governour of Berwick-upon-Tueed, whom King
Edward Third of England dealt fo unworthyly with, contrary to the
laws of warr and of all Chriftian nations. Upon this marriage Sir
Alexander Seaton changed his name and armes for the name and

THE HOUSE OF DRUMMOND.

armes of Gordone; and fince his time the fucceffion of the family wes thus: Firft, Alexander Gordon, fone to Sir Alexander Seaton alias Gordon, whom he begot upon the heretrix Elifabeth Gordon, was the firft Earle of Huntly, created by King James the Second, at Edenburgh, upon the 17th of Apryle 1449. He married, firft, Lady Honora Keith, daughter to Sir William Keith, Marifchall of Scotland, who dyed without children; he married again Elifabeth Hay, heirefs of Tulliebodie, by whom [he had] Seaton of Touch his anceftor; and the third time to Elifabeth Creichton, daughter to William Lord Creichton and Chancellor of Scotland: With her he begot the fecond Earle George Gordon. 1449.

He [the fecond Earl] married Lady Jane Stuart, daughter to King James the Firft, *sans* iffue; fecondlie, a daughter of the Earle of Erroll's; and dyed att Sterline anno 1501. 1501.

The third Earle of Huntly was Alexander, the fone of George. He married Lady Jean Stuart, daughter to John firft Earle of Athol of that name. He dyed at Perth anno 1525. 1525.

The fourth, was John Lord Gordon, the fone of Alexander. He married Lady Margaret Stuart, daughter to King James the Fourth, whom he begot upon Margaret Drummond, daughter to John Lord Drummond. He dyed before his father anno 1514. 1514.

The fifth, was George Earle of Huntly, the fone of John. He married Lady Elifabeth Keith, daughter to Earle Marifchall. He was Chancellor of Scotland, and by King Henrie the Second of France, made Knight of the Order of St. Michael. He defeat the Englifh at Haddenrig anno 1542; and was taken prifoner at the batle of Pinkie; bot killed at the fight of Corrichy, 1562, and lyes at Elgine. 1542. 1562.

The fixth, was Alexander, the fone of George. He dyed chyldlefs.

The feventh, was George, the brother of Alexander. He was Chancellor of Scotland in the time of Queen Marie. He married

2 G

Lady Anna Hamilton, daughter to John Duke of Chaftelherauld. He dyed at Straboggie, and lyes at Elgine.

The eighth Earle of Huntly was George, the fone of George; he, with Francis Earle of Erroll, beat the Earle of Argyle's army at the battle of Glenlivet, 1594. He was by King James the Sixth created Marques of Huntly, and Earle of Enzie at Holyroodhoufe anno 1599. He married Lady Henrietta Stuart, daughter to Efme Duke of Lennox.

1594.
1599.

The fecond Marques was George, fone to George; he married Lady Anna Campbell, daughter to Archbald Earle of Argyle. He fuffered death at Edenburgh for ferveing the King: his eldeft daughter was Lady Anna Gordon, Lady Drummond.

The third Marques wes Lues, the third fone of George; the two eldeft, George and James, haveing both dyed unmarried. He married Grant, daughter to the Laird of Grant.

The fourth Marques of Huntly is George, the fone of Lues; he married Lady   Howard, daughter to Henrie Duke of Norfolk, Earle of Arundale, and Earle Marifchall of England.

This Family of Huntly is twife defcended from the Drummonds. Firft, George fecond Earle of Huntly married Lady Jean Stuart, the daughter of King James the Firft; and Lady Annabella Drummond was the King's mother. Secondly, John Lord Gordon, the father of George fifth Earle of Huntly, married Lady Margaret Stuart, daughter to King James the Fourth; and Mrs. Margaret Drummond, eldeft daughter to John Lord Drummond, was her mother. And now the Houfe of Perth is come of the Marques of Huntly by this worthy lady, Anna Gordon, mother to James the prefent Earle of Perth.

THE HOUSE OF DRUMMOND.

CONCERNING JAMES THE FOURTH EARLE OF PERTH, THE SONE OF JAMES THIRD EARLE THEREOF.

PARTITIONE FIFTEENTH.

James the fourth Earle of Perth, eldeſt ſone of the former Earle James, had all the advantages of good breeding, that either his own country, France, or England could afford; and hes given large teſtimonie how capable he hes been to learn what ever was worthy there or elſe where. He married, firſt, Lady Jean Douglas, daughter to William Marques of Douglas, and fiſter-germane to William Duke of Hamilton. By her he hath a ſone, James, and tuo daughters, Lady Marie, and Lady Anna Drummonds. After the death of Lady Jean Douglas Countefs of Perth, he married Lillias Drummond Countefs of Tullibardine, the widdow of James, laſt Earle of Tullibardine, and daughter to Sir James Drummond of Machany. He hes by her tuo ſones, John and Charles Drummonds.

Of Lilias Drummond now Comteſs of Perth, mention is made in the accompt of the family of Machany.

James fourth Earle of Perth, the twentieth cheef of the family.

OFF LADY JEAN DOUGLAS, COMTESS OF PERTH, AND OF THE MARQUES OF DOUGLAS HER FATHER, AND HIS FAMILY.

The Douglaſſes are and hes been one of the eldeſt and confiderableſt Familys of the nation: They are from theire extraction native Scotſmen born, and theire begining to be noticed is very ancient.

228   THE GENEALOGIE OF

The firſt of them, whom we hear of, appeares to have been a man of no ſmal power, and of a ſingular courage and reſolution ; for, in a batle fought betwixt King Solvatius, the ſixty-fourth King of Scots,
707. about the year 767, againſt the firſt Donald Bane, that famous rebell, when the King's army was ſuccumbing before theire enimies, a valiant champion enters the liſts, recovers the day, and routs Donald Bane's army ; which was ſuch a ſurpryſe, that the King and the victorious army cried aloud, "What was the gallant that ſo nobly turned the chaſe?" It was anſwered, by theſe who had obſerved his activety, SHOLTO DOUGLAS: which is as much as, See, yonder black gray hero! And thus was Sholto faſtened on him for a name, and Douglas for a ſyrename to him and his poſterity : ſo that Sholto Douglas was the firſt remarkable beginner of the family of Douglas, whereof now James Marques of Douglas is the cheefe.

King Solvatius rewarded this Sholto for his ſervice with lands; which from him were called Douglaſdale, the river that waters it Douglas, and the caſtle for his palace built upon Douglas. Sholto had a grandchyld, called William Douglas and ſecond brother, who went with William, King Achaius brother, and 4000 Scotſmen under his conduct, to the aſiſtance of Charleſmaine, when he invaded Italy
800. about the year 800. This William Douglas made his abode in Italy, and was the father of that honourable family in Placentia, called to this day the Scotti, who keeps ſtill the coat of armes, or very near it, that belonged of old to the Douglaſſes. The cheefe of theſe Scotti ſent a tree of theire pedegree to William Earle of Angus, about the year 1622.

The firſt of the Douglaſſes who was nobilitat was called William ; him King Malcolm Keandmore, in a parliament holden at Forfar anno
1057. 1057, created a Lord ; and it was then that the firſt Earles, Lords, and Knights were made by that King. After this firſt Lord William, there followed nine ſucceſſions, all Lords of Douglas, worthy and

THE HOUSE OF DRUMMOND.

valiant men; untill William the tenth Lord Douglas, whom King David Bruce made Earle of Douglas in the field, that day whereupon the unfortunat batle of Durham was fought. William, the firſt Earle of Douglas, by marrying of tuo heretrixes, to wit, Margaret Marr and Margaret Stuart, was by right of them Earle of Marr and Earle of Angus. From this Earle William there ſprung the tuo great families of the Douglaſſes; of the firſt wife were the Earles of Douglas, and of the laſt, to wit, Margaret Stuart, the Earles of Angus. By the firſt wife, Margaret Mar, he had a daughter, Lady Iſſobella Douglas, who fell to be heretrix of Mar; ſhe married firſt Malcolm Drummond, Seneſchal of Lennox, who was by her right Earle of Mar, but had no children.

A LIST OF THE EARLES OF DOUGLAS.

The firſt Earle William, of whom we have now ſpoken, was the ſone of Archbald Earle of Galloway, the third brother of good Sir James, the eighth Lord Douglas, who was ſlaine by the Saracens in Spaine; for William ſucceeded to his uncle Hugh, the ninth Lord Douglas, who was the ſecond brother of good Sir James. E. of Douglas

2. James, the ſone of William. He married Euphame Stuart, daughter to King Robert the ſecond, whom he begot upon the Earle of Roſs' daughter, bot had no children. He dyed victorious at that bloody fight of Otterburn in Northumberland.

3. Archbald, the brother of James, called Archbald the Grim. He married the only daughter of Thomas Murray, Lord of Bothwell, and got with her the lands of Bothwell, &c. He dyed anno 1400.   1400.

4. Archbald, called Tynman, the ſone of Grim Archbald. He

married Margaret Stuart, daughter to King Robert the III., and was the firſt Duke of Turraine, created by Charles VII. of France. He dyed at the batle of Vernoil, anno 1424.

1424.

5. Archbald, ſone to Archbald Tynman, married Maud Lindſay, daughter to David Earle of Craufurd. Archbald was ſecond Duke of Turraine, and purchaſſed the Earledome of Wigtone from the Fleeming. [He] dyed anno 1438.

1438.

6. William, ſone to the former Archbald. He was third Duke of Turraine; a young man, unmarried. By the contriveances of Chancellor Creichton and Governour Livingſtone, in the reigne of King James the Second, he was execut in Edinburgh Caſtle, 1440.

1440.

7. James, the uncle of William and ſone of Archbald Tynman, called Groſs James; married Beatrix Sinclar, daughter to Henrie Earle of Orknay; and dyed anno 1443. He was fourth Duke of Turraine.

1443.

8. William, the ſone of Groſs James, married Beatrix Lyndſay, daughter to the Earle of Craufurd. He was fifth Duke of Turraine, and had no children. He wes ſtabbed by King James the Second, in Sterline caſtle, 1452.

1452.

9. James, the brother of William and ſixth Duke of Turraine. He and his three brothers, Archbald, Hugh, and John, with Beatrix, relict of Earle William, Alexander Earle of Craufurd, and James Lord Hamilton, were all declared rebells and forfaulted. At laſt, Earle James was taken priſoner and brought to King James the Third, who cauſed impriſon him in the abbay of Lundores, where he dyed 1488; and with him ended the Race of the noble Earles of Douglas.

1488.

THE HOUSE OF DRUMMOND.

A List of the Douglasses, Earles of Angus.

1. William, firft Earle of Douglas, was alfo by right of his fecond E. of Angus.
lady, Margaret Stuart, the firft Earle of Angus. Of him and his
diverfe marriages, whereof by the firft fprung the Earles of Douglas,
and by the laft the Earles of Angus, we have fpoken of before.

2. George, the fone of William and Margaret Stuart. His wife
was Mary Stuart, daughter to King Robert the Third, begotten upon
Queen Annabella Drummond, of whom mention is made already.
He [dyed] anno 1430.   1430.

3. William, the fone of George, beat the Percie at the batle of
Piperden. He married Margaret Sinclar, daughter to the Earle of
Orkney, and had a fone, James, who fucceeded. This William dyed
about the year 1437.   1437.

4. James, the fone of William. There is no mention of his wife
nor of his children, fo that it appeares he had neither. He dyed
about the year 1452.   1452.

5. George, uncle to James, and fone to William the third Earle.
He married Elifabeth Sibbald, daughter to the laird of Balgonie,
Thefaurer of Scotland, defcended of Sibbauld Earle of Northumber-
land in the dayes of King Malcolm Keandmore. George dyed 1462.   1462.

6. Archbald, the fone of George. He married Elifabeth Boyd,
daughter to Robert Lord Boyd, Chancellor, and one of the governoures of Scotland, anno 1468, in the minority of King James the   1468.
Third. This was Archbald Bel-the-Cat, and Chancellor to King
James the Fourth. He dyed 1514, the year after Floudon.   1514.

7. George, the fone of Archbald Bel-the-Cat. He married Elifabeth Drummond, daughter to John Lord Drummond. He dyed
before his father, and fo came never to be Earle, bot was called
Mafter of Angus; and killed at Flowdone 1513.   1513.

232   THE GENEALOGIE OF

  8. Archbald, the fone of George Mafter of Angus. He married, firft, Margaret Hepburn, daughter to Patrick Lord Bothwell. His fecond wife, in anno 1514, was Queen Margaret, relict of King James [the] Fourth. And his third wife was Margaret Maxwell, daughter
1557. to the Lord Maxwell. He left no fone, and dyed 1557.

  9. David, nephew to Archbald, the fone of his brother Sir George Douglas of Pittendrich. He married Elizabeth Hamilton, daughter to John Hamilton of Samuelftone, called John of Cliddefdale, brother
1558. to James Duke of Chaftelherauld, the Governor. He dyed anno 1558.

  10. Archbald, the fone of David. He married, firft, Margaret Erfkine, daughter to John Earle of Mar; bot had no children by her. He married the fecond time Margaret Leflie, daughter to George Earle of Rothes; neither had he any children by her. He married the third time to Jean Lyon, daughter to Patrick Lord Glames, Chancellor; neither had fhe any liveing child: he died in
1588. the year 1588. He was the laft Earle of Angus of the race of George the fone of Archbald Bell-the-Cat; wherefore the fucceffion followes from William Douglas of Glenbervie, fecond fone to Archibald Bel-the-Cat, and brother to George Mafter of Angus, flaine at Flowdone.

  This Sir William Douglas married Elifabeth Aufflect, heretrix of Glenbervie, and begot a fone, William Douglas of Glenbervy.

  11. William Douglas, grandchild to Archbald Bel-the-Cat, fucceeded to the tenth Earle Archbald by taylzie. He married Giles Grahame, daughter to Sir Robert Grahame of Morphie, and begot William.

  12. William Douglas, the fone of William, fucceeded to be Earle of Angus. He married Elifabeth Olyphant, daughter to Laurence Lord Olyphant, and begot with her William, who fucceeded.

Marques of Douglas.
  1. William Douglas, the fone of the laft William, was the thirteenth Earle of Angus: he was created Marques of Douglas by King

THE HOUSE OF DRUMMOND.

Charles the Firſt, anno 1633. He married, to his firſt wife, Lady 1633. Margaret Hamilton, fiſter to James Earle of Abercorne, and begot with her Archbald Earle of Angus. Archbald married, firſt,   and begot with her James, now ſecond Marques of Douglas. Archbald's ſecond wife was Lady   Weems, daughter to   Earle of Weems, who had to him   now Earle of Forfare; married to   Lockart, daughter to Sir William Lockart of Lie.

William firſt Marques of Douglas married to his ſecond wife Lady Margaret Gordon, daughter to George Marques of Huntly, and begot on her William, now Duke of Hamilton,   Earle of Dumbarton, and four daughters.

2. James, now ſecond Marques of Douglas, ſone to Archbald Earle of Angus, and grandchyld to William firſt Marques of Douglas, married Lady   Erſkine, daughter to John Earle of Mar; and hes by her a ſone,   Earle of Angus.

THE MUTUAL ALLYANCES BETWIXT THE HOUSES OF DOUGLAS AND DRUMMOND.

Firſt, Sir Malcolm Drummond married Lady Iſſobella Douglas, daughter to William firſt Earle of Douglas, whom he begot upon Lady Margaret Marr, heretrix thereof; and ſo Malcom becam Earle of Mar by right of his wife, who was alſo heretrix.

2. Archbald the fourth Earle of Douglas, called Archbald Tynman, married Lady Margaret Stuart, daughter to King Robert the Third, whom he begot upon his Queen, Annabella Drummond.

234   THE GENEALOGIE OF

3. George Douglas, fecond Earle of Angus, married Lady Mary Stuart, ane other daughter of King Robert the Third's, and her mother alfo was Queen Annabella Drummond.

4. George Mafter of Angus, eldeft fone of Archbald called Bel-the-Cat, who was the fixth Earle of Angus, married Elifabeth Drummond, daughter to John firft Lord Drummond.

Lastly, James, now Earle of Perth, married Lady Jean Douglas, daughter to William firft Marques of Douglas; and hes by her James Lord Drummond, Lady Mary and Lady Anna Drummonds.

THE ORIGINAL AND SUCCESSION OF THE RUTHVENS.

Raniminis Arrago, King of Arragon, his eldeft fone was Alphonfus, who fucceeded. His fecond fone Baldwine married Ruthia, daughter
1060. to the Duke of Ferrara: he dyed anno 1060; and begot Ruthowen.

He married Matildis, daughter to Rhyfe ap Griffith ap Leulin,
1102. Prince of Wales. Dyed anno 1102.

Fleanchus, the fone of Bancho, and father of Walter the firft great Stuart of Scotland, married Nefta, the fifter of Rhyfe ap Griffith ap Lewlin, Prince of Wales; of whom the Royal Family of Stuarts is lineally defcended.

Ruthowen begot Rhyfe ap Rothuen, who married Eupheme, neece
1130. to Richard Earle of Pembroke. He dyed anno 1130; begot

Riore a Ruthven. He married Emergarda, daughter to Gilchrift
1189. Earle of Angus: dyed anno 1189. This Riore or Rore a Ruthven was the firft of that family who came to Scotland with his brother William, anno 1159, in the reigne of King Malcolm Fourth: he begot

THE HOUSE OF DRUMMOND.

Sir William Ruthven, who married Alice, daughter to the Earle of Beaumont, in France; dyed anno 1224: begot 1224.

Sir John Ruthven; he married Lucina, daughter to the Lord Kinclevein; he dyed 1262: begot 1262.

Sir Patrick Ruthven; he married Annabella Campbell, daughter to the Knight of Lochawah; dyed 1296: begot 1296.

Sir William Ruthven; he married Marrion Ramfay, daughter to the Lord of Ochterhoufe; dyed 1320: begot 1320.

Sir Walter Ruthven; he married Marjory Carron; and was killed at the battle of Durhame 1346: begot 1346.

Sir Patrick Ruthven; he married Margaret Hay, daughter to the Earle of Erroll; dyed 1379: begot 1379.

Sir James Ruthven; he married Margaret Douglas, coufine to the Earle of Douglas; dyed 1420: begot 1420.

Sir William Ruthven; he married Eleonora Vaufs; he dyed anno 1454: begot 1454.

Sir Patrick Ruthven; he married Jean Boyd, daughter to the Lord Boyd; dyed 1470. He had a daughter Margaret, married to Sir Walter Drummond, the fone of Sir John Drummond, the ninth cheefe of the family of Drummond. Sir Patrick begot lykwife a fone 1470.

William, firft Lord Ruthven, created anno 1487 by King James the Third: married Elifabeth Lythington, daughter to the Barron of Saltcoats; dyed anno 1528: begot 1487.
 1528.

William, fecond Lord [Mafter of] Ruthven: he married Jean Hepburn, daughter to the Laird of Riccartone; dyed at Flowdone anno [1513]: begot

William, third Lord Ruthven: he married Jean, daughter and heretrix of George Halyburton Lord Dirleton, with whom he had eight daughters; firft, Elifabeth, Lady Bonington Wood; fecond, Lilias, Lady Drummond; third, Jean, Lady Strathurd, (he was Creichton); fourth, Catharina, Lady Glenurchy; fifth, Cicile, Lady

Weems; fixth, Margaret, Lady Elphingfton; feventh, Chriftina, Lady Lundy; eighth, Barbara, Lady Gray. He dyed 1551: begot (Alexander the firft of Freeland was his fone)

Patrick, fourth Lord Ruthven; he married Jean Douglas, daughter to Archbald Earle of Angus; dyed 1566: begot

William, firft Earle of Gourie; he married Dorrothea Stuart, daughter to Henrie Lord Methven. He was created Earle by King James the Sixth, October 24 1581, and made Lord Thefaurer of Scotland. He had eight daughters; firft, Marie, Comtefs of Atholl, who had four daughters; Dorothy, heretrix of Atholl; fecond, Jean, married to James Earle of Atholl, Lord Innermeath; third, Mary, Lady St. Colm Stuart; and Anna, Lady Ochiltree. William Earle of Gaury's fecond daughter, Jean, wes Lady Ogilvy; third, Lilias, Duchefs of Lennox, without ifhew; fourth, Dorothea, Lady Pittencreiffe, without ifhew; fifth, Margaret, Comtefs of Montrofe; fixth, Beatrix, Lady Coldingknows, now Earles of Hume; feventh, Elifabeth, Lady Lochinvar, now Vifcounts of Kenmuire; eighth, Barbara, unmarried. This William Earle of Gourie kept King James the Sixth a prifoner at Ruthven Caftle untill he figned a warrant to banifh his coufine Efme Duke of Lennox; for which he was convicted of treafon, and execut at Sterline, May 4 1584.

His eldeft fone James was fecond Earle; bot dyed young, about fourteen years of age, 1588.

William Earle of Gourie's fecond fone John was third Earle; who, with his brother Alexander, were killed at Perth anno 1600, upon the 5th of Aguft, for confpyreing to kill the King. They were forefaulted, theire lands annexed to the crowne, the fyrname abolifhed, Ruthven Caftle called Huntingtoure, and ane anniverfary thankfgiveing appointed to be keept on that day.

THE HOUSE OF DRUMMOND.

THE FAMILY OF SINCLAR EARLE OF ORKNAY.

1. William fecond fone to Voldefius Earle of St. Clarence or St. Clare, in France, came to Scotland either with King William, or to England with the Conquerour, and thence hither, bot moſt apparently with King William. He married Agnes Dumbar, daughter to Patrick Earle of March.

2. The fecond, Sir Henrie Sinclair; he married Catharina daughter to   Earle of Strathern.

3. The third, Sir Henrie; he married Margaret Mar, daughter to Gartney Earle of Mar.

4. The fourth, Sir William; he married Elifabeth Spar, daughter of Malicius Spar, Earle of Orkney and Shetland, whereby he became Earle of Orkney. Elifabeth's mother was Lucia, daughter to the Earle of Rofs. He went with James Lord Douglas to the Holy Land to convey the heart of King Robert the Firſt, anno 1330: vide Godfcroft. 1330

5. Sir Henrie Sinclair; he, after the forfaulture of his grandfather Malice, Earle of Strathern, was by King David Bruce created Earle of Orknay and Shetland. He married Florentina, daughter to the King of Denmark.

6. Henrie, fecond Earle of Orkney, married Giles or Egidia Douglas, only daughter to William the Black Douglas, Lord of Liddifdale, and the faire Egidia Stuart, who was treacheroufly flaine by the Lord Clifford, on the bridge of Dantzick. Elifabeth Sinclar, fpoufe to Sir John Drummond, was daughter to this Henrie. He was by the King of Denmark created Duke of Oldenburgh; he was Knight of the Thiftle, Cockell, Garter, and Golden Fleece, the cheefe orders of knighthood in Scotland, France, England, and Spaine. Egidia Stuart was the wonder of that age for beautie, fhe was

daughter to King Robert the Second, by Elifabeth Muire. Hector Boethius wryttes, that Charles the Sixth King of France, heareing of her fame, fent a painter privately to Scotland, who drew her picture, and prefented it to the King, who was therewith fo enamoured, that he difpatched Ambaffadoures to demand her in marriage; bot they came too late.

7. William Sinclair, third Earle of Orknay, &c. married Elifabeth Douglas, daughter to Archbald Tynman Earle of Douglas. His fone was William the Wafter, by her, author of the family of Ravenfheugh. Elifabeth Douglas, comtefs of Orknay, was begotten by Archbald Tynman, upon Margaret Stuart, daughter of King Robert [the] Third and Queen Annabella Drummond. This Earle William was
1453. Chancellor of Scotland to King James [the] Second, 1453, and got from the King the Earledome of Caitnes in compenfation for his clame to the Lordfhip of Liddifdale, offices, and penfiones contracted by King Robert the Second to William the Black Douglas, Lord of Liddifdale, with his daughter the faire Egidia.

It was this Earle William's fifter, Elifabeth Sinclare, who married Sir John Drummond, the ninth cheefe head of the family of Drummond.

William third Earle, after the death of Elifabeth his firft wife, married a fecond time to Marjory Sutherland, daughter to Alexander, Mafter of Sutherland; and had by her tuo fones, the firft, Oliver of Rofline, and William. This William was the firft Earle of Caitnes,
1470. 1470: he was f'aine at Floudon. This William Earle of Orknay was forefaulted by King James [the] Third, and the Earldome of Orknay, and Lordfhip of Zetland annexed to the Crowne.

THIS COPPIED FROM THE ORIGINAL MANUSCRIPT BY MR. DAVID
DRUMMOND, ADVOCAT, ANNO 1689.

APPENDIX.

APPENDIX.—No. I.

HISTORIE OF THE FAMILIE OF PERTH.
BY WILLIAM DRUMMOND OF HAWTHORNDEN.

[*The manuscript from which this History is printed belonged to Robert Mylne, writer in Edinburgh, who died at a very advanced age in the earlier part of the last century. In many places it is evidently inaccurate, and, like most other of his transcripts, interpolated. An attempt is made to distinguish his additions by printing what appears to be such, within brackets.*]

To The Right Honourable JOHN EARLE of PERTH.

My Noble Lord,

Though, as Glaucus sayes to Diomed, (in Homer,)

—— Like the race of leaves
The race of man is, that deserves, no question; nor receaves
His being any other breath: The wind in Autumne strowes
The earth with old leaves; then the Spring, the woods with new endowes.

Yet I have ever thought the knowledge of kinred, and genealogies of the ancient families of a countrey, a matter so farr from contempt, that it deserveth highest praise. Herein consisteth a part of the knowledge of a man's own selfe. It is a great spurr to vertue to look back on the worth of our line. In this is the memory of the dead preserved with the living, being more firme and honourable than any epitaph. The living know that band which tyeth them to others. By this man is distinguished from the reasonless creatures, and the noble of men from the baser sort. For it often falleth out (though we cannot tell how) for the most part, that generositie followeth good birth and parentage. This moved me to essay this Table of your Lordship's House, which is not inferior to the best in this Isle and greatest. It is but roughly (I confess) hewen, nakedly limned, and after better Informations to be amended. In pieces of this kind, who doeth according to such light as he receaveth is beyond reprehension.

Your Lordships humble servant and kinsman,

W. DRUMMOND.

EDGAR ATHELING, son to Edward, Prince of England, intituled the Outlaw, the nephew of Edward the Confessour, finding him selfe weake to resist the power and violence of William Duke of Normandie, who then was subdueing England, fearing to be impaired in honour and estate, with his mother, Agatha daughter to Solomon King of Hungarie, and his two sisters, Margaret and Christian, intendit a retreate into Hungarie, their native countrey. In their voyage they were driven by tempest on the coast of Scotland, and arryved on the northern syde of the river of Forth, at the place now named St. Margaret's Hope. Malcolme the Third, King of Scotland, having then his residence in Dumfermling, not farr from the haven, not only in all hospitable manner entertained them, his former sufferings in his exyle having taught him to compassionat others in lyke distresses, but with ane army assisting Edgar, raised great commotions in the North against Duke William, entered into league with Edgar for the publict saifty; and to inchaine it the stronger, took to wyffe Margaret, his sister, a lady indued with all blessed vertues. In the traine of thes Princes were many gentlemen, some English some Hungarians, who had used all endeavoures to recover the lost countrey: but the government being setled they prevailed nothing. Among which one eminent for his valour against the Normanes, who by his good service in the conduct of the Navie wherein the Royal strangers were embarqued, was gratifyed by King Malcolme with sundry lands, and honoured with a coat of armes, viz. three ondes *id est* weaves *gules* in a *feild* of *or;* crest, halfe ane gray hound, *gules*, with his collours, *or;* two savadges for supporters. About this tyme surnames in Europe beginning, which necessity first found out, this gentleman was named Drummond; which seemeth to have been the motto given unto him from the Tempests, Drum in the ancient language signifying hight, as the Drum of Athole, Blair, Lenrick, and other eminent places yet signifye; and *onde*, in all languages which come from the

No. I. APPENDIX. 243

Latine, a wave ; unless one would conjecture this name to have been given from the ships in which they were conveyed ; which some other before that were called Dromones, *Quasi cursoria navigia,* [for according to] Isiodorus, *Longae naves sunt quas Dromones vocamus :—cursum enim* Δρομον *Graeci dicunt.* The French yet call a caravall, or swift vessell used commonly by pirrates, a Dromant. Thus the Argonautae were named from the ship Argos, in which they sailed to Colchos. This happened about the year of our Lord 1067.

Of this Drummond lineallie descended the race of the Drummonds of Stobhall, of which the most apparent, about the year 1370, was,—

1. Sir John Drummond, whose linage in our tyme, is, by the blessing of God, numerous and floorishing. He marryed Eleonor Saintclair, daughter to Henrie Sinclair, Earle of Orkney, Earle of Caithnes, Lord Sinclair, Baron of Roselin, Piethland, or Pent land. And from him Glen-Orkney, a forest yet in the possession of the Lord Drummond had the name. This Henry Sinclair's mother was a daughter of William Douglas, Lord of Niddisdale, her mothers name was Geills, or Aegidia, daughter to Robert the Second, by his wyfe Elizabeth Moore : this is asserted [by] David Hume in the history of the Dowglasses. Eleonor Sinclair bore to Sir John Drummond of Stobhall, knight, fyve sons, and one daughter named Annabella, a lady born under a happy conjunction of starrs, if ever any. Robert the Third King of Scotland, enamoured with her vertues and singular beauty, made her queen, of which marriage a Poet of our tyme wrytteth : *Ecce autem quaerenda, &c.* [See page 76.]

From her in a direct lyne the Kings of Scotland are descendit till this year, [1649] which is the first of our Sovereigne Lord's reigne, Charles the Second. Annabella wes marryed to King Robert about the year 1391. She bare to him,

David, Prince of Rothesay. He marryed the Earle of Douglas' sister, and wes four years marryed befor his cruell Uncle starved him in the towr of Falkland, then twentie-four or twentie-fyve of age. He wes installed Duke 1396. She bare also,

James the First, King of Scotland of that name. And Margaret Steuart, who was maryed to Archbald fourth Earle of Douglas, and lyes buryed in the church of Lincluden with this inscription on her tomb :—

HIC JACET MARGARETA, SCOTIAE REGIS FILIA, COMITISSA
DE DOUGLAS, VALLIS ANNANDIAE ET GALLOVIDIAE DOMINA.

The Earle of Douglas had by her tuo sons. 1. Archbald Earle of Wigtoun. And, 2. James Earle of Abercorne, called Gross James. He had tuo daughters by her, 1. Margaret, maryed to William Sinclair Earle of Orkney. And, 2. Elizabeth, maryed to John Stuart Earle of Buchan, second son to Robert Duke of Albany Governour, and Constable of France. This is averd by David Hume in the History of the Douglasses.

King James the First of Scotland, married Jane, daughter to the Earle of Somerset, and cousine to Henry the Sext. She bore to him, 1. James the Second, King of Scotland. And daughters: 2. Margaret, (maryed to Lewis the Dawphine of France, after King Lewis the Eleavinth,) who dyed young without children, and is buryed at ..... 3. Elizabeth, maryed to the Duke of Bretaigne. 4. Eleonor, maryed to the Duke of Austria. 5. Mary, maryed to the Earle of Camphire. 6. Jean, Countess of Huntlie. 7. Annabella, Countess of Morton. She bare to the Earle of Morton a daughter, who was first maryed to the Earle of Cassills, and bare him, Kennedie Earle of Cassills; Kennedie, bishop of St. Andrews; and Sir Alexander Kennedy beheaded. She after maryed the Earle of Montrose, to whom she bare Patrick Grahame, first Archbishop of St. Andrews; and the Laird of Fintrie, of whose ofspring are the present Grahames of Fintrie.

King James the Second of Scotland, maryed Mary, daughter to the Duke of Gilders. She bare, 1. James the Third. 2. Alexander Duke of Albany. 3. John Earle of Marr. 4. Mary, Countess of Arran Boyd, thereafter Lady Hamilton 1479. 5. Cicile, maryed to William son to the Lord Crichtoun.

King James the Thrid maryed Margaret, daughter to Christian King of Denmark, who bare to him King James the Fourth.

King James the Fourth maryed Margaret, daughter to Henry the Seaventh of England, who bare to him James the Fyfth, King of Scotland.

King James the Fyfth maryed, first, Magdalen of Vallois, daughter to Frances the First King of France; and she dyeing *sans* ishu, he maryed Mary of Loraine, sister to Frances, daughter to Rheyne Duke of Guise, who bare to him Mary Queen of Scotland.

Mary Queen of Scotland was maryed to Hary Steuart, Lord Darnley. He begot upon her James King of Great Brittaigne.

King James the Sexth maryed Anna of Denmark, who bare to him, 1. Henry Prince of Wales, who dyed of 18 years of his age. 2. Charles the First, King of

England. And, 3. Elizabeth; she was maryed to Frederick, Elector Palatine of the Rhine, therafter vnfortunate King of Bohemia, and bare him many children.

King Charles the First maryed Mary of Burbon, daughter to Henry the Fourth King of France, who bare to him, 1. Charles the Second, King of Scotland. 2. James, Duke of York. 3. Henry, Duke of Glocester. 4. Mary, maryed to William Prince of Orange. 5. Elizabeth died vnmaried. 6. Henrieta maryed Philip Duke of Orleance, only brother of Lewis Fourteenth King of France.

Thus much for the Race of the Kings come of Annabella.

2. Malcolm Drummond was the eldest son of the forsaid first Sir John Drummond of Stobhall, and Helenor St. Clair. He maryed Issobell Douglas, daughter to the Earle of Douglas, and Margaret Marr, who wes daughter and heir to Duncan, or Donald Earle of Marr; she had no children to Malcolm, nor to Alexander Steuart, who, after the decease of Malcolme, maryed her. He was son to the Earle of Buchan brother to King Robert the Third.

3. Walter Drummond succeided to his brother Malcolme. He maried Montifixo, daughter to   This lady bare to him four sons. 1, John. 2, Mr. Walter. 3, James.

4. John succeided to his father, and was created Lord 1484. He married Elizabeth Lindsay, daughter to David Lindsay Earle of Crawfurd. She bare to him tuo sons and three [six] daughters. His eldest son wes named,

William, the first Master; his father long outliving him. This first Master wes married to [Isobel] Campbell, daughter to the Earle of Argyle. She bare to him   named the Second Master. It is told this first Lord Drummond lived to see the Thrid. The Second Master maryed   Grahame, daughter to the Earle of Montrose, who bare to him David second Lord Drummond; in whose chyldhead John his grandfather dyed, ane active vallourous man, famous in all our historyes: in Edward Hall, Buchanan, Hollinshed, Leslie.

Wee shall now follow furth John first Lord Drummond his children, before we come to David second Lord Drummond.

The Second son of John the first Lord Drummond, was John Drummond of Innerpeffrey, named John Bane, that is, fair and comelie: he maryed the Lady Saltoun.

APPENDIX. No. I.

He had tuo sons; the one was Sir John Drummond of Innerpeffrey, and Harie, who maryed [Janet] Crichtoun heiress of Riccarton. Sir John, the eldest, maryed Margaret Steuart, Lady Gordon, naturall daughter to King James the Fourth, who bare to him, 1. Margaret Countess of Eglintoun. 2. Anna Lady Semple. 3. Issobell Lady Elphinstoun; the genealogie of Elphinston calls her Margaret. 4.   Lady Laudon. 5. Jane Lady Cromlix—in whom the house of Innerpeffrey ceassed.

Margaret did beare the Master of Eglinton that was slaine by the Cunninghames, and Margaret Lady Setton. . . . . The Shirreffe of Air, first Lord Lawdoun. (¹)

Jane bare Sir James Chesme [Chisholme] of Cromlix, and the Bishop of Vestoun, [Vason] a learned and grave churchman. He was one of the prelats receaved Mary of Florence, Queen of Henrie Fourth King of France, in Avignon, 19th November 1600.

[Nota.—The lands of Innerpeffrey went with the above Jean to Chisholme of Cromlix. And it came back to James first Lord Madertie. He maryed Jean, daughter and heiress of Sir James Chisholme of Cromlix.]

Issobell was mother to Alexander Lord Elphinstoun, Mr. George Elphinstoun, Rector of the Scots Colledge of Dowie, and James Lord Balmirino, Secretar and President of the Colledge of Justice.

Hary Drummond, the second son of John Drummond of Innerpeffrey, wes a stout and vallorous man. He, by the endeavours of Mary of Loraine, Queen Regent of Scotland, with whom he wes in high esteem, obtained in mariage Janet Crichtoun, heretrix of Riccartoun, daughter to Hary Crichtoun Laird of Riccartoun, and then the Queen's waird, by whom the Drummonds have the tytle of thes lands. Janet Crichtoun's mother was a daughter of the Lord Livingstoun. She bare to this Hary, 1. Hary Drummond, Laird of Riccartoun. 2. William of Piteairne. 3. Sir Edward Drummond, a supreame Judge in Veson, a toun pertaineing to the Apostolick Sea, in France. He was one of the knights of Clement the Eight, and came to Scotland in anno 1600, for great matters, to King James, concerning his succession to the croun of England. 4. Mr. Ninian Drummond, Minister of Kinnoull. 5   Drummond, Lady Logy, the mother of that famous young gentleman beheaded by the Hollanders. —[Nota. Janet Crichtoun after this Haries death maried Monteith of Carss.]

(¹) Mylne, in one of his transcripts, has supplied the defect in this place by an extract from Freebairn's History.

No. I. APPENDIX.

Hary, son of the last Hary, married   Sandilands, daughter to the Laird of Calder, sister to Sir James Sandilands of Slammanno-moor, gentleman of the Kings Privie Chamber. She bare to him, 1. William Drummond. 2. Thomas Drummond.

William marryed   Stirline, daughter to the Laird of Keir; who bare to him William Drummond and daughters. [His son] William maryed Magdalen Dalziell, daughter to Thomas Dalziell of Binns and Magdalen Bruce [daughter] to my Lord Bruce in England, once Master of the Rolls. Thomas Dalziell was coussine to the Earle of Carnwath. [His son Thomas wes a great generall, and a man famous in the late warrs, and against the Whigs at Pentland Hills.]

John the first Lord Drummond had thrie daughters:

1. Margaret, the eldest, affianced to King James the Fourth, though he was not suffered to marie her, least the familly of Drummond sould have been raised too high; and she was cutt of by poysson, and tuo other of her sisters that accidentally shared therof. She bare to him Margaret Steuart, whom the King maryed to the Lord Gordon; unto whom she bare George Earle of Huntlie, who wes slaine at Corrichie. After the Lord Gordon's death Margaret wes affianced to Alexander Steuart, eldest son of Alexander Duke of Albany. This marriage was interrupted by his brother John the Governour, least he should come betuen him and the Croun of Scotland, if James the young King should chance to dye; and, to barr him from the succession, he wes turned a churchman, being made Bishop of Murray and Abbot of Scoon: ffor Alexander wes eldest son to their father Duke of Albany, born of the Earle of Orkney's daughter; whilst John was but borne of a second mariage, viz. the Earle of Bulloigne's daughter, a French woman. The Governour committed my Lady Gordon, for her fault, in the castle of Drummond, to John Bain Drummond, her uncle.

2. Elizabeth, the second daughter of John Lord Drummond, was marryed to George Master of Angus, and bare to him Archbald Earle of Angus; who maryed Margared Tudor, widow of King James IV. She bare to him Lady Margaret Douglas, mother to Henric Steuart Earle of Darnley father to James, King of Great Brittain, and Sir George Dowglas, of whom are the Earles of Angus and Morton.

3. The third daughter of John Lord Drummond was [Eupheme] Lady Fleyming, of whom the hous of Wigtoun is descended. Ther is a constant report that this Lady Fleyming, with her sister, Lady Margaret, and a younger unmaryed sister, were all thrie in one day taken away by poyson.

5. David Lord Drummond, after the death of his father, the second Master of Drummond, succeidit. He wes the son of the Earle of Montrose's daughter. He maryed, himselfe, first the naturall daughter of Alexander Steuart, Bishop of Murray, which Margaret Lady Gordon bore to him whilst she was affianced to him, and in promise of marriage. She bore to him Sybilla Drummond, Lady Powrie Ogilvie.

After the death of Margaret Steuart, this Lord maried, secondly, Lillias Ruthven, daughter to John Lord Ruthven, who bore to him, 1. Patrick Lord Drummond. 2. James Lord Madertie, who married Jean, daughter and heiress of Sir James Chisholme, [by whom (1.) John, his successor. (2.) Sir James Drummond, the first of Machany. (3.) Lillias, maryed to Lord Oliphant, to whom she bore only a daughter, his heiress. (4.) Jean, to Wood of Largo, *sans* ishu. (5.) Margaret, to Muirehead of Breadisholme, with ishu. (6.) Katharine, to Andrew Lord Rollo, with ishu.] and fyve daughters. 3. Lady Montros. 4. Countess of Marr. 5. Countess of Crawfurd. 6. Lady Tulliebairne. 7. Lady Keir.

John second Lord Madertie, maried Margaret, daughter of Patrick, first Lord Lindoris; [by whom David, his successor, and other four sons, and thrie daughters, Anne, Jean, and Margaret, maried to Rattray of Craighall, Grahame of Inchbrake, and . . . .]

[David, third Lord Madertie, maried first Alison, the eldest of the two heiresses of John Crichton of Airlywight, *sans ishu ;* secondlie, Beatrix, sister of James first Marques of Montrose ; by whom Margaret, Beatrix, and Mary, maried to   Grahame, Generall Post-Master, John Lord Carmichaell, and Hadden of Gleneagles.]

6. Patrick Lord Drummond married   Lindsay, daughter to the Earle of Crawfoord, who during his lyfe only enjoyed the tytle and honour of the earledome. And after his decease his son remained Laird of Ægle and a Lord of the Colledge of Justice. He had by her tuo sons and thrie daughters. 1. James first Earle of Pearth. 2. John second Earle of Pearth. 3. Lillias Lady Fyvie, maried to Alexander Setton, after Chancellor of Scotland, and Earle of Dumfermline, who bore to him Anne Countess of   , Issobel Countess of Lawderdale, Sophia Lady Balcarras, and Margaret, Countess of Seaforth. 4. The second daughter of Lord Patrick wes Jean Countess of Roxburgh. 5. The third daughter, Katharine, maried James, Master of Rothes, to whom she bore, (1.) John, Earle of Rothes, that great actor in the late civill warrs, who dyed at London, *non sine suspicione veneni.* (2.)   Lady Elphingstoun.

No. I.   APPENDIX.   249

(3.) Anna Lady Towie. [Nota, The Genealogie of Rothes sayes, this Katharine had only one daughter to this Master, that was Lady Weem in Athole.]

7. James succeeded his father, Lord Patrick. He wes imployed in that honourable embassie with the Earle of Nottinghame in Spain for the peace of the Low Countries. After his returne to Scotland he maried Issobell Seaton, daughter to the Earle of Winton. She bore to him one only daughter, Jean Drummond, who wes maried to the Earle of Sutherland. He wes created Earle of Perth, 4th March 1605. He died at Seaton, and wes buried in the chapell there : his Lady over him erected a marble monument with this inscription.

CONDITUM HIC EST QUICQUID MORTALE FUIT

JACOBI DRUMMOND, FAMILLÆ PRINCIPIS,

QUIQUE PRIMUS FAMILIAM TITULO PERTHIANI COMITATUS

ILLUSTRAVIT :

MONUMENTUM HOC POSUIT

AMANTISSIMA ET MOERENTISSIMA CONJUNX

D. ISSABELLA SEATOUN,

ROBERTI WINTONIAE COMITIS VNICA FILIA.

AN. SAL. M.DC.XI.

8. John, the second Earle, succeidet to his brother James. He maried Jean Kerr, daughter to Robert Earle of Roxburgh ; she bore to him 1. Henrie, who died a child. 2. James Lord Drummond, his successor. 3. Sir John Drummond. 4. Sir William Drummond. 5. Jean Lady Flyming. 6. Issobell Lady Tullibairne.

9. James Lord Drummond succeidit his father ; maried Ann Gordon, daughter to George, second Marquess of Huntly, execute for his fidelitie to his Prince in anno 1649.

David Lord Drummond his second son, by the Lord Ruthven's daughter, wes James Lord Madertie, who married   She bore to him   Lord Madertie, Sir James Drummond of Machany, Lady Oliphant, Lady Duncrub, Lady Largo.

Lord Madertie married   Leslie, daughter to my Lord of Lindoires ; who bore to him   Master of Madertie, and daughters. The Master of Madertie married   Grahame, sister to James Earle of Montrose.

Sir James Drummond of Machanie married   Hamilton, sister to my Lord of Barganie, who bore to him   And   Drummond, slain on the walles of Newcastle, at the taking of the toun, 1641.

2 K

GENEALOGIE OF DRUMMONDS OF CARNOCK, [NOW REPRESENTED BY SIR WILLIAM
DRUMMOND OF HAWTHORNDEN.]

Now, let us turne againe to the other sons of Sir John Drummond of Stobhall, who floorished about the year 1370; for Sir John had fyve sons by the Earle of Orkney's daughter. 1. Walter, who succeidit him. 2. Gawin. 3. Thomas. 4. Sir William, of whom in the next section. 5. John, the progenitor of the Drummonds in Portugall.

1. Sir William Drummond, the fourth son of Sir John Drummond of Stobhall, brother to Annabella the Queen, by her endeavoures apparently, acquyred one of the co-heires of Sir William Airth, knight of Carnock and Plain, to his wife; hir name wes Elizabeth Airth. He wes styled Sir William Drummond of Ermore. She bore to him

2. David Drummond of Carnock, who maryied Marion Cunninghame, daughter to the Laird of Wester Polmais; who bore to him

3. Robert Drummond, who married Marion Monteith, sister to William Monteith of West Kerse. She bore to him

4. Alexander Drummond, famous by his exyle and forfeiture with Archbald Earle of Angus, who maryed the mother of King James the Fyfth. This Alexander maried Marjorie, sister of Robert Bruce of Auchinbowy, by whom [he had] three sons and three daughters. 1. Sir Robert Drummond, Master of work, or Surveyor of King James the Sext his works. 2. Alexander Drummond of Meadop. The daughters were, the Lady Makerstoun, who bore Collonell Bartholomew Balfour, a valiant commander of the warrs of Holland, father to Sir Phillip Balfour; and the Ladyes Skelmor, and Froske Abercrombie, of whom was Sir Patrick Abercrombie, Sir David Abercrombie.

[Alexander Drummond of Meadop] maried   daughter of   Bruce; who bore to him Sir Alexander Drummond of Meidop, a Lord of Session, who died 11th July, 1619. Mr. John Drummond of Woodcockdale, a gentleman of the bed chamber to King James the Sext. Major William Drummond, slain at seige of Groll in Holland.

Sir Robert Drummond of Meidope, son of the said Sir Alexander, maried Hamilton, a sister of Binnie's; by whom [he had] only one son, killed at Aldern with

Montrose, in anno 1645; and the ladies of Kincavell and Kennet. The first was mother of the Bruces of Kincavell; the most renouned whereof was Mr. Robert, who travelled to Palistine. The second wes mother of Mr. Alexander Hay of Kennet and his brethren, &c.

5. Sir Robert Drummond maryed first Margaret Kirkcaldie, sister to the Laird of Grange, so famous in our Historyes, especiallie for keiping òf the castle of Edinburgh. By whom [he had] Margaret Drummond, who wes mother to
Areskine, Lord of Cambuskenneth, to Annabella Areskine, Lady Buchanan, and to   Areskine, Lady Tulliebody. Sir Robert his second wife was Marjorie Elphingston, sister to Robert Lord Elphingston, and neice to Alexander Lord Elphingston, slain at Flowdoun with King James the Fourth. Her mother's name wes   Areskine, daughter to the Lord Areskine. This Marjory bore to him, 1. Sir Patrick Drummond. 2. Sir John Drummond of Hawthornden, gentleman usher to James, King of Great Brittaine. 3. Margaret Lady Seafeild. 4. Jean Lady Lea.

Sir Patrick Drummond maryed Margaret Scot, heretrix of Monzea: He died before his father, the 17th August, 1587, leaving by the said Margaret, 1. Sir Alexander Drummond of Carnock. 2. Mr. James. 3. Patrick. 4. The Lady Kipponross.

6. Sir Alexander maryed Elizabeth Hepburne, daughter to Sir Patrick Hepburne of Wauchtoun, knight, by whom

7. Sir John Drummond, who maryed a daughter of Rollock, laird of Duncrub; in his person the lands of Carnock changed the sirname of Drummond. He, in the last civill warrs, wes slain at Alfoord, 1645. His lineall successor wes

8. Sir John Drummond of Hawthornden, who maryed Sussauna Fouller, sister to Sir William Fouller, secretarie to Anna, Queen of Great Brittain, who bore to him a son and tuo daughters.

9. Mr. William Drummond of Hawthornden. Anna Drummond, maryed to Sir John Scot knight, of Scots Tarvet, one of the Lords of the Session. [Anna Drummond bore to Sir John, Sir James Scot who maryed   Carnegie, sister to the Earle of Northesk.] Rebecca wes second daughter to Sir John Drummond, and maryed William Douglas of Bonjedwart, [and had issue.]

Another brother of Queen Annabella wes John, named in the Portugall genealogie, Johuan Escorcio, of whom are descended the Drummonds of the Isle of Madera.

This John came first to France, and from that to Spain and Portugall, out of which he hazarded, with the Portugall fleet, to sie Madera. Heire taken with the amenitie and plentie of the soyle, he forgot his native cold countrey, and marying, wes blessed with a fare race of children. The Portugall record sent to Scotland, in the reigne of King James the Fyfth, setteth down, that of gentlemen and women, small and great, 200 acknowledged ther descent and progenie from him. Such as we could find of his genealogie are Andreessa Goncalles Drummonda, a lady from Johuan Escorcio, Diego Pierez Drummondo, anno 1513.

Manuell Alfonso Ferrera, Martin Mendez de Vasconcelles, 1604. From these came many tokens of kinred to John Earl of Perthe, and Jean Lady Roxburgh and others. A new testification of their descent from the Hous of Stobhall wes sent to them. John Earl of Perthe sent this letter unto them. "*Quanta solent laetitia, &c.*" [See page 109.] Thus in English—

"What joy the meitting of friends and kinsmen, by tempest severed, disperst and distressed on seas, whom fame had many years reckoned amongst the dead, useth to bring the same in me wrought the sight of your unexpected but welcome letters. What greater contentment could I have wished, then to have found my House and Name after such a revolution of years, even scarce to have been limited by our ocean, and as it were overreached the pillars of Hercules. Not to recognize and acknowledge so ancient a kinsman, (so proved to be by such authentick witnesses as the registers of tuo Kingdomes) were not only repugnant to all humane civilitie, but even to the laws of nature, which in nothing more seemeth to delight then the conservation of ther kyndness; and not to extend my power for so worthy friends, who, in a strange and farr distant isle, in dispight of fortune, have continued ther race, were against the common precepts of vertue herselfe.

"I must yet challenge you of one thing, that ye should have suffered such a vast course of tyme over shadow your fame, and bury your rememberance in this your first native countrey; Scotland being a countrey better known to you then Madera to us; navigation being now more frequent. And this one letter of yours having had so good a fortune, I hope heireafter ye shall not prove so negligent. I regret by reason of my distance from court, my power can not equall my good will in performing your request with such expectation as I wish, by obtaining you the King of Great Britaignes recommendatorie letters, but [if] thes can serve your advancement, neather they nor the Great Seale of Scotland, with a gentleman of myne oun, shall be wanting. Direct your nixt letters to the Court of England, where many kinsmen and friends of myne are resident, who will occasion them to come to my hands. I have thus wrytten in Latine, at the desyre of the bearer, as he reporteth, being the language best understood in thes parts."

Of the other children of Sir John Drummond of Stobhall, except the names Gawen and Thomas, I have found no record.

REMAINS OF THE NAME OF DRUMMOND.

There is difficiencie in this genealogicall table of many gentlemen of the name of Drummond. We have had no information concerning the Drummonds of Concraig. Concraig is that rock upon which John first Lord Drummond builded the Castell of Drummond about the year 1470, and by ane excambion of certaine lands between the Drummonds of Boreland and Stobhall remained with the Drummonds of Stobhall. Of the Drummonds of Concraig are descended the Barrons of Boreland; amongst which the most famous was Malcolme Drummond, Boetius, and Leslie, p. 269, name him; John who, after the death of Robert the Third, whilst Mordoch governed, killed Patrick Earle of Strathern in anno 1411. The challenge wes, Patrick had talked that he had a better tytle to the croun of Scotland then King James, then prisoner in England, as being the race of Euphame Ross, first wyfe to King Robert, [she wes only his second wyfe] and to be preferred to the race of Elizabeth Moore; which injury Malcolme revenged by his death. [Nota. This wes not the real quarrell, but it wes because the Earle wes come in by force to remove him from the Steuart deputship of Stratherne.]

The last of this race wes Sir John Drummond, who seeking to repair his lost fortunes in Scotland by Ireland made a plantation ther. He had ane Uncle, famous for a librarie, which he first erected in Dumblane, and after in Stirling, *Blattis et tineis*; but more famous for his many years, haveing long since passed eighty, and now travelling towards the hundredth year of his age.

We have no instructions of the Drummond's [of] Blaze, potius Blaire in Angus, of which familly is Sir Patrick Drummond, Conservitour, and other gentlemen and ladyes of Milnab, Pitkellayne, [and] Samuell Drummond of Carlawrye ; of which family, Sir David Drummond and Sir Maurice were.

The race of Drummynerrioch is recordit to be from James the third son of Walter Drummond, Laird of Stobhall, called James of Coldoch. As the Drummonds of Coriwaughter [are] from the fourth son of this Walter. Corse Caplea is descended of Mr. Walter Drummond, Clerk Register.

John Lesly, in his history of Scotland, maketh mention of one Henricus Drummondus, anno 1560, a valiant and courageous commander of the Scots at Leith, who with one Kennedy, a stout man, wes their slain, page 568 and 561. Anno 1559 he nameth also one Drummondus Caduceate, page 566.

John Major in his history nameth only Annabella, fol. 122.; meaning King Robert, *In conjugem Annabellam filiam Joannis de Drummond ob mulieris pulchritudinem accepit,* anno 1391.

Hector Boetius maketh mention of Joannes Drummondus, (which should be Malcolm, or Malcolumbus, as Buchanan tenneth our names,) who killed the Earle of Strathern.

Buchanan makes mention of Joannes Drummondus, who wes the first Lord where he defeat the Earle of Lennox at Tylyemoss, lib. 13, p. 457. And of Alexander Drummond of Carnock, whom he nameth Alexander Drumanius, Carnocensis p. 511. lib. 14, and p. 513.

Edward Hall nameth only the Lord Stobhall, and Drummond L. of Stobhall Commissioner, with the Earles of Huntly, Angus, and Argyle, in the life of Richard the Third, fol. 20, and fol. 18.

Hollinshed maketh mention of the Drummonds in the lyfe of King James the Fourth, sie page 5. He maryed his daughter Margaret Steuart to George Lord Gordon. Her mother wes Margaret Drummond daughter to the Lord Drummond. Hollinshed maketh mention of John Lord Drummond, in the lyfe of King James the Fifth, the Governour of John Duke of Albany ; setting down at lenth how he wes forfeited and imprisoned for beatting ane herauld, but restored.

The Annales of England begun by John Stow, and continued by Edward Howes, makes mention, amongst the knights dubbed by King James at Westminster, 1602, of Sir John Drummond, Gentleman Usher, (fol. 827,) who wes Sir J. Drummond of Hawthornden.

No. I. APPENDIX.

Theodorus Beza, in ane Epistle prefixed to a piece of Mr. Robert Rollockes, maketh mention of David Drummonius.

Arthurus Johnstonus amongst his Epigrams, hath ane De Gulliemo Drummondo, page 21.—" *Quaesivit Latio*," &c. [See page 75.]

Michaell Drayton, a renowned English poet, maketh mention of Drummond of Hawthornden in his Elogie to Henry Reynolds esquire, of Poets and Poesie.

> So Scotland sent us hither, for our owne
> That Man, whose name I ever would have known
> To stand by mine, that most ingenious Knight
> My ALEXANDER; to whom in his right
> I want extremely, yet in speaking thus
> I do but shew the love that was twixt us,
> And not his numbers which were brave and hie,
> So like his mind, was his clear poesie:
> And my deare DRUMMOND to whom much I owe
> For his much love; and proud I wes to know
> His poesie, for which two worthy men,
> I MENSTRIE still shall love, and HAWTHORNDEN.

And the Author of the Vindication of Poesie named Drummond.

> Amongst the modernes came the Fairy Queen,
> Old Jeffrey, Sidney, Drayton, Randolph, Green,
> The double Beaumont, Drummond, Johnstoun, Brown;
> Each had his chaplet and his yule crown.

Cambden in his description of Great Britaigne, giveth a singular commendation to the ladyes of the Hous of Drummond, saying, that for ther unparalelled perfections and beautie the Kings of Scotland made choice of them for ther paramours.

Of all the ladyes in this genealogie nixt Annabella, Jean Lady Roxburgh appeareth to have been of most happy enduements and rare gifts, and even to the admiration of strangers. Antimo Galli, a famous Italian poet, haveing his residence a whyle at the English court, wrote this to her.([2])

([2]) Mylne's MS. contains a sonnet and two short extracts in Italian in praise of Lady Jean Drummond, and of James, Earl of Perth, from a volume of poems by this "Antimo Galli," or, as the name should probably be written, "Antonio Gatti;" but they are so extremely inaccurate and unintelligible, that it was thought proper to omit them, not being able to meet with a copy of the original work, from which they might have been given correctly.

Samuell Daniell, one of the gravest and statliest writters of England, either for verses or prose, did dedicate to her his pastorall tragicomedie, Hymen's Triumph, which was presented at the Queen's court in the Strand, at her nuptialls.

The brother Earles were not only great favourers of learned men, but very learned themselves, having spent some years in the most famous universities of France.

Thomas Dempsterus, that learned professor of Bononia, being in Scotland the time of the marriage of this Earle with the Earle of Wintoun's daughter, Issabell, presented him with an Epithalamium or nuptial verses; which the Earle rewarded with as much gold as defrayed his charges, till his returne to Italy, and a fair hecknay.

There wes no sound and solid knowledge in which Earle John was not taught and exercised in, witnes many volumnes market with his own hand, and thes many books he had not for ostentation but for use. He made a generall survey of all the best of man's learning, being compleat in all vertues and true worth. The ancient Hous by his industry wes increassed by the occasion of sundry fair lands which he purchassed. His loyaltie to his Prince was great, notwithstanding of great difficulties his sones were in during thes civill troubles in King Charles the First his reigne. His modesty and constancie wes praiseworthie, and his charity towards all men.

[Nota. He wes living the tyme that Hawthornden wrote this history, and wes past his great climacterick.]

APPENDIX.—No. II.

NOTES ON LORD STRATHALLAN'S GENEALOGIE
OF THE HOUSE OF DRUMMOND.

PAGE 1.—OF LORD STRATHALLAN'S work various manuscripts have been examined, and the text is taken from one which is probably the earliest that now exists, being "Coppied from the Original Manuscript by Mr. David Drummond, Advocate, Anno 1689." It is a folio volume of 66 leaves, somewhat injured by damp; and was purchased for the Advocates' Library, in the year 1818, at the sale of MSS. belonging to the Reverend James Scott of Perth. There is a transcript of the work in a modern hand in the Library at Drummond Castle, which has a continuation of the History of the Perth Family, afterwards enlarged, and published, by the author, under the title of "A Genealogical Memoir of the most Noble and Ancient House of Drummond, and of the several branches that have sprung from it, from its first founder, Maurice, to the present Family of Perth." By David Malcolm, A. M. Edinburgh, 1808, 12mo. pp. 254.

Pages 3. and 4.—COLLECTIONS FOR THE HISTORY OF THE FAMILY. Those of the three persons first named, Sir Robert Drummond of Meidop, Sir Patrick Drummond, and the Reverend Ninian Drummond, are not known to be extant.

The Genealogy by WILLIAM DRUMMOND OF HAWTHORNDEN, the distinguished poet, is now printed, for the first time, as No. I. of this Appendix. The letter of dedication, addressed to John Earl of Perth, has been frequently printed, but the lines with which it commences, and which are quoted from Chapman's spirited translation of Homer, have been hitherto misprinted, by not attending to its peculiar measure. It is uncertain at what time this Account of the Family was written. In the list of books presented by Drummond to the College of Edinburgh in 1626, is entered "The Genealogie of the House of Drummond, MS." As this manuscript is not now to be found in the Library, we can only infer that it was compiled by Drummond; but that he was engaged at a later period of life in such a work, is evident from his own words in the letter which is inserted in the Note to page 201. This letter being written in

1649, the year in which he died, it is very probable he did not live to render the Genealogy more perfect than it now appears.

Of Mr. JOHN FRIEBAIRN's work there are three manuscript copies in the Advocates' Library, agreeing very closely with each other; but from an earlier manuscript, communicated by HENRY HOME DRUMMOND, Esq. of Blair Drummond, it is evident that neither of these copies preserve the work entire, while it more fully confirms the truth of Lord Strathallan's observation, that Friebairn had come "nearest to the point, *if he had treated upon that head only.*" Mr. Home Drummond's MS. (like a similar transcript in the Library of the Antiquarian Society of Scotland) probably contains only the first half of the work, divided into eleven chapters; of which the other transcribers have omitted the title, dedication, and various long and tedious digressions, not illustrative of the History of the Family of Drummond. Thus, for instance, Chapter Seventh " Contains, be way of digression, the Resolution of the question, Whither Dundie was ever called Alectum? and so being, Whither it changed that name in Don-der or Don-tar, or if there be a better nor any of them?"

The title of the manuscript runs thus:—

" An Extract of the Noble Race of the Drommonds, from their first comming to Scotland out of Hungarie, to this present tym. Whercunto is added and intermingled, be way of digressione, an number of pretiouse and rare peeces of Storie, drawen out of authenticque evidences, which as they serve and concurre to the clearing of this taske, so to rectifie many errors and mistakes in our Scottish histories, never published before. Newly collected and emitted be Mr. John Friebairne, an old Minister and Preacher of the Gospell at Madertie, within the Countie of Stratherne."

The dedication, dated 20th Junii 1636, is sufficiently comprehensive, being addressed " To the Right Noble John Earle of Perth," &c. " To his noble children, William Earle of Roxburgh, James Lord Drommond, Sir John Drommond of Coldach, Ladie Jean Drommond Countesse of Wigtoune, Ladie Lilias Drommond Countesse of Tullibardin, and their hopefull Offspring." And

"To his honorable Cousins, David Lord Madertie, Sir James Drommond of Machanie, William Drommond of Riccartoune, their Ladies and Children, and All the Branches of that noble Stock within or without this Kingdome: the Author wisheth grace and glorie through Jesus Christ, blessed for ever, Amen."

Some extracts from Friebairn's History are inserted in the following Notes.

Page 15.—ORIGIN OF THE NAME OF DRUMMOND. The passage in Isiodorus, here quoted, is as follows:—" Longae naves sunt, quas Dromones vocamus: dictae eo quod longiores sint caeteris, quibus contrarius Musculus, curtum navigium. Dromo autem à decurrendo dicitur. Cursum enim Graeci δρομον vocant." Isiodori Origines, lib. xix. cap. i. Matriti 1599, folio.

Page 15.—In Drummond of Hawthornden's Works, p. 228, there is " A short Discourse upon Impressa's and Anagrams," addressed to John Earl of Perth. The subject is further pursued by him in the following letter to the same nobleman.

To the Right truly [Noble] Honourable Earle of Perth.

My Noble Lord,

After a long inquirie about the armes of your Lordships auncient House, and the turning of sundrye bookes of Impresses and Heraildrye, I found your VNDES famous and verye honorable. In our neighbour countrey of England they are borne, but inuersed vpside downe, and deversifyed. Torquato Tasso, in his Rinaldo, maketh mentione of a Knight who had a rocke placed on the waues, with the word, *Rompe ch'il percote*. An other hath the sea waues with a sirene rising out of them, the word *Bella Maria*, which is the name of some courtezan. Antonio Perenotto, Cardinal Granvella, had for an Impresa, the sea, a shipe in it, the word "*Durate*" out of the first of the Aeneades, "*Durate et vosmet rebus seruate secundis.*" Tomasso de' Marini, Duca di Terra Nuono, had for his Impresa, the waues with a sunne ouer them, the word "*Nunquam siccabitur aestu.*" The Prince of Orange vsed for his Impresa, the waues with a halcyon in the midst of them, the word "*Mediis tranquillus in undis,*" which is rather an embleme than impresa, because the figure is in the word. By reasone of your Lordships name, and the long continuance in your House, to none they apertaine more rightlie than to your Lordship. *Drum* is, in the old Celtique and British language, an height, and *Onde*, in all the countreyes almost of Europe, a waue ; which word is said to haue beene giuen in a storme, by Margarite Queene of Scotland, to a Gentleman who accompanyed her, the first of your Lordship's house. But to make an inquirie in surnames were now too long.

W. Drummond.

20th of Feburarye.

Ruscelli in his Impreses.

Page 17.—The armorial bearings, on the engraved plate opposite the title, are given in facsimile from a MS. of the Arms of the Scotish Nobility, emblazoned in the reign of Charles I., by John Sawers, a herald painter. The MS. is preserved in the Advocates' Library, and appears at one time to have belonged to the Lyon Herald Office.

Page 30.—LORD STRATHALLAN in the Second Partition of his Pedigree appears to have overlooked several of the heads of the Family. Their descent, during the 13th, 14th, and 15th centuries, is thus represented by later writers, omitting the references to authorities which are given in *Wood's Peerage of Scotland.*

SIR MALCOLM DRUMMOND, who flourished in the Reign of William I. Lord Strathallan (p. 29.) designates him as Fifth Thane or Seneschall of Lennox. He had two sons.

MALCOLM BEG DRUMMOND, Sixth Thane of Lennox, died before 1260. In a charter of Maldwin, third Earl of Lennox, in 1225, he appears as a witness, and is designed by the Earl, *Camerarius meus.* He witnessed other charters of a later date, of the same Earl, whose daughter Ada he married—leaving two sons :	RODERICK DRUMMOND, who, in an inquisition on the division of some lands in Dumbartonshire, is designed brother of Malcolm Beg, in 1234.

MALCOLM DRUMMOND, the eldest son, in a charter dated 1260, is designed son of Malcolm Beg Drummond and steward of Lennox. He witnessed other charters in 1273 to 1272—and left three sons.	JOHN DRUMMOND, also designed son of Malcolm Beg Drummond, in a charter of Maldwin, Earl of Lennox.

SIR JOHN DRUMMOND, (designed as filius Malcolmi) swore feallty to king Edward I. in 1296 ; was carried prisoner to England, and released the following year on condition of serving Edward in his wars in France, in 1297. He left three sons and two daughters by his wife, daughter of Walter Earl of Monteath.	GILBERT DE DRUMMOND, mentioned in several charters betwixt 1280 and 1290. Gilbert de Dromund, and his son, Malcolm de Drummond, swore fealty to Edward I. King of England in 1296. This Malcolm was father of Brice Drummond, killed by the Menteiths in 1330. See pp. 29 and 66.	THOMAS DRUMMOND of Balfrone, who is mentioned by Lord Strathallan, page 38.

SIR MALCOLM DRUMMOND, the eldest son succeeded about the year 1301, and died about 1325. He distinguished himself at the battle of Bannockburn. See note to page 38. He left by his wife, the daughter of Sir Patrick Graham of Kincardine—a son.	GILBERT, mentioned in a ratification by Malcolm, fifth Earl of Lennox, of the lands and church of Kilpatrick, in 1330.	WALTER DRUMMOND, Clerk Register, mentioned by Lord Strathallan, page 37. as one of the Commissioners sent to England, in 1328.

SIR MALCOLM DRUMMOND, who died about 1346. In a charter of Malise Earl of Strathern, he is designed Malcolm, son of Malcolm Drummond. David II. by two charters confirmed to him the lands of Tulliecraven and Dronan, and the coronership of the county of Perth. He had three sons.

No. II. APPENDIX.

SIR JOHN DRUMMOND, mentioned by Lord Strathallan, page 65, and who by his marriage with the eldest daughter and co-heiress of Sir William de Montefex, (See p. 84.) obtained the lands of Stobhall, Cargill, &c. which were confirmed to him by royal charter from David II., together with the office of baillerie of Abthain of Dull, in Athole. By her he had four sons and four daughters, the eldest of whom was Annabella Queen of Scotland.

SIR MAURICE DRUMMOND ancestor of the Drummonds of Concraig, (p. 39. Culqualzie, (p. 51.) Milnab, (p. 62.) Lennoch, Broich, (p. 61.) Balloch, (p. 59.) Pitkellony, (p. 55.) &c.

WALTER DRUMMOND, who had a charter from King David II. wherein he is designed *nostrorum Rotulorum registro, et a Consiliis.*

SIR MALCOLM DRUMMOND. See p. 86. He was at the battle of Otterburn, 1388, and succeeded to the Earldom of Marr, in right of his wife, Lady Isabell Douglas. He died in 1403, leaving no issue.

SIR JOHN DRUMMOND, who succeeded his brother.

WILLIAM DRUMMOND, married one of the daughters and co-heiresses of Airth of Airth, with whom he got the lands of Carnock. From him are descended the Drummonds of Carnock, Maidhope, and Hawthornden. (p. 71–75.)

ANNABELLA, married to John, Earl of Carrick, afterwards King of Scotland by the name of Robert III. He died in 1401. (See page 76.) Her second son was King James the First.

SIR JOHN DRUMMOND of Cargill, Justiciary of Scotland, in 1391, succeed his elder brother, (See p. 111.) and died in 1448, leaving by his wife Elizabeth, eldest daughter of Henry, Earl of Orkney, three sons and three daughters.

SIR WALTER DRUMMOND of Cargill and Stobhall, (See p. 111.) who died in 1455, leaving by his wife Margaret, daughter of Sir William Ruthven, three sons.

ROBERT DRUMMOND, who is said to have assumed the name of Moubray, on his marriage with the heiress of Barnbougle. (See p. 111.)

JOHN ESCORTIO DRUMMOND, who is said to have settled in Madeira. (See page 92.)

SIR MALCOLM DRUMMOND of Cargill and Stobhall, died in 1470. (See p. 118.) He married in 1445, Mariot eldest daughter of Sir David Murray of Tullibardine, and had by her six sons.

JOHN DRUMMOND, Dean of Dumblane. (See page 118.)

WALTER DRUMMOND of Ledcrieff, progenitor of the Drummonds of Blair and Gaerdrum. (See p. 113.)

SIR JOHN DRUMMOND, of Cargill and Stobhall, afterwards First LORD DRUMMOND. He died in 1519. (See p. 132.)

WALTER DRUMMOND, of Deanston. (See p. 118.)

JAMES DRUMMOND, of Corywauchter. (See p. 122.)

THOMAS DRUMMOND, of Drummond-Irenoch. (See p. 124.)

WILLIAM DRUMMOND, of Muthill.

ANDREW DRUMMOND, Vicar of Strageth.

Page 35, line 15.—" Copies of old Charters." Father Hay in his MS. collections, says, " The first Drummond that I find in records is Malcome Beg, and Roderig Beg his brother, who are mentioned in the chartular of Paslay, pag. 323 and 324, ad annum 1223." And he adds,—" I am curious to sie that writt [the Charter by Malcolm Earl of Lennox, to the church of Campsay, at p. 367,] before I give faith to what they advance." Memoires, tome ii. p. 85.

Page 38, line 14.—It will be apparent from the Table we have given, that Lord Strathallan's conjectures are not correct, as he has confounded the descent of several generations. Malcolm Drummond who appears as a witness to this charter in 1296, it may be inferred, was either the son or nephew of the Gilbert de Drummond whose name stands first. We are informed that "Sir Malcolm Drummond was a person of so great importance, that King Edward I. on the 25th of August, 1301, offered oblations at the shrine of St. Kentigern, in the cathedral of Glasgow, for the good news of Sir Malcolm de Drummond, knight, a Scot, being taken prisoner by Sir John Segrave. Adhering to King Robert I. he obtained from that prince in 1315, not long after the battle of Bannockburn, for his good and faithful services, a grant of several lands in Perthshire ; and it is conjectured that the caltrops were then added by way of compartment to his arms, as they were used in that memorable action with great success against the English horse, possibly under his direction." *Wood's Peerage*, ii. 358.

Lord Strathallan, at page 15, line 26, has referred to the disposal of Auchindonnan, by Malcolm Beg Drummond to Malcolm Fleming about the year 1290: there is printed in the Collection of Royal Charters, edited by Thomas Thomson, Esq. a charter of Robert the Bruce in 1316, confirming the resignation of the lands of Auchindonan, " quam Malcolmus de Drumond coram magnatibus nostris nobis resignavit." (Registrum Magni Sigilli, p. 16, No. 81.)

Page 39, line 21.—The words, " 2. This Sir Maurice," &c. should have formed part of the preceding paragraph ; and the new paragraph commenced at the middle of line 23. " 2. Sir Maurice Drummond, sone," &c.

Page 40, line 16. " Glasdun," read " Glaselun."

Page 41, line 19.—Johannes de Drommond de Concraig, miles, is witness to a charter dated last November 1406. (Registrum Magni Sigilli, p. 227, No. 14.)

Page 50, line 8.—The work by Rollok, to which Beza's epistle is prefixed, is entitled, Tractatus de Vocatione Efficaci, Edinburgi, 1597, 12mo. The letter, dated Geneva Cal. Novembris 1596, is addressed to John Johnstone, from which it appears that David Drummond was the bearer of letters to Beza's friends in Scotland. His words are, " Hanc verò tam beatam sortem, tibi, cæterisque istic venerandis fratribus, hisce literis gratulandi gaudeo præbitam mihi occasionem, tùm ab eo vestrate, D. DAVIDE DROMENIO, viro pio, et non indocto, cujus præsentia aliquot dierum nobis hic fuit jucundissima, ad vos revertente, cui has literas commisi."

Alexander Montgomery, author of the Cherrie and the Slae, has a Sonnet, written probably about 1590, addressed to M. David Drummond, which concludes,—

> Sa thou lyk Dido, Maister David Drummond
> Hes me to ansueir, by thy Sonnet summond.

The following epigram, " Ad Davidem Dromondum," occurs in a volume of Latin poems, by John Dunbar, London 1616, p. 193:—

> Qui Dromonde tribus dictum de montibus inquit
>   Esse tuum nomen, falliter haud dubiè ;
> Nimirum duplici Parnassi à vertice venit :
>   Hinc est quòd tantus esse Poeta soles.

Page 50, line 15.—Sir John Drummond of Bordland was served heir of his ancestor (attavus) John Drummond, son and heir of Maurice Drummond, August 5th, 1609. (Inquis. Retorn. Abbreviatio.—Inq. Gen. No. 429.)

Page 50, line 25.—William Drummond was served heir of his father, Malcolm Drummond, brother-german of Sir John Drummond of Bordland, knight, May 22d. (Ib. No. 4134.)

Page 54, line 14.—John Drummond of Coquhallie, was served heir male of his grandfather, John Drummond of Coquhallie, March 3, 1658. (Perth, No. 663.)

Page 54, line 23.—John Drummond of Coquhallie was served heir male of his father, John Drummond of Coquhallie, April 18, 1688. (Ib. No. 971.)

Page 58, line 7.—John Drummond of Kirkhill was served heir of his brother Daniel Drummond, April 13, 1602, (Perth, No. 93.); and heir of his father, James Drummond of Kirkhill, Aug. 1, 1605, (Ib. No. 149.)

Page 58, line 14.—James Drummond was served heir of his father, John Drummond of Pitzalloun, November 26, 1601. (Perth, No. 87.)

Page 59, line 12.—The Third Branch from the House of Concraig, omitted by Lord Strathallan, is probably that of Lennoch. John Drummond, second son of Sir John Drummond, third Knight of Concraig, (page 41. line 15,) was the progenitor of the

Family of Lennoch and Megginch, which latter title was assumed on purchasing the estate of Megginch in the reign of Charles II.—In the Index of Fines during the reign of Charles II. is the following: "Received from Mr. John Drummond of Meggins, as the fyne imposed by the Councill, for his lady and his eldest son being present at ane Conventicle, per discharge, dated 24th of July 1672, £6000 Scots."

Page 60, line 19.—In the Acts of Parliament, 1592, is printed the Ratification of the Charter of fewfarm granted by the late Roger Gordon, Deane of Dunblane, to George Drummond of Balloche, and the late Margaret Drummond his spouse. (Vol. iii. p. 591.)

The following notices of members of the Balloch Family are taken from the Retours:

Page 60, line 25.—Henry Drummond was served heir of his father, George Drummond of Balloch, March 27, 1600. (Perth, No. 61. See also Nos. 104, 121, 227.)

Page 61, line 2.—John Drummond of Balloch was served heir male of his grandfather, Harie Drummond of Balloch, October 21, 1657, (Perth, No. 653,) and heir of his father, George Drummond of Balloch, on the same day. (Inquis. Gen. No. 4282.)

Page 61, line 9.—David Drummond was served heir of his father, George Drummond of Balloch, March 3, 1665. (Ib. No. 4874.)

Page 61, line 15.—Mr. Henry Drummond of Balloch was served heir male of his grandfather, Henry Drummond of Balloch, April 11, 1662, (Perth, No. 690,) and of his father, George Drummond of Balloch, April 6, 1676. (Ib. No. 893. Inquis. Gen. No. 5990.)

Robert Drummond of Balloch, was served heir of his brother-german, Mr. Henry Drummond of Balloch, February 26, 1690. (Perth, No. 981. Inquis. Gen. No. 7003.)

One of this family, probably Robert, who is last mentioned, was the author of a volume of unpublished poems, containing a religious poem entitled "Phyllis, in four sections. 1. Age and Life. 2. Vertue and Fortune. 3. Death and Resurrection. 4. Hymns and Prayers." Together with Two Centuries of Riddles, &c.

"Conditur exigua lepidus Ballocus in urna,
"Cui natura parens, sorsque noverca fuit."

Page 61, line 19.—Patrick Drummond of Broich, was served heir of his father James Drummond of Broich, Sept. 10, 1663. (Retours, Perth, No. 722.)

Page 62, line 10.—This notice of John Drummond, "Master of Works" to James the Fourth and Fifth, is interesting; but whether he shall be entitled to the credit of designing and executing the fine carvings known as the "Stirling Heads," may be considered doubtful. In the Treasurer's Accounts during the latter part of the reign of James the Fourth, the name of "John Drummond wricht," frequently occurs. Thus, for instance,

"1512. August 4.—Item, to Johne of Drummond, wrycht, in part of payment of his awne wagis, and vtheris wrichtis hewand hemys, and vtheris werkis, to gud compt, L.7.

—— Aug. 24.—Item to Johne of Drummond, wrycht, laborand with his servitouris in the woddis, to gude compt, L.14.

—— Sept. 18.—Item, send be Wille Stewart to Johne of Drummond, wrycht, in compleyt payment of four wrychtis and four sawaris wagis and feys with the said Johne in the wod of Kincardine, hewand hem stokkis and quheill graith, fra the ferd day of August to this day, eftir his bill of compt gevin thairon, L.11.

1512-13. Feb. 24.—Item, giffin to Johne Drummond, wricht, to pas to Logan Wod in Anerdale, and to the Wod of Cambusnethane in Cliddsdale for tymmer, and certane seruandis with him, L.4, 4s."

His name also occurs in the Treasurer's Accounts during the reign of James V. Whether the first entry refers to the same person may be doubted, as we have no hint given that he ever appeared as the King's kemp or champion, although, it will be seen, he was employed to make the lists for some exhibition of knightly prowess at the time.

"1527. March 1.—Item, to Johne Drummond, callit the Kingis kemp, be his precept, L.15.—(About the same date.) Item, to Johne Drummond to by tymmer to make listis in the Abbey, L.30.—Item, in drinksiluer at the beginning of the said listis, 20s."

Page 63, line 14. Patrick Drummond was served heir of his father William Drummond of Milnab, June 30, 1603. (Retours, Perth, No. 115. See also No. 118.)

Page 63, line 22. Among the epitaphs subjoined to the "Funerall Sermon preached at the buriall of the Lady Iane Maitlane, daughter to the Right Honourable Earle, Iohn Earl of Lauderdail, at Hadington, the 19th of December, 1631. By Mr. I. M." Edinburgh, 1633, 4to. there is one beginning,

"When thy fair beautie like the blushing morne," (34 lines.)

which is signed "James Drummond of Millanab."

James Drummond, according to the late historian of the family, was forty years depute of Stratherne; and dying in 1664, in the 83d year of his age, a marble bust was erected to his memory in the church of Crieff, with the following inscription:—

> Juridici, nullo secli data crimine pessum,
> Obruta quin senio, busta verenda vides.
> Hunc juvenem amplexae musae charitesque, senectae
> Sed fuerat gravitas, consiliumque decus.
> Quantus adest Heros! viridi ipse pavesco juventâ,
> Ut cineres tanti ceperat urna viri!
> Obit Anno, M.DC.LXIV. Kal. Decembris xvii. aetatis suae LXXXIII.

In Malcolm's House of Drummond, p. 227, is inserted a translation of these lines "by a youth who was one of his descendants," but whose name is not mentioned.

Page 64, line 9. John Drummond of Mylnabe was served heir of his father Mr. David Drummond of Mylnabe, April 15, 1669, (Retours, Perth, No. 790. See also Jan. 27, 1681. Inquis. Gen. No. 6265.) John Drummond of Callendar, at the last mentioned date was served heir of his grandfather James Drummond of Mylnabe, (Perth, No. 907. See also Inq. Gen. No. 8088.)

Page 64, line 15. George Drummond was Lord Provost of Edinburgh in 1684, and was knighted in July that year. (Fountainhall's Chronological Notes, p. 91.) From the same authority we learn that he became bankrupt, (pp. 119, 120. 143. 200. 209.) The lands of Milnab which he purchased from his Nephew in 1677, he subsequently disposed of to James Earl of Perth.

Page 65.—" Sir John liv'd in 1325, in which year I find this record in the books of Aberbrothe, pag. 142,—Joannes Drumminus Vice-comes de Aberdeen, ac locum tenens nobilis viri Domini Alexander Frazer Camerarij Scotiae." Father Hay's Memoires, vol. ii. p. 86.

Page 66, line 1. David II. granted a charter "to John Drummond, of all lands quhilks pertained to Marie Montefixo." Robertson's Index of Charters, p. 33, No. 31.

Page 68, line 11.—The Indenture between the Drummonds and Menteaths in the year 1360, is alluded to by Drummond of Hathornden, in the dedication to John Earl of Perth, of his History of the Jameses, and is "published from the original copy" in the edition of his Works, 1711, folio, p. 241.

Page 69, line 24. In the Registrum Magni Sigilli, (p. 113, No. 3.) is printed a confirmation charter by Robert II. to Sir Alexander de Meneteth of the lands of Rossneth, in the Earldom of Lennox, which Mary Countess of Meneteth, in her widowhood, had granted to the late John Drummond, and by him disponed to Sir Alexander. It is dated the last of March, anno Regni 2do, or 1372.

Page 71, line 15.—"Archbald Earle of Douglas," an evident mistake for Archibald Earle of Angus.

Page 71, line 17. Alexander Drummond of Carnock was summoned to appear at the parliament held at Edinburgh, on the 4th of September 1528, and not appearing, was forfeited, (Acts of Parliament, vol. ii. 322, 326. Lesley's History, p. 140.) He was restored by an Act of Parliament, May 13, 1532, (ib. p. 336.)

Page 71, line 23.—Sir Robert Drummond of Carnock, Master of Works, is mentioned again at page 74, his second son by a second marriage, being the first laird of Hawthornden. He died in the year 1592, aged 74; and the following quaint epitaph on him occurs in the poems of Alexander Montgumery, author of the "Cherrie and Slae." Edit. Edin. 1820, p. 244.

EPITAPH OF THE MAISTER OF WORK, [SIR ROBERT] DRUMMOND OF CARNOK, [KNIGHT.]

Stay, Passinger, thy mynd, thy futt, thy ee ;
Vouchsaif, a we, his epitaph to view,
Quha left bot feu behind him, sik as he ;
Syn leirnd to de, to live agane aneu.
All knoues this treu, quho noble Carnok kneu.
This Realme may reu that he is gone to grave.
All Buildings brave bids Drummond nou, adeu ;
Quhais lyf furthsheu, he lude thame by the laiv,
Quhair sall we craiv, sic policie to baiv ?
Quha with him straiv to polish, build, or plante ?
These giftis, I grant, God lent him by the laiv ;
Quha mot resaiv his saull to be a sante !
To regne with him in evirlasting glore,
Lyk as his corps his country did decore.

Page 72, line 7.—Patrick Drummond "apperand of Carnock," is mentioned in the Acts of Parliament, in the year 1584, (vol. iii. pp. 332—334, *passim.*)

Page 72, line 9. Margaret Drummond, wife of James Kynros, fiar of Kippenros, was served heir of provision and entail, of her father's sister, Elizabeth Drummond, sister of the late Patrick Drummond, fiar of Kernok, Nov. 21. 1598. (Retours, Stirling, No. 367.)

APPENDIX. No. II.

Page 72, line 15. Alexander Drummond of Carnok, was served heir of his father, Patrick Drummond, fiar (feoditarius) of Carnok, Dec. 1, 1596. (Perth, No. 1079.)

Page 72, line 19. John Drummond of Carnok was served heir male of his father, Sir Alexander Drummond, May 16, 1627. (Perth, No. 351. Stirling, No. 121.)

Page 73, line 2. The name of Alexander Drummond of Medhop, in 1584, is mentioned in the Acts of Parliament, vol. iii. p. 287.

Page 73, line 4. Sir Robert Drummond, an evident blunder for Sir Alexander, who is thus correctly designated at lines 9 and 15.

Page 73, line 14. Sir Robert Drummond, it is said in Dedication, "left some Memorials" regarding the history of the Drummonds.

Page 74. FAMILY OF HAWTHORNDEN. The following account of the family is copied from the Manuscript Collections of Father Augustine Hay, who was grandson to Sir John Hay of Landes. For farther particulars, see the articles Drummond, in Kippis's Biographia Britannica, and in Douglas's Baronage.

" Sir John Drumond, sone to Sir Robert, fyfth Laird of Carnoke by his second wife, was first Laird of Hawthornden. He was gentleman uscher to King James the Sext ; and married Susanna Fowler, daughter to Sir William Fowler, secretary to Anna, Queen of Great Brittain. He had by her one sone, Mr. William, and two daughters. Anna, spouse to Sir John Scott of Scotstarveth, one of the Kings Secret Counsell, Director of the chancellry, and a Lord of the Colledge of Justice. She had to him Sir James Scott, who married . . . . . Carnagy, sister to the Earle of Northesk, upon whom he begot David Scott, now of Scotstarvett. Sir John his second daughter, Rebecca, married William Douglass, Laird of Bongedward. The Annalls of England begun by John Stow, and continued by Edward Howes, makes mention of Sir John Dromond, gentleman usher, who was dubbed Knight by King James, at Westminster, anno 1603.

" Mr. William Drummond of Hawthornden, sone to Sir John, was born anno 1585, was made Mr. of Arts att Edinburgh in 1606 ; past into France to study the laws, but sieing himself unfitt for the toiles, and difficultys of that study, he betooke himself to the softer intertainement of the Muses. Att 45. years of adge, he married unexpectedly Elisabeth Logan, a ministers daughter of Edliston, which church is within a quarter of a mile of Darnhill [Darnhall], principall dwelling house to Blackbarrony. Her mother was a shepherd's daughter. The family of Hawthornden pretends that she was daughter to the Laird of Cottfeild, and grandchild to Sir Robert Logan of Lestalrig: but no sutch matter. This William Dromond wrott the History of our Nation from 1425 till 1542, with severall Memorials of State dureing the reign of Charles the first, [and] divers pieces of poesie. He left a quantity of books to the library of Edinburgh, and died in 1649. Michael Dredan, [Drayton] a renown'd English poet, maketh mention of him in his Elogie of Poets and Poesy, to Henry Rynolds, Esquire. And the Author of the Vindication of Poesy nameth him. Arturus Johnstonus amongst his Epigramms hath one, page 21, De Gullielmo Dromondo. *"Quaesirit Latio, &c.* [See page 75.] He begott upon Elisabeth Logan, Sir William, Robert, and a daughter named Elisabeth, married to Mr. Henry Hendersone, a famous doctor of physick, by whom she had only a daughter, Elisabeth Henderson, married to Sir John Clerk of Pennycooke. Her childering are John, Henry, Elisabeth, and Barbara Clerk. Robert, Mr. William his second sone, married Anna Maxwell, sister to the Laird of Hills; died Roman catholick, left noe childering. He was a gentleman of the Guard; commonly he was stil'd Rachihomme, he was mutch given to drinke.

"Willielmus Drumond puer in politiori litteratura domi tum in juris scientia institutus, in historia concinnanda et pangendis versibus magnam laudem promeruit. Gentis namque suae historiam ornatissime perscripsit, cunctis haud dubie erepta laude qui id generis munus ante susceperant. Cum vix 56 aetatis annum attigisset excessit e vita cum diu pectoris angustia ex pituitae stillicidia laborasset, immatura sane morte, cum quisque ab uberi ejus ingenio plura sibi polliceretur fato functus est domi, relatusque inde ad fanum finitimum in specu subterranea conditus est. Sunt qui ereptum scribant cum accepto temere pharmaco, quo se adversus morbos praemuniret, vitae suae jocabundus illusisset, pervasurus haud dubie ad exactam aetatem, nisi intempestivis medicamentivis insanus medicus viscera corrupisset.

"William Dromond, whose fame reacheth no furder then the narrow bounds of some few climats of this small Globe of the Earth, lays buried in the dust at Leswade, without any monument, till the Almighty God raise and refine his scatter'd ashes, after soe many alterations on the Earth.

"Sr William, eldest sone to Mr. William, poet, as he pretends only representative of the House of Carnock; a man of a hideous bulke, if tallow and skins had become searse, he had been ane excellent purchase for some hungry starved courtier to have beg'd of the King; he had made infinit gains in selling as mutch skin out of each cheek, as would cloath'd up a pair of bag pipes. Sir William purchased the title of a Justice of peace by my Lord Lauderdale's favour, a place full of labour, charge, trouble, without any profitt to himself, only able to gratifie his own ambition, for he was fitter to set in privat parlors over the glass, whilst healths goe round, and to examine the condition of a pot of ale, which he hath good opportunity to discover, than the circumstances of any debate that comes before him. He married Sophia Auchamouty, daughter to Sir Alexander Auchamouty of Gosford, Master of the Rolls to King James the Sixt and King Charles the First. Upon whom he begot only one daughter, Sophia Dromond, matched with John Murray of Kringelty in Tweddale, eldest sone of the second marriage to Sir Alexander Murray of Blackbarony, a man of a bade shape, crookbacked, unfit for marriage and not without some distemper of spirit. She was divorced from him by law, and afterwards joyned in marriage with Robert Preston, sone to the Laird of Gorton, by his first lady. Sir William had for second wife Barbara Scott, daughter to Sir William Scott of Clerkington, a senator of the colledge of justice. He begot upon her William, Robert, Barbara Lady Abbayhill, Elisabeth, Anna, Margaret, Marie, and Jacobina.

" William Dromond, the poet, bore *Argent* three fasces, unde *Gules*, for supporters two wild men, with clubs, as the Earle of Perth ; above his crest, a Pegasus *Or* with displayed wings ; for motto, *Hos gloria reddit honores*, which words are taken from Petronius Arbiter in his Satyricon, pag. 273.

" As for Hawthornden it is upon the south of the river Esk ; it is thought ane ancient fortification, its tower seemeth to have been the worke of the Romans, by the doors of so mutch of that tower as remaineth being all without, which made them have the name of *Fores*. This place is renown'd for certaine cav's in the middest of a stippe rock ; in those caves there is a spyder which maketh a kind of silk ball of the greatness of a wallnutt, and is bred and nourish'd upon a certain ride minerall appearing in the clifts of the rocke. Besides, here are found of old characters numismata, medalls. Johannes Major makes mention of this Fort, in the life of King David, in his 5 booke *De gestis Scotorum*, cap. 13 and 16, about the year 1340."

The preceding extracts taken from " Memoires, or a collection of severall things relating to the Historicall account of the most famed families of Scotland. Done by Mr. Richard Augustin Hay, Cannon Regular of Sainte Genovefs of Paris, Prior of St Pieremont, &c. Tome Second, Anno Domini, 1700." MS. folio, Advocates' Library p. 105—107.

Page 74, line 17.—Mr. William Drummond was served heir of his father, Sir John Drummond of Hathorndene, knight, Aug. 24. 1611. (Retours; Edin^r. No. 1455. Linlithgow, No. 304. Peebles, No. 214. Stirling, No. 370.)

Page 75, line 15.—William Drummond of Halthorndean, was served heir of his father Mr. William Drummond of Haltherndean.—Decr. 29. 1652. (Ib. Inq. Gen. No. 3726.)

Page 74. l. 25.—Mylne's MS., written at a later period, says "sex daughters;" and in line 26, after the words Mary [and Jacobina] Drummonds, supplies this additional information regarding the Hawthornden family. "His eldest son, William, is now abroad, a pretty gentleman. I sie those letters of recommendation under the present Earle of Perth's hand, the first from Stirling Castle, the 8th of March 1689, direct to Monsieur Innes, principall du College des Ecoseis a Paris, is thus:

" May it please your   the bearer Mr. William Drummond, laird of Hauthornden is my cousine; his predecessor was a brother to that Queen of Scotland who was mother to one of our most famous Kings, James the First. He is a loyall honest young man and loves me. These are to recommend to yow to befriend him, &c.

"Ane other letter of the same date, to " Madame Madame la Countesse de Crollis, Rue St. Honore proche le Pallais Royalle a Paris." [This was Lady Anne Gordon, daughter to the Marquis of Huntly, and wife of the Count de Crolli.] " Madam, the bearer of this letter, Mr. Drummond of Hauthornden, whose grandfather was famous for his witt, and fidelitie to his prince, being (rather than live in Holland) resolved to spend some time where monarchie and good principalls are more in fashion than in a commone wealth, would gladly be under the protection of some great men, being of a religion that is not much favoured where yow are. He is my cousine, and the family he is of, since they were a familly, (that is to say, near 300 years, for the first of this house was brother to that Queen who was mother to King James [the] First) hes been royall, so I hope yow will procure him such a pass from the Bishop of Meaux as may be usefull to him, and give him your advice what to doe, and how to live, for his father does not allow him too much to live upon. In all this I hope ye will be so good as to oblidge me, and nothing the less that I writ from this place, where I have now lyen these 11 weiks. I am,

Your most obedient servant and brother,

PERTH."

" As also another letter to Monsieur Monsieur Herbbe Renaudet to the same purpose.

"Anne, Sir William his second daughter, maried John Corser, wryter in Edinburgh; Margaret maried   Nairne, a baillie in Dalkeyth; Mary maried Charles Mylne, eldest son of Sir Robert Mylne, Baronet, a captaine in the Foot Guards; Barbara maried Purves of Abbayhill—she was eldest." Pp. 58, 59.

Page 76, line 10.—The marriage of John Earl of Carrick, and Annabella, daughter of Sir John Drummond of Stobhall, took place at least twenty years before he ascended the throne of Scotland, by the title of Robert III. Abercromby has quoted a charter, the date of which, if correctly given, would fix the marriage to the year 1357, but it has been supposed he made an error by antedating it ten years. Robert III. and Annabella were crowned at Scone, August 14, 1390. Two letters written in French, by Annabella Queen of Scotland, to Richard II. of England, 28th May and August 1, 1394, are preserved among the Cottonian MSS. in the British Museum, and are printed in the Appendix to Pinkerton's History, vol i. pp. 446, 447. Queen Annabella died in the year 1401; and Robert III. died at Rothesay Castle, April 3, 1406.

Friebairn, in his MS. History, relates the following instance, " as an argument of the King's great justice." It is evidently copied from Bowar's continuation to Fordun's Scoti-Chronicon.   (Goodall's edit. ii. 418). " Robert " (he says) " entering to his Government after his Father's decease, was crowned at Scoon and his Queen Annabella in one day, in the month of September 1390, which coronation was so gracious and acceptable to the nation, be reason of the good hope they had of him and his noble Lady, whyle they were Earle and Countess of Carrict. that the greatest part of the Nobles, Barons, Knights, and many Ladies come, some called but moe voluntarly, to countenance that solemnity which wes very glorious; at which time there fell out a mirry accident which I cannot pass by. The multitude of horses being so many, that they did consume all the fruits upon the ground, or in the barn-yards, the graniter went to complain to the King; bot being repelled by the courtiers, who cared not for such things, one of the convent, being a witty fellow, called Robert Loggy, did advyse, that again the morrow, next day after, as they might provyde all the people, young or old, of whatsomever sex, should make the randevous at the Abby with all the violers. drumers, horns, or any other thing would make a noyse, and he sould head and direct; which being so sudden and unexpected, the King and Court being late at balling, were for the greatest part sleeping, the noise was so various and loud, that it put them all in ane affrighte, and many of them cryed treason; at last, their Leader being apprehended, and some of the specialls of them with him, they are brought before the King and Court, and questioned of that insolent behaviour. The Monk, without astonishment said, That that convention was out of joy and mirth of the tennents and laburers of their granges and fields who were wont, horsemen and women, to be burdened with gathering and inbringing of the fruits wherof now the Court had eased them. The Courtiers hearing of this were so offended, that they wold have them presently tortured to death, but the King and Queen taking up the matter more justly, forbad all insolence or violence, and commanded to search for so many honest men as wold appryse the lose, and wold not depart from the place, till all that was apprysed, sould be punctually payed; which thereafter he did practise in all the places where he resided any whyle, as at another time at his dukedome, whyle after some stay there."

Page 76, line 13.—The Latin verses, "*Ecce autem quaerenda*," &c. here quoted, are from a poem by the celebrated scholar Thomas Dempster, written upon the marriage of James Earl of Perth, and Isabella, daughter of the Earl of Winton, in 1608. See the Note to page 201.

Page 77.—In Hector Boece's Chronicle, and in later histories, will be found an account of the lamentable fate of David Prince of Rothsay, who was starved to death, at Falkland, in the year 1396. See also Sir Walter Scott's ' Fair Maid of Perth.'

Page 79, line 17.—Myln in his transcript alters this sentence to,—" The fourth, Mary Countess of Camphire ; the fifth, Jean Countess of Angus, then of Huntly ; and the sext, Annabella Countess of Morton."

79, line 26.—After the words, " Earle of Orknay," there is subjoined in Mylne's transcript :—" With her he had a son Alexander, who, to stop his succession to his father, wes made Bishop of Murray and Abbot of Scoon. His father divorced his mother   St. Clair ; and married, secondlie, the Duke of Bulloigne's daughter, in France, by whom he had a son, Duke of Albanie, governour of Scotland, in the minoritie of King James the Fifth. He, while Governour, procured a ratification of the foresaid divorce in Parliament 1516, wherin the said Alexander, his eldest brother, acknowledges his bastardie, and renunces all pretensiones to the Crown. And Duke John, his younger brother, is declared apparent heir therto, failzeing the King and heires of his body. The foresaid Alexander, the eldest son, begot on Margaret Stuart, naturall daughter of King James the Fourth, and relict of the Lord Gordon, (under promise of mariage,) a daughter Margaret, who was married to David Lord Drummond."

Page 80, line 14.—" Mathew or John Stuart Earle of Lennox: &c." corrected in Mylu's MS. to: " Mathew Stuart Earle of Lennox, and had to him Mathew or John Earle of Lennox."

Page 80, line ult.—" She bore him besyde Finrassie, Norman Leslie, fiar of Rothes, who was forfeitt for the murder of Cardinall Beiton, and wes elder then Finrassie ; and other children."—Mylne's MS.

Page 81, line 7.—In the Treasurer's Accounts, 1506-7, Feb. 20, is the following entry :—" Item, to Johne Beg, messingeir, passand to the Beschopis of Dunblane, Dunkelden, the Lordis Oliphant and Drummond, to cum to the Cristinnyng of the Prince, 10s."

Page 85, line 12.—There is a charter in the possession of the Earl of Mansfield, to Sir William de Montefixe et " domine Elene sponse sue," of the lands of Beyn and Cathochylle, granted by Willielmus de Freslaye miles, dominus de Fourgy, without date, but probably about 1320, in the reign of Robert I.

Page 86.—Sir Malcolm Drummond, who obtained by marriage the heritable title of Earl of Mar, is thus mentioned in Wyntown's Metrical Chronicle.

> Schyre Malcolm of Drummond, Lord of Mare,
> A manfull knycht, baith wyse and war,
> That long before then weddit was
> Wyth the Erlis dochtyr of Douglas.

About the year 1403, he was suddenly surprised by a band of ruffians, and imprisoned till he died of his hard captivity. Pinkerton attributes his captivity and death to Alexander Stuart, natural son of the Earl of Buchan, and " a noted leader of the Highland freebooters," who is known at least to have married the widow of Sir Malcolm Drummond, and in her right, to have succeeded to the Earldom of Mar.

Page 86, line 19.—In the Chamberlain's Books is a grant in the year 1390, " Et domino Malcolmo de Dromund percipien per annum, &c. ratione Sponse sue sororis quondam Comitis de Douglas," and in 1405, " Domino Johanni de Drummonde, fratri et heredi quondam domini Malcolmi de Drummonde."

Page 86.—Malcolm de Drummond, miles, in a charter of Robert III., is styled " dilectus frater noster." (Registrum Magni Sigilli, p. 198, No. 12.) There was granted a Charter by David II. to John Drummond of the office of Baillerie of Abthanie of Dull in Athole. (Robertson's Index of Charters, p. 46, No. 46.)

No. II. APPENDIX. 275

Page 113, line 22.—In Mylne's MS., the blank is thus supplied: " by the Lairds of Ardlarie [Ardblair] and Drumlochie; thar are ordered to be apprehendit, 4th June 1554." Hadd. Minutes of Parliament, &c. page 36.

Page 113.—SLAUGHTER OF JOHN DRUMMOND OF BLAIR.—Several original papers connected with this transaction, are still in the possession of HENRY HOME DRUMMOND, of Blair Drummond, Esq.; and as curious illustrative documents may be here inserted. The first paper is the Queen's Proclamation in Council, June 13, 1554, for apprehending and convicting the Laird of Gormok and his accomplices.

I. " MARIE be the grace of God Queine of Scottis, to oure Shiref of Perth and his deputis, and to Oure louittis Archibald Campbell, Thomas Drummond, messengeris, oure scriffis, specialie constitute greting, Forsamekle as it is humlie menit and complenit to ws be Oure louittis the Wiffe, Baruis, Kin, and Friendis of vmquhile George Drummond of Leiderief, and.Williame Drummond his sone vpoun Williame Chalmer of Drumlochie, Williame Rory, George Tullydaf, Williame Chalmer, &c., George M'Nesker, fidlar, his houshaldmen, Robert Smyth (and six others,) tennentis to the Laird of Drumlochie ; Johnne Blair of Ardblair, Andro Blair, Thomas Blair his sonis, David M'Raithy his houshald man, Patoun Blair, (and two others,) tennentis to the said Laird of Ardblair,—Williame Chalmer in Cloquhat, Alexander Blair, half bruther to Johnne Buttir of Gormok, Williame Buttir,—Dauid Blair of Knokmaheir, Johnne Blair, Patrik Blair his sonis,—Williame Young of Torrence, and Thomas Robertson, tennentis to the said Laird of Gormok, quhilkis with thair compleces, with convocatioun of Oure liegis to the nomer of lxxx personis bodin in feir of weir, with jakkis, coittis of mailze, steil-bonettis, lance staffis, bowis, lang culveringis, with lychtit lunttis and vthiris wappinis invasiue, recentlie vpoun Sounday the thrid day of Junij instant, befoir none, off the counsaling, deuysing, causing, sending, command, assistence, fortefeing, and ratihabitioun of the said Johnne Buttir of Gormok, come to the said vmquhile George Drummondis perroche kirk of Blair, to haif slane him, the said vmquhile Williame his sone, and vthirris being with him in company ; and becaus thai culd nocht cum to thair peruersit purpois, thai passit to the Laird of Gormokis place of Gormok, and thair dynit with him, and send furth spyis to await vpoun the said vmquhile George and his cumpany, quhen thai come furth of his place of Blair. And being aduerteiss by the saidis spyis, that he wes cumin furth of his said place, thai with thair compleces with the said Laird of Gormokis howshaldmen and seruandis, bodin in feir of weir, of his causing, sending, deuising as said is, with convocatioun of oure lieges to the nomer of lxvi personis, the samin day at twa houris or thairby eftir none, ischit furth of be said Laird of Gormokis place foirsaid, and vmbeset the gait to the saidis vmquhile George and Williame, his sone, quhair thai wer dowblate allane at thair pastyme play, and at the rowbowlis in the hie marcate gait beside the Kirk of Blair, in sobir maner, traisting na truble nor harme to haif bene done to thame, bot to haif levit vnder Goddis peax and ouris; and thair crewellie slew thame, vpoun auld feid and forthocht felony, set purpois and provisioun, in hie contemptioun of oure auctoritie and lawis gif sa be. OURE Will is therfoir, and we charge zow straitlie, and commandis, that incontinent, thir Oure letteris sene ze tak sicker souertie of the saidis personis and thair compleces committaris of the crymes abouewrittin in maner foirsaid, samony as the saidis complenaris will mak faith befoir zow, wer arte and parte thairof, and gevis thair names to zow in bill, that thai sall compeir and vnderly oure law for the samin befoir oure Justice or his deputis, in oure Tolbooth of Edinbur', the thrid day of Julij nixttocum, vnder the panis contenit in Oure Actis of Perliament. And that ze charge thame personalie gif thai can be apprehendit, and failzeing thairof, be oppin proclamatioun at the marcate croce of the heid bur' of Oure Shyre, quhair thai duell, to cum and find the said souertie to zow, within sex dais nixt eftir thai be chargeit be zow thairto, vnder the pane of rebellioun and putting of thame to Oure horne. The quhilk sex dais being bipast, and the said sourtie nocht fundin to zow in maner foirsaid, that ze incontinent thairafter denunce the disobeyaris Oure rebellis, and put thame to Oure horne; and escheit and inbring all thair movable gudis to oure vse for thair contemptioun; and als that ze summond ane assis heirto ilk persoun vnder the pane of fourty pundis; as ze will answer to ws thairupoun. The quhilk to do We committ to zow conjunctlie and severalie Oure full power be thir Oure lettiris deliuering thame be zow deulie execute and indorsate agane to Oure Justice Clerk: Gevin vnder oure signete at Edinbur', the xiij day of Junij, and of oure regnne the twelft zeire.

Ex deliberatione Dominorum Consilij.

In the original document, there is added the attestation of James Bannatyne, notary public, that the messenger had duly published the said Letters, &c. The next three papers contain the Offers, Answers, and additional Offers of the persons who were chiefly concerned in the slaughter.

II. "THIR AR THE OFFIRIS quhilk the LAIRDIS OF GORMOK, DRUMLOYCHYE, AND AHBLAIR, and thar Collegis Offinis to my Lord Drummond, and to the Soun of vmquhill George Drummond, his wyf and barnis, kyne and frendis, &c.

Item, In primis, To gang, or caus to gang to the four heid pilgramagis in Scotland.

Secundlye, To do suffrage for the sawll of the deid, at his Perroche kirk, or quhat thir kirk thai pleys, for certane zeris to cum.

Thridlye, To do honour to the kyne and frendis, as efferis, as ws is.

Ferdly, To assyth, The partye is content to gyff to the kyne, wyf and barnis, 1ᵐ. [1000.] merk.

Fyfthlye, Gif thir Offiris be nocht suffecyent thocht be the partye and frendis of the deid, we ar content to vndirlye, and augment or pair, as resonabil frendis thinkis expedyent, in sa far as we may, lefsumlie."

III. "THIR AR THE ANSWERIS THAT MY LORD DRUMMOND, his kyne and frendis makis to the Offiris presentlye gevin in be the Lardis of Gormok, Drumloychye, and Arblair wyth thar collegis.

Item, As to the first, secund, and thrid artickill, thai ar sa generall and sempil in ther self that thai requyr na ansver.

Item, As to the ferd artickill, offring to the kyne, frendis, wyf and barnis of Georg Drummond 1ᵐ. [1000] merk for the committing of sa heych crewell and abomenabill slaychtiris and mwtillationis, of set purpos devysyt of ald, be the Lard of Gormok; and Georg Drummond, his sone, nor nane of his frendis, nevir offending to thame nather be drawing of blud, takin of kirkis, takis, stedingis, or rowmis our ony of thair heidis, or thar frendis; sa in respect heirof, my Lord Drummond, his kyne, frendis, the wyf and barnis of Georg Drummond, cane on na wayis be content heirwyth."

Indorsed]. The Offeris offerit be the Laird of Gormok, to zoung George Drummond of Blair, for the slauchtir of his Fathir.

IV. "THE OFFERIS OF WILLIAME CHALMER of Drumlochy for hym self, WILLIAME
CHALMER his Cousing, GEORGE TWLYDAF, WILLIAME CHALMER, JOHNE FYDLAR, JAMES
KEY, JOHNE BURRY, JOHNE WOD his Seruandis.

IN the fyrst, the said William offeris to compeir befoir my Lord Drummond, and the
remanent frendis of vmquhile George Drummond, and thair to offer to his Lordschip,
and the party, ane nakit swerd be the poynt ; and siclike to do all vthir honour to my
Lord, his hous, and frendis that salbe thocht ressonabill in siclike caises.
    Item, Offeris to gif my Lord and his aris his band of manrent in competent and dew
forme, sik as may stand with the actis of Parliament and lawis of this realme.
    Item, Becaus throw extrame persecutioun be the Lawis of this Realme, the said
Williame hes nather landis, gudis, nor money, he thairfoir offeris his Sonis mariage to
be mareit vpone George Drummondis dochter, frelie, without ony tochir. And siclike
the mariage of the said Williame Chalmer his cousing, to the said George sister.
    Item, The said Williame offeris hym reddy to ony vther thing, quhilk is possabill to
hym, as pleis my Lord and frendis to lay to his charge, except his lyfe and heretage.

The next document is indorsed, "The Layrd of Drumlochie's Band of Manrent,"
and is written on vellum, with the seal preserved. This submission, with the alliances
proposed in the preceding offers, appear to have reconciled all the parties concerned.

V. "BE IT kend till all men be thir present Lettiris, me Williame Chalmir of Drumlochie, that fforsamekle as ane noble and michty Lord, Dauid Lord Drummond, and
certane vtheris principalis of the four brancheis and maist speciall and nerrest of the
kin and freindis of vmquhile George Drummond of Leidcreif, and Williame Drummond
his sone, for thame selffis and remanent kin and freindis of the saidis vmquhile George
and Williame, hes remittit and forgevin to me thair slauchteris, and gevin and deliuerit
to me thair lettiris of slanis thairvpoun ; and that I am oblist, be vertew of ane contract, to gif the said noble Lord my Band of Manrent, as the saidis contract and lettir
of slanis, deliuerit to me, mair fullelie proportis ; Thairfore to be bundin and oblist,
and be thir present lettiris, bindis and oblissis me and my airis in trew and anfald
Band of Manrent to the said noble and mychty Lord as Cheif, to the saidis vmquhile
George and William his sone, and the saidis Lordis airis ; and sall tak thair trew and
anfald part in all and sindry thair actionis and causis, and ride and gang with thame

thairin, vpoun thair expensis, quhen thay require me or my airis thairto, aganis all and sindry personis, oure Souerane Lady, and the auctoritie of this realme alanerlie exceptit ; and heirto I bind and oblis me and my airis to the said noble and michty Lord, and his airis, in the straitest forme and sicker stile of Band of Manreut that can be deuisit, na remeid nor exceptioun of law to be proponit nor allegit in the contrair. In witnes of the quhilk thing, to thir present Lettris and Band of Manrent, subscriuit with my hand, my seil is hungin. At Edinbur¹, the fift day of December, the zeir of God ane thousand five hundreth fiftie aucht zeris, befoir thir witnessis Andro Rollok of Duncrub, James Rollok his sone, Johnne Grahame of Gormok, Maister Johnne Spens of Condy, and Laurence Spens his bruther, with vtheris diuers.

          WILZAM CHALMIR
          off Drumloquhy.

Page 114, line 6.—" The following is an exact copy of a note in the hand-writing of James Drummond of Blair, son to the George Drummond with whom Lord Strathallan's Genealogy ends, [page 117, line 13.] The accuracy of it may be depended on :

" The lands of Blair were acquired by the second George Drummond of Leadercift, as appears by the charter of alienation by Patrick Bishop of Murray, perpetual Commendator of the Abbacy of Scoon, to the said George Drummond and Katharine Hay his spouse, and George Drummond their son, dated at Kinnaird the last day of October 1560.

" The tymes of the deaths of George Drummond, commonly called old George, of George his son, and of John his son, are marked in the Callender of a manuscript Missal or prayer-book, wrytten upon parchment or vellum, in the library of the Family of Perth, in these words :—

" George Drummond of Blair deceised 4th January 1596.

" 11th Aug. 1596, George Drummond, younger of Blair, departit frae this life.

" 2d May 1620, John Drummond of Blair deceis'd."

(MS. note communicated by Henry Home Drummond, of Blair-Drummond, Esq.)

Page 115, line 2.—Patrick Drummond of Gairdrum was served heir of his father, Mr. Henry Drummond, August 28, 1663, (Retours, Perth, No. 721.) James Drummond of Gairdum, mentioned by Lord Strathallan, was a younger son, and was served heir of his brother Patrick, August 13, 1693, (ib. No. 1001.)

Page 115, line 10.—Patrick Drummond was Conservator in 1638, and was knighted previous to October 1640, at which time he was suspended and deposed from his office by the Committee of the Estates of Parliament. Thomas Cunningham, who was afterwards appointed to this situation, held it till the year of his death, in 1655; and there was no other person appointed Conservator till after the Restoration of Charles II., when a commission was granted to Sir William Davison, Baronet, dated the 28th November 1661. He is called successor to Sir Patrick Drummond, who, in virtue of his previous appointment, probably may have retained the title, and Cunningham's commission been virtually disowned. There is a Sermon, printed in 1663, under the following title, which shows that Drummond at least officiated as Conservator two years previously to the date of printing: "The Honour of Kings Vindicated and Asserted in a Sermon preached before the Right Honourable Sir Patrick Drummond, late Conservator of the Priviledges of the Scots Nation in the Netherlands, &c. the 3d of May 1661, Stilo Novo, being his Majesty's Coronation Day. By Mr. Thomas Moubray, Minister of the Gospel at the Stapel Port in Camp-veer. Middleburgh, printed by Thomas Berry, 1663," 4to. The wife of Sir Patrick Drummond, Lord Conservator, was Margaret Porterfield, who survived him. (See Retours, October 4, 1681, Edinburgh, No. 1278.)

Page 115, line 25.—George Drummond of Boghall was served heir of his grandfather, James Drummond of Boghall, June 26, 1674. (Retours, Perth, No. 865). At line 27, Myln in his transcript gives this additional information: "Gawin lives in East New Jersey, and is ther maried; George dyed in Carthagena, being taken prisoner when he was upon the coast serving his country for the settlement of Darien. John, the factor, left   sons." p. 77.

Page 116, line 7.—The original Warrant to set at liberty George Drummond of Blair, "being at present in waird within our burgh of Perth," dated at Stirling 13th August 1589, and signed JAMES R., is in the possession of Henry Home Drummond, Esq.

Page 116, line 18.—Mr. Thomas Murray, Governor of Charles I. while Prince of Wales, was the third son of Patrick Murray of Newraw, afterwards of Woodend. He was appointed in 1621, Provost of Eton College, and died April 9, 1623, in the 59th year of his age. He wrote several Latin poems, inserted in the *Delitiæ Poetarum Scotorum*.

"He was a person," says Dr. M'Crie, "equally distinguished for literary accomplishments and the more valuable qualities of the heart," (Life of Melville, vol. ii. p. 410;) and Sir James Balfour mentioning his death, says: "He was first Master, and thereafter Secretary to Prince Charles; and because he lyked not the Princes jorney to Spaine, nor matche with Spaine, he was remoued from his office of Secretary to the Prince; and Sir Francis Cottingtone was put in his place,—a professed Roman, and ane. money hundereth degrees, inferior to him bothe in loue and integritie to his Master, and honesty to all men."—(Annals, vol. ii. p. 97.) The grand-daughter of his brother, William Murray, parson of Dysart, became by her second marriage Dutchess of Lauderdale. See page 195, line 19.

Among Sir James Balfour's collection of Original Letters, (preserved in the Advocates' Library), are two from a Jean Drummond; but she must have been a different person from the lady mentioned by Lord Strathallan, as the wife of Thomas Murray. One is dated May 7, 1615, and has lost the address, but like the other, which is here annexed, is also signed "Your loving wife *to command yow*". Her "Good Husband," it appears, was John Murray of Lochmaben and Cockpool, Keeper of his Majestie's privy purse, afterwards raised to the Peerage in 1622, by the title of Viscount of Annand, and who was probably twice married, although no mention is made by the Peerage writers of his wife, Jean Drummond. She evidently held some office about the Queen, who died May 3, 1619.

"Husband, yeesternight at 7 a clok at night your letter cam to my hands, presently I deliuered his Majesties letter. Her Majestie desires that yee will giue the King many thankis from her, for his letter, and excuse her not wretting to his Majesty at this tyme. Shee hathe commandet Monsieur de Mayarne to wret particulerly her estait to the King; so to his letter I will leaue it, only this I can assure yow, shee hath had much paine, and now, God be praysed, the paine is almost gone, bot the suelling continues so in her futte, as her Matie. is not able to sett it to ground, so sittis all day long in a chayre. God send her better, if it be his blessed will, and graunt to both ther Majesties long helth and happines; and your self, Husband, I shall euer be

Your very loueing wyff to comand yow,

JANE DRUMOND."

Greenwich, 10 of Maij [1618.]

APPENDIX. No. II.

[On the cover.] " To my honord. and worthye freend Mr. Johne Murrey, one of his Maties. bedchamber."

Page 116, line 24.—John Drummond of Blair was served heir-male of his grandfather, George Drummond of Blair, August 2, 1604, and of his father, George Drummond [younger] of Blair, on the same day. (Retours, Perth, No. 128, 129. See also No. 145, and 264.)

Page 117, line 4.—George Drummond of Blair was served heir of his great-grandfather, George Drummond of Lidcrieff, June 16, 1630. (Inq. Gener. No. 1701.)

George Drummond married Marjorie Graham, daughter of George Graham, Bishop of Orkney, who was brother to the Laird of Inchbraikie, and one of the Bishops who gave in their submission, on the restoration of Presbytery in 1638, and thus avoided the sentence of excommunication. The Bishop appears afterwards to have resided with his son who was minister of Holme in Orkney ; from whence is dated the following letter written by his son-in-law, the original of which is preserved among Wodrow's manuscripts in the possession of the Church of Scotland.

RIGHT REVEREND AND MUCH RESPECTED FREIND,

As I maide my first addres to yow at my cumming south from Orknay, whairin I receaved your kyndlie and loving acceptance, so I am bold now to give yow ane accompt, that I am called bak heir againe be ane Ordour from the Committee of Estaites, in commissioun with vtheris, for the leveing of a regiment to be vnder the command of Generall Quartermaister Stewart ; theirfore, Sr. I must intreate you, that I may haif ane warrand to the Ministeris heir to mary tuo of my Dochteris. The eldest of whom I had aggried to marie with ane gentilman named Patrik Blair, sone lawfull to vmquhill Johne Blair of Pitindreich, and whiche mariadge was condiscended to above sevin zeiris agoe. He hes a testimoniall from M. Johne Ross, his ordinar minister at the kirk of Lethindie, and ane vther testimoniall from his Presbitrie, and he has beine, and is, alwayes a frie man. My secund dochter is contracted with Patrik Monteith of Eglischaw in Orknay heir, who is a man frie of all imputatione, except onlie in what he did with the rest of the gentrie in Orknay, which, on his pairt, was meirlie passive, and he had no active part quhatsumever in that mater. Zit notwithstanding he is content to find sufficient cautione to giue what obedience sall be requyred be the Kirk of him. So althoch I had not my awin interest, I doe heauelie regraite the estaite of the haill cuntrie heir in this caise ; as the minister in the mayne land, Mr. James Moriesone, hes represented in his lettre; for the treuth is, thair hes never beine any mariadge heir since the troubillis began, how cleir and innocent soever the pairties desyring the mariadge haif beine, nether any celebration of the Sacrament of the Lord's Supper: which is a great greif to all Godlie persones, to be depryved of that benefite, all the Ministeris heir being depryved except tuo, and these tuo ar so dubious in the mater of mareing any heir, that they will doe nothing thairin without they be of new authorized thairto; and in the Kingdome thair ar none frier then thir persones that I requyre to be maried, quho ar laufullie contractit with the consent of parentis and freindis; whairof I haif sent ane authentick testificat vnder the hand wreiting of tua famous Clerkis heir, quha war the draweres vp of the securities matrimoniall.

Now, Sir, the justnes of my desyre, and the expectatione I haif of your guidnes, is suche, that it imboldines me to petitione a returne from yow warrantabill for this effect. This tyme being so doubtsome, and danger in delay for poore vnprovyded children; for presentlie at the wreiting heirof I am ready going a schipboord from Orknay to Zetland, for discharge of those commandis putt vpoun me be Publict authority. So commending yow, and the work of God in your hand, to his benedictione, I rest

<blockquote>
Your trew freind to serve yow,
</blockquote>

Holme this 2 Octo[ris] G. Drummond off Blair.
1650.

[On the cover] ffor the right reverend and his much respected freind
Mr. Robert Douglas, minister of Edinburgh.

Page 118, line 16.—Mr. Walter Drummond sat as one of the Commissioners of Parliament, in 1489. (Acts of Parliament ii. 212, 123.) He is styled Dene of Dumblane, in the Acts Nov. 26, 1513 (ib. 281.)

Page 119, line 19.—In the Treasurer's Accounts, July 27, 1508, we find this entry, "Item to Malcum Drummond to gif to iij[c] vj [306] men that wes at hunting with the King, L.5, 2s."

Page 120, line 2.—John Drummond was served heir of his father Thomas Drummond of Corscaplie, March 9, 1615. (Retours, Perth, No. 1110.)

Page 120, line 11.—John Drummond was served heir of his father Mr. James Drummond, minister of Fowlis, Nov. 26, 1642. (Inq. Gen. 1766. See also No. 458.)

APPENDIX.

The name of Isobella Drummond, daughter of the Reverend James Drummond, minister of Foulis, appears in the Retours under the date Sept. 23, 1623, (ib. No. 1088.)

Page 121, line 13.—The name of Patrick Drummond occasionally occurs in the correspondence of James Sharp, afterwards Archbishop of St. Andrews, while at London previous to the Restoration; but this person may have been Patrick Drummond of the Carnock family, (see page 72, line 11.) Among the Wodrow MSS. in the possession of the Church of Scotland, is a letter written from London, dated Feb. 28. 1661-2, by "P. D." supposed to be Patrick Drummond, and addressed to Robert Douglas, detailing a conversation he had had with " my Lord St. Andrews," in respect to Douglas and some others of the Edinburgh Clergy.

The following notice of him is taken from the unpublished account of Scotish Divines, by Mr. Laurence Charteris, written about the year 1700:—

" Patrick Drummond, a young gentleman, bred at Edinburgh, afterwards went to London, 1654, quhair he was much esteemed by all that knew him: he dyed of a consumption after he had languished 11 years: under it he published a short discourse on the life and death of Mrs. Beuly, 4to. 1659, and left diverse MSS., particularly a large Paraphraze on the first six chapters of Ecclesiastes; and the Life of John the Baptist. He was a wise and generouse person, and his death was much lamented by all that knew him."

Page 121, line 26.—" Has only a daughter." We find, however, that he had a son John Drummond, who was served heir of his father John Drummond of Deanstoun, Dec. 6, 1692. (Retours, Inq. Gen. No. 7316. See also Perth, No. 994.)

Page 123, line 16, should be, " Drummond of Boreland. His father Gavin was killed at the feild," &c.

Page 123, line 20.—David Drummond, called " Glauring Davie." See Nichols' Progresses of King James, vol. iii. p. 50.

Page 123 and 124.—In the Retours we find John Drummond of Kildees was served heir of his father, Gavin Drummond of Kildees, March 26, 1618, (Inq. Gen. No. 737). Gavin Drummond was served heir of his father Gavin Drummond, brother-german of Mr. James Drummond of Kildees, Feb. 26, 1671. (Perth, No. 816. Stirling, No. 257. Inq. Gen. No. 5403.)

Page 124, line 6.—Sir James Balfour informs us that, in June 1614, " Mr. John Murray being slaine in Dumblaine by Gawin Drummond of Kildrees, the Privy Counsell call the Earls of Perth and Tullibardine and Lord Madertie, (fearing some feud);

who declared they meaned not to interfere in the least to hinder, but would promote the ordinary course of Justice."—MS. Adv. Library. See also his Annals, vol. ii. p. 53.

Page 125.—Thomas Drummond, called "Tom Vnsained" or Unblessed, is so named in the Treasurer's Accounts under the date July 25, 1513:—"Item to Thomas Drummond, alias Thom Vusanit, at the Kingis command, the tyme the schippis past away, L.7."

Page 126, line 13.—Mr. Gregory in his "Earlier History of the Clan Gregor," printed in the Transactions of the Society of Antiquaries of Scotland, says, "The slaughter of Drummond of Drummondernoch, under King's Forrester of Glenartney, said to have been committed in 1589 or 1590, by some of the Clan Gregor, induced the Secret Council to grant in 1590 a Commission of fire and sword to various noblemen and gentlemen for pursuit of the whole Clan, of whom nearly 200 are mentioned *nominatim* in the commission; and which is said to have been executed with extreme severity in the district of Balquhidder especially, and around Lochearn." (Arch. Scot. vol. iv. p. 148.) See also some interesting particulars in the article (attributed to Sir Walter Scott) Culloden Papers, in the Quarterly Review, 1816. Among the Commissioners were the Earls of Huntly, Argyle, Athole, Montrose, the Lord Drummond and the Commendator of Incheaffray.

Page 126, line 21.—David Drummond of Drummondernoch, was served heir of his father John Drummond of Drummondernoch, July 29, 1669, (Perth, No. 796.)

Page 127, line 23.—Margaret, wife of Sir George Muschet, and three of their children died of the plague in 1647, as appears from the following inscription on the tombstone, in the orchard, where they were interred, near the house of Burnbank, now part of the estate of Blair Drummond.

"Here lyes the Corpes of Margaret Drummond, Third Daughter to the Laird [of Inver] may, and [Spouse to] Sir George Muschet of Burnbanke: Her Age 26 : Departed this Life in the Wisitation, with Her Three Children at Burnbanke, The 10 of August 1647."

Page 128, line 8.—James Drummond of Comrie was served heir of his father David Drummond of Comrie, Oct. 29, 1658. (Retours, Perth, No. 672.)

Page 128, line 21.—David Drummond of Cultmalindie was served heir of his father Mr. James Drummond of Caltmalindie, Oct. 6, 1676. (Perth, No. 889. Inq. Gen. No. 5937.)

Page 129, line 1.—James Drummond of Pitcairnis, was with the King at Perth on the 6th of August 1600, and was examined as a witness on the subsequent trial for the Gowrie Conspiracy. See his deposition, in the Acts of Parl. vol. iii. p. 211.

Page 129, line 10.—Thomas Drummond, brother-german of Sir William Drummond of Richarton, was served heir of entail and provision of his uncle William Drummond of Pitcairnie, Nov. 10, 1615. (Retours, Perth, No. 234.) William Drummond of Richarton is styled heir of conquest *fratris avi* of William Drummond of Pitcairnie, July 25, 1630. (Inq. Gen. No. 1754.)

Page 130, line 3.—Mr. James Drummond of Comrie was served heir male of his brother-german Dauid Drummond of Comrie, April 23, 1696. (Inquis. Gen. No. 7693.)

Page 131, line 21.—David Drummond of Halholl was served heir of his brother-german, William Drummond Clerk Seneschall of Strathern, Jan. 11, 1672. (Retours, Perth, No. 829.) In 1697 the name occurs of Francis Drummond of Halholl, (ib. Inq. Gen. No. 7884.)

Page 132, line 3.—The name of SIR JOHN DRUMMOND of Cargill and Stobhall occurs frequently in the Acts of Parliament from 1471 to 1487. Sometimes he is styled simply as Dominus de Stobhall, under which designation he sat in the Parliament of 1478, among the Barons; at other times, as Johannes Drummond, Dominus de Stobhall, or de Cargill. He was created a Peer by the title of LORD DRUMMOND, January 29, 1487-8:—"*Joannes Drummond de Cargill, effectus fuit Dominus Parliamenti, et in futurum nominandus Dominus Drummond.*"

Page 132, line 9.—Lord Strathallan and the Peerage writers have fallen into a mistake in regard to the sons of John first Lord of Drummond. He had a son David, (as rightly stated at page 125 line 3,) who was concerned in the burning of Monivaird Church in 1490. See the Notes to pages 157 and 160.

Page 136, line 3.—John Lord Drummond, at that time constable of Stirling Castle, was committed a close prisoner to Blackness Castle, July 16, 1515, by orders of the Regent Duke of Albany, on the allegation mentioned in the text. His lands and goods were forfeited to the Crown. The Queen Dowager accused the Herald of insolence in delivering his message; and presenting herself at Court "sore weeping," she vainly solicited at the time for Lord Drummond's pardon.

Page 136, line 11.—John Lord Drummond was restored 'to his honour, dignitie, heretage, &c.' by an Act of Parliament, dated Nov. 22, 1516. (Acts ii. 284.) This Act of Restoration was confirmed by a subsequent Act, dated June 8, 1537, and the confirmation has been also printed from the original, in Archiv. Comitatus de Perth, (ib. vol. ii. p. 393.)

Page 138.—LADY MARGARET DRUMMOND.—The King seems to have early become attached to this Lady, probably while Duke of Rothsay. Her name at least appears in the Treasurer's Accounts during the first year of his reign. A few extracts may be here inserted from this curious and interesting record.

1488, Sept. 15. and Oct. 3.—Item, for twa elne of franshe to be hir my Lady Mergatt a goune, L.5.—Item, for three elne of blak ryssillis for a goune till hir, L.5, 8s.—Item, for golde, aysure, silver, and colouris till it, and worken of it, L.6, 17s.—Item, for three vnce of sylkis to frenzeis till it, 13s.

1488, Dec. . Item, sende to Lady Mergret to by hir necessar thingis, L.2, 10s.

1489, June . —— to a servand of Lady Mergretis to by hir curcheis, sarkis, and oder small geyr, at the Kingis command, L.2, 10s.

1491, Dec. . —— to by small geyr to Lady Margret, L.2, 0s. 0d.

1496, May 11. —— that samyn nycht in Drummyn to the King to play at the bilis, 28s.

June 9. —— giffin to the Lady Mergret of Drummond, L.20, 0s. 12d.

—— that samyn day giffin to the Lady Lundy to mak Mergreit Drummondis costis, 40 markis.

17. —— to the Lard of Lundy to by wyn to send to Striuelin, L.11, 14s.

27. —— to the Lard of Lundy for the Ladyis costis, Mergret Drummondis costis, L.20.

Sept. 10. —— to the Lady Lundy for Mergret Drummondis costis L.40.

Oct. 28. —— to the Lady of Lundy for ditto, L.13, 6s. 8d.

30. —— to Sir David Kingorne to furnyse Margret Drummondis costis in Linlithquho, L.22, 3s. 6d.

Dec. 6. —— to Margret Drummond, at the Kingis command, L.10, 0s. 9d.

—— to Sir David Kingorne for Margret Drummondis expensis, L.40.

12. —— [Various sums for dresses to Margret Drummond, viz.]—Wellus (velvot), L.41, 8s.—damas to line hir cloke, L.2, 10s,—greendamas, L.9, 12s.— black damas, L.7, 14s.—Rissillis blak, L.9, 6s.—broune, L.12, 8s.—chamlet, L.5, 5s.—blak gray, 45s.—lynnyn clath, 18s.—schering the clath above writin, 7s.—a horse to turse (carry) it to Lithquho, 6s.

1496, Dec. 13. Item, for Sir David Arnotis and David Betonis biand the Ladyis clathis in Edinburgh five dayis, 38s. 8d.

1497, Jan. 13. —— to Sir David Kingorne for Mergret Drummondis expense, L.40.

19. —— to the Lard of Lundy of the rest of the hale payment for Mergret Drummondis costis, L.28, 13s. 4d.—(He also got L.5, on the 9th "of the taxt silver of Fiffe," for the same purpose).

Feb. 3. —— giffin Sir David Kingorne to furnish M. D. expensis in Linlithquho, L.20.

March 2. —— to Sir David Kingorne to furnish M. D., L.17.

12. —— to ditto, for part of payment of M. D. expense in Linlithquho, L.6.

31. —— giffin to the Lady of Lundy for M. D. expensis xj dayis scho was in Striuelin quhen scho passit hame, L.10.

May 17. —— to the King himself upon the stane in Striuelin quhen he passit to M. D.,—iij vnicorns, iiij French erovnis, and three Scottis crovnis, L.7, 10s.

1498, Feb. . —— in the Stobhall giffin to ane lutar at the Kingis command, 9s.

April . —— A variety of costly dresses for M. D. [Margaret Drummond.] bought of John Farnbae the merchant of Portingale.

In Douglas's Peerage, by Wood, vol. i. p. 51, and vol. ii. p. 361, she is mentioned as having been poisoned in 1501. This date is certainly inaccurate. In the Treasurer's Accounts, there are a variety of payments "for the Ladyis expenses in Stryuelin," from February 1501 to August 1502. That these refer to Lady Margaret, is evident from the following entry in a different portion of the same volume:—

1502. June 23.—"Item, the xxiij. day of Junij the King [wes in Drummonde] giffin to Mergret Drummond, be the Kingis command, xxx French crownis, summa, L.21.—Item, To her nuriss iij French crownis, summa, 42s."

Similar payments "for the Ladyis expenses in Striuelin," occur in 1503, but these must refer to " L. A." " L. A. M." or to some other Lady; as on the 1st February 1502—3, we find this payment :—" Item, to the priestis of Edinburgh for to do Dirige and Saule Mess for Mergratt Drummond, L.5."

The date of the catastrophe described by Lord Strathallan may therefore be placed at the end of the year 1502, or in January 1503.

On the 10th February 1502-3 is this entry, " Item, to the Priestis that sing in Dumblane for Margaret Drummond their quarter fee, L.5." As this payment occurs regularly every quarter for several years in the Treasurer's Accounts, during the reign of James IV., it may be held as testifying the King's affection in thus securing the stated performance of the service for the dead, in the appointment of two priests, whose office it was to sing masses for her soul, in the Cathedral church of Dunblane, where she was buried.

Some further particulars will be found in Mr. Tytler's History of Scotland, vol. iv. Note L.—It may be added, that there is a beautiful descriptive Scotish ballad, published in "Select Remains of the Ancient Popular Poetry of Scotland," Edinburgh, 1822, 4to, under the title of Tayis Bank, which is supposed to allude to Lady Margaret Drummond. It is by an anonymous author, and as James the Fourth is himself mentioned in the number of the Scotish Makaris, some zealous antiquary might be inclined to attribute to him its composition.

The last stanza may be quoted:—

> The rever throw the ryss cowth rowt,
> And roseris raiss on raw;
> The schene birdis full schill cowth schout
> Into that semely schaw;
> Joy wes within, and joy without,
> Under that vnlenkest waw,
> Quhair Tay ran doun, with stremes stout,
> Full strecht under Stobschaw.

Page 133, line 7.—As stated in the text, Castle Drummond was built about 1491, by John, first Lord Drummond, on removing from the ancient family seat at Stobhall. The Castle was besieged, taken, and garrisoned by Cromwell's forces; and, finally, at the Revolution totally demolished, excepting some remains which evince that it must have been a place of considerable strength. (Pennant's Tour, vol. iii. p. 100.) "Drummond Castle, a poem written in the year 1783," is printed in the Edinburgh Magazine, vol. iii. p. 448. The present building stands a little to the eastward of the Old Castle.

Page 136, line 20.—Burial place at Innerpeffray. See extract from Friebairn's MS. quoted at page 294. There is a Library at Innerpeffray, founded by David Lord Maderty, chiefly for the use of students of divinity.

Page 139, line 13.—James IV. after long protracted negotiations, was affianced to Margaret, eldest daughter of Henry VII. in January 1502, but the marriage ceremony did not take place till the 8th of August 1503.

APPENDIX. No. II.

Page 140, line 18.—In the Acta Dominorum Concilii, 3d March 1491, there is a notice respecting a suit for 1600 merks, the tocher of Elizabeth, daughter of John Lord Drummond, **wife of George Master of Angus.**

Page 141, line 27.—Lord Strathallan has fallen into a mistake in regard to the parentage of Dorothea Stewart, and some writers on the mysteries of the Gowrie Conspiracy have quoted his work as an authority to prove that Dorothy was the daughter of Queen Margaret by her third husband, Lord Methven. It has since been established beyond all doubt that she was Lord Methven's daughter, by his second wife, Janet Stewart, Countess of Sutherland. See the "Examination of the alleged descent of John Earl of Gowrie," by James Maidment, Esq. advocate, subjoined to a volume entitled, "A Chronicle of Perth," &c. Edinburgh 1831. 4to. p. 99.

Page 144, line 14 and 25.—"Another daughter," &c. Mylne asserts that this lady was not the daughter of the Master of Angus, but of John Lord Drummond.

Page 144, line 14—26. "There seems to be a mistake here be my Lord Strathallan, for there is ane infeftment in Duke Hamilton's charter chests to this Earle of Arran, and Beatrix Drummond, daughter of Lord John Drummond, his lady, bot she continowed bot short time, as appears by a second marriage to   .

"This I had from Wishaw, so that its probable that this Elizabeth and Beatrix may be the same person, bot whether first married to the Earle of Arran, or Master of Angus, is to be considered." (Note on the margin of Strathallan's MS. by David Drummond, the transcriber, fol. 42.)

Page 144, line 1.—In Mr. Pitcairn's Criminal Trials, is inserted an account of the sentence and execution of Janet Douglas, Lady Glamis, from the records of Justiciary, illustrated with extracts from the different historians who have given any detail of the proceedings.

Page 148, line 4.—Camden's words, as translated by Bishop Gibson, are as follows: "The bank of the river Ern is adorned with Drimein, a Castle of the Barons Dromond, who acquired considerable honours ever since King Robert Stewart III. married a wife from this their family, (the beauteous Annabella, mother of King James I.): the women of this Hous so far surpassing others in beauty and gracefulness, as to have even Kings for their admirers."

Page 152, line 9.—The words here quoted respecting Hary Drummond, second son of Sir John Drummond of Innerpeffray, are from Knox's History of the Reformation. Knox, after mentioning his being summoned to appear in the Blackfriars

No. II. APPENDIX.

Church, May 15, 1555, says of himself, that, on the same day, " he taucht in Edinburgh in a greater audience than ever befoir he had done in that toun. The place was the Bishope of Dunkellis his grit logeing, quhair he continowit in doctrine ten dayis both befoir and afternoone. The Erle of Glencairne allurit the Erle of Merschell, who, with Harie Drummond his counsaillour for that time, hard ane exhortation ; but it was upon the nicht ; who was so weill contentit with it, that they both wyllit the saide Johne to wrytte unto the Queen Regent sumquhat that mycht move hir to heir the Word of God. He obeyit their desire, and wreit that which was afterward imprentit, and is callit The Letter to the Queen Dowager," &c. edit. 1732, folio, p. 92.

This 'Counsaillour' was certainly no great clerk, as among the Balcarras Letters and papers in the Advocates Library is an original receipt, in French, for 500 crowns (Cinq cens escuz) which is thus signed " Hary Dromond wy^t my hand at the pen, led be my Lord Marschallis seruand maister Ihone Elder." It has no date, but was probably about the year 1560.

Page 153, line 19.—Lord Strathallan has committed a mistake in saying that the third son's name was David. The person referred to was Sir Edward Drummond.

Page 153, line 30.—An original letter of Ninian Drummond Parson of Kinnoul, addressed to Sir James Semple of Beltrees, of the date July 28, 1612, respecting the parsonage of Kinnoul, is preserved among Wodrow's MSS. in the possession of the Church of Scotland, vol. xviii.

Page 154, line 5.—Duncan Drummond of Culcrieff and Balhadie, was one of a tribe of the Clan Gregor, known by the name of Clan Jan-vallich. On the proscription of the name of MacGregor, A.D. 1603, he took that of Drummond. John Drummond of Culcreiff, was served heir-male of his brother-german Patrick Drummond, younger of Culcreiff, July 2, 1646, (Perth, No. 552.)—Duncan Drummond of Balhaddies, heir-male of his brother-german, John Drummond of Culcreiff, March 17, 1658, (ib. 667 ;) and as heir of his father Patrick Drummond of Balhaddies, July 26, 1666, (ib. 751.) Alexander Drummond of Balhadies was served heir of his father Duncan Drummond of Balhadies, March 6, 1685. (Clackmannan, No. 53, Inquis. Gen. No. 6623.) This Alexander was elected Chief of the Clan Gregor, in the year 1714, and was made a Baronet by the Ex-King James VIII. from whom he had likewise the commission of Colonel.

Page 154, line 21.—Mr. John Friebairn, minister of Madertie, the author of the " Extract of the Family of Drummond," already mentioned. See page 258.

APPENDIX. No. II.

Page 154, line 31.—Henry Drummond, was served heir to his brother of the same name, who is styled eldest son and heir apparent of the late Henry Drummond of Richarton, April 22, 1574. (Retours, Linlith. No. 7.)

Page 155, line 5.—Thomas Drummond in 1615. See Note to page 129, line 10.

Page 155, line 12.—Dominus William Drummond of Ricarton, was served heir of his father, Henry Drummond of Ricarton, August 14, 1606. (Linlith. No. 48. Edinburgh, No. 89.)

Page 155, line 18.—William Drummond of Ricartoun, was served heir of his father Sir William Drummond of Ricartoun, January 26, 1626. (Retours, Linlith. No. 116, Perth, No. 363.) See also Note to page 129, line 10.

William Drummond of Ricarton was sent as one of the Commissioners of the Estates to London to attend Parliament, in November 1640.

Page 155, line 19.—Thomas Dalzell of Binnes, died February 10, 1642, as appears from his epitaph by Drummond of Hawthornden, printed in the Archaeologia Scotica, vol. iv. p. 113.—General Dalzell, according to Lord Fountainhall's chronological notes, died suddenly, "and was buried splendidly after the military form, being attended by the standing forces, and six piece of cannon drawn before his herse, with his led-horse, and his general's battoon, August, 1685." p. 63.

Page 156, line 12.—Thomas Drummond of Ricarton was served heir of his father, Thomas Drummond of Ricarton,—and of his grandfather, William Drummond of Ricarton, May 2, 1668. (Retours, Linlith. No. 225. See also Stirling, No. 245.)

Page 157.—William Master of Drummond, according to Douglas, (Peerage, vol. ii. p. 361), was apprehended and sent prisoner to Stirling, where he was tried, convicted, and executed in the year 1511, for this offence. The date is undoubtedly erroneous, and also the person; as it was David the second son who drew down upon himself the infliction of such punishment for his being concerned in the burning of Monivaird Church, which took place in the year 1490.

William Master of Drummond was twice married. By his second wife Mariot Forrester, he had a son John. In 1512, there is a charter to her and her son, in fee of Glentarkin in Strathern. See Note to page 160, line 16.

Page 158, line 5.—BURNING OF THE CHURCH OF MONYVAIRD. Lindsay of Pitscottie says, "In this mean tyme the Drummondis brunt the kirk of Monivaird, quhairin was six scoir of Murrayes, with thair wyffes and childraine, and few escaped thairfra, bot war all aither brunt or slaine, except one David Murray; quhilk fact the King punisched condignlie thairefter, for he headed monie of the principall actouris thairof at Stirling."

The following extract from Friebairn's manuscript may also be added, as it contains, along with some particulars omitted by Lord Strathallan, a copy of the paper to which he refers. In his account of John Lord Drummond, he says:—

"Bot as ther is no constancie in earthly things, adversity alwayes following (to the best) upon the heells of prosperity, so it fell out that there wes a fearfull breach of amitie betwixt him, at least his children and friends, and his Mothers kin of the hous of Tullibardine, upon what grounds hes been variouslie reported; but as the triviall proverb goes, The mother of mischiefe may be less nor a midges wing, so it fell out in this quarrell, which once begining continued to wax eager for a long space; but as I desire not, since it is still in all mens mouths, to slip it altogidder, unless I should seem partiall, so I mynd not to be curious, seeing they themselves were on both sydes put to such disadvantages, that none of them had caus to glory, but only touch it in the by; for all that I have sein upon record, is this, a Complaint given into William Bishop of St. Andrews, by George Abbot of Incheffrey, wherin he most pittiefully layes out his grievances, supplicating for a remedy, and relating that some of the Drummonds whom he calls Sathans souldiers and rotten members had most barbarously killed and brunt in the Kirk of Monyvaird a number of his kinsmen, friends, and followers, without either regaird to God, or that place which they had taken upon them as a sanctuarie and refuge; whose names are expressed as follows:—

BARTHOLOMEW MURRAY.	NICOL ROBERTSON.	LAURENCE MURRAY.
DAVID MURRAY.	PETER KEUSE.	JOHN OF FENTON.
JOHN OF MURRAY.	NICOL ELDER.	WALTER COUAN.
JOHN MURRAY.	JOHN ROLLOCK.	PATRICK DAW.
NICOL HALDEN.	ALEX^r. ROLLOCK.	PETER LUTEFUTE.
JOHN HALDEN, with his two Sons.	ANDREW MENTEITH.	

"The Bishop of St. Andrews does, with all aggravation of the fact, recommend the anathematizing of the saids persons to the Bishop of Dumblane, within whose diocie that deid was committed, by all the solemnities requyred in the rubrick of the great excommunication, sic as book, bell and candell, and ordains him to cause intimate the same to all the congregations in the country: This is all that I have sein in wreate, but the tradition of the parties does say, that my Lord Drummond was frie hereof; bot one of his sons, called David, and Thomas Drummond [of] Drummenernoche, with some others, being provocked by some vendictive instrament, to goe along where those men were conveined in a bragging manner at Monyvaird, that the very whyle they were lyke to ingadge, that the Captain of Dunstaffnage, with a company comeing by, did syde with the Drummonds, ther Masters neir allya, which the other partie seing, they took them to the kirk, which they conceaved would gaurde them from any harm, out of which one of them unhappily did shoot and kill one of the highlandmen, whereat the rest were soe cruelly enraged, that without respect or compassion, they set fire on the kirk, which was theiked with hedder, and brunt them every man that wes within. This barbarous crueltie comeing to the King's ears, David Drummond was brought to Stirling, and was drawn blood of, notwithstanding that his Mother and Sister, the King's mistress went along with him to beg his lyfe; which is said might have been obtained, were not some unreasonable words uttered by her Mother, which irritat the King so, that he wold have justice done upon the principall actor and some others, togither with a great asythment to the wyfes and children of the defunct, which bred such heart sore to them, that for a whole age they could not be heartily reconceilled, but upon the least occassion given, be any of the sydes, the old quarrell was renewed; till at last it pleased the Lord so to sodder them togidder by such strong bands, that they live alse close and kyndly united as any trybes in the kingdome."

"John Lord Drummond having reedifyed the Chappell of Innerpeffrey from the ground, and erected it in a Colledge of some few prebendars, to pray for requiems for him and his hous, he ordained it to be ther Buriall place for all tymes comeing; and being near eighty yeares of age, he framed one of the most materiall and perfyte Testaments that ever I saw, and syne closed his eyes and tyme togidder, and was most honourably buried at Innerpeffrey." This Testament is no doubt the paper inserted in Lord Strathallan's work. See page 136.

Page 160.—This sad outrage was at length compromised, and on the 14th of January 1500-1, a letter, under the Privy Seal, was "maid to the Lord Drummond and Schir William Murray of Tulebardin, knicht, thare kyn, men, frendis, and seruandis, *for hertlines to be had amangis them in tyme to cum;* renunceand and forgevand to the said kin and frendis of baithe the said parties, al actions and crimes of the Birnyngis of the Kirk of Moneivard, and slauchter of the Kingis lieges at that tyme," &c. Reg. Secr. Sig. quoted in Pitcairn's Criminal Trials, Part ix. p. 101.

It may be added, that in the Acta Dominorum Concilii, October 22, and November 3, 1488, are notices respecting the right of David Drumond, son to the Lord Drumond to Dry Ile in Straithern. November 27, 1490, Lord Drummond's second son was put to the horne for the burning of the Kirk of Monyvaird, February 24, 1491. David Drumond was "at our Soucrane Lords horn," when Dry Ile was sacked by the Murrays.

Page 160, line 15. "Trybes of the nation." Mylne in his transcript adds the following " Nota. It seemes ther is a mistake heir, for ther is a chartor to William Drummond, and Marion Forrester, his spous, on his resignation of Callocht and others in Menteith, 21. March 1502. Lawson's Coll. page 744. And ther is another chartor to Marion in liferent, and John Drummond, her son, of Fordie, and Glentarkie, and Balmuk, 24 May 1511, page 242. So it would appear this William hes been thryse married, and Forrester's children to him hes died *sans* ishu."

Page 163, line 18.—John Drummond was served heir-male of his father, John Drummond of Balmaclone, April 30, 1644. (Retours, Perth, No. 539.)

Page 167, line 9. "Nota. Ther is no certaintie of his being Lord till 1487, which is long after King Robert the Third's days; and that year is the first he is remarked sitting as Lord of Parliament on the articles," &c. Mylne's MS.

Page 170, line 6.—"The Governour;" there is added, "who died *sans* ishue. His father's divorce against his first wyfe Kath. St. Clair is dated 1477, and ratified in Parliament 1516." Mylne's MS.

Page 179, line 31.—Archibald Napier of Merchiston, created first Lord Napier in 1627, was the son of the inventor of Logarithms, by his first wife, Janet, daughter of Sir Francis Bothwell, one of the Lords of Session.

Page 186, line 10.—Lt. Col. Andrew Drummond was succeeded by his grandnephew, Sir John Drummond, in 1678. See Note to page 187, line 3.

Page 186, line 27.—John Drummond of Machaney was served heir of his granduncle, Lt. Col. Andrew Drummond, October 31, 1678. (Retours, Perth, No. 902. Inq. Gen. No. 6106). And in January 1679, he was served heir of his father Dominus Jacobus Drummond de Machaney miles, (ib. Perth, No. 903).

Page 186, line 28.—In Lord Fountainhall's chronological notes, it is stated that the Chancellor Earl of Perth, obtained for his brother-in-law, Drummond of Machany, a gift of the estate of Nicolson of Carnock, in 1687, which had fallen into the King's hands as *ultimus haeres*, p. 219.

APPENDIX. No. II.

Page 186, line 29.—John Lord Madertie was served heir-male of his father, James Lord Madertie, March 17, 1624. (Retours, Perth, No. 317.)

Page 187, line 13.—There is a sonnet by Sir Robert Ayton, written on the death of this Lady Maderty, who died about the year 1630.—(Watson's Collections, Part III. p. 41. Bannatyne Miscellany, vol. i. p. 311.)

Page 187, line 21.—WILLIAM DRUMMOND, who is here mentioned, was the Author of the present work. He was the youngest son of John Lord Maderty; and was created Viscount of Strathallan, September 6, 1686. At the time of his death, which took place in January 1688, he held the high appointment of General of the Forces in Scotland. He was buried at Innerpeffray; and as the Sermon preached at his interment, April 4, 1688, by Dr. Monro, Principal of the College of Edinburgh, contains various interesting particulars of his life, the following extracts may not be deemed superfluous.

"My Lords and Gentlemen, so far have I discours'd of this consolatory argument, to ease our mind upon this sorrowful occasion. But you see another text, viz. the earthly remains of the noble Viscount of Strathallan. When I remember his true vertues, I despair to say any thing proportionable to his worth; the naming of him once, suggests greater thoughts than ordinarily occur. When we form to ourselves the most perfect idea's of valour, and honour and generosity, then we have not the best notion of that great soul that once lodged in that tabernacle; all the projects of his mind were beyond the common level. The generous inclinations he derived from his

Earl of Perth. ancestors began to appear very early: A family too well known in Britain for every thing that is great, ancient, loyal, and generous, to need any particular descant of mine; I am not to act the part of a herauld from this place, there is none capable to be my hearer, but knows already how needless it is to tell Scotchmen of the noble atchievements and many illustrious branches of that Cedar of which our deceased General is descended. He began to bear arms when as yet he had not strength enough to manage them, the vigour and alacrity of his spirit out-running the growth of his body; he then, when but a child, lodged no thought in his breast, but such as

St. Andrews. were daring, great and difficult. When he was a boy at St. Leonard's College, he gave all the proof of a docile and capacious spirit, far above any of his school-fellows: but his mind (that always entertain'd extraordinary enterprises) began to be weary of an unactive life. Then it was that he was made Captain in that regiment that went to
Sir Rob. Monrow. Ireland against the rebels, under the command of an old and experienced officer,

In that expedition, he behaved with so much life and resolution, as drew upon him the eyes of all men, and every body concluded the young Captain was calculated for the greatest actions.

"He came over from Ireland some years after, and assisted those forces that beat the rebels once at Stirling; and all those loyal gentlemen, engaged in that expedition, upon all occasions bestow'd upon him the most ample applause, and unforced commendations that were truly due to his skill, conduct, and fidelity. *Argyle beat at Stirling, by Sir George Monro.*

After this, General Drommond and all his associates became so odious to the prevailing faction of the Covenanters, that (until the mock-repentance after Dunbar fight) he was not suffered to engage in his Majesties service. Mean while, he went to London, and the forces commanded by his friend were disbanded: and there he was a spectator of that tragedy that pierced his soul with the most exquisit grief, I mean, the martyrdom of King Charles the First. The scene he saw, and the preparations to the fatal blow, but more he could not endure." *Sir George Monro.*

[After some reflections on the fate of Charles the First, and an account of the Battle of Worcester, where General Drummond was taken prisoner, but afterwards made his escape, and joined Charles II. at Paris, Dr. Monro proceeds:]

"At Paris he received his Majesties commands, and many letters and commissions for the nobility and gentry that yet adhered to the afflicted cause of true honour and loyalty: He came over then himself in the quality of Major-General, he landed near Yarmouth in England, with a double bottom'd trunk in disguise, in which were laid his Majesties letters and commissions: From thence he came to Newcastle, then to Kelso, from Kelso to the Earl of Roxburgh's house, from thence to Edinburgh, in the habit of an ordinary carrier: From Edinburgh to the Westferry, where he was almost discovered to be another man than what he appear'd, by one of the usurpers spies: but the divine Providence watched over his person; he got rid of this fellow, and went to Elplingstoun, and being provided of a boat that afternoon, he came quickly to this country, so wearied and disguised, that his nearest relatives could not know him. *General Drummond in disguise.*

"Now though he had most dexterously disfigured his complexion, yet how difficult was it to hide and obscure his noble genius; notwithstanding of his sorry horse and his load of cheese, he could not persuade the people with whom he lodged upon the road, but that he was some extraordinary person; upon every turn they saw something

in him above their level; they knew not what he was, but they were sure he was none
of their gang; he was out of his element as a fish upon dry land; and though his cap,
perruque, and his beard made him appear another thing, yet he could not hide his
looks; and the poorest of the people saw in him something they could not name, but
still above servility and meanness; the artifice of his design could not raze out the
signatures of greatness that God had stamped upon his soul and body.

"Why should I enter upon the history of that unfortunate expedition? You all
know the event of it. . . . . . .

"But all hopes being lost at that time, to serve his Majesty, the General and
Dalyell beg'd leave to go for Moscovia; which they obtain'd, and accordingly took
their journey. And when he arriv'd at the imperial camp, the emperour of Russia
was then lying before Riga, and now we have this generous soul in Moscovia, a
stranger, and you may be sure the cavaliers Coffers were not then of great weight; but
he carried with him that which never forsook him till his last breath, resolution above
the disasters of fortune, composure of spirit in the midst of adversity, and accomplishments proper for any station in court or camp that became a gentleman.

"The emperour of Russia quickly took notice of him, and immediately he was
made a Collonel, and soon after Lieutenant-General of the Strangers. He served the
emperour of Moscovy against the Polonians and Tartars in many rencounters, with great
conduct and fidelity. But I must be allowed to mention one instance of his valour,
in which he saved the whole army that was then sent by the emperour of Russia
against the Poles, and commanded by Knez Joury, who was of extraordinary reputation
among the Russians; but in this encounter when he marched too near the enemy, he
withdrew all the cavalry, and left our Scots here with a small body of foot, to the
mercy of the Polonian horse, (perhaps the best in Europe,) what shall he do in such
circumstances, must he fly? But that was it he was not acquainted with; he drew up
his handful of men behind some shrubs which had a marsh at each end of them, and
planted the swans feathers before them: The Polish horse came to assault them in
that post with extraordinary briskness, but were received with so much order and resolution, that the first and second salutes of the General's musketeers, put the enemy
in great disorder, and in defiance of their number, strength and quality, he managed
his retreat with so much success and conduct, that he got under the covert of the
nearest wood, by which he saved the whole army; for if he had been beat, the main
body, (which Knez Joury had too hastily withdrawn) would certainly fly, if assaulted

whiles they were in confusion. To manage a retreat with so small a body of men, in view, and upon the nose of so strong an enemy, was a proof of conduct and valour equal to any thing that we meet with in history."

We must refer to the Sermon itself, for additional passages in the life of this very able and accomplished person, who is there said to have died at the age of seventy. It is contained in a volume of "Sermons, preached upon several occasions. By Al. Monro, D.D. (then) Principal of the College of Edinburgh. London: 1693," 8vo. pages 447—502.

Page 189, line 24.—David Drummond, Master of Maderty, was married to his first wife, Alison Crichtoun, at Perth, February 6, 1638. (Chronicle of Perth, p. 36.) At her death she left an only daughter, Margaret Drummond, who was served heir of her mother, March 19, 1642. (Retours, Perth, No. 499.) She did not survive long, as David Drummond, Master of Maderty, was served heir of his daughter, Margaret Drummond, January 14, 1643, (ib. No. 522.)

Page 191, line 1.—Patrick, Master of Drummond, eldest son of David Lord Drummond, sat in the Convention of Estates in 1567. In a List of the Scotish Nobility about the year 1595, Patrick Lord Drummond is said then to have been "Of 45 yeares: his mother, daughter to the Lord Ruthven: his wife, daughter to Lindsay, laird of Edzell: and his religion Protestant." In a previous list, (for the year 1583,) where he is misnamed David, instead of Patrick, Lord Drummond, he is thus described: "Maryed the laste Erle of Craufourde's doghter: of an auncient house; and hath a Iland of frendes in Strathern: himself unhable in his hearing; and is presently in Fraunce."—(Bannatyne Miscellany, vol. i. p. 65.)

Page 195, line 29.—Lady Jean, third daughter of Patrick third Lord Drummond, was the second wife of Robert, then Lord Roxburghe. On occasion of their nuptials, February 3, 1613-14, was given a magnificent entertainment at Court, when Hymen's Triumph, a beautiful pastoral by Samuel Daniel was represented. The autograph manuscript was given to the College of Edinburgh, with other books, by Drummond of Hawthornden in 1626. (Auct. Bibl. Edinburg. 1627, p. 10). It was printed along with "The whole Workes of Samuel Daniel Esquire, in Poetrie," under this title, "Hymens Triumph, a Pastoral Tragicomaedie, presented at the Queenes Court in the Strand, at her Majesties magnificent entertainment of the Kings most excellent Majesty, being at the nuptials of the Lord of Roxborough. By Samuel Daniel. London, 1623." 4to.

300 APPENDIX. No. II.

Page 196, line 7.—Jean Lady Roxburghe is the lady to whom was addressed the Italian sonnet mentioned in Drummond of Hawthornden's Account of the Family. (See note, page. 255). Since that sheet was thrown off, the following transcript has been made from the original volume, a copy of which is preserved in the British Museum. The title is: "Rime di Antimo Galli. All 'Illustrissima Signora Elizabetta Talbot-Grey. Londini excudebat M. Bradwood, 1609." 12o.

PER L' ILL^MA SIGNORA GIOUANNA DI DRUMOND.

Quella prudenza, e quel valor, che regna
In te Giouanna, è tal, ch' altrui stupore
E riuerenza in vn reca, et amore ;
Com' ad alma immortal sol del ciel degna
Donna tu sei, e tal, ch' à te non sdegna
Gran diua, i gran sergeti aprir del core :
Onde fatto piu chiaro al suo splendore
Tuo bel pensier' à Dio poggiar n' insegna.
Non Artemisia, non Zenobia, ò quali
Altra più celebrata, ò noua, ò antica
Donna hebbe mai qual tu grazie cotanti.
Tu d' Eroica virtu, di gloria amica,
 Posti i mondan piacer tutt' i non cale,
 Fai de l'alma tua bella il Cielo amante.

Page 196, line 16.—Dominus Gulielmus Drummond, youngest legitimate son of John Earl of Perth, now William Earle of Roxburghe, was served heir of entail and provision of his grandfather, Robert Earl of Roxburghe, May 2d, 1650. (See the Retours.)

Page 196, line 23.—Robert, third Earl of Roxburghe, the year after this work was written, was one of those who accompanied the Duke of York in the Gloucester frigate, and perished when that ship was lost near Yarmouth, May 7th, 1682. His widow survived him no less than 71 years; and died January 22d, 1753, in the 96th year of her age.

Page 200, line 12.—Family of Seton.—The curious and interesting History of the House of Seytoun, written about the year 1559 by Sir Richard Maitland of Lethington, with a Continuation to 1687 by Alexander Viscount Kingston, was printed at Glasgow in 1829, 4to., for the Maitland Club. Sir Richard's work has also been published from a different MS., with notes by Charles Kirkpatrick Sharpe, Esq. Edinburgh, 1830, 4to.

Page 201, line last.—Issobella Seaton, Comtess of Perth. The marriage of the Earl of Perth with this Lady, in 1608, was celebrated by Thomas Dempster, in a Latin poem inserted in the Delitiae Poetarum Scotorum, 1637, 12o, vol. i. p. 310. It was originally published under the following title:—"Epithalamion in Nuptiis generossimorum Jacobi Comitis Perthani, Domini Drommondi, Baronis Stobhalliæ, &c. & Isabellae, unica Roberti Comitis Wintonij, Domini Setonii, &c. filiae. Fvndebаш Thomas Dempstervs a Muresk. I. V. Doctor, Scoto-Britannus. Edinburgi: excudebat Robertus Charteris, Typographus Regis. MDCVIII." 4to.

The following extracts are from Mr. Sharpe's edition of "The Chronicle of the Hous of Setoun." Edin. 1830, p. 51.

"Upon the last of November 1593, Dame Isabell Setoun, Countess of Perth, was borne, being Fryday, at ane efter midnight. Upon the 19th of Apryle 1608, being Tysday, James, first Earle of Perth, was mareit vpon Dame Isabell Setoun, dochter to Robert, first Earle of Wintoun. Upon the last day of Apryle, my Ladye Perth was deliverit of ane dochtor, at 6 hours at evin: her name callit Jean, zeir of God 1611, and was baptised vpon the   of Maij 1611. Upon Wednesday the 18th of December 1611, the Earle of Perth departit this lyfe. Upon the 2d of August 1614, being Tysday, Francis Earle of Bothwell mareit the foirsaid Dame Isabell Setoun, Countes of Perth."

The following letter from Drummond of Hawthornden, addressed to this Lady, is to be found in the edition of his History, 1655 folio, p. 244; but is here printed from the original in the Museum of the Society of Antiquaries of Scotland.

Madam,

Your courtesie hath prevented me, it being mine to offer you thanks, both for esteeming me worthy so honourable a task, and for measuring those lines according to affection, and not their worth; for if they had any, it was all (as the moon hath her light) borrowed from the rayes of your Ladiship's own invention. But this quality becometh well your sweet disposition, and the generosity of that noble stem of which you have your birth, as doth the erecting of that notable Monument to your all-worthy Lord; by the which ye have not onely obliged all his kinred now living, but, in ages to come, the unborn posterity, to render you immortal thanks. Your defert and good opinion of me have, by a gracious violence, (if I can be so happy as to do you service) won me to remain your Ladiships,

    Ever to command,

            W. DRUMMOND.

In the same collection is the original of the following letter, which shows that Drummond at the close of his life was engaged in drawing up the Genealogy which is inserted in this Appendix, see No. I. page 241.

MUCH RESPECTED FREIND,

    These are to intreate you earnestlie that when occasion and your leasure serueth, yee would be pleased to doe mee the favour, as to take the paines to transcriue the Iuscription which is vpon my Lord of Perth's tombe in the chapell of Seatoun. I haue drawen up a Geneologicall Table of the House of Drummond, with many ornamentes and some garnishing of the persones. In this the inscriptions of my Lord's tombe will serue me for some light. My noble Lord of Wintown is descended linealie of this Race, and shall not be overpassed in what I can doe him or his aunceint familie honour and seruice. When this piece is perfeeted it must come under your hand, to giue it the last lustre. Thus, my commendations remembred to your bedfellow and selfe, I remain

    Your assured and loving friend, to serue you,

            W. DRUMMOND.

[April 1649.]

This letter is addressed on the cover "To his uorthye and much respected freind Maister William Ansterre at Tranent ;" and the other side has the inscription, written in a different hand, as follows:

        D. O. M.

ET VIRTUTI ET MEMORIAE CLARISSIMI JUVENIS JACOBI DRUMMOND QUI VT PRIMUM IN NOBILLISSIMA FAMILIA LOCUM OBTINEBAT ITA FAMILIAM PRIMUS COMITATUS PERTHIANI TITULO COHONESTAVIT: FORMA, INDOLE, INGENIO, MORIBUS, OMNIUM BONARUM ARTIUM PERITIA, INTER EXIMIOS PRIMI; QVEM IMMATURA MORS NE IMMORTALEM RERUM GESTARUM LAUDEM AETERNUMQUE DECUS RELIQUERET SUMMO BONORUM OMNIUM MOERORE INTERRUPIT.

ISABELLA ROBERTI WENTONIAE COMITIS FILIA CONJUGI CHARISSIMO MOERENS POSUIT. VIXIT ANNOS XXIX. HIC OBUIT ANNO SALUTIS [DECEMBRIS XVIII M.DC.XI.] FILIAM EX SE RELIQUIT JOANNAM.

> INSTEED of Epitaphs and airye praise,
> This Monument a Ladie chaste did raise
> To her Lord's living fame, and after death
> Her bodie doth vnto this place bequeath
>> To rest with his, til God's shril trumpet sound,
>> Tho' time her life, no time her loue can bound.

Page 202, line 3.—Isobell Seaton married to the Earle of Perth, by whom she had one daughter only, Lady Jean Drummond, who married the Earle of Sutherland, in anno 1629, " who gott in tocher with her 50,000 merkes, the greatest portion that was ever given in Scotland, before that time." (Lord Kingston's Contin. of the History of the House of Seytoun, p. 60.) Lady Jean Drummond, Countess of Sutherland, was served heir of her father, James Earl of Perth, March 23, 1632. (Retours, Perth, No. 409.)

" In Balfour's Annals (says Mr. Kirkpatrick Sharpe) we read, that Lady Perth's daughter, Lady Sutherland, who was married to her Lord at Seton, died, Dec. 1638, at Canowgaite, neir Edinburghe, of a hectick fever, and wes interred at the Collegiat Church of Setton, without any funeral ceremony, by night." Gilbert Gordon, in his Genealogy of the Earls of Sutherland, says, that " her corps was carryed home into Sutherland, and there buried at Dornogh, as she hade appointed in her latter will and testament."—Chronicle of the Hous of Setoun, foot note, p. iii. The date of her death, however, is stated to have been December 29, 1637. See the " Genealogical History of the Earldom of Sutherland, from its origin to the year 1630; with a Continuation to the year 1651." Edinburgh, 1813, folio, p. 486.

Page 208, line 1.—John Earl of Perth was served heir-male of his brother-german, James Earl of Perth, March 11, 1612.

Page 208, line 12.—Drummond of Hawthornden composed no less than three sonnets on the Portrait of this Lady Jean, Countess of Perth, the last of which, entitled " Vpon that same [Pourtrait] drawne with a pansie," runs thus:—

> WHEN with brave Arte the curious Painter drew
> This heavenly shape, the hand why made hee beare
> With golden veines that Flowre of purple hue,
> Which followes on the Planet of the Yeare?

> Was it to show how in our hemispheare,
> Like him Shee shines? Nay, that effects more true
> Of power, and wonder doe in her appeare,
> While Hee but flowres, Shee doth brave minds subdue
> Or would Hee else to Vertue's glorious light
> Her constant course make knowne, or is it Hee
> Doth parelell her blisse with Clytias plight?
> Right so, and thus, Hee reading in her eye
>   Some woefull lover's end, to grace his grave,
>   For Cypresse tree this mourning Flowre her gave.
>
>   (DRUMMOND'S POEMS, Edinburgh, 1616, 4to.)

He also lamented her death in the following Sonnet, entitled " To the Memorie of the most excellent Ladie, IANE, COUNTESSE OF PERTH."

> THIS Beautie which pale Death in dust did turne,
> And clos'd so soon within a coffin sad,
> Did passe like lightning, like to thunder burne;
> So little life, so much of worth, it had!
> Heavens, but to show their might, heere made it shine,
> And when admir'd, then in the World's disdaine
> (O Teares, O Griefe!) did call it backe againe,
> Lest Earth should vaunt, Shee kept what was divine.
> What can wee hope for more? What more enjoy?
> Sith fairest thinges thus soonest have their end;
> And, as on bodies shadowes do attend,
> Sith all our blisse is follow'd with annoy!
>   Shee is not dead, Shee lives where she did love,
>   Her Memorie on Earth, her Soule above.
>
>   (FLOWERS OF SION, Edinburgh, 1630, 4to. p. 103.)

Page 209, line 2.—Drummond of Hawthornden, who frequently acknowledged in his writings the obligations conferred on him by John Earl of Perth, dedicated to him his History of the Five Jameses, with the following eulogium: " And I may say about your Lordship, without flattery, which I abominate, that, even in these worst of times, you are eminently conspicuous for piety and prudence, for loyalty towards the King, for real affection towards your Country, for kindness towards your Friends, and for the care you take in preserving your Family, and managing your affairs so justly and frugally."

In the "Chronicle of Perth," John Earl of Perth, is said to have died at Drymen, at 'the age of fourscore zeires and mair,' June 11, 1662.—(p. 46.)

Page 209, line 13.—"The marriage-contract of Sir John Drummond of Burnbank, afterwards of Logie Almond, and Grizel, daughter of Sir Thomas Stewart of Grandtully, is dated 18th August 1664.

"It is a mistake that he was succeeded by a John, father of Thomas. Thomas was not his grandson, but his son. He married, 1. Anne, daughter of Patrick, second Lord Kinnaird. 2. his cousin-german, Grizel, daughter of David, second Lord Newark, but had no children. Thomas Drummond of Logie Almond held the estate for 80 years, from 12th December 1678, when he was served heir to his father, Sir John, till 11th February 1758, when his nephew, John, was served heir to him at Perth.

"Thomas's brother, Mr. William Drummond of Ballathie, who died before him, was forfeited, and was therefore passed over in the entails of Grandtully in 1717 and 1724, but his sons were put in. Mr. William's wife was Elizabeth, daughter of Mr. George Oliphant of Clashberry, second son of John Oliphant of Bachilton."—MS. Note communicated by Alexander Sinclair, Esq.

Page 209, line 15.—Thomas Drummond of Logie Almond was served heir of his father, Sir John Drummond of Logie Almond, Dec. 12, 1678. (Retours, Inq. Gen. No. 6115.)—The estate of Logie Almond, by the death of the late Right Honourable Sir William Drummond (one of the most learned and accomplished scholars of his time) came into the possession of his nephew Sir John A. Stewart of Grantully, Baronet.

Page 214, line 4.—Spalding, in his Annals, mentioning the Lord Drummond's marriage with Lady Anne, eldest daughter of the Marquis of Huntly, in October 1638, says, she "was ane preceise puritane, and therefore weill lyked in Edinburgh. This marriage (he adds) was celebrated with great solemnity. Many nobles and knights were there. Amang the rest, the Lord Gordone came frae Strathbogie to the samen, &c."—4to. edition, vol. i. p. 178.

Page 215.—JOHN FIRST EARL OF MELFORT.—John Drummond of Lundy, the second son of James, third Earl of Perth, before he was raised to the peerage, held several offices of great importance in Scotland. He was Deputy-Governor of Edinburgh Castle in 1680, when James, Duke of York, and his Duchess visited this country. Macky says, "Being very handsome, and a fine dancer, he got into her Royal Highness's favour, as to be made Lord Treasurer Deputy; and on their Highnesses arrival at London, he was sent for to Court, and made Secretary of State." (Memoirs, p. 243.) He continued one of the chief favourites at Court during the reign of James VII., by whom he was created Viscount of Melfort, August 14, 1685, and Earl of Melfort, August 11, 1686.

After the Revolution, he adhered to the fortunes of King James, and for several years "had the chief administration of St. Germains." Macky, describing his person, says, "He is tall, black, stoops in the shoulders, thin, and turned of fifty years of age." His pictures and prints represent him as remarkably handsome. He was usually known by the title of Duke of Melfort; and died at St. Germains in January 1714.

Page 215, line 9.—The second wife of John Drummond of Lundy, afterwards Earl of Melfort, was Euphemia, daughter of Sir Thomas Wallace of Craigie, Lord Justice Clerk of Scotland. It may be noticed that 'I Padri, e gli Alunni' of the Scotish College at Rome, in republishing Father William Lewis Lesley's "Vita di S. Margherita Regina di Scozia," Rome 1691, 18mo. dedicated the volume "All' Illustriss. et Excellentiss. Sig. la Signora Eufemia Wallas Drumont, Contessa di Melfort,"— and these Reverend Fathers, while complimenting her on her beauty and accomplishments, allude to her alliance with "un Cavaliere—perche trahe apunto l' origine da quel Signore Inglese, che hebbe l' honore di condurre S. Margherita nella Scozia."

Page 215, line 14.—"The Countess of Arrol, sister to the Earl of Perth (says Sir Robert Sibbald, in 1682) sent me a Description of Buchan; and was pleased to doe me the honor to grave two plates, ane of silver, another of copper, she sent to me, and the draught of some fowles, done by herself, admirably fine."—(Memoirs of his own Life, MS.) These two plates were introduced by Sir Robert Sibbald into his Scotia Illustrata; and the Description of Buchan is preserved in his MS. Topographical Collections, in the Advocates' Library.

Page 216, line 4—28.—Hay of Luncarty, the ancestor of the Earls of Errol, whose noted exploit against the Danes is commemorated in a Latin poem, by James Ross, entitled "Origo gentis Hayorum: seu Danorum ad vicum Loncartem excidii, virtute cujusdam Hayi, rustici vulgo crediti, sed revera ex antiquissima Cantii regum prosapia oriundi, parti, historico-poetica narratio." Edinburgi, 1700, 8vo.

The following Sonnet, addressed to the Countess of Erroll, probably soon after the year 1600, by William Fowler who was Secretary to the Queen Anne, wife of James

No. II.   APPENDIX.   307

the Sixth is transcribed from the Hawthornden MSS., in the Library of the Antiquarian Society of Scotland.

> Hee quho to Hauen gaue starrs, and winds to Aire,
> Flouers, hearbs to Earth, and waues vnto the See,
> Doeth to our Age his wounders more declaire,
> Since things more strange then these we see in Thee;
> Yea, that we suld cast bothe our mynds and ee
> Upon his gracious and his glorious frame,
> In you He hathe maide placed for to be
> Quhat most was raire, quhat most is fair Madame:
> Whense Love his flammes doth fetche, and netts doth make
> Bright haire and eyes, that starrs and sunn doth schame
> Sueit smyles, chaist wourds, that peace and weres proclame
> Graue port, auld witt in youngest yeares, but lak,
>   With store of graces and off beautyes strainge,
>   Which giues to Nature law, and stay to chainge.

Page 227.—JAMES, FOURTH EARL OF PERTH, to whom this work is dedicated, succeeded to the estates and honours of the family, on the death of his father, in the year 1675. In 1682, he was appointed by Charles II. to the office of Lord Justice-General, and in 1684 to that of Lord High Chancellor of Scotland. On the accession of King James VII. he was continued in all his places; had the chief administration of affairs, and declared himself of the King's religious persuasion. After the Revolution, being obnoxious to the populace, he attempted to make his escape in disguise, but the vessel in which he had embarked was pursued, and being brought back, he was thrown into the common prison of Kirkaldy, and afterwards confined in Stirling Castle till August 1693, when he was liberated on giving his bond to leave the kingdom under penalty of L.5000. He went abroad, and adhered, with the utmost fidelity, to the changed fortunes of the exiled monarch, who appointed him Governor to the Prince of Wales, and created him Duke of Perth. In Macky's Memoirs he is described as "of middle stature, with a quick look; of a brown complexion, and towards fifty years of age." He died at St. Germains, 11th March 1716, in his 58th year, and was buried in the chapel of the Scots College at Paris. (Douglas's Peerage by Wood, Art. PERTH.)

Sir Robert Sibbald, in the Memoirs of his own Lyfe, which still remains unpublished, gives the following account of his first acquaintance with the Earl of Perth:—

"About this time [1678] the Earl of Perth began to employ me as his Physitian to his family, and introduced me with his friends. I had been recommended to him by his cusin, Mr. Patrick Drummond. I had payed my respects to him, upon his comming from his travells; bot Doctor Henderson, who maried Hawthrondale, his sister, was his Physitian whill he lived, and had been his Fathers. So I succeeded him.

"The Earl was of great partes, and of a serious temper, read much, and was very observant of the rites of the Church of England, and had the English service always in his family; he was temperate, and was of excellent conversation, and very desyrous to learn. I, by his order, acquainted him with the curious books, especially pieces of divinity, history, poemes, memoirs of ministers of state, and discourses in philosophy. There was a great friendship contracted betwext us, which was entertained by correspondance of letters; and few weeks past without letters, either when he was in England, or here. I gave him account of the parts of learning he affected most. He not only wrotte ane excellent style of English, but upon occasions, made verses, and translated some of the psalms of Buchannan, and some odes of Horace. I gave him the best advice I could, for ordering of his life, and wrotte many letters to him, and had many discourses with him, to diswade him from medling with the Court, and had publik employment, and to follow the directions left him by his grandfather, a man of great prudence and learning, who did advise his descendents to keep at home, and to manage y^r own private affairs aright. Bot the low condition of his estates, (haveing sustained great losses, and payed many fines in ye late troubles, and payed out great portions to the bretheren and sisters), and the persuasions of his friends that expected great advantage by his Court, prevailed with him to embrace publick employment, and goe frequently to Court; which at first occasioned his being made Justice-General, and after that he was made Chancellor, which ingaged him in the interests of the Court, and occasoned much trouble to him, and persecution and lose to me."

There is a poem addressed "To James Earl of Perth, &c. Lord Chancellor of His Majesties most ancient Kingdom of Scotland, as "*The Congratulatory Welcome of an obliged Quill;*" which is reprinted in a volume of Fugitive Scottish Poetry of the 17th century, Edinburgh, 1825. 8vo. The author, who signs himself M. M., was Mungo Murray, not Mary Morpeth, as erroneously stated in that volume.

"Among the epistolatory correspondence of the Logie Almond family are letters announcing, that James Earl of Perth had a son born 19th February 1673, and a daughter born 13th July 1675. Lilias, Countess of Perth was widow of James, fourth

Earl of Tullibardin, who died in January 1670. Her second marriage was in 1679; and she died in September 1685. In January 1686 the Earl of Perth married thirdly Lady Mary Gordon, daughter of the Marquis of Huntly."—MS. Note by Alexr. Sinclair, Esq.

"In the possession of the family of Perth there still remains the literary correspondence between this nobleman [the Lord Chancellor Earl of Perth] and their majesties, Charles, James, and his son. There are also preserved the Royal appointments of this great statesman to his high offices. And there is also a collection of his private letters to his friends in Scotland during his imprisonment and exile in foreign lands. These breathe a spirit of exalted piety, submissive resignation, and heroic magnanimity; and while they unfold the character of the man, they present the remains of the able statesman, the ingenious politician, and the accomplished minister." Malcolm's House of Drummond, p. 154.

Page 238, line ult.—Mr. David Drummond, Advocate, the transcriber of the manuscript of Lord Strathallan's work, as mentioned at page 54, line 4, was the son of Mr David Drummond, Minister of Linlithgow, and afterwards of Moneidy. In the account of the family of Smythe of Braco and Methven, inserted in Douglas's Baronage, the Father is called John Drummond. His son, David, was appointed one of the Advocates-Deputes, July 16, 1684, when the Earl of Perth was made Lord Chancellor. (Fountainhall's Notes, p. 93.) The Viscount of Dundee, in a letter to the Earl of Melfort, dated from Moy in Lochaber, June 27, 1689, says, "I was extremely surprised when I saw Mr. Drummond the advocate, in a Highland habit, come up to Lochaber to me, and gave account that the Queen has sent L.2000 sterling to London for the King's service, and that two more was a-coming. I did not think the Queen had known any thing of our affairs." (Letters of Lord Dundee, printed for the Bannatyne Club, 1827, p. 47.) The Editor, George Smythe Esq. Advocate, in a note, says, "It appeares, from letters in the possession of the Editor, that Mr. Drummond did not escape the suspicion of the government. In the beginning of December 1689, he and Cockburn of Langton were apprehended by an order of the Council, and detained for some time close prisoners in the Tolbooth of Edinburgh."

David Drummond, as a Jacobite, having declined taking the oaths to government, ceased to practise at the bar, but still retained his title of Advocate; and was afterwards appointed Treasurer of the Bank of Scotland. He held that office in 1704, December 20, on which day his wife, Jean Leirmont, addressed a letter to his cousin,

the laird of Methven, from which the following curious extract is made, describing a
run upon the Bank, occasioned by what would now be considered a very trivial loss:—

"DEAR SIR.—My Husband is in such confusion and trouble about ye affaires of y^e
Bank y^t he could not ans^r you himselfe. This day eight days one of the tellers,
Mr. Pringle, ran away; he hade more than L.1000 sterling in his hands. But he was
so discreet y^t he took w^t him only eight thousand merks, q^{ch} his cautioners have given
bond for to pay, so y^t my Husband will come to no trouble. His running away, and
the noise of crying up money, made all people runn upon ye Bank for money, so that,
upon Munday last, they were forsed to stop pay^{tt} for want of money, which is grown
very scarce of late, by reasone of great exportations, ther being no course taken to
hinder it houever. Immediately ye Directors applied to ye Privy-Council, who appointed a Committee to inspect ye Bank books, who, upon a full inquiry, found y^e
stock in ye Bank to bee far above al ye Bank bills y^t ar running, which being reported
to y^r Councell, they approved ye same, and ordered it to be printed to satisfy those
concerned; and furder, ye Directors have resolved y^t al bank bills, where or housevers
hands they ar, shal bear annualrent from Munday last, which was ye day they stopt, so
y^t no body can bee losers y^{r}by."

The celebrated Dr. Pitcairn was an intimate friend of David Drummond, and from
some of his poems, which are addressed to him, it appears that both of them were born
on Christmas-day. He is also celebrated in poems by Allan Ramsay and others 'On
the Royal Company of Archers.' He succeeded his brother, Dr. John Drummond, an
eminent Physician in Edinburgh, who died in December 1740, aged 78; but he did
not long survive, as his name occurs in the Obituary of the Scots Magazine for February 1741.—It may be added that Margaret Blair, of Balthyock, the wife of David
Drummond, now Blair, son of David Drummond, Advocate, Treasurer of the Bank of
Scotland, was served heir of her father, John Blair, October 3, 1723. (Regist. Retorn.
vol. lviii. p. 859.)

APPENDIX.

ADDITIONAL NOTES.

Page 4.—In the Accounts of the Family may be noticed the article Drummond, in Bayle's "Dictionnaire Historique et Critique," communicated in 1695, by the Chancellor Earl of Perth.

Page 45, line 9.—Drummonds of Concraig.—The following notice of documents regarding this branch of the family, preserved in the charter-chest of his Grace the Duke of Athole, has been communicated to the Editor.

No. 1. Charter by " Malcolmus de Dromond dominus de Conchraig," of ten merks of lands in his Lordship of Tulichrawyn, in the county of Strathern, granted " Donaldo filio Gilberti"—" causa matrimonii contrahendi inter eundem Donaldum et Elissabeth sororem meam," at Perth, August 14, 1421.

No. 2. Confirmation of the preceding charter by Walter, Earle of Athole and Caithness, tutor of Malise Earl Palatine of Strathern, in which Malcolm Drummond of Concraig is styled " consanguineus noster ;" dated Methven, August 26, 1421.

No. 3. Instrument of sasine, May 17, 1453, of the lands of Kilauch, &c. in the territory of Tulichrawyn, " propriis manibus," granted by Maurice Dromonde of Conchrage, " consanguineo suo dilecto Mauricio Donaldi." Among the witnesses is John Dromonde Gylach, who is mentioned in this work, page 47, line 8.

No. 4. Charter of woodset of the lands of Daleherach and Scrimer, in the Earldom of Strathern and County of Perth, granted by Maurice Drummunde of Concrag, with consent of John, his son and heir, and Andrew Mercer of Inchbreky, " amico meo carissimo Johanni Dromund de Culquolly," dated April 20, 1453.

No. 5. Ratification by Margaret Mersar out of presence of " Moryss of Drummund," her husband, of grants of the lands of Dalquhilrach, Serymbyr, and the Katkyne, which lands the said Moryss has woodset to John of Drumunde and Malcolmeson his cussynes. To this deed the seal of Andrew Mersar of Inchbrecky, her " dearest father," is appended : dated Inchbrecky, April 20, 1453.

No. 6. Charter of the lands of Kilach to James Murray, son of Sir David Murray of Tulibardine, by Maurice Drummond, son and heir " quondam Malcolmi Drummunde de Concrag," dated at Strowan, January 26, 1468.

No. 7. Instrument of sasine of the lands of Kilach, in favour of John Drummond, son of umqll. Maurice Drummond of Cowquhalzhee, November 2, 1468.

Page 55, line 17.—James Drummond, Sherriff-Clerk of Perth. The following is an extract from Sir James Balfour's MSS. :—29 Aprilis 1614, " His Majesties letter concerning James Drummond, schyref-clark of Perth, and preferring of Maister Hary Kynrose to his office and place, wes this day presentit and red in Counsell, and it wes thoght be the Counsell that they could not recommend ane other to be preferred to his office and place while first himselve wes hard ; and, therefore, the Shireff of Perth, the said James and Harie Drummond, his sone, who pretendes a right to that office, ar ordained to be summond to the next counsell day, at whiche tyme so far will be done in that mater as may stand with equitie and justice."

James Drummond of Cardnies, Sheriff-Clerk of Perth, had a sister, Margaret, married to Alexander Soutar, portioner of Wester Banchrie, September 7, 1560 ; and three daughters, Jean, Helen, and Isabel, Feb. 19, 1572. (Sheriff Records of Perth.)

Page 61, line 5.—George Drummond 'cruelly shot to death by order of the Committee of Estates.' On the 4th June 1650, " Letters from Lt. General David Lesley were read in the House, shewing that George Drummond, Ballows brother, and Captaine Mellweill wer apprehendit in Jutland Castle in Orknay, and ther persons sceured."—(Balfour's Annals, vol. iv. p. 44.)

Page 62.—Mr. David Drummound, Prebendarius de Crieff, is witness to a paper dated February 23, 1611. (Acts of Parl. vol. iii. p. 506.)

Page 63.—Mr. David Drummond, son of the preceding, was also minister of Crieff. On October 26, 1641, "The Estates of Parliament ratified the presentation of Mr. David Drummond to the Kirk of Crieff." (Ib. vol. v. p. 441 and 443.) There is printed in the Acts of Parliament 1662, " An Act and Decreit against Dowgall Macpherson of Powrie, and Mr. David Drummond, late minister of Crieff, in favour of Rorie M'Leod of Dunvegan." (Ib. vol. vii. p. 400.)

Page 73, line 9.—Sir Alexander Drummond of Medope was admitted an Extraordinary Lord of Session, May 17, 1608. Sir James Balfour thus notices his death :— " The 15th of Julij 1619, deyed Sir Alexander Drummond of Medope, one of the Senators of the Colledge of Justice, a werey learned judge." (Annals, vol. ii. p. 76.)

Page 123, line 23.—Captain Drummond, who was appointed leader of the left wing, is said to have been the principal cause of the defeat at the battle of Aldearn ; and he suffered by martial law for his conduct. The following extract may be compared with Lord Strathallan's account.—" The victorie at Alderne was chiefly attributed to the Gordons and their heirs. When Vrrie returned to Inverness, Captain Drummond was accused to have betrayed the armie. He confessed that he hade spoken with the enemie after the word and sign of battle was given; whereupon he was adjudged by a Councell of Warre to be shot to death, which was done." (Geneal. Hist. of the Sutherlands, p. 525.)

Page 129.—Drummonds of Pitcairnes. Janet Crichton, spouse of Hary Drummond of Riccarton, was infeft in the mill lands of Pitcairns in liferent, January 28, 1544. She is mentioned as his relict in the Records of the Sheriff-Court of Perth, March 3, 1570. William, his son, fiar of Pitcairns, is mentioned January 20, 1570; and Jean Hepburn Lady Riccarton March 14, 1574. Hary Drummond of Pitcairns had a son christened Andrew, March 3, 1642. (Kirk Session Records of Perth.)

On April 15, 1644, "The Convention of Estates ordaines and commands Harie Drummond, Rootmaister, to marche with all expedition with his troop from Perth to Dumfries, and to be there on Thursday nixt, the 18th of this instant, to attend Colonell Campbellis regiment." (Acts of Parliament, vol. vi. p. 87.) In December 1650, Lord Drummond was named Lieutenant-Colonel, and Harie Drummond of Pitcairnie his Major. (Ib. p. 575.)

Page 144, line 11.—One of the earliest authors of the name, of whom we have any notice, was a Jonas Drummond, settled probably as a physician in England, during the first half of the 16th century. He published a little tract under this title :— "Here is a New boke, called the Defence of Age, and Recoverg of Youth, translated out of the famous Clarke and right experte mebgegne Arnold de Noba Qilla, berg profgtable for all men to knowe." It is dedicated "Unto the noble and vertuous my Lady Marget Dowglas, Nice vnto the most noble and crysten Prynce Henry the VIII., King of Englande and of France, Defender of the Fayth, and under God the Supreme Heid of the Churche of Englande; Syster vnto the moste noble and chrysten Prynce James Kynge of Scottes; Daughter vnto the noble Countie Archebald Erle of Anguysshe." The translator says, "Sorry am I to offer vnto your noble and vertuous Ladyshyp so small a boke, were it not so that I am purposed to recompense your Ladyship with a greater, so that this may favourably be receyued." Whether this intention was ever fulfilled is uncertain. It has no date, but was undoubtedly printed in the reign of Henry VIII., probably before 1544, as otherwise, the name of James V. would not have been noticed in the dedication. The said little "Boke," of eight leaves, only contains the notice that it was "Imprinted by me Robert Wyer, dwellynge in Saynt

Martyns parysshe, at the sygne of Saynt John Evangelyst, besyde Charynge-Crosse." A transcript occurs among Sir H. Sloane's MSS. in the British Museum. The printed copy is very rare.

Page 162, line 20.—There is a letter, probably to this Sir Maurice Drummond, dated May 12, 1630, from William Drummond of Hawthornden. (Works, p. 146.)

Page 163, line 14.—In Balfour's Annals it is stated, that the Committee of Estates of Parliament ordered "Johne Drumond of Baleclone to be dismissed, he finding cautione for his good behaviour for 6000 markes in tyme coming." February 21, 1645. (Vol. iii. p. 278.)

Page 186, line 6.—Sir James Drummond of Machiney, in Perthshire, was knighted by Charles the Second, at Scone, January 2, 1651. (Balfour's Annals, vol. iv. p. 256.)

Page 187, line 22.—William Drummond, brother to Lord Maderty, was named Colonel, by the Estates of Parliament, December 23, 1650. (Balfour's Annals, vol. iv. p. 216.) In the Memoirs of Sir Ewan Cameron of Lochiel (MS.) mention is occasionally made of LORD STRATHALLAN, then General Drummond, and the present work is also alluded to: "He was (speaking of his Lordship) AN HONEST MAN, A FAITHFUL AND SINCERE FRIEND, AND AN UNCORRUPTIBLE PATRIOT; besides, he distinguished himself by his learning and parts, and wrote a GENEALOGICAL ACCOUNT OF THE DRUMMONDS with judgment and spirit, but it has not yet been printed."

Page 196.—Jean Drummond, afterwards Countess of Roxburghe, was Governess to the children of James the First, and received L.2200, as a free gift, in the 3d year of the King's reign, 1605-6, and a similar gift of L.3000 in 1617. (Nichols' Progresses of King James, vol. ii. p. 747. n.) As stated, in a preceding Note, she was married in February 1614; and died in October 1643.

Page 214, line 15.—In the Treasurer's Accounts, 1506-7, Feb. 27, we find the following payment:—"Item to James Lundy, the Lard of Lundyis son, be the Kingis command, quhen he passit in France, xx French crownis, summa, xiiii Lib."—and 1512, April 16,—"Item, to the Lard of Lundeis sone, quhilk come fra the King of France with lettrez to the Kingis grace at his returnyng, xlv Lib."

INDEX.

INDEX.

ABERCROMBIE of Cassie, 127.
— of Abercrombie, 116.
— of Skemor and Frosk, 71, 250.
Aberdeen, Bishops of, 21, 36, 40, 133.
Abernethie, Lord ABERNETHIE, 198.
— — Lord SALTON, 140.
— William, (Minister at ———,) 182.
Abthane and Thane explained, 16, 32.
Abthanie of Dull, 32, 274.
Ada of Huntingtoun, 33, 34, 36.
— of Lennox, 65.
Airth of Airth and Carnock, 70, 250.
Albanack Crinen, 31, 32.
Allan Lord of GALLOWAY, 33, 219.
ARBUTHNET, Viscount, 175.
Areskine. See Erskine.
ARRAN, Earl of. See Boyd, Hamilton, Stuart.
ARUNDELL, Earle of, 33.
ASHBY, Allan, (Lord de la Zough,) 219.
Atcheson of Gosfoord, 121.
Auchmutie of Gosfoord, 75, 270.
Auchterarder, Goodwife of, 60.
Auchinleck (Auffleet) of Glenbervie, 232.

Baine (Ben) of Findall, 63, 124. 57.
Balcanquil of that ilk, 62.
Balfoure, Lord BURLEIGH, 185.
— of M'Creistoun, (Makarestowne,) 71, 250.
— James, 154.

Banco Thane of Lochaber, 32.
Barclay of Colerny, 51.
— of Towie, 151, 197, 249.
Barton of Over Barton, 21, 92, 131, 169.
Battle of Aldern, 73, 123, 312; Alfoord, 72; Corrichie, 225; Durham, 68; Flowdone, 232; Glenlivet, 226; Haddenrig, 225; Harlaw, 31, 65; Murthlake, 31; Otterburn, 88, 229; Pinkie, 123, 142, 225.
Beaton of Creich, 184.
— Cardinal, 199, 200.
BEAUMONT, Earl of, 235.
Becket, Thomas a, 218.
Bell, —, (Provost of Linlithgow,) 49.
BELLENDINE, Lord, 196.
Belshes of Tofts, 127.
Beton, James, (Bishop of Glasgow,) 57.
Bet, —, (Merchant in Stirling,) 51.
Bisset of Glasclun, 40.
— of Logie, 62.
Blacater of that ilk, 140, 144.
Blair of Ardblair (Ardlair), 275-277.
— of Kinfauns, 54.
— of Tarsappie, 54.
— John, (Minister of Kilspindie,) 54.
Boyd, Earl of ARRAN, 80.
— Lord BOYD, 148, 200, 231, 235.
Boyle, (Bool) —, (in Comra,) 58.
Bramstone, Sovereigne of Belfast, 181.
BRECHIN, Lord, 41, 43.

2 T

Brodie of Lethen, 175.
— of Pitgeveny, 175.
Brown, Bishop of Dunkeld, 118.
Bruce of AILESBURIE, (Elgin,) 155, 247.
— of Airth, 55, 151.
— of Auchinbowie, 71, 250.
— of Baldridge, 154.
— of Kincavel, 73, 251.
— Blanch, 73.
— Rob. (Minister of Aberdour,) 73, 251.
Buchanan of Buchanan, 66, 67, 71, 186, 251.
— of Lenie, 181.
— of Shirrahall, 155.
Burnet, Archbishop of Glasgow, 197.
Butter of Gormok, 275-277.

Cameron, Mr. Archibald, (Clerk,) 54.
Campbell of Aberuchell, 155.
— of ARGYLE, (Lochawah,) 21, 24—26, 51, 67, 68, 133, 134, 157, 160, 161, 185, 194, 195, 203, 214, 226, 297.
— of Arkinlas, 52.
— of Auchinbreck, 172.
— of Caddel, (Calder,) 200.
— of Dunstaffnage, 159.
— of Glenurchie, 146, 162, 176, 235.
— of Kethick, 163.
— of Lawers 57, 155.
— of Lochinzel, 53.
— of Lochawah (Lochow,) 65—68, 83, 160, 161, 235. See Campbell of Argyle.
— of LOUDON, 148—150, 197, 246.
Campbells, their origin, 22, 160, 161.
Cants, Andrew, (Ministers,) 182.

Cardenie, Marion, 65, 83.
Cargill of Haltown, 116.
Carmichael, Lord CARMICHAEL, 190, 248.
Carnegie of NORTHESK, 74, 194, 251.
— of SOUTHESK, 168, 213.
— of Phinheaven, 194.
Carron, Marjory, 235.
Cavendish, Sir William, 80, 141.
Chalmer of Drumlochy, 275-279.
Charters, (Writs,) 35, 36, 38, 40, 47, 70, 83, 133, 134.
Charters of Amersfeild, 21.
— of Kinfaunes, 181, 183, 200.
Chancellor's Office, first in Scotland, 217.
Cheesholm of Buttergask, 151, 183.
— of Cromlix, 56, 122, 127, 151, 163, 177—184, 246, 248.
— Parson of Comrie, 181, 182.
— Baylie of Dumblane, 49, 181, 182.
— Bishop of Dumblane, 56, 122, 178-181.
— Bishop of Vason, 151, 153, 181, 183, 246.
Christie, Tho. (Minister of Wigton,) 154.
Cleeland of that ilk, 185.
Clerk of Pennicook, 74.
Clerk,—(Admiral of Sweden,) 54.
Cochrane, Earle of DUNDONALD, 192, 207.
Cockburn of Langton, 151, 185.
Colquhoun (Caluhoune) of Luss, 59.
Colt (Coult) Minister of Inneresk, 182.
Colvill of Cleish, 145.
Colvill, Alex. (Justice depute,) 25, 26.
Comrie of that ilk, 58.
Commissioners for Peace, 37, 133.
Constable, Office of, first in Scotland, 217.

INDEX. 319

Cornwall of Bonhard, 119.
Corser, John, 272.
Cossans, Lady, 60.
Cowan, Provost of Stirling, 172.
Craig of Rosecraig, 182.
Cramond of Aldbar, 60.
Craufurd of Carse, 146.
— of Lochnorris, 148, 153.
Creichton of Airlywight, 189, 248.
— of CREICHTON, 80, 225, 230.
— of DUMFRIESS, 146, 153, 189, 192.
— of Lugton, 154.
— of Riccarton, 152, 153, 246, 313.
— of SANQUHAR, 132, 146.
— of Strathurd, 235.
— Ceeillia, 170.
— Bishop of Dunkeld, 152, 153.
— Sir Robert, 189.
Cumin, Earl of BUCHAN, 33, 219, 220.
— of Inveralachie, (Lyon King at Arms,) 135.
Cuninghame of Capringtoun, 148.
— of Drumwhasel, 151.
— of GLENCAIRN, 21, 152, 174.
— of Glengarnock, 50, 52, 146.
— of Wester Polmais, 70, 250.

Dalzell of Binns, 123, 155, 156, 247, 292, 298.
— Earle of CARNWATH, 155, 247.
— Sir Robert, 194.
Danielstoune, Hugh, 69.
Davidson (Minister of Muthell,) 57.
Denmark, (Norway,) King of, 90, 91, 237.
Dickson of Ballachaster, 162.
Dog of Ballingrew, 121, 128.

Douglas of ABERCORN, 78, 244.
— of ANGUS, 21 46, 57, 71, 78, 79, 87, 93, 134, 135, 140-145, 174, 206, 227, 231-233, 236.
— of Bonjedward, 74, 251.
— of Coldoch, 112.
— of Dallenie, 120.
— of DOUGLAS, 29, 67, 77, 78, 87, 88, 91, 199, 227-230, 235, 238.
— of Drumlanrig, 140, 145.
— of DUMBARTON, 233.
— of FORFAR, 233.
— of Glenbervie, 140, 232.
— of Kilspindie, 142.
— of LIDDISDALE, 166, 237, 238.
— of Lochlevin, 152.
— of MAR, 78, 86.
— of MORDINGTON, 184.
— of MORTON, 79, 140, 143, 145, 149, 168, 196, 213, 273.
— of NIDDESDALE, 89, 90.
— of Pittendreich, 140, 142, 143, 232.
— of Placentia, 228.
— of SPINIE, 117, 145.
— of Whittingham, 144.
— of WIGTON, 78.
— Provost of Banffe, 182.
— Prior of Coldinghame, 140, 144.
— Bishop of Dunkeld, 142.
— George, (Master of Angus,) 140-145, 290.
— Jean, (Lady Glamis,) 144, 145, 290.
— Margaret, 144, 313.
Douglasses, Alliances of, with the Drummonds, 233, 234.
— their origin, 227, et seq.

INDEX.

DRUMMOND, Chiefs of the House of,
— Maurice, the Hungarian, First Thane, or Seneseall of Lennox, 5, 9, 14-19, 27.
—Maurice, and the next four Senescalls of Lennox, 9, 27—29. (See p. 260-1.)
— Malcolm Beg, 6th Seneseal, 9, 15, 29, 30-38, 65.
— Sir John, (of Cargill,) 7th Seneseal, 9, 65-70, 245, 266, 267, 272.
— Malcolm, Earle of MAR, 8th Chiefe, 9, 86-88, 245, 274.
Sir John, 9th Chiefe, 9, 15, 88-92, 235, 238, 245, 274.
— Sir Walter, 10th Chiefe, 9, 111, 235, 245.
— Sir Malcolm, 11th Chief, 10, 118.
— Sir JOHN, 1st Lord DRUMMOND, 12th Chiefe, 10, 16, 48, 62, 79, 132-138, 158, 231, 245, 274, 286, 293-295.
— William, Master, 13th Chiefe, 10, 157-160, 245, 292, 295.
— Walter, Master, 14th Chiefe, 10, 164, 167, 245.
— DAVID, 2d Lord, 15th Chiefe, 10, 79, 93, 167, 169-171, 200, 235, 245, 248, 273-279, 299.
— PATRICK, 3d Lord, 10, 122, 150, 191, 193, 194, 197, 204, 213, 248, 299.
— JAMES, 1st Earle of PERTH, 10, 100, 201, 206, 248, 249, 273, 301-303.
— JOHN, 2d Earle, 10, 16, 50, 100, 105, 196, 208, 248, 249, 259, 300, 303, 305.
— JAMES, 3d Earle, 10, 214, 249.
— JAMES, 4th Earle, 10, 186, 227, 306-309.
— JAMES Lord Drummond, 10, 227.

DRUMMOND OF
— Achlaick, 125, 130.
— Auchterarder, 62.
— Auchtermuthill, 60.
— Balhadie, (Culcrieff,) 154, 291.
— Ballathies, 305.
— Balloch, 45, 49, 59-61, 122, 154, 181, 264.
— Barnbougal, 92.
— Belliclon, 124, 157, 162, 163, 295, 314.
— Blair, 61, 111, 113-117, 233, 275-283.
— Boghall, 115, 116, 280.
— Boreland, 48-50, 57, 58, 181, 263, 284.
— Broich, 45, 60, 61, 133.
— Bruntihill, 131.
— Callendar, 64, 266.
— Cardnies or Hehill, 55.
— Cargill, (see 7th Chief,) 46, 48, 69, 89, 124, 132.
— Carlowrie, 254.
— Carnock, 70-72, 129, 142, 185, 250, 251, 267-269, 284.
— Coldoch, 56, 122, 147, 179.
— Concraig, 35, 38-48, 89, 253, 262, 263, 311.
— Comrie, 126, 128-130, 285, 286.
— Corrivauchter, 60, 118, 122, 123.
— Corskeplie, 119, 150, 180, 283.
— Creiff, 122.
— Cuilt, 124.
— Culcreiff, 291.
— Culqualzie, 39, 47, 51-54, 57, 63, 125, 263, 311, 312.
— Cultmalundie, 127, 128, 285.
— Dalcheefic, 39.
— Dalwhynie, 57

INDEX.

DRUMMOND of
— Deanstown, 58, 118-121, 283, 284.
— Dilpatrick, 58.
— Drumduy, 49, 53.
— Drummawhence, 53.
— Drummonerinoch, 52, 118, 119, 124-126, 285.
— Eremore, (Carnock,) 70, 76, 250.
— Fintelich, 56.
— Fliskhill, 113.
— Gardrum, 115, 117, 280.
— Gassingall Wester, 154.
— Giblistown, 119.
— Halholl, 131, 286.
— Hawthornden, 4, 45, 72, 74, 75, 241, 250, 251, 268-272.
— Hehill, or Cardnies, 55.
— Inchchaffray, (Lord Maderty,) 177.
— Innermay, 126-129, 184, 186, 285.
— Innerpeffrey, 48, 122, 140, 147-151, 169, 183, 197, 245, 246.
— Innerramsay, 40, 47, 51.
— Kilbryd, 48, 52, 122.
— Kildees, 58, 122-124, 284.
— Kingsfeild, 71.
— Kirkhill, 58, 263.
— Ledcreife and Blair, 111, 113, 133, 275-283.
— Lennoch, 41, 47, 60, 150, 264.
— Logie Almond, 209, 305.
— Lundin, (MELFORT,) 194, 214, 215, 305.
— Madera, 20-22, 91-110, 250, 252.
— MACHANY, 178, 184—186, 227, 248, 249, 295, 314.
— MADERTY, 151, 171, 177-190, 246, 248, 249, 289, 296, 299.

DRUMMOND of
— Maler, 126.
— MAR. See 8th Chiefe.
— Meggor, 52, 122.
— Meginsh, (Mewie,) 41, 47, 264.
— MELFORT, (Lundin,) 305, 306.
— Midhope, 3, 71, 73, 250, 268, 312.
— Milnab, 45, 53, 60, 62—64, 264-266.
— Muthell, 55, 118.
— PERTH. See the Chiefs.
— Pitcairnes, 126, 129, 153, 285, 286, 313.
— Pitzallonie, 40, 50, 52, 55-59, 124, 133, 150, 179, 185, 263.
— Riccarton, 60, 129, 152-156, 177, 246, 290-292, 313.
— Smithiestowne, 130, 131.
— Stobhall. See Cargill and Perth.
— Strageth, 60, 150.
— STRATHALLAN, 187, 296-299, 314.
— Ward, 125.
— Woodcockdale, 73, 250.

DRUMMOND,
— QUEEN ANNABELLA, 8, 20, 24, 65, 76-83, 243-245, 272-274.
— Anna, (Countess of Errol,) 306, 307.
— Annabella (Lady Graham,) 147.
— Alexander, W. S., 119.
— Andrew (Lieut.-Col.,) 186, 295.
— Andrew, Rector of Kirkconnel, 52.
— Andrew (Minister of Panbryde,) 114.
— Andrew (Vicar of Strageth,) 55.
— Arch. (Minister of Ochterarder,) 120.
— Bryce, 29, 38, 66.
— David, 49, 50, 263.
— David, (Advocate,) 54, 309, 310.

DRUMMOND,
— David, (Major-General,) 162.
— David, (Minister of Creiff,) 62, 63, 312.
— David, (Minister of Linlithgow,) 54, 309.
— David, (Edward, Judge) 153, 246, 291.
— Dean of Dumblane, 111, 112, 283.
— George, (Minister of St. Madoes) 58.
— George, (shot by order of the Committee of Estates,) 61, 312.
— George, (Provost of Edinburgh,) 57, 63, 64, 266.
— James, (Minister, Co. Durham,) 115.
— James, (Minister of Fowlls,) 58, 120. 283, 284.
— James, (Minister of Muthill,) 121.
— James, (Sheriff-clerk of Perth,) 55, 312.
— James, (depute of Strathern,) 63, 265, 266.
— Jane, 281.
— Jean, (Countess of Perth.) See Kerr.
— Jean, (Lady Roxburgh,) 195, 248, 252, 255, 299, 300, 314.
— Jean, (Lady Sutherland,) 202, 303.
— John, (Sheriff-depute of Aberdeen,) 266.
— John (Minister of Fowlls,) 54.
— John, (shot after battle of Olderne,) 123.
— John, (Master of Works,) 62, 264, 265.
— Jonas, (Physician,) 313.
— Colonel Lodowick, 187.
— Malcolm, (Judge,) 42.
— Lady Margaret, 138, 139, 247, 287-289.
— Ninian, (Minister of Kinnoull,) 4, 154, 246, 291.
— Sir Patrick, (Conservator,) 3, 115, 252, 280.

DRUMMOND,
— Patrick, (at London,) 284, 308.
— Patrick, (Minister near Newcastle,) 121, 284.
— Robert, (Master of Works,) 71, 250, 267.
— Sybilla, (Lady Kinclevin,) 147, 148.
— Walter, (Clerk Register,) 37.
— William, (the Poet.) See Hawthornden, 4, 45, 74, 75, 257, 259, 268, 301-304.

DRUMMONDS allied with Douglasses, 233, 234. Flemings, 211, 212. Gordons, 207, 226. Stuarts, 5, 7, 8, 34, 80, 140, 234. Foreign Princes and Sovereigns, through the Stuarts, 79-83, 273.
— their Arms, 17, 21, 23, 95, 242, 243, 259.
— Collectors of their History, 3, 4, 257.
— their Name and Origin, 14, 22-26, 258.
— their Settlements, 15, 16, 69, 88, 92, 132, 133.
— Chiefes omitted, 260, 261.
Drummond Castle, 125, 133, 159, 289, 290.
Dumbar of Auchtermonsie, 199.
— of Balduine, 192.
— of Lothian, 16, 31.
— of MARCH, 16, 91, 165, 203, 205, 237.
— of MURRAY, 205.
— Bishop of Glasgow, 179.
Dumblane, Bishop of, 21, 165, 178-181, 274, 293.
Dundas, Lyon King at Arms, 133.
Dunkeld, Bishop of, 118, 152, 153, 274.

INDEX. 323

Earls first in Scotland, 12, 16, 18, 242.
Edgar Athelin, 12, 13, 18, 242.
Edmonston of Duntreath, 79, 172, 179.
— of Ednim, 79.
Eglington, Sir Hugh, 40, 67.
Elphingston of BALMERINOCH, 151, 192, 246.
— of COWPEN, 151.
— of ELPHINGSTON, 71, 74, 150, 151, 153, 187, 197, 206, 207, 236, 246, 251.
— Bishop of Aberdeen, 133.
— George (Rector of Scots College, Rome,) 151, (Douay,) 246.
Erskine of Alloway, 67.
— of Balhagartie, 39, 40, 47.
— of CAMBUSKENNETH, 71, 251.
— of KELLIE, 193.
— of MARR, 72, 143, 145, 147, 173, 174, 191, 232, 248, 251.
Erskine, ——, 58.
—Lyon King at Arms, 194.
Escortio. See Drummond of Madera.

Faussyd, Thomas of, 40.
— of Glenegask, 190.
Fenduy, Baron of, 62.
FERRERS, Lord, (Constable,) 219.
Fit of Gleusheris, 60.
Fleeming of Biggar, (Boghall,) 173, 211.
— of WIGTON, 78, 145, 146, 173, 196, 210—212, 247, 249.
— Malcolm, 15, 262.
Fogo, Wm., Minister of Callender, 154.
Forbes, Lord FORBES, 135, 151.
— Lord PITSLIGO, 174.

Fordon, Laird of, 48.
Forrester, Lord CORSTORPHINE, 89.
Fouller, Sir William. 74, 251, 307.
— Susanna, 74, 251.
France, Donald, 55.
Frazer, Lord LOVET, 140, 175.
— Lord MUTHELL, 197.
Friebairn, John, (Minister of Madertie,) 4, 34, 154, 258, 291.

Gall, Alexander, (Minister of Gask,) 57.
GALLOWAY, Lords, Earles of, 33, 218.
Garrie, Andrew, (in Perth,) 49.
Gilchrist, Earl of ANGUS, 217, 234.
Glasgow, Bishop of, 36, 57, 197.
Gordon, of ABOYNE, 175, 206.
— of Buckie, 148.
— of Cairnbarrow, (Drummond,) 148.
— of HUNTLY, 21, 79, 93, 111, 135, 139, 140, 148, 175, 198, 199, 203, 204, 206, 214, 224—226, 233, 249, 309.
— of LOCHINVAR, (Vis. Kenmure,) 236.
— of SUTHERLAND, 140, 151, 202, 206, 207, 249, 303.
— Anne, (Countess of Perth,) 214, 220-223, 226, 249, 305.
— Abbot of Inchaffray, 177.
Graeme, Grimus, the name, 31, 32, 164. See Graham.
Graham of Abercorn, 166.
— of Arbenie, 162.
— of Balgowan, 186.
— of Boultone, 154.
— of Braco, 168, 172.
— of Cairney, Cairnie, 60, 154.

Graham of Callendar, 57.
— of Cambuskenneth, 168.
— of Dundaffmure, 79, 165, 166.
— of Fintrie, 79.
— of Gartur, 49, 53.
— of Garvock, 56, 61.
— of Gorthie, 54, 61, 117.
— of Innermeath, 173.
— of Inchbrakie, 60, 127, 188—190, 248, 282.
of Killeren, 168.
— of Kincardine, 67, 166.
— of MENTEITH, 16, 121, 200.
— of Monorgan, 176.
— of MONTROSE, 41, 58, 61, 72, 120, 123, 125, 145, 147, 164—168, 172, 179, 181, 185, 189, 193, 236, 248, 249.
— of Monzie, 127.
— of Morphie, 232.
— of Ochterarder, 57.
— of Orchill, 58, 184.
— of Pitcairnes, 127, 186.
— of Raterns [Roterns] 58, 168, 172.
— of STRATHERN, 41—45, 167.
— Commis. clerk of Dumblane, 173.
— Bishop of Orkney, 282.
— Archbp. of St. Andrews, 79.
— Post-master-general, 189, 190, 248.
Grant of Balhagells, 117.
— of Grant, 174, 175, 226.
Gray of Balledgarney, 175.
— of Easthill, 53.
— of Pittendrume, 64.
— of GRAY, 64, 191, 199, 236.
Grier of Lag, 74.
Guthrie, Thane of Cathnes, 205.

Hacket, Colonell, 175.
Hadden of Glenegask, (Gleneagles,) 175, 190, 248.
— Sir Bernard, 42.
Halliday of Tulliboole, 185.
Hallyburton, 56.
— of Buttergask, 113.
— of Dirletoun, 171, 203, 235.
— of Piteur, 186.
Hamilton of ABERCORN, 233.
— of ARRAN, (Chastleherauld, Hamilton,) 80, 142-145, 149, 199, 226, 227, 232, 233, 290.
— of Baderston, 50.
— of BARGENIE, 186, 249.
— of BINNING, (Haddington,) 73.
— of Blair, 50.
— of Cadzow, (Arran,) 80.
— of Cliddisdale, 143, 232.
— of EVENDALE, 191.
— of HADDINGTON, 193, 250.
— of HAMILTON, (Arran,) 143, 227.
— of Samuelston, (Cliddisdale,) 232.
— of Sanquair, 204.
— Archbishop of St. Andrews, 149.
Hay of ERROL, 143, 173, 174, 186, 196, 199, 204, 206, 213, 215-217, 220, 225, 226, 235, 306, 307.
— of Keillour, 186, 215.
— of Kennet, 73, 251.
— of Meggins, 114.
— of Moncktown, 64.
— of Pitfowre, 129.
— of Tulliebodie, 225.
— of YESTER, (Tweeddale,) 132, 140, 144, 195, 196, 204.
Henderson, Henry (physician,) 74, 308.

Hepburn of BOTHWELL, 141, 203, 206, 232.
— of Humbie, 187.
— of Riccartoun, 235.
— of Wauchton, 72, 251.
— Patrick, 155.
Herring of Lenings, (Lethintie,) 116.
— of Westergormoch, 148.
Hirdman, (Stedman,) Sir William, 147.
Houston of Bearlaw, 154.
— of that ilk, 179.
— John, 149.
Howard of NORFOLK, 226.
— of Nottingham, 100, 249.
Hume, Lord HUME, 80, 132, 195, 199, 201, 236.
— of Wedderburne, 140, 144, 177.
HUNTINGTOUN, Earle of, 19, 34, 36, 219.
Hurrie, Major-General, 123, 312.

Ibret, ———, 126.
Inglis of Byres, 53, 55.
— John, 52, 125.
Innes of Coxtoun, 186.
— of that ilk, 151, 196.
Johnstoun of Waristoun, 187.
Isles, Donald Lord of the, 51, 65.

Keith of Ludquhairne, 172, 188.
— Earl MARISHALL, 135, 167, 172, 188, 225.
— Sir James, 172.
Kennedy of CASSILLS, 78, 145, 146, 174, 187.
— of Dunure, 78.

Kennedy, Alexander, 78.
— Bishop of St. Andrews, 78.
Kenneth of the Isles, 31.
Kerr of Cessford, (Roxburgh,) 213.
— of JEDBURGH, 213.
— of Kersland, 148, 213.
— of LOTHIAN, NEWBATTLE, 174, 200, 213.
— of ROXBURGH, 100, 120, 146, 168, 195, 196, 208—210, 212, 213, 248, 249, 299, 300.
— Jean, Countess of Perth, 208, 303, 304.
KINCLEVIN, Lord, 235.
Kings of Scotland. See Stuart.
King David II. 39, 66—69, 205.
— James III. 134, 135.
— James IV. 135.
— Malcolm III. 5, 13—16.
— Robert I. 37.
— Robert II. 65, 83, 90, 198.
— Robert III. 8, 65, 87.
— William, 35, 214, 217.
Kinghorn, David, 21, 287, 288.
Kinnaird of KINNAIRD, 91, 305.
Kippenross, Lady, 72, 180, 185, 251, 267.
Kippon, Christian, 56.
Kirealdy of Grange, 71, 251.

Lauder of Bass, 140, 144.
— of Hattone, 194.
— Sir Robert, 37.
Laurie, Robert, Bishop of Breichen, 53.
Lea, Lady, 72, 251.

Lennox, Earles of, 34—37, 65, 66. See Stuarts of.
Leslie of Balquhain, (Buwhain,) 162.
— of Findressie, 80, 170, 274.
— of LEVEN, 192.
— of LINDORES, 187, 248, 249.
— of NEWARK, 305.
— of ROTHES, 80, 168, 187, 191—193, 232, 248.
Lidderdale of Ile, 123.
Lindsay of Auchtermonsie, 199.
— of BALCARRAS, 194, 195, 248.
— of Balgayes, 200.
— of BYRES, 21, 200, 203.
— of CRAWFOORD, 78, 132, 151, 174, 191, 193, 194, 197—200, 230, 245, 248.
— of Edzell, 191, 194, 199, 200.
— of Kinfaunes, 151, 200.
Livingston, of LINLITHGOW, 146, 150, 151, 175, 210, 230.
— of Glentirran, 126.
Lockart of Lie, 233.
Logan of Coatfeild, 74.
— of Restalrige, 62, 74.
Logie, Laird of, 154.
Logie, John, 42.
Lundin of that ilk, 194, 214, 236, 314.
LYLE, Lord, 69, 133, 135.
Lyon of GLAMES, (KINGHORN, STRATHMORE,) 144, 145, 174, 175, 232.
Lyon King-at-Arms, 133, 135, 194.
Lythington of Saltcoats, 235.

M'Aula of Arncapell, 71.
M'Beth, 13, 31.

M'Carter of Thorowrige, 48.
M'Donald of the Isles, 51, 65, 83, 205.
— of Ross, 199.
M'Duff of FIFE, 16, 42, 43.
M'Greigors, (Clan,) 126, 285, 291.
M'Gruder, James, 126.
MACHANY. See Drummond of Machany.
M'Kenzie of SEAFORTH, 53, 173, 195, 248.
— Colin, 53, 175.
M'Kingie, Duncan, 125.
M'Kie, of Kilbryde, 48, 122.
M'Mesker, James, 58.
M'William, John, (Judge,) 42.
MADERTY. See Drummond of Maderty.
Maine of Bruntimiln, 56.
Maitland of Haltone, 194, 197.
— of LAUDERDALE, 146, 194, 195, 208, 213, 214, 248.
Malcolm, John, (minister of Perth,) 120.
Malloch of Cairnies, 63.
MAR, Earl of. See Douglas, Drummond, Erskine, Marr, Stuart.
Marr of MAR, 35, 40, 86, 205, 237.
Marischall, Gillycallum the first, 217.
Margaret, Queen of Malcolm III. 13, 242.
Mauld of Melgum, 53.
— of PANMURE, 174, 196, 210.
Maxton of Cultowhay, 62.
Maxwell of Hills, 74.
— of MAXWELL, 141, 143, 232.
— of Newark, 185.
— John. See Malcolm, John.
MELFORT. See Drummond of Melfort.

INDEX. 327

Menteith, Earl of, 38. See Graham, Monteith, Stuart.
Menteith, Sir Alexander, 266.
Menzies of Weem, 191, 249.
Mercer of Clevadge, 185.
— of Innerpeffrey, (Inchbrekie?) 46, 52, 311.
Methven, (Meffen.) See Stuart of.
Midelton, Earl of Midelton, 175.
Milne, provost of Linlithgow, 49.
Mitchell of Kincarrochie, 177.
Moncreiffe of that ilk, 154.
— of Westwood, 54.
Monipennie, Captain William, 163.
Monteith of Alcathy, 49.
— of Arran, 67.
— of Carse, 45, 49, 151, 246.
— of Eagleshaw, 117, 282.
— of Manor, 49.
— of Menteith, 38, 266.
— of Westcarse, 70, 250.
— Sir John, 34, 37, 38, 65, 66.
Monteiths, 15, 24, 25, 29, 66—69, 266.
Montgomery, Earle of Eglington, 148—150, 192, 197, 204, 246.
Montifex, (Montefichet,) 36, 38, 65, 68, 69, 84, 85, 274.
— Lady Mary, 65, 69, 84—86, 111, 266.
Monzie, Lady, 60.
Morison, Helen, 154.
Morvill, Constable, 36, 218.
Mowbray of Barnbougal, 92.
Muire, Captain David, (in Kintyre,) 50.
Murehead of Breadisholme, 184, 248.

Murray of Abercairnie, 47, 48, 132, 173, 186, 188.
Murray of Annand, 281.
— of Atholl, 80, 176, 212.
— of Balvaird, 177.
— of Blackbarony, 270.
— of Bothwell, 33, 41, 188, 229.
— of Carden, 173.
— of Cringelty, 270.
— of Dollorie, 63.
— of Dysert, 195.
— of Drumshergort, 41, 188.
— of Kildees, 122—124.
— of Lochland, 60, 64, 180.
— of Ogilvie, 41—44, 46, 48.
— of Polmaise, 179, 185.
— of Stanhope, 173.
— of Stormont, 74, 177, 213.
— of Strowan, 49, 60, 180.
— of Tullibarden, 35, 46, 52, 66, 80, 118, 145, 159, 160, 165, 172, 174—176, 186, 212, 227, 248, 249, 309.
— George, (Abbot of Inchaffray,) 158, 293.
— John, (Minister in England,) 154.
— Thomas, (Governour to Prince Henry,) 116 280.
Murrayes, burned at Monyvaird, 56, 157—160, 286, 292—295.
Murray, Bishop of, 36, 248, 279.
Muschampe. See Muschet.
Muschet of Burnbank, 127, 285.
— of that ilk, 53 85, 112, 127, 151, 183.
— of Wester-Cambsheeny, 112.
Mylne, Captain Charles, 272.

Nairne, Lord Nairne, 188.
— Bailie, in Dalkeith, 272.
Napier of Burnbank, 129.
— of Kilcreuch, 155, 183.
— of Kilmahew, 69.
— of Merchistoun, 61, 151, 179, 180, 183, 295.
— of NAPIER, 61, 173, 295.
— Duncan, 69.
Nicoll, — (merchant in Edinburgh,) 189.
Nicolson of Carnock, 156, 173, 295.
Notary-Publics, 22, 43, 45, 47, 55, 58, 84, 112, 147.

Ochtertyre, Lady, 179.
Ogilvie, Lady, 236.
Ogilvie of AIRLEV, 199.
— of Balfour, 188.
— of FINLATER, 151.
— of Powrie, 171, 248.
Oliphant of Aberdagie, 60, 166.
— of Bachelton, 53, 305.
— of Clashberry, 305.
— of Coltewcher, 128.
— of Gask, 57, 58, 124, 184.
— of Newton, 179, 180.
— of OLIPHANT, 133, 184, 232, 248, 249, 274.
Olyffards, 32, 36, 45.
Orkney, Earl of. See Spar, Sinclair.

Panter, (Panitier,) David, (Secretary,) 142.
Pearson of Kippenross, 127.
Percie, Earl of Northumberland, 162.

Percie Randolf, 88.
PERTH, Earl of. See Drummond.
Pitcairn of Pitlour, 49.
Polwart of Cowstowne, 154.
Pittencreiffe, Lady, 236.
Porterfield of Comistoun, 115.
Powfowlls, Lady, 180.
Purves of Abbeyhill, 272.

Queen Annabella. See Drummond.
— Margaret Tudor, 119, 135, 141, 232, 247, 286, 289.
Quincie, Earle of Winchester, Constable, 33, 36, 219.
— of Nether Gask, 33.
Quhytelaw, Archibald, (Secretary,) 133.

Ramsay of Balmane, 178.
— of Bainffe, 117.
— of Ochterhouse, 235.
— of Wauchton, 192.
Ratray of Craighall, 116, 188, 248.
Reid of Pitnacrie, 56.
Riddoch of Aberlednock, 53.
Riddoch (Redheuch) of Cultabregan, 55, 126, 180.
Rollo of Bannockburn, 127, 128, 185.
— of Duncrub, 60, 72, 163, 185, 249, 251, 279. See Lord Rollo.
— of Powes, 59, 185.
— Lord ROLLO, 53, 59, 72, 185, 186, 248. See Rollo of Duncrub.
Ross of Craigie, 41, 60.
— of Ross, 41, 237. See M'Donald Stuart.

INDEX. 329

Roxburgh, Jean, Lady. See Drummond.
Ruthven of Frieland, 236.
— of RUTHVEN, (Gowrie,) 114, 117, 132, 144, 168, 171, 172, 176, 234—236, 248, 290.

St. Andrews, Bishop of, 21, 35—37, 40, 77—79, 81, 149, 158, 197, 293.
Sandilands of Calder, (TORPHICHEN) 146, 155, 247.
Scot of BALCLEUGH 143, 192, 193.
— of Balweery, 119.
— of Clerkingtoun, 75.
— of Monzie, 72, 125, 251.
— of Scotstarbet, 74, 251.
— of TANNAS, 192.
— Alexander, 21.
— David, (Apothecarie,) 56.
— John, 54.
Scrimgeour, Earle of DUNDIE, 213.
— James, (Minister of Currie,) 182.
Seaton, (Seytoun, &c.) of DUMFERMLING, 191, 193—195, 201, 204, 210, 248.
— (alias Gordon) of HUNTLY, 224, 225.
— of Touch (Tyllibodie,) 180, 225.
— of WINTOUN, 150, 192, 193, 201—204, 249, 300.
— Sir Alexander, (Governor of Berwick,) 203, 224.
— Isabella, (Countess of Perth,) 202, 249, 273, 301—303.
Semple, Lord SEMPLE, 184, 246.
Shaw of Sauchie, 147, 200.
Shevez, Archbishop of St. Andrews, 158.

Sheyffield, (Seafield,) Lady, 72, 251.
Sibbald of Balgonie, 231.
— of NORTHUMBERLAND, 231.
— David, 64.
— Sir Robert, 306—308.
Sinclair (St. Clair,) of Ardoch, 180.
— of CAITHNES, 182, 195, 200, 238.
— of Dryden, 178.
— of Glassingall-beg (Galdwalmore), 122, 180, 182.
— of ORKNEY, 78, 79, 89—91, 170, 230, 231, 237, 238, 243, 244.
— of Ravensheugh, 199.
— of Rosline, 186, 238.
— of Ulbster, 182.
Smyth of Methven, 54, 126, 189, 300.
— of Rapnes, 188.
Spalden, William, 41, 42.
Spar, Earl of ORKNEY, 237.
Spens of Wormistoune, 162.
Stanley, Earl of DERBIE, 176.
Sterline (Stirling) of Ardoch, 120, 175, 180, 184.
— of Ballindooch, 63.
— of Harbertshyre, 189.
— of Keir, 21, 63, 155, 177, 179, 180, 247, 248.
Steuart, Stewart. See Stuart.
Strageth of Strageth, 55, 123.
STRATHALLAN, Viscount. See Drummond of Strathallan.
Strathern, Earles of, 16, 31—36, 165. See also Graham, Stuart.
— Thane, (Seneseal,) of, 16, 30—35. See Drummond of Concraig.
Stewart, Seneseal, 5, 16, 32, 37.

Stuart Royal Stock, 7—9, 76—83, 243.
— of ALBANY, Alexander, 79, 140, 169—171, 244, 247, 273. Henric, (Darnlie,) 81. John, 57, 71, 80, 136, 141, 169—171, 247, 273, 286, 295. Robert, 51, 91, 243, 244.
Stuart of ANGUS, 29, 67, 87.
— of Ardworlich, 126, 129.
— of Arntullie, 83.
— of ARRAN, 143, 144.
— of ATHOLL, 8, 45, 91, 140, 146, 176, 206, 225, 236.
— of AUBIGNIE, 80.
— of Ballathy, 209.
— of Banchrie, 54.
— of Blackhall, 177.
— of BOTHWELL, 202.
— of BRECHIN, 41, 43.
— of BUCHAN, 51, 78, 87, 203, 244, 245, 274.
— of Buite, 8.
— of CARRICT, 83, 272.
— of Dalguissie, 116.
— of Duallie, 65, 83.
— of Dundonald, 7, 34, 66.
— of EVANDALE, 25, 134.
— of Foss, 123.
— of FYFE, 42, 83.
— of GAIRLIES, 200.
— of Garntullie, 128, 187, 209, 305.
— of Innernytie, 186.
— of Kinnaird, 61.
— of Ladywell, 128.
— of LENNOX, 21, 34, 80, 135, 141, 143, 206, 236, 247, 274.
— of MAR, 51, 80, 81, 87, 274.

Stuart of MENTEITH, 83.
— of METHVEN, (Meffen,) 141, 236, 290.
— of Minto, 184.
— of MURRAY, 120, 143.
— of OCHILTRIE, 120, 143, 236.
— of ORKNAY, 187.
— of Ross, 57.
— of ROTHSAY, David, Duke, 77, 243, 273.
— of St. Colme, 236.
— of STRATHERN, 29, 39—41, 67, 68, 87.
— of Tarbolton, 34, 66.
— of TRAQUAIR, 141.
— Ægidia, 90, 237.
— Lady GORDON, 139, 140, 246, 247.
— William, 50.
Surnames, their ryse, 14.
— that came with Queen Margaret, 20.
Sutherland, Earl of SUTHERLAND, 68, 204—206, 238.

Thane, 16, 31. See Abthane.
Thomson, 123.
Tosheoch of Pitenzie, 53.
Toures of Innerleith, 21.
Traile, Bishop of St. Andrews, 77.
Tulliebody, Lady, 71, 251.
Tyrie of Drumkilbo, 116.

Urquhart of Cromertie, 151.
Urrie. See Hurrie.

Vauss, Eleanora, 235.

Wales, Prince of, 234.
Wallace (Coll. James) of Achens, 50.
— of Craigie, 148, 215, 306.
Weems of Bruntisland, 193.
— of Weems, 175, 193, 206, 233, 236.
Weems, George, (Minister of Scoon,) 54.
— John, (Minister of Dumbarnie,) 54.
Whitson, Thomas, 116.

Witnesses to Charters, &c. 35—38, 40, 43, 47, 91, 133, 134, 165, 167, 172, 202, 203, 279.
Wood of Bonnington, 235.
— of Largo, 184, 248, 249.

Young, (Minister of Abbotshall,) 186.
— David, (Minister of Lethendie,) 154.
Youngman, Thomas, 55.

www.ingramcontent.com/pod-product-compliance
Lightning Source LLC
Chambersburg PA
CBHW030745250426
43672CB00028B/784